a People's History of the Hmong

a PEOPLE'S HISTORY

OF THE HMONG

PAUL HILLMER

 MINNESOTA HISTORICAL SOCIETY PRESS

*To Julianna Marie, who lives on
in the hearts and memories of her parents*

www.mhspress.org

The Minnesota Historical Society Press is a member of the Association of American University Presses.

Manufactured in the United States of America

10 9 8 7 6 5 4 3 2 1

⊗ The paper used in this publication meets the minimum requirements of the American National Standard for Information Sciences—Permanence for Printed Library Materials, ANSI Z39.48–1984.

International Standard Book Number
ISBN-13: 978-0-87351-726-3 (cloth)
ISBN-10: 0-87351-726-1 (cloth)

Library of Congress Cataloging-in-Publication Data
Hillmer, Paul, 1960–
    A people's history of the Hmong / Paul Hillmer.
        p. cm.
    Includes bibliographical references and index.
    ISBN-13: 978-0-87351-726-3 (cloth : alk. paper)
    ISBN-10: 0-87351-726-1 (cloth : alk. paper)
    1. Hmong (Asian people)—History. I. Title.

    DS509.5.H66H55 2010
    909'.0495972—dc22

                                                    2009034511

contents

Laos Region during and after Secret War

Military Region 2 in Laos during Secret War

abbreviations appearing in text

AAHWM	Association for the Advancement of Hmong Women of Minnesota
ANL	National Army of Laos (Armee Nationale Laotienne)
BV	Volunteer Battalion
CAT	Civil Air Transport
CDNI	Committee for the Defense of the National Interests
CIA	Central Intelligence Agency
CINCPAC	Commander in Chief, Pacific Command
CMA	Civilian Military Assistance
CPT	Communist Party of Thailand
EAO	ethnic affairs officer
FAR	Forces of the Royal Army (Forces Armee Royale)
GCMA	Mixed Commando Airborne Groups
HAP	Hmong American Partnership
IATF	interagency task force
ICC	International Control Commission
INS	Immigration and Naturalization Services
IRC	International Rescue Committee
IVS	International Voluntary Service
JVA	Joint Voluntary Agency
LPDR	Lao People's Democratic Republic
LPLA	Lao People's Liberation Army
MACTHAI	Military Assistance Command, Thailand
NSC	National Security Council
NVA	North Vietnamese Army
OSS	Office of Strategic Services
PARU	Police Aeril Reinforcement Unit
PEO	Programs Evaluation Office
PDR	People's Democratic Republic
RDD	Rural Development Division
SF	Special Forces
SGU	Special Guerrilla Units
SOT	Special Operations Teams
TACAN	tactical air navigation system
ULNLF	United Lao National Liberation Front
UNHCR	United Nations High Commissioner for Refugees
USAID	U.S. Agency for International Development

a people's history of the hmong

INTRODUCTION

In January 1961, Bill Lair, a quiet Texan (and a Central Intelligence Agency—CIA—officer already in Thailand for nine years), approached Hmong military leader Vang Pao with a proposition. Lair offered "VP," a colonel in the Royal Lao Army, American-financed training, arms, and supplies, not only to defend his people and their homes but also to participate in a larger struggle against the spread of Communism in Laos, South Vietnam, and Thailand. In the ensuing years, the Hmong people—one of several minority groups in Laos covertly recruited, trained, equipped, paid, and deployed by the United States—impressed Lair. He was convinced they could shoulder greater responsibility and learn new skills, despite their isolated and impoverished mountain existence. He took one of his ideas to a friend, Colonel Harry C. "Heinie" Aderholt, commander of the 1st Air Commando Wing at Hurlburt Field in Florida, seconded to the CIA and stationed at Udorn Air Base in Thailand. The United States was running a program called "Water Pump," designed to train South Vietnamese, Thai, and Lao men to fly single-engine planes in combat. As Lair recalls,

Bill Lair (above, in hat and sunglasses) quietly following General Vang Pao on a tour through a Hmong village in Laos and (facing page) decades later, before speaking at the dedication of the Lao, Hmong and American Veterans Memorial in Sheboygan, Wisconsin, on July 15, 2006.

*I asked [Aderholt], "Do you think I could get somebody in [the program]?" And he said he'd go over and talk to 'em . . . They said, "Aw, hell, those people [the Hmong] . . . never saw anything more than the ass end of a buffalo. They can't fly." But [Aderholt] kept talking to them, and I kept pushing him. And those air force guys . . . could do whatever they wanted to do, so they finally said, "OK, send us a couple of those guys. They won't make it, we'll get rid of 'em, and you all will shut up."**

Of course, the air force was unaware that Hmong recruits for this project were quite well educated and accustomed to traveling in planes. They were also unaware that Lair already had a training program up and running, led by a Thai colleague and pilot named Somboun. As Lair saw it, "'The Americans are going to pull out of here some day. It would be good if we could train Hmong to be pilots' . . . So I asked VP, 'Do you think the Hmong could learn to fly?' And he would always say, 'Oh sure, no problem! They can do anything.' And you know, I began to believe him . . . Even if they didn't have much education, they were . . .

---

* While this book is about the Hmong, it would be inaccurate and irresponsible to suggest that the Hmong did all or even most of the fighting against Communism in Laos. In addition to the ethnic Lao themselves, the Khmu (also known as the Lao Theung), the Brao, and the Mien (also called the Yao) all fought against Communist forces in the country—often alongside the Hmong.

unusually bright people, and they picked up things so quickly." On a trip to Okinawa, Lair found and commandeered two unclaimed, disassembled Piper Cubs and had them sent on the next C-46 heading his way. As the planes were being rebuilt by a Thai mechanic, Lair told Somboun, "'Start teaching [the Hmong recruits] English, teach 'em what makes an airplane fly, how the engine works, all that stuff, and then start 'em flying.' I never said anything to the American government . . . And as time went on, Somboun said, 'These guys are doing really good. They can fly.'"

Despite the somewhat justifiable opinions of U.S. Air Force personnel, Hmong men learned to fly. They sent, received, and decoded radio messages and repaired radios, translated for U.S. personnel who interrogated prisoners, guided bombers to their targets, monitored and reported on enemy activities, and carried out a number of other functions few—including the Hmong themselves—ever expected them to perform at all, let alone well.

The most frequently celebrated Hmong fighter, apart from Vang Pao himself, is pilot Lee Lue. A schoolteacher who answered the initial call for trainees in 1967, Lee and his classmate Vang Toua were the first two Hmong to complete their training. Neither could drive a jeep when they began. (Vang Toua was shot down shortly after he began flying in combat.) Even Americans marveled at Lee Lue's accomplishments. He flew over five thousand combat missions, more than any other pilot in history. He risked as many as ten missions a day and averaged 120 a month. Unlike their American counterparts, Hmong pilots had no specified rotation or tour of duty. They took little or no R & R and flew until they died or were injured beyond hope of recovery.[1]

The Hmong, given their need to relocate—sometimes because of their tradition of slash-and-burn farming, sometimes because of war, disease, or persecution—have frequently managed to adapt to new en-

vironments and circumstances. Their history is fraught with challenges—not only in terms of the many trials and tragedies they have
endured and overcome but also because the history itself is difficult to
recount. Though legend suggests the Hmong had their own written
language centuries ago, lost as a result of Chinese persecution and
forced segregation but preserved in Hmong needlework, they certainly
had no way of recording their history throughout their time in Laos.
Accounts written by others are less than reliable as well. According
to Robert Cooper, "Most reports and writings on the Hmong, until recent years, have been made by . . . writers . . . often intent on killing,
taxing, or converting the Hmong, activities which tend to make partial
history."[2]

Hmong oral history accounts must also be used with caution.
Though we tend to think of oral history as history shared by word of
mouth, it is more correctly defined as the history of people's memories. And as study after study has shown, the human memory is a no-
toriously unreliable or at least incomplete source. Thomas Spencer
Jerome reminds us that "entirely faithful testimony is not the rule but
the exception." After all, "the human mind is not primarily an organ by
which man determines the real objective truth . . . but is rather a tool by
which one accomplishes one's desires."[3]

Nonetheless, Hmong oral history is valuable and perhaps on average a little more reliable than accounts provided by Westernized, mod-
ernized minds. First, in the absence of a written language, their reliance
on memory and oral communication makes it more rather than less
likely that they would remember specific details. Second, the intensity
of their lives and the frequent traumas they endured increase the likelihood that Hmong who lived in Laos can't forget what they experienced—even if they want to. Recent studies have shown a correlation
between adrenaline and memory retention, and there is no doubt that
Hmong who lived through the "Secret War" must have had adrenaline
coursing through their veins on a regular basis.[4]

On the other hand, given the nearly unfathomable loss that the pro-
Western Lao Hmong endured, it is reasonable to assume that survivors
are more apt to seek and identify scapegoats to blame for their troubles.
Every memory is subjective, personal, and—when discussing matters
of this intensity—often the subject of violent disagreement from some-

one else whose memories are very different. These stories may also change as subsequent circumstances reframe the memories or as a particular audience changes one's sense of how the story should be told.

In the midst of analyzing the extraordinary circumstances that have surrounded the Hmong from the 1940s to the present, it is easy to paint them either as super- or subhuman: "super" because of their ability to survive in the high mountains and to serve first the French and then the Americans so well and for their remarkable adaptability; "sub" because they have been dominated by other groups and governments, fled Laos, and usually arrived in the United States—as well as other countries like Canada, Australia, France, Argentina, and French Guiana— with little or none of their new country's language skills, schooling, or social and cultural orientation. But the Hmong, most Southeast Asians, and a few other refugee groups came to this country as a result of failed U.S. policies that gave them little choice but to flee their homes.

Suffering the indifference, scorn, or even hate of so-called natives has been the fate of numerous immigrant groups in American history. The Irish were reviled first for their Catholicism and then for their abject poverty as they escaped the ravages of the potato famine. An old Italian proverb recounted, "Before I came to America, I heard the streets were paved with gold. When I arrived, I learned three things. The streets were not paved with gold; the streets were not paved; and I was expected to pave them." Chinese, Japanese, Poles, Slavs, Russian Jews, Central and South Americans, and numerous other immigrant groups, including the more recently arrived Somali and Sudanese, have all been met with a mixture of hospitality and hostility.

As readers might have surmised by now, my take on the Hmong experience and Hmong migration to the United States is influenced by immigration history. While their history and culture are unique in numerous ways, many problems the Hmong have faced in this country are not much different from those experienced by previous immigrants. Challenges associated with the process of adaptation; fierce debates over the loss of tradition; particularly acute generational conflicts and gangs who not only defy parental authority but break the law—all are experiences nearly every immigrant group has endured. Some of these conditions become even more poignant in communities of refugees fleeing a war-torn or strife-ridden homeland. All the aforementioned problems are compounded by worries about the family members, friends, and cherished places left behind and the fate they may be suffering. Questions about if and under what conditions one might return to the motherland can persist for decades. And these struggles are even greater when, like the Jews (until 1948) or the Hmong, one has never had a "home country." Lacking a sense of "state," living outside modern communities with buses, libraries, and markets, the Hmong instead developed a deep and abiding sense of kinship and community.

All of us, whether recently or hundreds (even thousands) of years ago, have immigrants somewhere in our family tree. Our ancestors may have crossed an Aleutian ice bridge, been brought against their will as part of the Atlantic slave trade, or left their country of origin as a result of either crisis or opportunity. But somewhere back in our past, whether still recorded or long forgotten, our families underwent experiences that resemble what present-day immigrants and their children are going through now. My mother's parents, one an immigrant and one the son of immigrants from northwestern Germany, spoke *Plattdeutsch* at home and maintained a relatively isolated existence in a small northwestern Iowa farming community where they lived, worked, and worshiped with other immigrant families. Living in the country kept them from being considered too clannish or un-American and spared them many of the ills suffered by those who settled in urban environments. But even so, my maternal grandparents had certain expectations for their children, dreams for their success, a mixture of pride, anger, and envy concerning their facility with the English language and the American values that came along with it, fears that they might abandon or water down the one true Lutheran Missouri Synod Christian faith (or worse, become Catholic!), and so on.

I am now only two generations removed from Germany. I speak no German and have no particular affinity for the German people, German cuisine, or German culture. I am in many ways, I imagine, exactly what my grandparents feared my mother and her brothers might become. My ethnic ancestry has been all but erased. Though the Hmong, lacking my entirely unearned advantage of having white skin, will have less success in "blending in" to mainstream American culture (this country still sorts people by race), Hmong refugee parents still face many of the same struggles my grandparents did. First-generation American Hmong serve as a bridge between the old world and the new, as my parents did. And second-generation American Hmong are, even as I write, letting their history, their culture, and their language slip between their fingers, just as I did.

For those not yet familiar with the history of the Hmong people, this book will serve as an introduction to the Hmong experience from about 1945 to present. For those Hmong who have grown up in America and heard incomplete or half-believed stories from parents, grandparents, and other elders, I hope this book will serve as at least partial corroboration. The stories you have heard may be truer than you ever thought or they ever wished.

In this book, I will share the story of what I have come to call the "Six Cs": Section 1 will discuss the history and **culture** of the Hmong people in the days leading up to their recruitment by the French in the waning months of World War II. Sections 2 and 3 will define and delineate the **conflicts** that divided not only the Hmong people in Laos, Vietnam, and Thailand but also the Lao leadership, the regional and colonial powers in Southeast Asia, and the superpowers that emerged in the wake of World War II. Section 4 will examine the **catastrophe** (at least from the pro-Western Hmong point of view) that culminated in the expulsion of General Vang Pao from Laos in May 1975 and the resulting exodus of tens of thousands of Hmong people. Section 5 will describe the horrors, struggles, and stifling boredom of living in a Thai refugee **camp** and the circumstances that made it possible for the Hmong to find new homes. Section 6 will share the challenges and rewards that led up to **citizenship** in a new country, and in the Epilogue I will review **contemporary issues** of concern to the worldwide Hmong community. Throughout I will rely not only on close consultation of scholarly resources currently available but also on more than 220 interviews conducted over the course of the last seven-plus years (see appendix for a list of interviewees). These interviews are not only with Hmong soldiers and elders but with U.S. personnel who served in Laos and Thailand in military, intelligence-gathering, and humanitarian capacities and with younger, more Americanized Hmong. We will also hear from Hmong who still live in Southeast Asia and who, in some cases, fought for the so-called People's Revolution—that is, on the side of the Communists.

1 | "THIS WAS THE LIFE OF OUR HMONG PEOPLE"

THE GOOD OLD DAYS

When exactly *were* "the good old days"? Listening to my parents, it must have been the 1930s—no, wait, that was during the Great Depression. That can't be it. The 1940s? Well, we spent the first half worrying about and then fighting in a world war and the second half fearing global obliteration during the Cold War. How about the 1950s? My parents remember them as a time of bedrock values, strong families, and near-perfect unity. Yet scholars like Stephanie Coontz have demonstrated this was not the case. The fifties also had the Korean conflict, Joe McCarthy, racial violence, and the continuation of an anti-Communist foreign policy that led the United States into war in Southeast Asia. Of course, plenty of positive events occurred during these decades as well, but they were rarely the Edenic times many purport them to be. Still, many older Americans long for the "good old days," even though their exact location is difficult to pinpoint.[1]

This same kind of nostalgia dwells in the hearts of Hmong who grew up, got married, raised children, and buried loved ones in the hills of Laos. "I miss the freedom," lamented Karry Moua in 2002. "We didn't have a lot of clocks or watches in Laos, so time was not important. In Laos, we were free. The weather was great . . . It was like spring all the time." The children and grandchildren of people like Moua, who grew up in the United States, may have a difficult time understanding how their elders could possibly pine for a life devoid of modern medicine, running water, a cornucopia of dietary options, regular leisure time, or efficient communication and transportation—even the wheel. But conversations with older Hmong almost inevitably turn to a not-so-hidden longing for the old days, the simple life, the traditional way.

Some associate the old ways with their childhood, a time when life was simpler, when responsibilities weighed less heavily on them. Others remember life in Laos as a way that embodied and preserved all that was good about Hmong culture and life, a repository of a pure, received wisdom that is now disappearing. Still others are so unhappy and uncomfortable with the changes they have experienced since coming to America that they have adopted a sort of "we were better off as slaves in Egypt" philosophy, ignoring many of the ills suffered in Laos. This kind of reinvention of the motherland is common in the immigrant experience and begins practically from the minute one leaves one's home behind.[2]

"This was the life of our Hmong people," remembers Pa Seng Thao.

We lived freely and independently. There was no one to boss us around. We were farmers, and we worked in the field all day. We raised cattle, horses, and other live-stock . . . A cow or bull of four or five years could be sold for one or two silver bars — enough to buy salt [which preserved food and warded off sickness], yards of cloth, and items for our homes . . . We had enough to live from year to year. We used our horses to transport our goods, and we took care of our gardens. Our children played freely, and all our neighbors were close and related. There were no arguments or squabbles over anything. One or two villages would pool resources and start a school for the children. There was no crime in our land, not like here in America . . . [I]f our children wander off they are hurt or killed . . . That's why we are constantly worry-ing about life in America.

But the life Hmong elders remember leaving behind was not necessarily one of ease. Though clearly desiring to return to Laos, Khu Thao confessed life "wasn't easy, like living here in the United States . . . No matter how far or near, we would have to walk, and all we used were our backs and shoulders to carry things. But then there was a lot of free-

Unidentified Green Hmong family, ca. 1959–60. Note the only male (center) wears his hair in the traditional braided style.

dom during that lifetime. There were no debts to pay, no taxes to pay
... and no one to tell me what to do. The only thing scary back then ...
were the tigers." Xai Thao told her daughter, "There was little free time.
Only after the harvest season was over were we able to celebrate ... our
New Year. This was the only time we were given new clothes to wear."

So what was life really like for the Hmong back in Laos before the
days when the *Fackee* (as the Hmong called the French) asked for their
assistance to fight against the occupying Japanese? What was lost, never
to be recovered, for those who cast their lot with the West's battle
against Communism?

IN THE BEGINNING ...

The Hmong people can be traced back four thousand or more years in
China, though their exact origins are unclear. Since the Chinese referred
to almost any southern minority as *Miao,* a term they now reserve
largely for the Hmong, it is difficult to know in many cases which "Miao"
are Hmong and which are not. Keith Quincy, Jane Hamilton-Merritt,
and Anne Fadiman, for example, all regale their readers with the en-
thralling legend of the Hmong king Sonom, who supposedly defeated a
vastly larger Chinese army in 1772, sparking a vengeful and expensive
counteroffensive by the Manchu dynasty. After four years of failure, the
Chinese convinced Sonom that if he surrendered, his family would be
spared. When they were brought before the emperor, however, Sonom
and his entire family were chopped to bits, their heads placed in cages
for all to see. This compelling story helps set a dramatic tone for discussing the Hmong's life of hardship in China, but Robert Entenmann
has largely proved not only that Sonom was not Hmong but that many
other details of the account shared by Quincy and others are inaccurate.[3]

Even so, China was a far from tranquil home for the Hmong. As
Yang Dao (widely recognized as the first Hmong to earn a PhD) has
written, "The vicissitudes of history uprooted them from the plains of
the Huang He (Yellow) and the Yangzi (Yangtse) rivers in China and
made them, unwillingly, into resigned mountaineers whose reserve has
struck more than one observer. Generally peaceable, but with a wild,
proud spirit of independence, the Hmong people two centuries ago
pulled up stakes from imperial China under expansionist pressure from
the Han, and ahead of massacres of their members." In light of these

numerous clashes it is not surprising that one widely known Hmong folktale involves a god named Tswb Tchoj, the offspring of a mystical coupling between a wild boar and a human maiden, who in various incarnations fought against the Chinese, eventually becoming emperor. Though tricked out of his throne, he vowed to return and help his people. In the ensuing decades, numerous individuals would claim to be the next incarnation of the Hmong messiah.[4]

In the early 1800s, after centuries of persecution in China, hundreds of thousands of Hmong began migrating into the highlands of Burma, Laos, Vietnam, and Thailand. Wherever they settled, the Hmong were independent but marginalized, living apart from mainstream society, engaging in slash-and-burn farming, and practicing their own form of animistic spirituality.

To understand any group of people, one must become acquainted with their stories. What do they believe? How do they define themselves and the world in which they live? How do they explain the forces larger than themselves? Where and how do they send their loved ones when they die?

Like Jews, Christians, and Muslims, most Hmong believe that an almighty being, Tswv Ntuj, whom they often refer to as King of the Universe, Lord of the Sky, or Master of the Universe, created all things. But they also believe in numerous major and minor deities or spirits, many of whom were present at creation. When in great need, many Hmong appealed to Saub "the Benevolent," though he was usually depicted as rather disinterested in the affairs of mortals.

The Hmong also believe that a massive flood once covered the earth. As Chong Toua Lo tells the story,

Saub told the Hmong people that the world was going to be flooded. One man went looking for a mole . . . He dug deep, and when he found one, the animal said, ". . . Why are you wasting time? I am trying to dig a hole deep enough to protect me from the flood that is coming! Go and build a boat and put your children and all of your animals in it! Dig a deep hole and put into it all of the seeds that you will need to start your lives over."

But when the man came back to his village and told the people what he had been told, they thought he had gone mad . . . [H]e started to build his own boat, but his neighbors still didn't believe him. The man found a tree bigger than the redwoods here in America, and into it he put all of the seeds he would need to plant after the flood was over. He put all his chickens and pigs and other animals on his boat, and also a drum into which he planned to safeguard his two children, a boy and a girl.

The ground began to dry up and crack open; the floodwaters burst forth, killing everyone except those who were on the boat. After three days of rain, the waters rose so high that the drum resting on the boat hit the top of the sky . . . The father said, "Has it flooded this high already? We must find a dagger and pierce the earth so that the water can drain away."

So the father pierced the earth, and the water started to drain away—but as he was doing this, the drum containing his two children fell overboard and was swept into a whirlpool created by the draining water. The ship was caught in the branches of a great tree, preventing it from following the drum into the whirlpool. Then the waters receded, and the boy and girl could see the dry land. Then Saub . . . said, "Black hawks, take some logs . . . and bring them to dry land," and so . . . the hawks did. And as the logs were brought to dry land and the sun came up, they crumbled and became mulch that created a pathway so the boy and the girl could leave the drum and walk on the earth.[5]

The story has many versions, but in the end the brother and sister were forced to marry because they couldn't find other humans. The child born of their incestuous relationship looked not so much like a child as a big ball of flesh. It had feet but no legs, hands but no arms, eyes but no face. Saub told the couple to chop their misshapen child into eighteen pieces and scatter them across the landscape, which they did (one would guess with no small amount of hesitation). From these pieces, like bits of a potato, grew the eighteen clans of the Hmong people.

As the couple strove to discover the size of the world in which they lived, they met a frog. He claimed the world was very small—so small that he could jump all the way around it in three great leaps. Instead he only landed helplessly nearby. Angered by the frog's vain boast, the couple killed him. In death he cursed them. The world in which humans and spirits easily communicated with one another was forever divided. Humans, who once lived in a paradise and rose from their graves thirteen days after their deaths, now lived in a world where weeds infested their fields, weather was unpredictable and often cold, and in death they were subject to the malicious Ntxwj Nyug, who judged and reincarnated them into the human, animal, or plant form he deemed appropriate. Perhaps the cruelest fate was to be reborn as one of the host of cattle penned up near Ntxwj Nyug's lofty mountain home, which were regularly slaughtered to satiate his prodigious appetite. Ntxwj Nyug's "chief of staff," Nyuj Vaj Tuam Teem, was charged with issuing each soul's license for rebirth. Writing his decrees from a great desk while seated on a majestic and terrifying throne, he fixed not only the souls' dates of birth but their deaths as well.

These two gods exercised their authority with abandon, collecting souls more quickly than humans could reproduce. In order to save humanity, Saub deigned to share some of his instruments of healing with a mortal man named Siv Yis, who until his death passed on the miraculous skill he was given. Like the human/boar emperor Tswb Tchoj, Siv Yis pledged to return to earth—in his case on the last day of the last lunar month (the New Year), and bring healing once again to his people. But when Siv Yis descended from the heavens, instead of the ardent welcome he had anticipated, the Hmong people were all fast asleep. In fury and disgust, he hurled to the earth the tools he'd inherited from Saub and stormed off to his spiritual home, never to return. Those who happened upon the implements Siv Yis had abandoned discovered their properties, becoming the world's first shamans. Only shamans, called by a healing spirit to serve their people, can engage in *ua neeb*, direct communication with (really, actual presence in) the spirit world. At their best, shamans can even negotiate with Nyuj Vaj Tuam Teem to extend another person's "mandate of life."

In simpler cases a shaman will perform *ua neeb muag dawb* (light-faced shamanism), requiring no extraordinary spiritual communication. But in times of great need or severe sickness (usually involving the loss of a soul or affliction by a spirit), the shaman must use *ua neeb muag dub*, or "dark-faced shamanism." For this ritual the shaman stands blindfolded (to focus his attention on his journey to the spirit world) on a bench, chanting and bouncing as if astride a mystical horse, working himself into a trance that will banish the separation between the seen and the unseen worlds. He is guided on this journey by the spirit that first called him to be a shaman, along with a host of otherworldly allies who guard him against evil forces. While in this trance, the shaman might well refer to himself as Siv Yis, the original healer.

"My father became a shaman at a very young age—I would guess . . . around ten," remembers Keith Vang. "[Shamans] are not the richest, but they are considered very humble." Indeed, shamans are seen as individuals who serve others in the community, though like doctors in Westernized countries they do not treat members of their own family. If anything is troubling a person other than an obvious physical injury that can be treated with herbs or simple first aid, the shaman will be asked to spiritually analyze his patient.

The Hmong people have traditionally believed that every person has at least three souls and numerous spirits. Sickness is often explained by the loss of one or more of these souls, which can wander off like a child to play with other souls, get bored and take a trip while one is asleep, or be scared off by some traumatic event. At death, the three souls separate. One remains at the deceased person's grave. Thus family members bring food to the graves of their loved ones to feed the spirit that remains there. Another soul is judged by Ntxwj Nyug, assigned a new incarnation, and issued a new mandate of life by Nyuj Vaj Tuam Teem. The last soul must travel back to the place of its birth before resting eternally in the land of its ancestors.

Losing a soul in life is no laughing matter. Dia Cha, professor of cultural studies at St. Cloud State University, explains:

> [W]hen a person has not injured him- or herself, but just suddenly cannot sleep at night, has lost weight, or is depressed, and has started to feel weak, that's when they think it's been caused by spirits . . . And then the shamans or the other spiritual healers will try to diagnose . . . Are all of your souls with you? . . . [H]ave you been put in a situation that might have frightened your spirit away, or might your soul be lost? . . . So if you should happen to fall down accidentally, then when you get up, you need to call, say, "Oh, come, get up, go, let's go, don't stay here! This is not a place for you to stay!" . . . When [parents] have babies or small children, when they go visit their in-laws or to other places that's not their home, when they come out they always call by saying, "Let's go home, don't stay behind" . . . [I]f people don't understand they will ask, "Why are they talking to themselves?" But it's really for the purpose of [summoning] the soul that you call. Sometimes young couples . . . have their first baby and they don't do that and they come back home and the child will cry all night. And they couldn't figure out why until they will bring a flashlight to the door, and they will say, "Come! We forgot to call you! We are home, so now come back. We are home, so don't wander around."

Though only a shaman is said to possess the power to travel into the unseen spirit world, spirits of all kinds regularly manifest themselves in the visible human world. Keith Vang remembers a story his father and his uncle told him. After casting an evil spirit out of a person from a nearby village, the two men were returning home, crossing a valley bisected by a river.

> When they came across this valley, that demon appeared . . . in the form of a fox . . . and wanted to confront [my father] . . . [W]hen [my father] called for help, the un-

cle could not see, and could not help him. Then my father summoned the shaman spirit . . . and he sort of spit some form of water into my uncle's eyes . . . And after that my uncle started seeing this creature and they battled. And the creature obviously left them, and that night came into a dream to let him know that this was not the last that he would see of this creature.

These evil spirits densely populate the human world, affecting not only shamans but all people. Many of the most troublesome, *dab qus* or wild forest spirits, inhabit specific locations in the wild, waiting for souls to capture or kill. It is believed, for example, that dragon spirits reside in the bottoms of lakes and deep pools. Dragon spirits take the form of a rainbow; even American-born or -raised children have been warned by their parents not to go outside when they see a rainbow or the dragon spirit will take them away.

"Even though you and I cannot see the other dimension, the spirits can see us," explains Dia Cha. "So we cannot say bad things about the other spirits or the other gods, or our ancestors who are long gone, because they are always with us . . . [Y]oung people will throw rocks into the forest or into the water, and the parent will stop that . . . And usually the children won't understand, and will keep asking, 'Why? Why? I just threw the rock in the water!' And [the parents] say, 'No, you're going to harm [or anger] the spirit who lives in the lake.'"

Much of what happens in life is explained by the activities of evil spirits and the intervention of "guardian angels" who first escorted each soul from the desk of Nyuj Vaj Tuam Teem to his or her life in the visible world. Almost any significant activity, any journey, might involve some interaction with or placation of some spirit. As Xao Vang Vue explains,

If you walked a full day and rested in a neighboring town . . . when you ate, you would have to call upon dab teb dab chaw *[spirits of the land]. "We have arrived at this location and we ask for you to help protect us to arrive at our destination. Please do not harm us. Now that we are eating, please come and join us in your share. Whether we eat in small or large portions, we are eating with you. Please come join us in exchange for our protection and help get us to our destination." . . . If you do not call upon them in my home country, when you arrive to a town or city that is far away, surrounded by jungle, and you go there, there are bad spirits called* pe kong quoi *and* pe yu vai *. . . that drink blood. If you call upon them, you sleep throughout the night without any disturbances—also if you don't set up a fire that has a sour stench. I've heard [the spirits] before, especially in places that are cold and in towns surrounded by jungles. You have to remember to call upon them to* *protect you from even greater threats like* dab ku haj *or any kind of* dab *that are really evil and mean.*

When you go into places . . . when it is the wrong time to be there, you will become very ill. They say that you have found dab qus. *When you get home, you become very sick. Some will go and return home dead . . . Others who travel in good times will return home without a problem . . . [W]hen you arrive in such a place, you should not kill any kind of animal that has always lived there . . . These animals belong to the* dab qus . . . *[Y]ou should burn incense and say that you want to eat one of their animals. . . . [I]f you go and kill the animals without asking or deliberately slaughter the animals for fun, when you return home, you will become very ill . . . [Y]ou deliberately killed their animals without permission. They want someone's head in return.*

When Khu Thao mentioned that the only dangerous things around her village were the tigers, she wasn't only referring to actual tigers. The Hmong have a wide range of beliefs and legends about spiritual or were-tigers who play the mouth harp and speak with the voice of a lost child, luring unsuspecting people into their ravenous grasp. There is also Poj Ntxoog, a dreaded, unkempt female spirit about the size of a small girl, who lives in the forest and is often associated with tigers.[6]

"Now that we live in a modern country, we must change with the times," says Sao Lee, an Australian Hmong.

I understand why we believed so much in spirit things. There were no hospitals, we lived far from civilization . . . We grew up with those ideas . . . [But] even now, when I go to some strange place or some place that people don't go to very often, I still think that there could be some bad spirit there. I don't do a bad thing; I don't want to hurt any spirit that might make me sick . . . Before we make a long trip to the U.S. or to Laos to visit relatives we usually burn tree incense . . . We always ask the spirit of the house and the ancestor, the grandparent who passed away already, for protection.

Given the pantheistic nature of Hmong cosmology, one would expect shamans to be plentiful and extremely busy, but in fact the most important rituals of all, associated with birth, marriage, and death, require no special or exclusively shamanistic participation at all.*

MATTERS OF LIFE AND DEATH

When a Hmong child is born, the parents conduct a "soul-calling" *(hu plig)* ceremony to ensure that the souls intended to inhabit his or her body have found their way. If the child survives for three days (some-

---

* This is not to say that shamans never perform these ceremonies—they often do. But their participation is not *required*.

thing never taken for granted), the ritual is performed on the house's front stoop. The *hu plig*, which also serves as a christening, begins with the placing of four sprigs of maple in the four corners of the stoop which are then girded in hemp twine to form a "dwelling box" for the soul caller. Facing the lowlands, he holds a chicken and burns incense and paper money (symbolizing an appeal to the spirit world). Standing in front of an egg and a bowl of rice set on a stool, the caller recites and repeats a sweet, winsome incantation inviting the child's souls into his or her body. When the ceremony is complete, the officiant eats with the family and ties hemp strings around everyone's wrists. (String-tying, or *baci*, is also a common ritual performed, for example, on the recently sick and those about to take a long journey.) Parents might attempt to more firmly bind their children's souls in place by adorning them with silver necklets. The father buries the child's placenta, thought of as the "golden jacket" that delivered the baby's soul into this world, under one of the hut's supporting poles (the main pole if it is a boy, the pole in the sleeping area if it is a girl). Years later, when the person's mandate of life has expired, the soul destined for eternal rest with its ancestors must first travel back to all of the places it has lived, ending with the place the placenta was buried, before it can complete its journey.

Another important ceremony is the *Chai Cha Kai*—the reading of the chicken, here described in a fictional account by Piriya Panasuwan:

Dang Lee killed one black chicken and gave it to the [shaman] to pluck out the feathers without dipping it in hot water first . . . [T]he chicken was cooked . . . and placed in a bamboo tray in front of everyone.

There are three points on the chicken that have to be read, they are the eyes, the head, and the fingers. If both eyes . . . were not tightly closed, it meant that the newborn baby would be difficult to raise. He would have all kinds of illnesses and might die while still young . . . [T]he [shaman] had to split [the head] open. If there was no fresh blood left in the veins, it meant that the baby would grow up to be a clever man . . . Should all of the fingers stretch out straight, it meant that the baby would be very successful and would become a very important member of the family. Generally it is almost impossible for all three parts of the chicken to turn out good.[*][7]

When the *hu plig* ceremony is complete, no outsider is allowed to enter the home for thirty days. And every person in the community knows better than to compliment the child, no matter how attractive

---

[*] The chicken's tongue is another important sign. If it pulls out straight, all will be well. If it breaks or comes out crooked, it is a sign that the spirits are displeased.

he or she may be, since these remarks might invite the interest of evil spirits.

Those who have observed Hmong rituals may notice the frequent presence of chicken sacrifice. The importance of the chicken—more specifically the rooster—is traced back to the tale of Kaj Yuam, the Heavenly Archer, who made the first crossbow and shot down nine of the ten suns and eight of the nine moons that originally circled the earth. The last sun, fearing for her life, fled into hiding, plunging the world into darkness and chaos. As humankind teetered on the brink of destruction, the rooster crowed, coaxing the sun back into the sky. The first thing touched by the sun's rays was the rooster's head, which now bears a bright red plume. The rooster, then, is seen as a savior of humanity, a powerful spiritual force, and also a "heavenly herald that leads the soul of the deceased into the Otherworld."[8]

Sacrifices of animals are not made lightly. First, of course, these resources are precious. But even more important, a life is being taken. "When Hmong sacrifice an animal for different ceremonies," says Dia Cha, "they always ask for permission. They always tell the chicken or the pig or the cow that 'We sacrifice you because God created you to serve this purpose. We do it, and we know it is a life that we're taking, and we apologize for it.' And so they have this kind of 'respect ritual' that reminds the animal that they don't just make the sacrifice without a purpose . . . It's a way to recognize that their lives are precious and valuable as ours, that they are just as significant as we are."

The Hmong child is born into a patriarchal, patrilineal community. Most societies controlled by men have stories explaining why this is so, and the Hmong are no exception. According to one legend, an aging, childless Hmong king looking for a successor secretly gathered all the Hmong men together. He announced that he would pass on his position to the first man with the courage to kill his wife and bring him her head. The next day when they returned, each man confessed that despite the ruler's remarkable offer, he didn't have the heart to kill his wife. One said, "I thought to myself, 'If I kill her, and someone else does too, only one man will get the throne. So what's the point of killing my wife and not becoming king?'" Another said, "If I killed my wife and married another woman, would my new wife love my children the way their mother does?" Others told similar stories. After repeated attempts to convince at least one man to rise to his challenge, the ruler hit upon a new strategy.

Chia Choua Vang (center) and two sons: Yeng, the oldest (right), and Wa Toua, the second oldest. All three would eventually fight in the Secret War.

He summoned all of the women, once again in secret, and made the same pitch: kill your husband, bring me his head, and you will inherit my kingdom. The next day every woman stood at his door waiting to cash in on his offer. Each one had gone home and hidden a knife under her pillow. There were more heads than the king could possibly accommodate or allow in his home, so he ordered the women to place them in a nearby ditch, which filled to the brim in short order. Every woman insisted that since she had done as the king desired, she deserved his throne. The king angrily denounced them. "You evil women! Don't you realize that I must have first made this offer to your husbands? And though I tried for three days to convince even one of them to kill even one of you, none of them would do it! I made you this offer only once, and every single one has committed murder without hesitation! What else are you capable of? Who else might you kill once you become ruler of my kingdom?" In disgust the king declared that no Hmong woman would ever have power over men. He wrote a list of their crimes in lurid detail and required every woman to carry a copy on her back. (The small extension on the back side of a Hmong woman's collar—her *dab tshos*—supposedly still commemorates this ancient offense.) From that time forward, men were allowed to do as they pleased, including marry more than one wife, while women would always be the wife of only one husband.[9]

Xao Vang Vue was asked to explain why her father took a second wife:

"He liked her, so he married her."

"He just liked her. It wasn't that there was heavy work for the family that he married her? Or was it that your mom couldn't have any boys or girls that he married again?"

"He liked her, so he married her."

"So there was no problem of any sort?"

"No. He liked her, so he married her."

In 1965, Carol Mills was in Laos with the U.S. Agency for International Development, working with several Hmong leaders to assist refugees. One of them was taking a second wife. "And I was very upset . . . growing up in an American culture, and I said to his wife, 'Aren't you upset Nhia Ying's taking another wife?' And she basically said, 'Oh no, it'll make my life so much easier. One of us will work in the field, one of us will watch the children, and I don't have to do both.' So you realized there are different ways of looking at things."

Obviously, not all plural marriages were accepted so easily. During the years of the Secret War, Mai Lee Yang's father was helping a team of Hmong soldiers remove land mines. She was not yet born. When the team accidentally detonated a mine, her inexperienced father stayed standing as his comrades hit the dirt. He was struck by shrapnel and evacuated to a hospital in the south. Soon after, the Nong Het region where Yang's family lived was taken over by Communists and her father was unable to return. She was born, but her older sister died from some unknown disease. Living with her husband's family, as Hmong custom dictates, Mai Lee's mother asked for and received permission to return to her own parents' home. Yang and her mother sustained each other with stories of one day reuniting with their lost husband/father. "I just remember my mom took me with her to the opium field . . . [S]he would need company, and I would just tell her stories, she would tell me stories . . . about her mother, about her parents, about her young childhood, about my father, how they met . . . [I]t was only myself and my mother, so she didn't want me to do anything—maybe she was lonely."

One night in 1969, almost ten years after her father had been wounded, a man arrived in the village, announcing that Mai Lee's father had sent him to rescue them. The two could hardly believe their ears. They hurriedly packed, said their good-byes to the family that had nurtured them for so long, and followed their guide through hostile territory for their long-awaited reunion. Finally arriving at the Hmong stronghold of Long Tieng, they were told her father was in the nearby village of Sam Thong. They were put on a plane—an experience foreign to both of them, and one that made Mai Lee violently ill—only to discover that her father was back in Long Tieng.

As soon as we got to Sam Thong . . . my uncle, my father's sister's husband, was there, and they knew my mother . . . [He] said, "Oh! You are here!" And he took us to their house. My mother and I stayed there, and I played with their kids . . . And every car that came past . . . they said, "Oh, maybe it's your father's car!" and we would all run out to have a look. But I didn't know who my father was, or what he looked like . . . And as we were playing outside my father came. He was wearing army dress, and a green hat. First [when] we saw him, I didn't know it was him, but my cousin knew it was him—"Oh, your father's here! Your father's here! Oh, Uncle's here!" I was so scared, I ran back inside to my mother, and he was chasing me! And I was crying, and he grabbed me and said, "Don't worry, don't be scared, don't be afraid. I am your father" . . . And he was crying, and he was hugging my mother and me at once. I remember, he said, "Don't be scared. Look at me and let me look at your face." [E]verybody was crying at that time. Like I said, they were apart for nearly ten years.

But soon we got to the place where . . . they came and picked up with the planes. At that time they told my mother, "Oh, your husband's married and got two children" . . . He didn't let the army tell my mother he's remarried already: "Just tell my wife to come" . . . And my mom is crying her eyes out . . . She didn't want to come

*anymore, but she couldn't [go back], because that place was [in enemy hands] al-
ready . . . And then my father came, and my father said, "I'm sorry I married, but I
still love you . . . Don't worry, I'll look after you. You are my first wife. I will love you
until we die." I remember what my father said . . . [T]wo hours later we reached his
house — and his wife's home, his two children . . . [I]t was hard at home. And we had
to sleep with them at the same house. And he has two children — very nasty, very,
very nasty. I had never seen children like that in my life. Even now I still haven't seen
any children as nasty as that.*

Yang remembers her later childhood, with a clear but understandable lack of objectivity, as a series of gut-wrenching confrontations between herself and her shotgun-adopted stepsiblings and a slow but in-
exorable alienation between her mother and father.

Hmong custom dictates that a man's first wife is the "head wife,"
having authority over any who follow, but a woman with a strong personality, aided by the effects of ten years of separation, can easily upset
this largely unenforceable tradition.

While any man could marry more than one wife, this practice was
limited by a few factors. Since a man was expected to provide a bride
price for his intended, often paid in silver worth about six hundred dollars, only those wealthy enough to afford this expense more than once
would think about marrying again. The relative poverty of the Hmong
people meant that polygamy was for the most part a wealthy man's practice. The main exception to this rule was *levirate.* If a woman lost her
husband, she had the option of marrying her husband's younger brother
and moving her children in with him, even if he was already married.

Another factor working against polygamy in some areas was the introduction and acceptance of Christianity. PaMang Her, who later
trained to become a pastor, claims that his father foretold the arrival
of missionaries bringing a new message to his people:

*The Thao clan believed first, and the Moua, Her, and Thao clans all lived by each
other, but in different villages. And the Thaos would spread the news when there
was someone in need or sick. During that year, many people became believers. Before
my parents were believers, my father [Zong Chue Her] was a shaman . . . and a
prophet . . . [H]e said that a day would come when everyone would believe in God
and all the evil spirits would go away . . . Christ is going to come. The relatives decided he was crazy, and they moved him from Pa Kad to Tum Thoa . . . [A]fter a while
the missionaries came and my father told them that he was talking about this all
along . . . [M]y father took all his old ways and laws and burned all of them, and
everyone still said he was crazy and if they didn't do anything to fix him, he was go-*

ing to die . . . But then my father didn't die and told them that God had told him to become a believer and he didn't die, so we all should become believers.

Christianity, another messianic belief system, was appealing not only for its message but also because of its apparent imperviousness to evil spirits. As Her recalls, missionaries "rented a house from a shaman [and our mayor] . . . which was haunted by ghosts . . . [T]he shaman told them that they could not live there, but the missionaries told him that their God was with them and they were not scared. When they lived in that house, they prayed so the ghosts all went away . . . That was when [the shaman] wanted to know the missionary more and see how God was more powerful than the ghosts."

Though they had encountered Christianity in China, it was in Laos and Vietnam that Hmong, especially Green Hmong, were converted in significant numbers. In addition to bringing the Gospel—and a good dose of Western culture—religious figures like Father F. M. Savina, Dr. William Smalley, Father Yves Bertrais, and Dr. Linwood Barney carefully observed Hmong culture, speculated on Hmong history and ethnographic origins, and helped create a Hmong writing system based on Roman letters. But to be sure, no Christian missionary tolerated polygamy.[10]

Most Hmong marriages—at least first marriages—began with courtship, and the best time for this activity was during the New Year, a celebration normally tied to the end of the harvest season, roughly at the close of the lunar year. While courtship outside of the New Year was certainly possible, most families kept their courting-age children quite busy during the remainder of the year. Khu Thao describes only the agricultural part of her busy schedule:

In January or February . . . we would go and cut down the forest and prepare the field for another year of rice paddies and cornfields . . . [W]e would let it dry for about one month. Then we would go back and burn it. If all of it did not burn away, we would have to go and pick up the remains and put it in a pile and burn it. We had to do that so the field would be nice and flat and clear to plant, and when weeds started to grow, it would be easier to pull them out . . . First we would plant the corn seeds, then the rice patty. After we were done planting the rice patty, the cornfields were already full of weeds for us to pick. After we were done weeding the corn, the rice needed weeding, too . . . [W]e would have to weed the fields twice before the corn and rice fields started to grow. The corn was the first to be ready, and then the rice. After we had put the corn away, then we would go back and harvest the rice . . . [I]f we had the time, we would [put the grains in a cloth bag and] hit it for the [seed husks] to come down, and then we would have the New Year. If we didn't have time, then we would just bring it in and stack it up in the storage room until after the New Year. Then we would go back and hit the rice. . . When I learned how to garden I was probably around six or seven years old . . . We would have to burn in the sun, get wet in the rain, get bit by little bugs and mosquitoes. We would start our day every morning at about five in the morning until seven at night. This is if we lived far from the field and would sleep over there. If we were going from our house, we would start at about seven in the morning and come back home at five at night . . . The only time we would rest was after we finished a row of rice or corn or when we took a break to eat lunch for about thirty or forty minutes.

Another crop commonly grown by the Hmong was opium. Despite the fantasies spun by movies like *Air America,* which bore almost no resemblance to the book by Christopher Robbins that "inspired" it, the Hmong did not grow opium for recreational use by themselves or others. It had limited use as a folk remedy, stimulant, and pain reliever. (Before dismissing this assertion too quickly, think of the vast array of "folk remedies" in the United States that were little more than high-octane alcohol.) While opium addiction did exist, it was rare and socially stigmatizing. No sane woman would marry an opium addict, and fathers would only rarely give an addict son the bride price he needed to wed. Opium was primarily used as a cash crop—both to pay taxes, a practice encouraged by the Lao government and the French colonizers, and to trade in exchange for other necessities. Opium netted a family more wealth per acre than the other crops they grew. A ball of unrefined opium carried in one's hand was much easier to haul down the side of a mountain than its financial equivalent in rice or corn, and most if not all of the other two crops were needed just to feed one's family and livestock.*[11]

If there were forces that reduced polygamy, Australian anthropologist William Geddes believed opium tipped the scales in the other direction. Geddes, one of the first Western non-missionaries to study the Hmong, made this assertion in his groundbreaking book, *Migrants of the Mountains.* Gary Yia Lee, pursuing his master's degree in social work

---

* The Hmong were already growing opium in China and brought the practice to their new homes. Robert Cooper has surmised that the Hmong eschewed the highly populated lowlands and moved into areas where opium markets were being created. They might well have moved into the mountains in no small part to take advantage of this ideal cultivation environment, growing opium in large quantities to maximize profits.

from the University of New South Wales, heard about the imminent publication of Geddes's book and rang him up. Quite pleased at the prospect of meeting an educated Hmong in his native land, Geddes congenially invited Lee over and offered him a copy of the book's galleys.

[H]e said that the Hmong institution of polygamy arose directly from the opium economy. And I said, "Why did you say that? Even Hmong who don't grow opium have many wives."... But now I go back to read his book and I agree with him ... because he's not talking about opium, but he's talking about economic success ... [I]n those days the Hmong only made money from growing opium, and no other commodity, because they ... didn't have the means to do otherwise. But what he's trying to say is that rich people can afford more than one wife ... And this is true.[12]

So the cultivation of opium created wealth, supported the practice of polygamy, and was yet another chore required of children who were also busy planting, weeding, tending, and harvesting a variety of crops, caring for livestock, and preparing each morning for their journey into the field—the females usually getting up an hour earlier than the males to fix the meals for the day. If they had younger siblings, they would often have to look after them. So upon arriving home, if they returned at all, teenagers were likely to be quite tired.

For those who still had the energy for courtship, there were clear, socially prescribed rules to follow. "In the old days, you did not tell each other verbally that you liked each other," says Xai Thao,

but used the traditional pipe instrument and other means to tell them. The passions in the tunes of the instruments expressed feelings that no words could. These tunes would tell how much you loved someone and that you wanted to marry her. We were too embarrassed to talk openly to someone that we were attracted to, not like you children today. We did not date; there was only courtship. The man would never enter our house. At midnight, the man who likes you will come like a thief to talk to you ... [through] the thin bamboo walls of the hut.

If a girl reached the point where she liked the boy enough, she might sneak out of the house for the evening, though she had to return in time to rise the next morning and help with the cooking and preparation for work. While premarital pregnancy did not always lead to marriage, the man who refused to wed the mother of his child would have to pay a penalty to the girl's parents, and the child would stay in the girl's family. Being the mother of an illegitimate child hurt a girl's reputation but did not erase her prospects for marriage, since the ability to bear children was seen as an essential attribute for a potential bride.

Still, the primary means for members of the opposite sex to meet and engage in lengthy romantic conversation remained the New Year—about the first of December. "When we were kids we were poor, we didn't eat meat every day—we ate it once a week or maybe once a month, depending on how rich your family was," remembers Sao Lee. "When New Year came, it didn't matter how poor or how rich a family was, everyone had to prepare for the New Year, had to buy new clothes, at least each kid had to have new clothes, a pair of new shoes, and at least we must have a few chickens for the New Year celebration."

Like many in the West, the Hmong saw the New Year as a time of reflection and renewal. They offered sacrifices to ancestral and household spirits who watched over and dwelt in various parts of the house. At least one highly adorned paper altar was dedicated to these spirits in each home. Every New Year that altar received a kind of spring cleaning and redecoration with new ceremonial paper. "They will thank the household spirit for protecting them over the year, explains Dia Cha, "and they will ask him to continue to protect the family in the New Year."*

For young people, New Year was primarily about fun and—for those of the appropriate age—flirting. "Everyone was looking forward to the New Year in Laos," says Sao Lee, "Ninety-nine percent of our life was spent at the farm; only at New Year were we allowed to stay at home for a minimum of three days. That's the only time you can see many girls!"

The primary means of communication between boys and girls was the ball tossing ceremony. Girls would each bring a ball—when possible made of hand-sewn silk—to toss with a suitor of their choosing. Hmong are not allowed to marry anyone sharing the same clan name, but other than this prohibition, only mutual attraction and the often vain efforts of parents to match up certain children to each other limited one's prospects. "Usually on that day," says Lee,

---

* This paper, called "joss paper," was traditionally handmade. "They used the young bamboo shoot," explains Cha, "and pounded it . . . They would carve and decorate it, and sometimes they would put chicken feathers [on it] if they were sacrificing chicken . . . [T]hey may put a few drops of blood from the chicken on it to sparkle the paper. But today the Hmong cannot do that anymore, so they buy commercially made [paper] . . . used for the household spirit, and they hang it up on the wall. That symbolizes the altar for the house spirit to occupy, and then in that area you are not supposed to do anything to disturb it, like children should not be playing there. People should not go in and lean against it. It is considered very rude if you go into a Hmong home and you just go stand so close or to lean against it or to touch it."

Girls ball tossing during a New Year celebration in Laos

you put on your best clothes . . . [Y]ou always looked for a flat area to toss the ball . . . Just say you are a boy: you walk around, you see a beautiful girl that you like. The first thing you do is ask what clan she belongs to. She could be a Yang, a Vue, or a Lor . . . If she says "I'm a Lee," I say, "Oh, you are my sister! Sorry!" . . . But if she says, "I'm a Yang," then you ask for her name, her age, and she will tell you. "Do you have a boyfriend?" If she says, "No," then you can ask if she wants to toss the ball with you.[13]

Many of these exchanges, depending on the age and comparative gregariousness of the individuals involved, began shyly and modestly. If the couple was mutually attracted, their interactions could last for the entire New Year and culminate in marriage. Others kept looking and might even travel to a nearby village to see if the pickings were better elsewhere. (Since most Hmong villages consisted of as few as twenty to thirty households, about half the time individuals found their future spouse outside the village.)

While the ball tossing ceremony has often been depicted in a romantic light, it had its darker or more scatological moments. Former CIA officer Vint Lawrence lived with the Hmong in Long Tieng for four years during the Secret War. He remembers the Hmong courtship ritual less sentimentally as "a sort of a gang wooing ritual . . . They toss the ball back and forth, and . . . there's a lot of sexual banter that goes on . . . I spoke enough Lao to understand it, but they were going back and forth in Hmong, and basically it's one sexual joke after another with the young girl."

In addition, it is customary that people who, intentionally or not, drop a ball tossed at them must surrender an article of jewelry or clothing to their partner. These items can be retrieved in exchange for a song. A poorly performed song or a too-hasty retrieval is a clear but not too insulting sign that the person wishes to move on to someone else. "As the day moves into evening, all but the determined have left the field," writes Robert Cooper. "Catchers become increasing maladroit and clothing changes hands and is not immediately retrieved. As darkness halts the game, each couple comes together to retrieve clothing and exchange songs. Not everything is retrieved and if a girl is wearing a man's watch the next day, it's a clear sign she is no longer to be the target of serious courtship." Unfortunately these customs, which can be interpreted to say that a girl in possession of an item belonging to a young man has entered into a binding contract of marriage, have been used on at least a few occasions to force girls away from their homes and into undesired unions. But no marriage, even one approved under duress, is considered binding until the parents of the couple have agreed on a bride price.[14]

"When both were ready for marriage and were [ideally] in love," explains Xai Thao,

representatives of the groom's family would bring some rice wine over and would try to offer a dowry for the girl's marriage. Sometimes the groom would come and "kidnap" the bride. In Laos, the dowry is to compensate for the loss of a valuable worker in the bride's family. The dowry would normally be five silver bars, worth about six hundred American dollars. Sometimes the bride's parents will give marriage presents that will be as valuable and as expensive as six hundred dollars. In Laos, the marriage age usually was around sixteen years old. If you were younger than this, the in-laws considered that you were still too young to do work.

Negotiating a bride price remains a delicate act of diplomacy. It was expected that no one would feign poverty, make excessive demands, or draw attention to real or imagined faults in either family's lineage. In the early stages, no contact between actual family members was involved: the male's father designated two emissaries to negotiate on his son's behalf. If discussions proved unsuccessful, then no one lost face.

If circumstances looked promising, the parents would meet to finalize arrangements. These discussions, even when agreeable, usually dragged on for several days, culminating in a promised payment due on the wedding day. If the couple feared the boy's parents might balk at the bride price or her parents might say no, they might have arranged a kidnapping, which was often, though certainly not always, a coconspiracy. (This strategy was also helpful if the girl was pregnant.) If the boy's family was poor, he would probably have to work off the bride price to his father-in-law for an unspecified period after the marriage.

Under normal circumstances, the bride would keep her own clan name (perhaps in part to maintain the clear message that husband and wife are not from the same clan) but live with her husband's family and adopt their family spirits as her own. "It is by tradition," says Xai Thao, *that the new bride cannot work for three full days when she first enters into the groom's house . . . The in-laws would go kill some chicken or a pig to offer to their ancestors so that the bride would be accepted into her new clan family. The groom was expected to work and help out at the in-law's house and farm as much as he worked on his or his parents' farm. The newly wedded are to call their in-laws "mother" and "father." It is an unspoken law and tradition that the bride must put her new family before herself, no matter the circumstances.*

To express the love of the family she leaves behind, the bride's parents often provided their daughter with "bride wealth" *(phij cuab)* to ensure short-term security and respect in her new family. This wealth, which usually included livestock, would remain entirely under her control, continuing to serve as a reminder of her parents' love and keeping her from feeling completely dependent on her in-laws.[15]

Most newlyweds lived with the husband's parents for the first years of their marriage—usually until they had a child or two of their own. In the meantime, they contributed to the economic well-being of the husband's family, though the son also possessed and controlled his own fields. What little leisure time Hmong families enjoyed was usually after supper. If the family had guests or was simply too large to eat together, the men always ate first, followed by the women. Men tended to gather around the fire, drinking tea and smoking their pipes (filled with tobacco, not opium), discussing everything from local politics to economic activities, from hunting to prospective new lands where they might relocate once their own fields played out. Women would often assemble for conversation and sewing.

Vint Lawrence marveled at the sewing skill of Hmong women:

It was one of those things where you realize that the people you're with have a different matrix of intelligence . . . I watched a woman embroidering one of these enormous Hmong skirts that are heavily pleated so that they are just enormous . . . [T]hey would start literally in one corner . . . and the patterns would get more and more elaborate, and then they would get all the way around the circle and come back to the original point in about a year's time, and it would end up perfectly symmetrical. And how they did that without patterns, without any kind of . . . aforethought whatsoever, I found absolutely remarkable.

In Laos the Hmong are divided into at least three subgroups whose names correspond to the women's clothing. Green employ batik in their highly ornate dresses. White usually wear blue pants, donning white skirts during the New Year. Armband or "Striped" incorporate distinctive marks on their sleeves.

A mother (third from left), her three daughters, and her grandson: Ge Vang, Bla Vang, Mai Thao, Mee Vang, and little Lee Pao Xiong, who eventually studied political science and public policy in Minnesota and is currently director of the Center for Hmong Studies at Concordia University, St. Paul.

Hmong people also have an affinity for music that seems almost unearthly to the average Westerner. Gretel Schwoerer-Kohl writes, "In the West . . . nursery rhymes [like] 'Jack and Jill' . . . or 'Frere Jacques' are (or were) sung by mothers to children without musical accompaniment . . . [I]t is almost impossible to hum or hear such songs without the words forming in the mind. In a very simple way, the hummed version represents a musical language code." The Hmong way of communicating through music is "about a million times more sophisticated." Hmong people can hear sounds and know what they mean without having heard them before. Though preliterate, the Hmong have for centuries been "eminently literate in terms of interpreting musical sounds." Hmong songs played on the flute, the mouth harp, or the *qeej*, the traditional reed pipe, can be performed without lyrics but still convey a very clear verbal message.

Even so, singing is prized by the Hmong. A village visitor may be surprised at the strength of the voice emanating from an old Hmong man or young Hmong girl. Hmong often sing just because they feel like singing. Some songs are known to everyone; others, especially those employed during courtship, are usually improvised. Still others of an arcane and complex nature serve specific ritual functions, especially at funerals, and are painstakingly learned and performed by community specialists.[16]

As skilled as the Hmong were at music and communication, their most serious shortcoming was in medicine. It was all too common for babies or mothers to die during birth, for dysentery to decimate a village, or for a seemingly routine accident to end in tragedy. Zong Khang Yang remembers going into the forest with his older brother to cut firewood.

He wanted to chop wood, and he accidentally cut his foot between the toes . . . [In the United States], we learned that when there's bleeding, you put some cloth on it and put pressure on it. That's it! . . . At that time Hmong people believed in magic — khou gong . . . [T]hey use, burn small incense and they recite the magic and blow into it, and it's supposed to stop the blood. Or they . . . put water over the wound, and it's supposed to stop the blood . . . [B]ut he was bleeding like crazy. And even though we raised his foot up, it's still bleeding . . . They do not put any pressure on it. Everybody's literally watching him bleed to death. So at that time, in that place, there's no hospital, no doctor. So we used a shaman, we used a medicine man . . . and it's not working. And then he died.*

The death of a loved one set in motion a series of events and actions involving the immediate family, the community, and numerous relatives from villages near and far. Funerals were significant occasions, not only because of the importance of saying final good-byes, lending assistance to the survivors, and helping with rituals, but also because they provided an opportunity to reinforce lineage ties, expand contacts with other family members, and even learn about new land or other agricultural resources.

Much help was (and still is) required for the traditional Hmong funeral. At least one cow, perhaps many more, would be slaughtered to show respect for the departed—and because it was believed that these animals would follow him into the Otherworld. People might burn ceremonial paper money, signifying the wealth they hoped to pass on to

---

* This tragedy, which occurred well after the Hmong's alliances with the French and the United States, indicates that modern medicine did not always penetrate down to the village level. Most medical care was focused on soldiers, though the United States did provide treatment to villagers through an organized system of dispensaries.

their loved one in his new life. It was also traditional to bring some kind of gift—a form of social welfare—to the family. As the departed's family profusely shared their thanks with the guests, the guests simultaneously and adamantly replied that no thanks were necessary.

The funeral itself lasted at least three days and involved a number of important rituals. The body, for example, would be shod in special hemp slippers designed to withstand the stress of the spirit's long walk through a forbidding, craggy landscape covered by poisonous caterpillars and leading to the home of Ntxwj Nyug.

"In the whole funeral," says Chia Deng Lor, "there are three important components. The first [is] the guiding of the spirit . . . If a person passed away . . . [and] that person happened to be born in China, moved to Laos, to Thailand, and to the U.S., and died in the U.S., then the person who guides that person['s soul] . . . should know all about his history . . . and guide him backwards towards his birthplace," stopping at any place where he spent more than one year. For each place, "the person who guides that spirit has to . . . thank all the spirits . . . that provided food . . . firewood, rice, water, whatever . . . until he reaches China." When it reaches the place where he was born, his spirit must be reunited with the placenta his father buried—his "golden jacket."

"They have to go back and get that clothing," says Lor, "put it back on, and then they can enter the spiritual world to stay with their ancestors." According to Keith Vang, "[W]hen they're done playing the song, and if you are one of the brave ones, you watch closely and you will see a color change in the dead person from a tan to black or blue . . . [Y]ou feel the spirit has left the body or that that person is really gone—or you really see there is a corpse."

"[U]sually it was during the second day," continues Chia Deng Lor, "that [the family] invited all his friends and relatives to . . . pay respects and maybe to say something to thank him for his help when he was still alive . . . And then the second part was the blessing back to his or her descendants." A highly skilled singer is hired to convey the wishes and blessings of the deceased back to his or her family. This time, called *Qhua txws*, is one in which the living pay respects to the dead but the dead also share blessings and advice with the living. The family of the deceased, says Keith Vang, "also pay respect by bowing down or kowtowing." They often feel that the blessings they received from their beloved relative will also pass on to him in his new life.

"The last day," says Chia Deng Lor, "is the *sam-sab*—that is to get ready to bury the person. And then they will have some *qeej* songs and some other rituals to send . . . the body of the person for burial." A large funeral drum is beaten, and people start to loudly, openly wail and mourn.

Back in Laos, remembers Vint Lawrence,

There was a . . . group of keeners, who were hysterical to watch. These women started keening and wailing; then [they] would . . . go out and . . . start laughing and talk about something else. And then they would go back in and immediately start [wailing again] . . . [Funerals] were daylong if not weeklong events where it was a personal good-bye said by all the relatives. That was why the body was left on the table, was that everyone who was related to that person had to basically come and touch the body one more time.

Just as the soul of the dead is forced to search for its home with the help of its relatives, so too those who lived in Southeast Asia regularly needed to find a new home. The practice of slash-and-burn farming or swidden agriculture eventually depleted the soil, requiring families to relocate every dozen or so years. But whole villages did not just pull up stakes and move elsewhere. Moving, after all, was a great deal of work and disturbed longstanding ties of family, kinship, and friendship.

The process was sometimes initiated by an adult married child who left his father's house to establish his own home. If no land was available nearby, he would try to move to land close to another relative. If such an arrangement was not possible, the family would establish a new home on the frontier—a prospect both frightening and full of potential. If successful, they would eventually be joined by other family members who would form the core of a new village.

If a larger component of the family was moving at once, decisions regarding when and where to move were made by the eldest member of the *tsev* or household, which usually included three generations of the family, as well as any widowed, divorced, or unmarried aunts or uncles. Younger members of the family might go first, allowing elders to live in greater comfort, though at least one son—usually the youngest— would stay behind to care for his parents and ensure that proper funeral and burial rituals were observed if one or both of them died.

Most Hmong lived in several places over the course of their lifetime, leaving behind the bodies and souls of departed family and friends, as well as the golden jackets (placentas) of their and their family's souls.

They took their ancestral altar and a bit of ash from the depleted earth they left behind. But they also fervently believed they would return one day when, in death, their souls traveled to all of the places they had called home in life.[17]

THE OTHERS

"Hmong culture never excludes any friends or any outsiders," says Gary Yia Lee. "If we are in the middle of a ceremony, some stranger just walks into the village, 'Come' . . . [T]he Hmong have no word for 'privacy' or 'personal' . . . Everything is communal, group, family. Most of the things we do, like funerals—if you go there and you're not a Hmong . . . they are very, very happy to see you. The more the better. It just means you care about our dead person."

But as people with a rather strong libertarian impulse, the Hmong bristled under the taxation of the Lao and the French. Laos had been under the political control of its ethnic majority, the lowland Lao, since the kingdom of Lan Xang ("Land of a Million Elephants") was established by Fa Ngum in 1353. Since the Buddhist king held both religious and political power, the royal city of Luang Prabang was also the nation's capital. But the kingdom's history was riddled with invasions from neighboring countries. According to Sucheng Chan,

Vietnamese armies marched through Xieng Khouang [province] all the way to the capital at Luang Prabang and held that city for a time before they were expelled. During the sixteenth century, Siam (the old name for Thailand) and Burma [now called Myanmar] invaded Lan Xang five times, causing the reigning monarch to move the capital to Vientiane. Toward the end of the seventeenth century, disputes over succession broke the kingdom into . . . three kingdoms: Luang Prabang in the north, Vientiane in the middle, and Champassak in the south. The eighteenth century saw Burma sack Luang Prabang in 1753 and again in 1771, and Siam attack Vientiane in 1778. In the early 19th century, the Siamese again invaded Vientiane and reduced it to ruins, while the Vietnamese claimed the provinces of Xieng Khouang and Khammouane. The Laotian kingdoms managed to survive by recognizing the suzerainty of both Siam and Vietnam.[18]

The Hmong played an important role during the conflicts of the early twentieth century, says Vint Lawrence, who heard the following story from numerous elders in Laos. In the 1920s, "the Vietnamese invaded northern Laos, and the Hmong, who were then in the Plaine des

Jarres . . . banded together and resisted, and in effect saved . . . the Luang Prabang king . . . [T]he king then gave to the Hmong of Xieng
Khouang a greater degree of self-governance than they had, than any
other minority group had."

In the midst of this bubbling cauldron of turmoil lived dozens of distinct ethnic groups, the Lao majority constituting only about half of the
country's population. The Hmong, who began arriving in the early nineteenth century, passed through the lowlands, on through the lower
mountain elevations populated by groups collectively known as the *Lao
Theung* (Lao of the Mountain Slopes), and into areas above three thousand feet. The ethnic Lao called the Lao Theung *Kha* (Slaves) and the
Hmong *Meo* (Savages).*

By 1858, the French had a presence in Indochina. They annexed
southern Vietnam (Cochin China) and established a protectorate over
Cambodia in 1864 and over central and northern Vietnam (Annam and
Tonkin respectively) by 1884. By the late 1890s, France also controlled
Laos. The French had few problems ruling the relatively easygoing Lao,
save when they attempted to import Vietnamese into the country as
civil servants. Long-standing animosities between the Lao and their
more aggressive neighbors boiled over but failed to stanch the flow of
foreigners. One of France's strategies to solidify its control over the region was "race mixing." France calculated the population density of Laos
as four people per square mile. In Vietnam's Mekong Delta it was close
to fifteen hundred. The French brought Vietnamese into Lao cities as
traders and merchants and midlevel bureaucrats, swelling the numbers
of those who would later participate in the Communist movement in
Laos, run by Hanoi.[19]

In 1896, the French instituted new draconian taxes intended to
make up the more than 50 percent budget shortfall in Laos. They left
collection of these new taxes to the existing Lao bureaucracy. "During
our grandparents' generation," says Pa Seng Thao,

*the taxes could be collected in the form of human labor [corvée], field taxes and live-
stock taxes . . . The French wanted the payment in opium . . . [T]he Laotians [also]
wanted taxation in the form of opium from us . . . whether we had opium or not.*

---

* One must distinguish between *Miao*, used by the Chinese, and *Meo*, used by the Lao and
adopted by the French and Americans. Both of these words are widely considered offensive by
the Hmong people in America, though there is disagreement about this.

[They collected taxes for the French.] The Laotians wanted one kilo of opium per [household] . . . Some of us were naïve and they overtaxed and cheated us by taxing for everything else not required. They even took our livestock and money . . . Some of the parents had to sell their children to pay for the taxes. Some parents were so upset that they committed suicide by taking poison . . .

My father told me that the Laotian authorities often came and took more than the required taxes and made profit from it . . . We found out when some of the Hmong leaders went with the Laotian authorities to deliver the taxes to the government in the city and saw how they kept half of the taxes for themselves . . . They even forced us to pay a special tax called Tah La [market place] . . . The Laotian tax collectors . . . would go to the market to buy themselves a cow [worth almost a year's wage]. This was the reason why we didn't care about going to war with them.

The Hmong attacked a French post northwest of Nong Het, an important trading community tucked into a forty-five-hundred-foot mountain pass on the Laos-Vietnam border. The Hmong were armed only with crossbows and flintlocks; the French mowed them down with their modern carbine rifles but were shaken by the ferocity of the Hmong attack. The colonial government investigated the situation and discovered the incident was fomented by a Lao governor attempting to shift blame from himself. They unseated him, met with a *kiatong* (little king) of the Moua clan, and negotiated a settlement. Taxes were reduced, and a few Hmong were even awarded positions in the provincial bureaucracy. The *kiatong,* Tong Ger Moua, became the first *tasseng* (district chieftain) of Nong Het. Several others were made *naiban* (village head).

But this new era was short-lived. Local Lao officials, deprived of money now going directly to the French, decided to reinstitute the taxes they collected themselves. Hmong appeals to the French went unanswered. In fact, France started collecting taxes twice a year instead of only once and expanded taxes to teenagers as well as adults. In 1917 the French once again began demanding *corvée* from Vietnamese and Lao farmers to build a road system they vainly hoped would finally make the region profitable. The Lao and Vietnamese usually had enough money to buy themselves out of *corvée,* but the countries' minorities did not.

In 1918, humiliation, resentment, and anger boiled over into a violent revolt led by Pa Chay (Batchai) Vue, a Hmong chieftain many believed to be the long-awaited messiah. But while hundreds took up arms and pledged an "oath to heaven" to follow him, other Hmong who benefited from their or their clan's new standing within the colonial bureaucracy stood against him. This was the first but certainly not the last time that Hmong across Vietnam and Laos would take sides against one another.

Pa Chay's rebellion began in Vietnam, near the border town of Dien Bien Phu. Villagers were convinced he could perform miracles. Leading their enemies on a frantic chase, Pa Chay's forces raided and burned villages at such a pace that the French finally abandoned the chase and focused on negotiation. Refusing compromise on every point, Pa Chay finally ordered that the French negotiator be executed. Incensed, the French pursued Pa Chay with a vengeance. But Pa Chay and his recruits not only were more familiar with their environment but received intelligence and needed provisions from sympathetic villagers. French forces suffered numerous humiliations. The tide began to turn after two years of fighting, forcing Pa Chay to seek new recruits and safe haven in Laos.

But there were Hmong who opposed him, most notably Lo Blia Yao, *kiatong* of the Lo clan and *tasseng* of Nong Het. Lo worked tirelessly to keep the Hmong of his region in line but was frustrated by his own nephew, who recruited for Pa Chay behind his back and even led an unsuccessful assassination attempt on his uncle.

By March 1921, the revolt seemed destined for failure, and Pa Chay retreated northward.* The French began burning mountain crops and relocating whole villages into French-controlled areas, steadily extinguishing the fires of dissent. But to ensure no resurgence of the "Madman's War," the French also put a bounty on Pa Chay, literally demanding to see his head before the reward was paid. French bribery succeeded where French diplomacy and military technology had failed. Assassins trudged to his hideout and shot him. Pa Chay's head and flintlock were taken to the French, and the killers received their due. Even a French colonel who helped suppress the revolt admitted, "Sometimes the warrior temperament of the Meo reveals itself for good reason: crushing taxes, heavy impositions on opium, horses requisitioned without being paid for," but this and similar admissions didn't stop the French from decapitating numerous rebels in front of captive Hmong audiences.[20]

But a curious thing occurred over the next several decades. As the

---

* Sources disagree about where Pa Chay ended up. Some say Phong Saly, which would be quite a ways to travel, while others say Luang Prabang.

Hmong contemplated their overall post-revolt treatment by the French, many of them considered the French better rulers than the Lao or the Vietnamese.

One of the keys to Hmong advancement was education. Under the French, Hmong children in Laos and Vietnam whose parents were willing and able to spare them from their chores could attend local schools, many administered by the French and taught in French. Under this system, men like Moua Lia, the first Hmong district school superintendent in Laos, and others who eventually served in the Lao bureaucracy would rise to prominence.

Admission to elementary school was not determined by age but by a much less exact test necessitated by a widespread reality: parents simply did not keep track of their children's birth dates. Ask a Hmong person born in Laos but living in America for his birthday, and he can provide it. Chances are very good, however, that the date was invented when his family prepared to migrate to this country. When was artist Seexeng Lee born? "Officially it's September 9, 1975," he replies. Officially? "They said I was born in the harvest time . . . [after the evacuation of] Long Tieng . . . It's kind of humorous for me to share this: my dad was born [January] 1—legally—my mom March 3, my brother May 5, my sister July 7—guess what, I'm 'nine-nine,' and then my baby brother, eleven-eleven! So at least they put me in the right time of the year!"

As Fungchatou Lo recalls, "[T]he first day . . . we went and met with the principal. The principal said, 'So how old is your son?' And my father said, 'I'm not sure, but I think he's ready for school.' And then the principal . . . had me . . . put my right hand over my head and touch my ear on the other side without bending my head to the right arm. And I couldn't do it! My hand was too short, and I couldn't do it . . . so he said, 'Your son's not ready.'" Lo's father found another principal to take his son, but most parents just waited until their children fulfilled this rudimentary requirement.

Sao Lee went to a small village school during the war. Most families were on the run, so schools had to be "portable."

Some of the buildings were just very small sheds in poor condition. We had so many kids there, all the classes were crowded . . . I didn't have shoes or warm clothes. When it was wintertime, it was very cold; there was plenty of frost outside. If you put a bowl of water outside the house overnight, it would turn into ice in the morning . . . We sat on these benches made from bamboo . . .

The teacher had all the authority—it's nothing like what we've got here in Australia at the moment. The teacher could punish you any way he wanted. Usually they made you stand with one leg up and two hands stretched out [straight out in front of you] in front of all the students for about half an hour, or they would write bad signs such as, "This is a lazy student" or "This is a bad student," and they put that sign around your neck; you walked from class to class so people could look at your face. I didn't know what sort of punishment that was, but it was very humiliating. Sometimes the teacher wanted you to put your hand out [puts hand out, palm up, fingertips together], and they hit on your fingertips with . . . a very long, hard stick . . . Now when I look back it seems to be a little bit rough, but at that time we just thought it was normal.

"[T]eachers commanded a lot of authority and respect," says Lee Pao Xiong. "I remember . . . my teacher taking the whole class to cut bamboo for him, to build his house. And people didn't question that. The teacher was sort of an extension of the parents back then, and commanded a high amount of respect."

Students who showed real promise had the opportunity to attend a French-run school or *lycée*. "Mr. Touby LyFoung, Mr. Tou Lia LyFoung, Mr. Touger LyFoung went to study in Vietnam, in Hue. Many Lao leaders went to study in Hanoi," recalls Yang Dao. "In French you have to pass three times: seventh grade—at seventh grade you have to pass the examination to go to the sixth [French schools number their grades in descending instead of ascending order, as in the United States]. Then in the third grade you have to pass an examination to be able to go to the second. If you don't pass, you stay for one or two years. And if you fail, 'Get out!' That's the French system of education."

THE GREAT DIVIDE

As Yang Dao mentioned, Touby Lyfoung and his two brothers were among the very first Hmong in the region to complete a modern French education. Gary Yia Lee, Touby's nephew, describes him as "the only Hmong who could speak and think as a French." Unfortunately, he was also caught in a clan rivalry begun by his father, Ly Xia Foung, and Lo Blia Yao, the *tasseng* of Nong Het who had tried to suppress support for the Pa Chay revolt.[21]

Discussing this rift between Ly Xia Foung and Lo Blia Yao makes the head of even a casual reader spin. Here is Touxa Lyfoung's description of his grandfather:

Since the age of twenty, he enjoyed getting involved with his community to share people's concerns about illness and well-being. He encouraged villagers to build [a] school, urged relatives to compete in making a better life for themselves, and helped Kaitong Lo Blia Yao settle Hmong peoples' disputes . . . When he saw that his friend, the well-known monk in the town of Ban-Bane, had a very old book about illnesses and ways of healing, he also asked for the book . . . When villagers became sick and when they used Hmong healing methods but did not get any good result, they always came to see Ly Xia Foung . . . [H]e also liked to visit and cheer up villagers who were in pain because of death in the house.[22]

By contrast we have the account of Keith Quincy:

In 1922 [Lo Blia Yao's] . . . favorite daughter, May, committed suicide. Four years earlier she had married a Ly clansman named [Ly Xia] Foung . . . LoBliayao had been against the marriage from the start. Foung was in his late forties, already had two wives, and was a social climber. LoBliayao was certain Foung was interested in May only as a way to advance his fortunes . . . To save face, LoBliayao demanded a large bride price, leaving the impecunious Foung with no option but to work it off as LoBliayao's employee . . . Soon [Foung] was serving as LoBliayao's personal secretary, learning the ropes and cultivating friendships with French bureaucrats. LoBliayao might have given Foung even more responsibility, but relationships between the two cooled when he learned Foung was beating May.[23]

So what do we believe? Is it all true? Is none of it true? Certainly all of us can recognize that we are capable of (and often demonstrate) both great evil and marvelous good. But neither of these sources offers us the kind of reliability and objectivity we would like. Touxa Lyfoung is obviously interested in telling a tale that reflects well on his family. Quincy's sources are untraceable, giving us no idea whether they had any direct knowledge of the events he describes. And in the footnote following the account above he reveals "some Hmong . . . place the rift after LoBliayao's death. In this account May Lo was still alive and so overwhelmed by her father's death that she insisted a lock of her hair be buried with him."[24]

Whatever doubts remain about the circumstances leading to their feud, the two men clearly had it in for each other. The conflict reached such a state that elders from other clans and French administrators intervened, dividing the Nong Het district in two, giving charge of one half to the Lo (Keng Khuai) and the other to the Ly (Phak Bun). "The Lor clan still wanted to retain their former position and the Lee clan would not allow this," remembers General Vang Pao. "The Lee clan said to the Lor clan, 'When one of your clan members was *tasseng,* we didn't say anything; now one of our clan members is a *tasseng*, you want us to divide the position?' This caused the clans to disagree and they split."

Even after Lo's death, Foung took advantage of his son Song Tou's profligate habits (and his failure to collect taxes for the French), convincing the French to award him control of Keng Khuai. Song Tou's younger brother Faydang was beside himself, pleading his case first to the French, and when they failed to act, to Prince Phetsarath, overseer of political spoils in Laos. Faydang offered the prince a wondrous bribe: his father's polished rhinoceros horn, an artifact believed to have mystical, protective powers. Phetsarath's support was won, but upon Foung's death in 1939, the French awarded control of both Nong Het districts to his son, Touby Lyfoung. Faydang would spend the rest of his life fighting against the French, the United States, and the Ly clan.[25]

Deep-seated, almost gravitational forces divided the Hmong of Nong Het and surrounding regions. It had begun with Pa Chay and Lo Blia Yao, expanded with the Lo-Ly rivalry, and would continue on in tensions between Touby Lyfoung and one of his young assistants, Vang Pao.

The presence of the Hmong in Western countries today is a direct result of this gradual but intentional decision by some to benefit from French colonialism (in many ways more of a vote against Lao tyranny and corruption) and this escalating feud between Ly and Lo. One side ultimately chose to hitch their destinies to the West: first France, then the United States. The almost superhuman wealth, technology, military might, and educational opportunity, and the fantastic potential it all seemed to portend, led tens of thousands of Hmong to work ever harder, learn new skills—even new languages—and struggle, innovate, and sometimes fail in a number of previously unimaginable ways to fit into the new world they would help to forge.

Lo Faydang and his followers chose, whether simply out of spite or out of some deeper sense of kinship or practicality, to side with fellow Asians, though in both cases these allies were invaders. The first was an aspiring empire-builder; the second a longtime aggressor whose newest incursion had begun, ironically enough, with the help of the French and the United States.

2 | "THEY WERE PERFECT"

geography, not politics

Most Americans, it's often said, couldn't pass the test immigrants take to become U.S. citizens. Most people don't study political philosophy and have trouble naming their state's senators and representatives, to say nothing of the rules that govern their legislative proceedings. Despite all the rhetoric trotted out on the Fourth of July or during political campaigns, most people really aren't that interested in politics. If one is a Democrat or Republican (still the only viable choices in this country), it's usually not because one has memorized the party platform and subscribed to a lengthy list of policy statements. It's more a feeling of what's right and what's wrong or a result of living in a part of the country where most people are loyal to certain leaders or particular ways of life. Likewise, when talking about the wars in Indochina between 1945 and 1975, one must be careful not to dwell on the rhetoric and propaganda that often accompanied them. People rarely chose sides because they'd studied Engels, Marx, and Lenin and thought Ho Chi Minh was a visionary political philosopher or because they'd looked into Western representative government and the laws that allegedly regulated capitalism and exclaimed, "Where do I sign up?"

The fortunes of the Southeast Asian Hmong people were, in many ways, an accident of geography—where they lived, who controlled the surrounding territory, and the extent to which those powers, whether French, Japanese, or Vietnamese, had access to their leaders and brought positive change or firm control to the region. While many, perhaps most, who know the Hmong in the United States believe all of them fought on the side of the West, Hmong in Thailand, in Vietnam, and yes, even in Laos, sided with the "people's revolution," whether in the form of the Communist Party of Thailand (CPT), the regime of Ho Chi Minh in Vietnam, or the Lao Issara and Pathet Lao movements, which most say were under Vietnamese domination. To expect all Hmong to make a single, monolithic choice is like expecting all Americans to vote the same way in an election or all members of a church, synagogue, or mosque to have exactly the same beliefs. But Western views of the Hmong are often skewed, in part by Americans' own ethnocentrism and nationalism; in part by our narrow understanding of the conflict in Southeast Asia, focused mostly or only on Vietnam; and partly because almost all of the Hmong who live in the West fought on our side.

KEY INDIVIDUALS AND THEIR ROLES

LAOS	Court of Luang Prabang 　King Sisavong Vong (1904–59) 　King Savang Vatthana (1959–75) Court of Vientiane 　Prince Phetsarath—founder of the Lao Issara 　Prince Souvanna Phouma—French-educated "Neutralist" 　Prince Souphanouvong—Vietnamese-educated "Red Prince" Political/military leaders 　Kong Le—leads a military coup in late 1960 　Phoumi Nosavan—conservative military figure, cousin of Sarit Thanarat ANL *(Armee Nationale Laotienne)*—National Army of Laos
VIETNAM	Ho Chi Minh—Nationalist, Communist, leader of Viet Minh Vo Nguyen Giap—commander of Viet Minh forces
THAILAND	General Sarit Thanarat—stages coup, takes over Thai government in 1957; 　supported Phoumi Nosavan, his cousin, in Laos
HMONG	Touby Lyfoung—leader with ties to old French colonial system Lo Faydang—leader with ties to Japan, then Vietnam Yang Thao Tou—Pathet Lao military leader Vang Pao—military leader who sides with Royal Lao Government 　and United States *Tasseng* (district chieftain) *Naiban* (village head)
FRANCE	Maurice Gauthier—helps recruit Hmong to fight against Japanese Captain Desfarges—saved from the Japanese by Touby, helps establish 　Hmong Mixed Commando Airborne Groups (GCMA) in northern Laos Lieutenant Max Mesnier—leads GCMA in Xieng Khouang General Henri Navarre—commander, French Expeditionary Force Captain Jean Sassi—tries to lead mission to take pressure off Dien Bien Phu
UNITED STATES	Office of Strategic Services (OSS)—precursor of the CIA General Claire Chennault—signs photo to Ho Chi Minh Major Allison K. Thomas—trains Viet Minh guerrillas Archimedes Patti—present when Ho Chi Minh declares 　Democratic Republic of Viet Nam Harry Aderholt—trains U.S. pilots to fly missions in Laos Bill Lair—meets with Vang Pao; uses Thai PARU (Police Aeril Reinforcement 　Unit) to train Hmong soldiers

RECRUITS

On January 23, 1945, Maurice Gauthier, a young, orphaned French commando, arrived in Laos. The tide of World War II was swinging decidedly in favor of France's allies, and it was time to reclaim French Indochina from the Japanese. Gauthier parachuted in with the second half of his detachment. Their orders were to find a French garrison located near the village of Khang Khay, gather intelligence, and organize a military resistance against the Japanese using indigenous recruits and loyal French personnel.

In the course of his daily intelligence-gathering and networking with French officers in the region, Gauthier met Tiao (Prince) Saykham, whose family had ruled over Xieng Khouang province until they were deposed by the Japanese. Retained by the French to gather intelligence, Saykham pointed Gauthier toward a group of mountain people in Nong Het province led by a district chieftain named Touby Lyfoung. It was certain Touby and the Hmong were no friends of the Japanese, whose Lao tax collector Phoumi Vongvichit had made a habit of overtaxing them.[1]

Gauthier was guided to the home of Touby Lyfoung, son of Ly Xia Foung, the blood rival of Lo Faydang. Gauthier promised him weapons and the training needed to use them. Other Hmong leaders joined Touby, including his brother Tou Geu, Chia Xiong ("from the Moua clan"), and Moua Chong Toua from Phou Duu village, to recruit and lead their kinsmen.[2]

At only five foot three, Gauthier fit right in with the Hmong, who called him "Little Fackee."* Phou San, Hmong-controlled land stretching from Ban Ban to the northern edge of the Plain of Jars, became a French base and staging area for reconnaissance or attack on Route 7. Hmong boys ran messages back and forth between the French and Hmong leaders mobilizing their men. Gauthier quickly grew impressed by the Hmong. He gave them used silk parachutes, which the women turned into clothing, and replaced the men's old flintlocks with modern rifles. Gauthier came to call the Hmong "warriors" rather than soldiers. They fought bravely and tenaciously but also only when they wanted to. Their speed and endurance amazed him. Acclimated to an oxygen-deprived elevation, they could march at a pace of eight to ten miles an hour for up to two days straight, Gauthier claimed. When asked why they climbed straight up a mountain instead of using switchbacks like he would, they stared at Gauthier in disbelief, replying, "Because that's where we're going."[3]

The men of Phou Duu helped the French retrieve airdrops, which arrived at night to avoid Japanese guns, leaving the women and children to do the farming. In January and February, seven more groups

---

* As noted earlier, *Fackee* is the Hmong word for "French."

of commandos were dropped into Laos to help raise a larger *Maquis* force capable of opening the door for an expected twelve-hundred-man Free French task force assembling in North Africa.*

But on March 10, writes Kenneth Conboy, before the force could be deployed, the Japanese "launched a *coup de main* throughout Indochina. Merciless in its execution, the Japanese killed or imprisoned nearly the entire European population." Most Hmong, who lived in isolated regions of little interest to the Japanese, had no great stake in the battle between France and Japan. But this crackdown won the French the sympathy of at least a few Hmong, who risked their own lives to save them. "Our family went to the village to trade for salt and necessary goods," Pa Cha Kong recalls. "The Japanese didn't give us any trouble. But when my father was in town, he saw the Japanese rounding up the French. They stuck something like fish hooks through their noses and led them by [pulling on strings connected to the hooks]. My father was a *tasseng*, so he started hiding the French in his area. And pretty much my whole side of the family started hiding the French. After all, *tassengs* were elected by the French government, so my father's loyalty was with the French . . . [O]ur family decided to go hide in the forest also."[4]

Nor Lue Lee had finished only two years of school when the Japanese arrived. He was in a Lao village when a company of Japanese soldiers stopped to ask for directions to a settlement where French soldiers were hiding. The villagers feigned ignorance but told them Lee's "village was in that direction . . . I was young and naïve, so I went with them as a guide . . . After we got to my village, I did not know the way any further . . . When I told them so, one of the Japanese officers hit me five or six times with the back of his long sword." The local canton chief agreed to guide the Japanese, but Lee was forced to accompany them. Marching all night through a driving rain, they finally reached the village of Nam Mo, "where they surrounded some Hmong houses used by the French to hide in. They speared and killed four Frenchmen that way . . . The rest of the French soldiers [about one hundred] ran away . . . The Japanese fired five or six rounds of mortars at them, then stopped . . . The French had many things air-dropped to them at Nam Vang, but they left them to the Japanese to burn." As they returned, they met Tong Khue Vang, who

* *Maquis* is a French honorific describing indigenous armed resistance fighters.

had a French man with him . . . [who] was trying to find out where all the French soldiers had gone . . . Tong Khue met him and told him that he wanted to take him to his rice field to hide him from the Japanese. But . . . Tong Khue went to see the Japanese and told them where the Frenchman was . . . He tried to run away, but they shot him and wounded him in the leg . . . They forced the Frenchman to take off his shoes, then made a hole into the palm of his hands and put a steel ring through it so they could attach a rope to the ring and lead him by the rope to go with them.

While circumstances in Xieng Khouang often elicited sympathy for the French, Hmong in other parts of Laos and Vietnam saw things differently. Holding no love for the Japanese, Zong Xeng Vang viewed the French not as liberators or partners in progress but as oppressors whose taxes laid a heavy burden on the Hmong and other Vietnamese. Some of the Hmong in Vietnam "followed Ho Chi Minh's revolution because they saw that he was someone who brought happiness and freedom to the poor people . . . We didn't know anything about Communist theory . . . We felt like if we followed Ho Chi Minh's revolution, then we would be able to stand in our own country and keep our own houses and villages." Even so, the allegiance was conditional. Vang says Ho's representatives met with his grandfather in early 1945 to see if the family would help fight against the Japanese. An agreement was reached, but only a month later the Japanese arrived. They "sent one battalion to fight against us. But we could simply hide in the mountains . . . and shoot them one by one. After three battles, the Japanese negotiated with Hmong leaders . . . [and] agreed to compensate for the damage they made to our village, including houses and animals . . . [They] had to get out of the Hmong village immediately . . . The Hmong had to let the Japanese move around their village without doing anything." So much for helping Ho Chi Minh.

By May, most French forces who'd entered Laos before December 1944 were captured or fleeing into China, often guided and given sanctuary by Touby Lyfoung's Hmong allies. Remaining French commandos and their partisans could do little more than harass Japanese convoys or launch guerilla attacks against Japanese installations. But even as they struggled to keep a toehold in the country, others were laying their own plans for Laos's future.[5]

Blackmailed by the Japanese kidnapping of his son, Crown Prince Savang Vatthana, Lao King Sisavong Vong publicly declared a formal end to his country's status as a French protectorate on April 8, 1945. Freed from the king's control, three princely siblings, along with a core of Laos's intelligentsia, explored their own brand of nationalism and self-determination. As Conboy describes them,

The oldest, Phetsarath, was a European-educated viceroy who . . . had toured the kingdom on horse and foot, gaining a solid reputation as both a patriot and a peacemaker. This, combined with a widely believed rumor that he could transform himself into a tiger to wreak vengeance on the unjust, made Phetsarath by 1945 the second most powerful man in Laos . . .

The second brother, Souvanna Phouma, had earned two engineering degrees in France before returning to Vientiane as chief of the Architecture Bureau in the . . . Public Works Service.

[Their half-]brother . . . [Souphanouvong] was [a]mbitious, flamboyant, and academically brilliant . . . [He] had earned a reputation as a rebel, his resentment of authority fanned by childhood discrimination because his mother was a commoner.[6]

Touby Lyfoung, whose clan came out the political winner in a feud with the Lo clan, benefited from his associations with the French colonial government.

Sisavong Vong's authority emanated from the Kingdom of Luang Prabang, the old royal capital; the three brothers were from the Kingdom of Vientiane, the administrative capital. Though all chose different paths and tried to bring the rest of the country with them, the king's reputed preference for France helped encourage anti-Japanese insurgency in Laos. The Japanese, in turn, sold or gave weapons to those willing to oppose the French. Most of those who responded belonged to Ho Chi Minh's followers, the Viet Minh.

Events in Vietnam had a direct bearing on the fortunes of Laos. If not for the support of Vietnamese Communists, the Lao Issara/Pathet Lao movements had little chance of success. The Viet Minh, in turn, were supported not only by the Japanese but also the U.S. Office of Strategic Services (OSS), a precursor to the CIA formed during World War II. As a former colony, the United States stood opposed to any attempt by France to reestablish a colonial sphere in Southeast Asia. But in searching for avowed anti-colonialists, the OSS unwittingly aided Communists.

The OSS heard that Viet Minh rescued downed American pilots and helped them safely into China. (Only one rescue can be definitely attributed to the Viet Minh, but they were happy to accept credit for the rest.) Having taken no initiative to gather their own independent information, the OSS's primary source of information about the Viet Minh was the Viet Minh. In the end, the two were drawn together by the OSS's need for information and the Viet Minh's desire for weapons.

Cashing in on U.S. pilot William Shaw's rescue, Ho Chi Minh sent a delegation to the OSS to request weapons, exaggerating the number of his forces and the number of times they engaged and defeated the Japanese. On March 29, Ho met General Claire Chennault, head of the U.S. Army Air Force in Asia. The meeting was arranged with the proviso that Ho ask for nothing. After a congenial conversation in which Ho displayed an impressive knowledge of the general's career, Chennault thanked Ho for Shaw's rescue. When their conversation concluded, Ho made one surprise request: could he please have a photograph of the general? Chennault obliged, signing it, "Yours Sincerely, Claire L. Chennault." The picture, says A. J. Langguth, "served Ho better than any visa. Brandishing it at Chinese officials and U.S. intelligence agents, Ho could prove that he enjoyed a close relationship with America." It wasn't the last time he exploited a misunderstanding to his advantage.[7]

On July 16, 1945, the OSS sent a six-man team led by Major Allison K. Thomas to train Viet Minh guerillas to attack Japanese road and rail traffic. On his second day with the Viet Minh, Thomas wrote in his report that the group was "not Communist." Forsaking his mission, he indulged a Viet Minh request to train guerillas in the Cao Bang region, essentially providing the Viet Minh with two hundred troops who later served as the backbone of a coup d'état begun in Hanoi less than a month after Thomas and his men landed in Vietnam.[8]

When, on September 2, Ho Chi Minh announced the establishment of the Democratic Republic of Vietnam, he was accompanied by Viet Minh general Vo Nguyen Giap and Archimedes Patti, the deputy of OSS's chief in China. As the new Viet Minh flag was raised, photographers snapped pictures of Patti and two aides standing next to Giap, saluting. Then as Ho spoke, American aircraft flew overhead, leading the crowd to believe the United States was saluting Ho and the new government. Patti later confessed, "I knew he was using us, and I didn't mind frankly, because the use he made of us was more one of image rather than substance. Really, what he was trying to do was to say: 'Well, look, even the Americans believe in my cause.'" It is hard to know what was insubstantial about that message. But the United States was still in full anti-colonial mode, trying to bar France from retaking its former holdings in the region. By the time American policy shifted 180 degrees, it had already helped the Viet Minh become a potent force.[9]

FRANCE RISES, FRANCE FALLS

The treaty ending World War II sent Chinese troops south to the sixteenth parallel to disarm the Japanese. Hoping to ward off China's influence, France moved back into Laos. Hugh Tovar, who twenty-five years later became CIA station chief for Laos, had already been in the U.S. Army for two years when he was recruited by the OSS. He was first sent to China: "I spoke schoolboy French, [so] they sent me down to Indochina in a parachute, and I ended up in Vientiane in late '45 and got my first direct involvement in what became . . . the Indochina War." When Tovar reached Vientiane,

the French were already coming back in . . . Some were coming in by parachute on British aircraft . . . My boss then was Major Aaron Bank, later one of the cofounders of the Special Forces . . . All the key people we met in Vientiane . . . were French-educated, very nice people . . . They were very Francophile in a true sense . . . but they didn't want the French back in . . . [Bank] told me, "I'm sending you down to Savannakhet in the south. I'm going to Hanoi to see Ho Chi Minh," which threw me a bit . . . But he sent me because I could manage in French . . . [and] I had met some of the British who were involved in the southern operation . . . I [also] had a Chinese captain who . . . spoke good French [and] all the other local languages . . . Here I'm a second lieutenant telling a French colonel, "You stay the hell out of this place."

The standoff persisted for two or three weeks.

But when Major Bank went to Hanoi, he left the rest of the group under his deputy . . . And they let them in . . . at . . . Thakhek, . . . midway between Savannakhet and Vientiane . . . The Viet Minh were very strong around Thakhek, and the British major . . . leading the French into Thakhek began to push them very hard . . . "Look, I'm Major Kemp . . . and these French officers . . . are to come in." The Viet Minh told him very bluntly, "You can come in any time. But if a Frenchman comes in, we're going to kill him." Well, about two or three days later . . . Kemp brought them in, and *they stopped him at the edge of the Mekong. He tried to go through by pure bravado, [but] they killed the French officer. [It] was very unpleasant because they felt that our people right there nearby could have stopped it . . . All hell broke loose between Kunming and Kandy, Ceylon [Allied headquarters for Southeast Asia], Paris and London and Washington . . . Not long after that we were sent a message . . . to get the heck out of there . . . After I left, the French went in and the shooting began.*

Hmong and Lao forces under the command of Touby Lyfoung and Lao forces led by Tiao Saykham attacked Lao Issara positions in Xieng Khouang, asserting control over the region on January 26, 1945. According to Gary Yia Lee, "Touby and Tiao Saykham liberated Xieng Khouang town from the Lao Issara. Touby sent a group of 50 Hmong (including his brother, Toulia) to help liberate Luang Prabang. Just before arriving, they sent a message ahead that there were 500 Hmong coming to take Luang Prabang—a nice ploy—and the Lao Issara all fled without a fight." Touby's Hmong also successfully attacked Viet Minh positions in the Nong Het area. Touby was asked to organize larger numbers of Hmong to halt the Vietnamese advance. The French even imposed a new tax on opium, collected by Touby, to help finance the operation.[10]

Lo Faydang's bitter feud with Touby Lyfoung led him to support first the Japanese and then the North Vietnamese.

Touby focused most of his attention around Nong Het, where Viet Minh attacks were most likely. For his efforts, he was promoted to *chao muong* (mayor) of the Hmong in Xieng Khouang, his former title passing to an older half-brother. Longtime rival Lo Faydang continued to challenge him. Whatever "Touby's men do, Faydang's men must do the opposite," observed missionary Linwood Barney. Lo had significant contacts within the Viet Minh, who in turn had many loyal members amongst the approximately fifty thousand ethnic Vietnamese in Laos. In April 1943, ethnic Vietnamese residents of Khang

Khay had made their loyalties clear when they tried to seize Xieng Khouang province (known by the Vietnamese as Tran Ninh) and make it a part of Vietnam.[11]

As if French and Vietnamese ambitions did not complicate Laos's situation enough, Prince Phetsarath also moved to capitalize on the postwar chaos. Only twenty days after Japan forced the king to break ties with France, Phetsarath sent a telegram to all Lao provincial governors, asserting that Japan's surrender had not abrogated the king's proclamation and insisting they resist interference by any foreign power.

On September 3, Phetsarath received a message from his half-brother Souphanouvong, who had spent the previous sixteen years in Vietnam working as an engineer. Souphanouvong had flown to Hanoi—in a plane provided by the OSS—to visit Ho Chi Minh. "I am in a position to negotiate on behalf of our country," he told his brother in a telegram, requesting instructions on how to proceed. But Phetsarath wanted nothing to do with Vietnam.

The king also wanted nothing to do with Phetsarath's plans for Lao sovereignty. On October 10 he dismissed him as prime minister and viceroy. Phetsarath and the Lao Issara responded two days later by declaring themselves Laos's new government, "deposing" the king. Souvanna Phouma was named minister of public works. Though originally

Prince Souphanouvong meets with Ho Chi Minh, ca. 1947, to discuss possible partnership between the Viet Minh and the Lao Issara.

the minister of foreign relations, Souphanouvong found his meetings in Hanoi had alienated him from his brothers but raised his own sense of self-importance. He came to Laos as the self-proclaimed "Lao Issara chieftain of the panhandle."

Having fallen short in its first two attempts to reassert control over Laos in the fall of 1945, France aggressively recruited and trained more troops, sweeping first across the Bolovens Plateau and then into Savannakhet. By May 18, they received orders to retake Thakhek. Eager to demonstrate his leadership, Souphanouvong ordered his men to dig in, but in the face of a massive force including artillery and ex-British Spitfire bombers, they fled. Souphanouvong, though wounded, escaped in a canoe across the Mekong River. By August 1946, the French had reincorporated Laos, along with Cambodia and Vietnam, into their Indochinese federation. The three princes and their compatriots brooded in Thailand.

The United States, now firmly convinced that Communism, not colonialism, was the greatest threat to Southeast Asia, lost its taste for anti-French intrigue. Even worse for the Issara, Laos was proclaimed a constitutional monarchy with a national assembly in May 1947 and an equal partner in the French Union in July 1949, granting it the right to raise its own army. The Issara's very *raison d'être* seemed to be disappearing. When the royal government offered amnesty later that year, Souphanouvong returned to commiserate with the Vietnamese, Phetsarath remained in Thailand, and Souvanna Phouma formally dissolved the Issara in October, leading the bulk of his comrades back to Vientiane "in peace."*

To cement this new era of influence, France trained the Armee Nationale Laotienne (ANL), even establishing an officer candidate school

---

* Phetsarath returned to Laos in March 1957 to wild acclaim. According to Nor Lue Lee, stationed in Kene Thao at the time, "Uncle Touby [Lyfoung] told me to go down and receive him with my troops." Despite considering himself "too dumb with little education to do such a big honorable job," Lee complied. "[H]e came through Kene Thao. So I went to meet him there. He was a bit scared of me because I was a soldier, but I told him that he was a prince and I was a commoner; I would protect him and take him to work with the king . . . When we got to Sayaboury town, I asked the prince if it was true that he could not be killed, that he was invincible (he was nicknamed the Ironman of Laos). He replied 'Son, do not believe it. At the time, I had power, so I spread rumor to that effect so people would be fearful of me. Right now, if you shoot me, I would just die,' he said. I was so surprised that he was so open and frank. I said to him that I would never kill him. I took him back to Vang Vieng." Any aspirations Phetsarath had of being a force in Lao politics died with him in October 1959.

at the village of Dong Hene, southeast of Savannakhet. But a new an-
tiroyalist independence movement was growing on both sides of the
border. The Pathet Lao, "reared by the Viet Minh as a wholly responsive Lao subsidiary," had already fielded its first guerilla unit by January 1949. Souphanouvong, ousted from the Lao Issara, joined the Pathet Lao, adding "appeal and legitimacy to an otherwise obscure, Viet
Minh-backed splinter movement." Operating from the mountainous
terrain along the Laos-Vietnam border, they recruited hill tribes like
the Hmong and put special emphasis on attracting minority leaders
like Yang Thao Tou, Lao Foung, and Nhia Vue.[12]

Vang Pao, Touby Lyfoung's young messenger who rose to become
the most powerful military leader in modern Hmong history, believes
at this time a conspiracy was already afoot to unseat the king. "After
one year of asylum in Thailand, these princes . . . created a new plan . . .
Prince Souvanna Phouma [would] go back and live in Vientiane. He was
to 'cut off the feet of the King.'" Souvanna Phouma became prime minister in 1951.

*Prince Souphanouvong was to go to Vietnam. When he came back, he would bring
back the Vietnamese to "cut off the head of the King" . . . Once a year . . . the king
would travel . . . to Vientiane. When the king visited the first year, all the military
and civilians were there to greet and pay homage to him. But the second year, [the
two princes] did not allow everyone to greet and pay their respects to the king. There
were only minor officers that were there to meet him. This is how they tried to undermine the king's power and authority.*

Grant Evans, an Australian anthropologist living in Laos, has heard stories like Vang Pao's before, and not only from the Hmong. He believes
the idea of Souvanna Phouma returning to Laos as a mole is "silly in the
extreme, without a single fact or even serious argument to back it. Souvanna Phouma was committed to neutralism and to the monarchy."[13]

By the early 1950s, large-scale conflicts were breaking out between
Communist and non-Communist Hmong. As Nor Lue Lee remembers,
it became difficult to live in his village of Nam Keng because of raids by
Pathet Lao Hmong led by Yang Thao Tou, Lo Faydang's cousin. Thao
Tou brought a company of thirty Hmong and thirty Lao soldiers to con-
fiscate property and take prisoners, but people were out cutting rice or
cultivating opium: "Thao Tou and his men could not capture us, so they
burned our houses." Nor Lue Lee's house was spared because one of his
cousins was married to Lo Faydang's sister. They were, in Hmong terms,

Nor Lue Lee in the mid- to late 1950s, dressed in a uniform provided by the French. Lee now lives in Sydney, Australia.

brothers-in-law. "They emptied our oil pans on the ground, cut down our smoked meat from the ceiling, opened up our corn granary for the pigs . . . They emptied our house of all valuables like new Hmong costumes, money, opium" and took adults into captivity.

Because Lee's nephew Ga Nou was only a boy, the soldiers did not take him, so he ran to the fields to tell everyone what was happening. Lee and Ga Nou's older brother Txai ran to the nearby village of Tham

Thao and spoke to the *tasseng*. They were given weapons and sent with eight others to pursue Yang Thao Tou and his men. They searched several villages before coming to Hav Kuj Yem [Palm Leaf]. "We nearly caught up with them . . . [b]ut the people there said 'Oh! They left three days ago' . . . That was a lie. They only left a few minutes before." Discouraged and angered, they took target practice on a nearby tree stump in front of the villagers. "We returned home and decided to leave. We killed our chickens, gave away our hens and pigs . . . Touby said for us to join him in Xieng Khouang town, so we left to go there." It was difficult to depart. Nor Lue Lee had grown rich by Hmong standards harvesting rice and opium: he left the village with sixteen silver bars and five balls of opium.

For Hmong with clear family ties to Touby, the reason for siding against the Pathet Lao is obvious. Families like Won Chuck Yang's were often split by divided loyalties. "At that time my grandfather's brother was an officer on the [Pathet Lao] side. My grandfather was on the city council on our side . . . My grandfather's brother said . . . 'Souphanouvong and the others gave me [the rank of] major, and sooner or later I will become a general. So I'm willing to work for them' . . . Half the city of Nong Het, all my dad's family, went with him north, to Vietnam." But his grandfather's younger brother was Touby Lyfoung's brother-in-law and a city official in Nong Het. "He said, 'If you people want to go with my brother Thao Tou, then you go ahead, but we're not going. We want to go with my brother-in-law, Touby Lyfoung. And whoever wants to come with me, come with me' . . . And that's why they split the family."

For other Hmong like Pa Cha Kong, as well as members of other hill tribes, the decision had to do less with clan loyalty than a fear of what Communists did or might do:

I decided to fight because when the Communist Laotians came into the village, they were very disrespectful. We were scared of them because they had weapons, so we would hide in the forest. But then they came and took our livestock and killed our chickens . . . My father, a tasseng, said, "We have to fight them. I am too old, so my sons . . . have to do my bidding." We didn't have special weapons or formal training. We were just villagers with Hmong flintlock rifles. After a while we asked for and received old French-supplied weapons . . . We even got a hold of some submachine guns . . . Touby Lyfoung was living in Xieng Khouang so . . . that's where all the weapons and supplies were handed out . . . In my area, all the Hmong were united to fight against the Communists. But just three-day's walk away there was a leader named Yaw Lor, and he and the rest of his clansmen . . . sided with the Communists . . .

> It wasn't just the Hmong alone who were fighting the Communists; it was the
> [Khmu] and other lower hill tribe people . . . The Communists were everywhere, so
> we hid in the forests all day, sneaking out in the morning to feed our livestock . . .
> Our village was on one side of the valley, and on the other side were . . . the [Khmu]
> . . . About fifty Communist soldiers came to the [Khmu] village . . . Instead of just
> shooting at them, they wanted to talk to them first. There was a huge disagreement
> that turned into a firefight, and the [Khmu] killed three of the Communists . . . Af-
> ter that, the Communists came back with a larger force and burned their whole vil-
> lage down. So the [Khmu] just hid in the forest.

As the stakes of the conflict in Laos rose, the United States began
arming the royal government's troops. Almost fifteen thousand were
scheduled to be in place by the end of fiscal year 1953, supplemented by
a peasant-trained national guard. Indigenous Mixed Commando Airborne Groups (GCMA, for *Groupe de Commandos Mixtes Aeroportes*),
trained in "raids, psychological warfare, reconnaissance, pacification,
sabotage, kidnapping, assassination, and raising indigenous airborne
commandos and *Maquis*." The two most valuable GCMA were Hmong
teams in Sam Neua and Xieng Khouang provinces, created after a meeting between Touby Lyfoung and Captain Desfarges, one of the first
French to parachute into Laos in late 1944. Touby, who had protected
Desfarges from the Japanese in March 1945, agreed to recruit Hmong
for the GCMA on the condition that they fight only in their home areas.
By late 1953, about one thousand Sam Neua Hmong served in three
French-led companies known collectively as "Groupe Servan." The GCMA
were further supported by partisans—mostly hill tribe farmers—who
provided an informal security zone of about six miles around the
guerillas. The French rewarded their assistance with airdrops of rice.
So effective were the GCMA that the Pathet Lao were forced to move
their headquarters from Sam Neua town to the village of Vieng Sai. In
Xieng Khouang, "Groupe Malo," led by Lieutenant Max Mesnier, established six separate companies surrounding the Plain of Jars. The
leader of a one-hundred-commando team protecting the strategically
important border town of Nong Het was Vang Pao, Touby's former
messenger, the first Hmong to graduate from the Lao military academy
at Dong Hene.[14]

But even with its many successes, the government's hold on most
of the Lao frontier remained tenuous—a reality apparently lost on the
king and crown prince. Indeed, in November 1952, two frontier out-

posts in Sam Neua province fell to "marauding elements" of the Viet Minh. Over the next four months, Viet Minh troops, accompanied by about three hundred Pathet Lao, overwhelmed Lao and French forces. One column seized most of Sam Neua province, while a second pushed toward Luang Prabang. By April 27, 1953, despite an emergency airlift of Lao, French, and Moroccan troops, U.S. diplomats were predicting the fall of the royal capital. The king refused to flee, leaving the French no choice but to defend him.[15]

Suddenly the United States was paying close attention to a country previously beneath its notice. During an April 28 National Security Council meeting, President Dwight D. Eisenhower made his opinion clear: if Laos fell to Vietnam, the West would "likely lose the rest of Southeast Asia and Indonesia. The gateway to India, Burma, and Thailand will be open." Though the president advocated no direct action, the United States sent six C-119 transports, hiring civilian pilots from General Chennault's Civil Air Transport (CAT), to fly them. By the first week in May, CAT was dropping cargo to French-held garrisons in northeastern Laos.[16]

While French and Lao forces fought to defend Luang Prabang, pro-French Hmong were protecting their villages along the route from Nong Het to the Plain of Jars. Nor Lue Lee was charged with command of Hmong troops in Xieng Khouang:

> The third route taken by the Viet Minh [was through] Xieng Khouang town . . . The initial group . . . came through Nong Het. The Hmong showed them no mercy. [When they] arrived at Faydang's village at Tiaj Louj Cuab . . . the Hmong cut off their rear . . . so the Viet Minh couldn't go back, and both sides [of the road] were lined with cliffs . . . At Nam Kong the Hmong stopped [the enemy's] advance with eight or nine machine guns . . . We fought for three days. Nearly all the Viet Minh were killed . . . The Hmong used Touby's buffalo to drag all the Vietnamese bodies to dump into a pit. It took three days to finish the job. The French had two jeeps, so we used them to carry bodies . . . There must have been about eight hundred or a thousand bodies.

It was a different story to the northwest. By May 10, the Viet Minh stood only nineteen miles from Luang Prabang. Only a relentless monsoon beginning on May 12 forced the Viet Minh to withdraw to Dien Bien Phu. French commanders were convinced that the Vietnamese and their Lao allies would be back with the next year's dry season.

In late November, the French Expeditionary Force dropped about forty-two thousand men into the Vietnamese valley of Dien Bien Phu.

Over the next several days, they built a new fortification and, with the help of hundreds of airdrops, prepared an airstrip suitable for receiving any class of plane. Hundreds of Algerian, Moroccan, and other troops were flown in to reinforce the new base, which by Christmas held twelve thousand men.[17]

General Henri Navarre, commander of the French Expeditionary Force, expected Dien Bien Phu to serve as a counter-guerilla staging base. Between intelligence and firepower on the ground and air support above, his men would mow down any Vietnamese force that sought to invade Laos. Instead, the Vietnamese—some already repelled from other positions in Laos—surrounded the base, brought in artillery more powerful than the French anticipated, and shelled the network of fortifications unmercifully. Antiaircraft fire also made aerial resupply of the fort extremely dangerous.

President Eisenhower, fearing a Korea-like invasion of Southeast Asia by the Chinese, authorized CAT pilots to fly two missions a day into Dien Bien Phu. World War II veteran Fred Walker had flown missions in India and Burma. With Mao Zedong's soldiers firing at him, he took one of the last U.S. planes out of China. But flying into Dien Bien Phu was terrifying. On May 5, with the situation on the ground truly desperate, CAT pilots gathered for their usual briefing. Chief pilot Hugh Marsh told them they would be dropping loads to one of the last remaining outposts at forty-five hundred feet instead of the usual nine thousand. After a period of shocked silence, someone blurted out, "Jesus Christ! You trying to commit suicide?" Marsh retorted, "Shut up. I'll be leading the parade." That, Walker reported, "was the end of that rebellion." In the morning mission, all eight planes sent out returned to base safely. But in the afternoon run, pilot James McGovern, originally matched with Walker, was hit and crashed along a riverbank in Sam Neua. He and his copilot were killed. The following day, every pilot refused to fly; CAT's vice president came down to give them a pep talk. When it became clear that he wouldn't fire anyone, seven pilots followed him back to Taipei the next day. "I didn't blame them," said Walker. "It was the damnedest operation I've ever been in in my life. It was terrible. Terrible!"[18]

On the ground, Captain Jean Sassi, who parachuted into Laos with Maurice Gauthier in 1945 and returned in October 1953, was trying to find a way to divert Viet Minh forces away from Dien Bien Phu. Victory was now out of the question, but Sassi hoped to open up a gap in the Vietnamese line through which French forces could escape. Though in different places, Nor Lue Lee and Pa Cha Kong were both preparing to go to Dien Bien Phu. Kong, who spoke French, Hmong, Lao, and Khmu, had become a translator. In late 1953 he went to Saigon for six months of Morse code training. "Our company consisted of Hmong, lowland Laotian, and [Khmu], and we were commanded by some Hmong officers, some Laotian sergeants, and French officers . . . I was a Morse code operator for a company of about 103 soldiers [and] was about to be dropped into Dien Bien Phu when I heard the news of [its] fall." Nor Lue Lee remembers,

When the French were about to face defeat, Hmong soldiers were sent to help. We went to the Bamboo Plain near Dien Bien Phu. There were many of us, so many that when we killed a buffalo to feed the Hmong soldiers, the food became cold and the fat became hard before everybody arrived on the scene. The Hmong were to guard this big empty plain for thirty thousand French soldiers to parachute into as reinforcement for those already stationed in Dien Bien Phu. We could hear bombs exploding and even French fighter-bombers could be seen flying over our heads.

French officials denied the use of their own paratroopers for a mission this dangerous: only the *Maquis* would do the fighting. "We stayed up all night while the battle raged nearby," recalls Nor Lue Lee. "At the first crow of the roosters, the people at Dien Bien radioed to say that the Viet Minh had won . . . and for the thirty thousand reinforcements not to come anymore . . . We had been marching for days and our feet were all stiff and sore. But upon hearing the news that we could go home to our wives and children, many of us just got up and danced."

"At Dien Bien Phu," says Pa Cha Kong, "the French were holding back the tidal wave of the Communists. When that collapsed, everybody came into Laos . . . Out of the forty or so Morse code operators that the French trained, only four of them survived after that . . . Prior to '54, I would estimate that in a company of [one hundred] Laotian Communist soldiers there were probably about three Vietnamese advisors . . . After '55, the Communist Vietnamese started pouring into Laos."

For the Hmong in Vietnam who sided with Ho Chi Minh, the fall of Dien Bien Phu was a triumphant day. "After the French and the Japanese withdrew from the Hmong villages," recalls Zong Xeng Vang, "the Hmong saw that there was no one to control them anymore . . .[T]hey didn't have to pay taxes to anyone, and they could grow their own plants

The qeej, or Hmong reed pipe, is a traditional instrument most commonly used in funeral rituals to help guide the deceased's soul to the ancestors. It is also played during the New Year and other celebrations.

and trees and rice." But there were thousands of others, both in Vietnam and Laos, who took no side at all. To them, people like Souphanouvong or Vang Pao were equally bothersome. Ideology meant nothing. Neither side was worth fighting for. They sought, as their ancestors had for centuries, to simply be left alone.

France's final report on Dien Bien Phu, issued on December 3, 1955, would sound eerily prophetic to Americans thirty years later:

The fall of Dien Bien Phu, in a strictly military perspective . . . did not upset the balance of forces present in Indochina. It only assumed the aspect of a definitive defeat of our forces by reason of its profound psychological effects on French public opinion, which, tired of a war that was unpopular and seemingly without end, demanded in a way that it be ended.

The end itself was in fact, both in terms of public opinion and of the military conduct of the war and operations, merely the end result of a long process of degradation of a faraway enterprise which, not having the assent of the nation, could not receive from the authorities the energetic impulse and the size and continuity of efforts required for success.[19]

FLIRTING WITH PeaCe

The Agreement on the Cessation of Hostilities in Laos, part of a larger series of treaties signed in Switzerland, went into effect at midnight Geneva time on July 22, 1954. It decreed the withdrawal of all French and Viet Minh forces—though a French training team of no more than fifteen hundred soldiers was permitted. Pathet Lao troops were to move into Phong Saly and Sam Neua provinces and reintegrate into the national army (ANL) within four months' time. Neither of these stipulations ever came to pass. Instead of disbanding, the Pathet Lao appointed their own local officials in the two provinces, establishing their own schools, print shops, and military academy. Their reliance on North Vietnam and antagonism toward the Royal Lao government only grew. The ANL was ill-prepared to defend king and country. Five hundred French commanders and noncommissioned officers were leaving; half of its thirty-five thousand troops were volunteers whose tours of duty were ending. Even the fifteen-hundred-man French training team was eventually eliminated for budgetary reasons. Enforcement of the Geneva Accords was left to a three-member International Control Commission (ICC) composed of Communist (Poland), democratic (Canada), and neutral (India) countries. Intended to "rush tripartite teams to the scene of cease-fire violations and, with the weight of its office, make objective observations that would presumably lead toward peace," the ICC was instead constrained by its pro-Communist member as well as by shortages in staff, transportation, consensus, and cooperation from the Pathet Lao.[20]

Of course, the French were not entirely forthcoming either, consistently denying the existence of the indigenous guerilla teams now fighting for their lives. Hmong and Khmu *Maquis* were between a rock and a hard place. Since they officially did not exist, it was easier for the French to cut off their aid. And Geneva ordered the Pathet Lao into Sam Neua, where they could effectively crush guerrilla groups.

In Sam Neua, for example, isolated Hmong guerrillas were supplied only by air. The Pathet Lao, who could easily spot these drops, contacted the ICC. Fearing his men would be slaughtered by the enemy before the ICC found them, the French commander invited the observers to his camp, exposing France's diplomatically "secret" operations. As the inspectors prepared to file their report, the commander left the country; the Hmong hid their weapons in caves surrounding a mountain called Phu Pha Thi. Next door in Xieng Khouang province, French helicopters kept Hmong guerrillas fed but refused to evacuate their wounded. Prior to his imminent departure, Captain Sassi worked to transfer his capable and much-needed fighters into the national army. But after initially positive signals from the government, the attitude toward "tribal guerrillas" soured. Most of the original guerrillas disbanded and returned to their homes. One of the few exceptions, Lieutenant Vang Pao, took his all-Hmong unit back to the Plain of Jars and formed the national army's Volunteer Battalion (BV) 21.[21]

Even as the French were leaving Laos, the United States assumed the mantle of keeping what it saw as Soviet and Chinese ambitions at bay. Tens of millions of dollars in American aid began pouring into the country. Souvanna Phouma was uneasy with this new partnership. In mid-1954 he met Souphanouvong in Khang Khay, offering him the chance to field Pathet Lao candidates for the 1955 elections. If Pathet Lao candidates won seats and incorporated themselves into the Lao government, they might cut their ties to Vietnam and avert a bloody civil war. Instead, the Pathet Lao chose not only to boycott the elections but to intensify their military attacks.

Nevertheless, the elections were a smashing success. As Arthur Dommen observes, "for the third time since 1945, Laotians did their civic duty and voted . . . in record numbers and in the total absence of violence." The process left the Pathet Lao with no way to declare elections—or the government—illegitimate. Laos was welcomed into the United Nations in December 1955, the royal government successfully countered the Pathet Lao's political attacks, and in January 1956 the ICC published a report stating "the sovereignty, independence, unity, and territorial integrity of Laos" were recognized by the Geneva settlement.[22]

Still, Souvanna Phouma worried about the United States, despite its significant investments in his country. Per capita, Laos received more U.S. aid than any other country in the world. But that money hardly ever reached beyond the capital. Instead of building new roads, increasing crop production, or improving medical services, most was absorbed by corrupt government officials and merchants. Those problems were still endemic by the time Roy Wehrle, a foreign service officer assigned to economic aid and development programs, arrived in Laos in early January 1960: "There was corruption everyplace. And we

Americans abetted it because we were so naïve; we just gave them all this stuff, and it was like candy. They did with it what you would expect children to do. And I don't mean *children* in a dismissive way. That's just exactly the way they looked at it. Somebody was giving them stuff, so, 'OK, we'll take whatever you give us' [and use it however we want]."[23]

On May 29, 1956, Souvanna Phouma accepted an invitation to visit China, seeing an opportunity to establish solid relations with an important neighbor and insist on their pledge to stop aiding the Pathet Lao. The U.S. ambassador, who should have been present when Souvanna Phouma departed for China in August, was conspicuously absent. This slight was only the beginning of an antagonistic relationship that seriously damaged America's relationship with the prime minister as well as Laos's chances for real and lasting peace. The United States repeatedly threatened a wholesale reevaluation of its relationship with Laos—even, in extreme cases, the immediate cancellation of all economic assistance. Aid payments were regularly delayed, angering soldiers entrusted with the country's defense, whose displeasure would later be expressed at the ballot box. Worse, the CIA, bent on ferreting out Communists in Southeast Asia, conducted operations in the region without the knowledge or approval of U.S. ambassadors, who found themselves trying to explain policies and embarrassing events about which they knew little or nothing.

Perhaps in part because of frustrations and concerns with U.S. policy, Souvanna Phouma once again reached out to Souphanouvong. This time, over American objections, the brothers agreed to supplemental elections in which Pathet Lao candidates would participate.[24]

Despite American hopes to delay or cancel the elections, negotiations between the Royal Lao government and the Pathet Lao moved swiftly, in part because Pathet Lao leaders were noting with alarm the large numbers of people abandoning the areas they controlled. Refugees were fleeing from Sam Neua, alienated by the Pathet Lao's empty promises and angered by the forced conscription of their sons.

Then, across the border in Thailand, another event occurred that would have lasting consequences for Laos and its hopes for peace and unity. On September 16, 1957, General Sarit Thanarat, deputy minister in the Thai cabinet, executed a bloodless coup, instituted martial law, forbade political parties to hold meetings, and commenced an efficient but harshly repressive regime that was recognized in short order by most Western nations. In Laos, the chief beneficiary of this coup was Sarit Thanarat's first cousin, an ambitious young lieutenant colonel named Phoumi Nosavan. If dissatisfied with the political direction in his own country, Phoumi knew he could turn to Sarit Thanarat for assistance.[25]

Laos's first coalition government, including two Pathet Lao members, was established in November 1957. During November and December, control of Sam Neua and Phong Saly provinces was officially turned over to the crown. But numerous Pathet Lao units were reportedly crossing back into North Vietnam. And America's interference in Lao politics, its ham-fisted attempts to use money as a weapon, and the widespread corruption associated with that aid were giving Pathet Lao candidates plenty of campaign material.

The results of the May 4 elections sent shock waves through the capital. Thirteen of the twenty-one contested seats were won by the Pathet Lao's political wing, the Lao Patriotic Front, or its allies. In addition to their anti-American campaign, Pathet Lao candidates benefited from nationalists who ran against each other, splitting their constituency and opening the door to victory for their enemies.

In the elections' wake, the U.S. State Department scrambled to beef up its military aid to Laos and to undermine the new coalition government. At the same time, more conservative civilian and military elements, led by Phoumi Nosavan, formed the Committee for the Defense of the National Interests (CDNI) and took a hard-line stance against the Pathet Lao, no doubt with the CIA's encouragement.

Crown Prince Savang Vatthana asked Souvanna Phouma to make another attempt to form a government. To no one's surprise, the Pathet Lao supported a Souvanna Phouma cabinet only if it excluded the CDNI while the U.S. embassy and the CDNI insisted the cabinet be kept free of potential Communists. In an August 5 cable, U.S. ambassador Horace Smith shared concern that his country was putting too much pressure on Laos's fragile government. He thought the CDNI too green and unlikely to garner broad national support: "[A]ny effort at a military coup at this time would almost certainly play into Communist hands . . . The two northern provinces might again split off in open rebellion and in the other ten provinces with aid and 'volunteers' from the Viet Minh, all but the few central points covered by the 300 paratroopers and such additional ANL units as are effectively armed, supplied, and trained might be openly taken over by the [Lao Patriotic Front] . . . The choice of ministers is for the prime minister to make."[26]

After months of fruitless discussion, Souvanna Phouma abandoned his quest to form a new government. His successor, Phoui Sananikone, acquiesced to U.S. demands, excluding the Lao Patriotic Front from his cabinet. The French ambassador tried to convince Smith of the prudence of putting Souphanouvong, the top vote-getter in the May elections, in the cabinet. There he would be constrained by the duties of his office and the vigilance of his colleagues to act in the national interest. In a country where Communism and class struggle were still alien concepts, his ties to Hanoi would be a liability rather than an asset. Smith was unconvinced.

Where Souvanna Phouma remained circumspect in his anti-Communist rhetoric, Sananikone invited a diplomatic officer from Taiwan into Vientiane, a grave insult to mainland China. In return for such provocatively anti-Communist measures, Phoui expected the United States to strongly express its support, but it did so only tepidly.

On December 14, a Vietnamese battalion established three posts in Tchepone province, near the demilitarized zone between North and South Vietnam. The commander refused requests by local Lao military and civil commanders for a meeting, captured two royal army soldiers on December 30, and had the audacity to fly a North Vietnamese flag on Lao soil. The battalion's arrival was the first step in a plan to open a trail or series of trails along the border to help supply North Vietnamese allies in South Vietnam. Crown Prince Savang appealed to the United States for aid but received a reply so noncommittal that the prince ceased to believe the United States would defend his kingdom.

Excluded from the cabinet, Pathet Lao officials began reneging on their pledge to join the royal government. On May 11, Constitution Day, fifteen hundred Pathet Lao soldiers were to participate in a ceremony celebrating their reintegration. Taking advantage of a monsoon storm, Pathet Lao battalions on the Plain of Jars and in Luang Prabang disappeared. While Dommen ascribes these moves to Communist machinations rather than government deceit, it is clear the fragile coalition was also upset by American inflexibility.[27]

military option

The Pentagon had contemplated sending military training teams to Laos since May 1958. That summer, with the king's blessing, four groups of U.S. "civilian" advisors were sent in to revamp the military. Later that year, the commander in chief of U.S. military forces in the Pacific (CINCPAC) ordered a small number of military advisors in to assist with road, airfield, and bridge projects. Select junior officers in the ANL were sent for training at Fort Benning, Georgia.

In November, retired Brigadier General John Hentges flew to Laos to inspect the U.S. Programs Evaluation Office (PEO) and found a Lao army in such a low state of readiness and whose stewardship of supplies was so poor that he returned to Washington recommending the swift deployment of U.S. Army Special Forces advisors and a much larger PEO staff, which he filled with nonactive veterans of his own World War II unit. CINCPAC also sent twelve mobile training teams composed mostly of Special Forces personnel (also removed from active duty) for six months' temporary duty in Laos. By the time they arrived in July 1959, their would-be trainees were in the field trying to retake four border outposts in Sam Neua province. The army was eager to pin their loss on the Viet Minh, but according to Conboy, the force responsible was the same Pathet Lao battalion that had fled the Plain of Jars two months earlier.

Though the Lao army (FAR)* succeeded in recapturing two of the four outposts originally lost, the Phoui Sananikone government reacted harshly to "the Sam Neua incident," arresting sixteen Pathet Lao leaders, including Prince Souphanouvong. A massive—but ineffective— sweep into Sam Neua province was ordered. One of the few competent, disciplined, and ambitious men in the field was Kong Le, an American-trained executive officer of the 2nd Parachute Battalion (2 BP). During his exercises in Sam Neua, Kong Le concluded that the incident was being overblown. He traveled to Sam Neua town to brief his superior, General Amkha Soukhavong, and found it abandoned. Disgusted, Kong Le radioed word of the general's retreat. Though he was joined the following day by two Lao generals and American CIA case officer Jack Mathews, Kong Le's respect for his leaders was dimming.

* In July 1959 the ANL (Armee Nationale Laotienne) was rechristened the FAL (Forces Armees du Laos), then changed again in September 1961 to FAR (Forces Armee Royale).

On October 29, after more than fifty-five years of rule, King Sisavong Vong died. Always overshadowed by his more dynamic and capable father, Crown Prince Savang Vatthana ascended to the throne. Though honest and well known, most believed he lacked the energy and respect needed to control the factions warring within his country. Less than two months after he became king, he got a taste of the coming storm. Generals Phoumi Nosavan and Ouane Rathikoun and the CDNI, dissatisfied with the prime minister's handling of anti-Communist activities, staged a coup on December 25. Troops and armored vehicles surrounded the prime minister's home, and for good measure Phoumi called in Kong Le's 2 BP, which seized the radio station, Wattay air base, the ministry buildings, the national bank, and Vientiane's power plant. On December 31, the National Assembly was dissolved; Phoumi and the CDNI rose to power, and Captain Kong Le received a first-rate lesson in how to stage a coup d'état.[28]

In 1959, Continental Air Transport, now a private contractor for the CIA, changed its name to Air America. With the advice of Harry C. "Heinie" Aderholt, a crusty World War II and Korean War veteran and unconventional war expert, it began to employ Helio Couriers: small, single-engine planes designed for short take-offs and landings (STOL) in rough, mountainous terrain. Based in Okinawa, Aderholt received two Helios and sent one of them to Air America for evaluation in Laos. But when he was transferred to Thailand's Takhli Royal Air Force base in January 1960, he learned the pilots in Laos refused to fly it. He volunteered to land the Helio on the most difficult strip the pilots could pick. They chose Phong Saly, short and narrow with a fifteen- to twenty-degree turn in the middle. Aderholt made an impressive landing, but he and his copilot soon discovered they were in Pathet Lao–held territory. After a forced overnight stay, the two men were released, and the Helio Courier was well on its way to becoming an essential component of America's operations in Laos. "[W]e modified it the way the pilots wanted it," remembers Aderholt, "[W]e put a bigger engine in it before it ever got there."[29]

The new Lao government, under the leadership of Prime Minister Kou Abhay, did everything in its power—and beyond—to avoid another Pathet Lao victory in the April elections. They distributed leaflets, gerrymandered voting districts, and raised educational standards for candidates, significantly reducing the number of eligible Pathet Lao. Air America pilots flew village chiefs to the capital, where government officials urged, even demanded that they deliver votes for government candidates. The Pathet Lao screamed foul, though they had resorted to similar tactics themselves. To no one's surprise, right-wing candidates scored big victories in the April elections, proving in the minds of the left that the new government was little more than a puppet of the United States.* In May, "Red Prince" Souphanouvong and others still in Phone Keng prison escaped during a squall. Many in Laos believed the government had actually arranged the escape, hoping to avoid the political mess that would no doubt accompany their trial. Others loyal to the Pathet Lao insist they were broken out of jail by Yang Thao Tou's soldiers and the complicity of several prison guards.[30]

On August 8, CIA case officer Jack Mathews and Filipino advisor Eduardo Perez traveled to see Kong Le and his 2 BP. After receiving no pay for their service in Sam Neua, Kong Le and his men had spent most of the following year in the field. Tired, abused, and unappreciated by their commanders, they had just been ordered back into battle. Mathews knew they were fuming. When he and Perez arrived, they noticed an unusually high level of security. "We could see at least a dozen trucks parked at the base, reportedly to be utilized for [operations] the next morning. Kong Le, who was not the jovial fellow he had been during our almost two-year relationship, . . . said he would remain at the base, and [his lieutenant] would be in command of the troops during the mission." After speaking with the lieutenant and a few officers, Mathews and Perez left the base believing all was normal.[31]

In the wee hours of the following morning, Kong Le and his men launched a coup, following tactics remarkably similar to those they had used to support Phoumi Nosavan in December 1958. Once his men took over the radio station, Kong Le sent instructions to them through small receivers the Americans had given them. He also broadcast numerous speeches that ordered all foreigners to leave the country.[32]

Now an internationally regarded linguist and anthropologist, Jim Chamberlain met Kong Le when he came to Laos as a community development officer for International Voluntary Services in 1964. "I knew [him] quite well, and he was a good guy . . . He was a real leader. He was the only person in Laos that I've ever seen before or after who had any

---

* Perhaps the most blatant sign of election tampering was in the Pathet Lao stronghold of Sam Neua, where the Lao Patriotic Front candidate received only four votes.

kind of oratory capability such that people would listen to him speak and they'd get fired up—and Lao people don't get fired up about political things very easily . . . [W]hat he was saying was, 'be neutral, and don't get involved in all this superpower stuff.'"

Tensions in the aftermath of the coup ran high. The French were suspected of aiding Kong Le in the hopes of reinserting Souvanna Phouma into the government. From Thailand, Marshal Sarit Thanarat worked to support his cousin Phoumi Nosavan, who had formed a counter coup d'état commission and branded both Kong Le and Souvanna Phouma Communists.* The U.S. Department of Defense and CIA guaranteed Phoumi a steady stream of supplies flown into Vientiane aboard Air America planes.

A fragile new government commenced on August 31, with Souvanna Phouma as prime minister and Phoumi Nosavan as deputy prime minister and minister of the interior. Though it was supplying Phoumi with weapons, the United States also officially recognized Souvanna Phouma as prime minister. But the government had barely formed when it began to fracture.† As Lao leaders jockeyed for position and Souvanna Phouma held negotiations with various parties, Viet Minh and Pathet Lao forces launched strikes against Sam Neua and Xieng Khouang. By September 28, Sam Neua was in Communist hands. Souvanna Phouma, seeking a nation that might support his continued quest for neutrality, appealed to the Soviet Union for aid. Word leaked out in late September that the U.S.S.R. would open an embassy in Vientiane.[33]

One man still living in Laos grew up in a village about forty-five miles north of the capital:

Kong Le's general took over this region and came to our village. They tied a red [cloth] to [show they had] taken over my village. After he passed, we were under Souvanna Phouma's group, so we followed him because Kong Le passed [through our] region . . . Then General Nosavan followed him, and then our village collapsed . . . [My family]

---

* Of course, in retrospect, General Vang Pao asserts that the Vietnamese put Kong Le up to staging the coup.

† On the same day Phoumi formally announced the dissolution of his counter coup d'état committee, Kong Le went on the air to protest Phoumi's presence in the cabinet. Though he broadcast a retraction the next day at the behest of Souvanna Phouma, Phoumi stayed out of Vientiane and went to his military base in Savannakhet. On September 2 the government, minus Phoumi, took their oaths of office; three days later Phoumi reactivated his counter-coup committee. The battle was joined.

went to the Nam Ngum Dam, upper side. There we met with the Neo Lao Hak Sat [Communist] side. We stayed there about three years in one village . . . [near] the mountain Phu Se, beside the Nam Ngum Dam.

This man's account provides insight into the broader Hmong experience in Laos. Living outside Xieng Khouang, where many Hmong had sided first with the French and then with the United States, his family and neighbors found their lives disrupted by a conflict they neither understood nor had a particular stake in. Their village was overrun first by Neutralists and then by Rightists. Their escape ultimately placed them in a secure location. Politics mattered far less than safety. This man's future, which as of 2007 included a successful career in Communist-controlled Laos, was shaped not so much by any political allegiance or philosophical bent but simply by an escape that led to a place of security.

But even the Hmong in northeastern Laos, whose leaders had repeatedly cast their lot with the West, often had little or no idea of the political events that had transpired over the preceding six years. Nonetheless, they were once again dragged into the growing conflict.

BILL LAIR and VANG PAO

In Xieng Khouang, Touby Lyfoung, Tiao Saykham, and their young protégé Vang Pao, a lieutenant colonel in the Lao army, heard that Lao soldiers in their region were throwing their support to Souvanna Phouma. Touby's political influence had grown. He and his brother Toulia had been elected to the National Assembly in 1958 (along with Faydang's relative Lo Fong Pablia). In 1960, Touby became the first Hmong to gain a cabinet position as minister for social welfare. Lyfoung, Saykham, and Vang all disliked the idea of accommodating the Pathet Lao, but Saykham advised caution. Better to wait and see how things unfolded than to act rashly. But Vang Pao was a man of action, a trait that had gotten him into trouble in his youth.[34]

Stories told by Vang Pao supporter and activist Jane Hamilton-Merritt in *Tragic Mountains* emphasize his heroic qualities: a man of the people, serving the French already at the tender age of thirteen; a thoughtful, canny intelligence gatherer who learned what the French needed to know by slowly, patiently befriending strangers and learning about their own experiences and needs before asking them for information about enemy movements; a fearless soldier who chased down enemies fleeing with important information in hand; a warrior who developed a well-deserved reputation as a field commander. More than thirty years after the war officially concluded, the CIA officer who first offered to arm the Hmong still asserts that Vang Pao "was probably the best you could have found anywhere at that time . . . He was just a simple mountain man [but] . . . he became a real expert at guerilla warfare, and he was very good at controlling the units . . . in the field . . . [H]is best capability was being the commander on the spot, meeting with the individuals, 'cause he could inspire them all . . . [H]e could almost lift them off the ground with the power of his speech." Former CIA detailee in Laos General Richard Secord asserts, "Vang Pao . . . is one of the best field generals I've ever observed, and I've seen a hell of a lot of field generals. He had a feel for the fight . . . that was eerie. He didn't have modern intelligence, overhead cameras, and all this kind of stuff, but he sure knew the enemy, and he knew what they were likely to do in certain circumstances."[35]

But this is only one side of Vang Pao's story. Many say that by age sixteen or seventeen he had earned the nickname Vang Pao the Liar. Tiao Saykham often claimed Vang Pao was a misdirected young man until Saykham all but forced him to go to school. Even his entry into Dong Hene Academy, they say, was a result of his indiscretions. Vang Pao and a friend had stolen thirty silver bars from a wealthy Lao family living inside Vietnam. When the crime was reported to a French military court in Xieng Khouang, Vang Pao's family appealed to Touby for aid. To save Vang Pao and salvage the broader reputation of the Hmong, Touby sent him to Dong Hene, much as a medieval European criminal might have been given sanctuary in a church.[36]

While Vang Pao is often depicted as a man with impeccable anti-Communist credentials, elder Hmong in Southeast Asia and America also point to an early friendship with Pathet Lao leader Yang Thao Tou. "They were friends a long time ago," says Won Chuck Yang,

And then [in] 1958, Souvanna Phouma and [his government said] if Vang Pao caught Yang Thao Tou, they would give [him] a big, high rank . . . Vang Pao went to Nong Het, on the other side, trying to catch Yang Thao Tou. But Yang Thao Tou's soldiers caught [him] there and took him to Yang Thao Tou. [He] told Vang Pao, "What the hell are you doing here? . . . You're lucky they brought you to me, and you're lucky you're alive! If you were with somebody else, they would shoot you and kill you . . . [G]et your ass back to Phonsavan before you get killed!" . . . These words

A rare photo of Yang Thao Tou, one of the most prominent Hmong Pathet Lao leaders until his death in 1961

came from General Vang Pao's mouth. [He said,] "If he was not a good friend to me, I think he would have killed me right there, but . . . he let me go."

A Lao Hmong historian claims Yang Thao Tou, who was closer to Touby Lyfoung's age, was a kind of older brother to Vang Pao. If Yang Thao Tou had not been killed in January 1961, he asserts,

Vang Pao might have come to the other side . . . Touby Lyfoung was afraid that Vang Pao was going to take his position, so there was . . . severe tension between them . . . When Yang Thao Tou died, Vang Pao . . . ordered a cease-fire for a period of mourning . . . Vang Pao was in a very difficult position . . . [H]e wasn't sure that the people would accept him on the revolution side, either . . . Then the Americans came along, and that was his way out . . . Vang Pao said he was fighting for freedom and all of that, but he was really fighting only for himself and the glory of his own clan. Just look at how many officers in his army were his relatives.

But in piercing the mythology that often surrounds Vang Pao, one must be careful not to overreach. It is not surprising, after all, that Hmong who fought for or who now live under the current government in Laos would be critical of Vang Pao, one of their chief adversaries. Numerous Hmong in the West, however, tell the same stories. For those who try to accurately describe Vang Pao, striking a proper balance between hero worship and character assassination remains a daunting task. One may question his motives, but there is no doubt that Vang Pao sided with Phoumi Nosavan and the conservatives. It was the only way he would have come to the CIA's attention.

After completing his education at Dong Hene, Vang Pao became the commander of the 10th Battalion in Xieng Khouang, but he had a difficult time gaining respect from the Lao. "There were many . . . Lao officers [who] tried to kill Vang Pao," remembers Nor Lue Lee. "Vang Pao was the commanding officer to some of these Lao officers, and they didn't like him for that, so they rebelled against him at the Plain of Jars . . . [H]e . . . [and] three or four other Hmong who were in the Lao army with him escaped to Lat Houang on the Plain of Jars. He went [into] hiding on Dong Dane. There were many Hmong living there at that time, including many of his wife's relatives. So the Hmong leaders mobilized many Hmong with guns to go back to the Plain of Jars." Vang Pao and his men ran off the Lao soldiers and captured a number of high-ranking officers.

"We went into the barracks, and after a while there was a big Dakota plane flying overhead," remembers Vang Pao. When the plane taxied to a stop,

Out came General Amkha and his second lieutenant Dam Douane. There were two pilots, one mechanic, and one radio officer . . . I went to greet [Amkha], and he said, "Vang Pao, why are there so many Meo around here?" I said, "General, I told you . . . that if Kong Le sent his paratroopers from the air and the Pathet Lao on the ground, then I would resist" . . . [The general replied,] "In that case, you're going to cause a lot of trouble" . . . I took him to the officer's club . . . and I phoned Savannakhet. They told me, "When [General] Thao Ma gets there, put all those people in his plane." At that time, one of the local Lao commanders was Phouthasinh. But he went to his home town in Muong Kham to celebrate Kong Le's victory. When he came back, we seized him, too, and bundled him in Thao Ma's plane as well.

"[T]he Hmong were treating them a little bit harshly," says Nor Lue Lee, "kicking them, beating them up, even though they were very high ranking. But this was not done by Vang Pao. They were all tied up and could not do anything to defend themselves because their subordinates all ran away. They were all put back in one plane to go to southern Laos to General Phoumi in Savannakhet."

On the morning of November 21, 1960, General Phoumi Nosavan launched his countercoup against Kong Le and his "Neutralists." Despite having five times the manpower, superior weaponry, American advice, and support from Thailand, his men suffered heavy losses and required reinforcements, including artillery fire from the Thai side of the Mekong River. The attack killed four to five hundred and wounded between one thousand and fifteen hundred civilians. Kong Le, who stayed with his troops to defend the capital, sent his deputy to Hanoi to request aid, which came the next day in the form of six American 105 mm howitzers that the Vietnamese had captured from the French.

Hanoi summoned French, Indian, and Indonesian diplomats, informing them that in light of Thailand's intervention on behalf of Phoumi,
they were now free to act. The Soviet Union, too, launched a full-scale
airlift to help Kong Le and Souvanna Phouma. Western diplomats in
Hanoi reported massive troop movements toward Laos, including Pathet Lao units crossing back across the border. Kong Le's troops withdrew from Vientiane and made their way toward the Plain of Jars.[37]

As Kong Le's men advanced toward a steel bridge spanning the Nam
Ngum River, Vang Pao was busy celebrating the New Year, tossing the
ball with a young woman he intended to make his next wife. He had
left one of his officers in charge of a few hundred Hmong soldiers, but
they were overwhelmed by Kong Le's forces.

"The day before Kong Le arrived," says Nor Lue Lee, "the Americans
dropped . . . a lot of weapons for us . . . But we didn't know how to use
the big guns [105 mm artillery] . . . so we just abandoned them." Kong
Le's success at the bridge was due in no small part to the presence of
North Vietnamese soldiers, who—unlike Kong Le's men, their Pathet
Lao allies, and their Hmong enemies—*did* know how to use the "big
guns." With their assistance, Kong Le and his men seized control of the
strategically important Plain of Jars. North Vietnam never announced
its participation in the war, referring to its soldiers in Laos as "volunteer Vietnamese troops."[38]

Watching his cousin Phoumi's failures in the field with alarm, Marshal Sarit of Thailand decided to commit elements of his security force
to the defense of Laos. Oddly enough, one of the architects of that force
was an American. A tall, slender, quiet Texan who had served in a tank
battalion in World War II, James William "Bill" Lair returned to Texas
A&M after the war expecting to work in the oil fields, as his father had.
In his senior year, pursuing a degree in geology, Lair was recruited by
the CIA. He was sent to Thailand for his first assignment in 1951 and
had been there ever since. The CIA used Lair to train Thailand's national
police to defend the border on the remote chance that China or Vietnam would march through Laos and into Thailand. When the fear of
invasion subsided, Lair transformed his unit into a commando team,
the Police Aeril Reinforcement Unit or PARU. Though he'd never worked
with Asians before, writes Roger Warner, "he found to his surprise that
it was easy to relate to the Thai policemen, who were about his own age
. . . He learned to speak their language from them, though with a Texas

twang. They parachuted from planes together and learned to live on wild foods from the indigenous people of the forest."[39]

Americans who later worked with Lair in Laos and Thailand accord him universal respect. "I really believed in Bill Lair then, and I still do," says Mike Lynch, a provincial advisor in Sam Neua during the war. "Bill was a remarkable person. I think that his understanding of the people and his way of doing things rubbed off a bit on all of us . . . Bill's credo with us was, 'This is their country, their war. We're here to help.'" Jokes Lynch, "He was so infectious and convincing that I think if Bill had come out and said, 'I've decided we're on the wrong side, we're going to switch,' many of us would have switched with him."

"I spent a lot of time with Lair in the early months," remembers Vint Lawrence,

and he talked about his life as a young officer, having his bride picked out for him [by the CIA]. And we talked a lot about his early formation of the PARU . . . I just don't think any of this would have occurred if the PARU had not been able to go in and quietly become our surrogates with the local population . . . Bill very quickly . . . became a paragon of how a secret service should operate . . . [He] found in the Thai a country and a people that he truly loved, and I think he turned down any efforts to move him on . . . And to somebody's great credit, they let him stay . . . Bill, to this day, is honored by Thais of every stripe . . .

Bill had become Thai. [T]here was very little of the Texas A&M guy left, except when he wanted to pull it out of the back closet. And he . . . [worked] through indirection as opposed to in your face—"this is what the fuck I want." He had really made that transition, and he was very adept and very careful at keeping at least the face of the person he was going after clean—and his own—and yet getting what he needed.

Lair scoffs at claims by former CIA colleagues that he became "more Asian than the Asians," insisting his persuasive skills were already honed in childhood: "I don't think it's something you can acquire . . . As a kid, I used to talk my mother into doing things, and she used to say, 'Bill if I could just find somebody to shut you up' . . . I could talk her into doing al[most anything]. So I say it was a natural trait."

Lair's trip into Laos first took him to Savannakhet to see Phoumi Nosavan, who told him there was no room for compromise or accommodation with the Pathet Lao. If war was going to break out, Lair would need to find a group in Laos interested in fighting against the Communists.

THe meeTInG

After their failure to stop Kong Le's advance, Vang Pao and his men moved south toward Vientiane. After about two days, says Hmong scholar Gary Yia Lee, they stopped to reassess their situation: "That's when they were contacted by Bill Lair."

At least two CIA officers had already met Vang Pao. "The first American who came to meet General Vang Pao," says Lieutenant Colonel Gao Moua, "was named Captain Jack F. Mathews"—the same case officer who later worked with Kong Le. "They met in 1958."

The second American to contact Vang Pao was Stuart Methven, a member of the first CIA class trained at Camp Peary, a wooded facility just south of Washington, DC. Brought to Laos because of his serviceable French, Methven became the "civic-action contact" with the Hmong. Like all CIA officers in Laos at the time, Methven traveled with a member of the Lao army: "We were trying to get government representatives out to the countryside, to say . . . [we're] working for you . . . [T]he Lao officer would say to a district chief, 'What can we do for you?' And the guy would say we need seeds, we need this, we need that . . . I would jot it down and say maybe we could help him out. The Lao weren't ashamed to turn to you like that, but we preferred to stay farther out, to let them handle it alone and carry the ball." While traveling in the Plain of Jars, Methven made some inquiries to see

if there were any Meo who were part of the Laotian government. I learned that they had a big chief down in Vientiane named Touby Lyfoung. But he had sort of gone soft, and they had him in some kind of ceremonial position. So I didn't feel he was the guy to work with . . . But we had to work through somebody connected to the government, not just an ordinary Meo, because that was the only way we could get the Vientiane government to support it. Then I heard about a Meo captain, farther north, who was in the Laotian army. I sent word that I would like to meet him, and he came down two days later. He was . . . a Chinese-looking guy, very dynamic.

Methven remembered Vang Pao as remarkably direct, brave, charismatic, and honest. "I asked him if there was any way, in conjunction with the Lao government, that we could help him and the Meo. Most people asked for all kinds of things. We had these big radio sets, and people would ask for things like that, or they'd ask for a pistol. But Vang Pao asked for an anvil . . . The Meo were great at working with metals. So I went back and walked into the station and said, 'I need an anvil.'"

Vang Pao, eventually commander of all forces in Military Region 2

It was cold up in the mountains, Vang Pao added, and the Hmong had few clothes. Methven found a military depot overstocked with olive green sweaters from World War II and bought five thousand of them for a nickel apiece. He had the items loaded in a plane and a Hmong guide showed him where to take them. "The anvil went down by parachute, the sweaters we kicked out. As they hit the ground, they fell all over the place. It was a sea of olive drab down there. I later went back to the Plaine des Jarres and walked back up to Vang Pao's position. I think it took two days to get there. And the Meo were lined up along the road waiting for me, wearing those green sweaters."

When asked how the Americans contacted him, Vang Pao described events very similar to those recalled by Methven:

They never came to make this agreement or that agreement. They just came looking around. They saw the Hmong were very poor in many ways—no salt to eat . . . no clothes to wear, so when the Americans came, they said, "Do you want salt for the Hmong?" So the Americans dropped salt everywhere for the Hmong. And when the winter came and it was very cold, the Americans asked, "Do you need clothes for the Hmong?" The Hmong are very poor, so they dropped clothes from the sky for the Hmong . . . Then one day they brought carbines . . . And then they brought in . . . communication radios and gave one to each Hmong chief. At that time we already had communication everywhere. So slowly, slowly, that's how we did it . . . All they did was say, "Do you need this? Do you need that?" Yes, we needed this, we needed that, we were poor . . . So when the war came, they asked for our help, and we helped . . . [T]he king also gave his consent. So that's why I helped the Americans.

Vang Pao, said Methven, feared the United States, like the French, would train and arm the Hmong, let them fight, but ultimately leave and force the Hmong to give up their weapons. When Methven told Vang Pao he wanted to introduce him to Bill Lair, he says Vang Pao "looked me in the eye and said, 'You aren't going to do what the French did, are you?'" Methven replied, "'Listen, this is the United States government you are talking to. When we make a commitment, we keep it. How can you compare us to the French?' I was convinced we'd never let them down."[40]

Pa Cha Kong was the radio operator, "so I knew about the meeting . . . [It was] in a Laotian place called Tha Thom, between Xieng Khouang and Vientiane . . . My understanding was that . . . General Vang Pao wanted . . . more weapons, more ammunition, more medicines, and food—that's it . . . I didn't think anything about losing. I thought as soon as we won the Americans were going to come in, develop our country, and we were going to have business together."

Despite stories from many quarters to the contrary, Bill Lair insists,

We didn't promise them anything. They didn't want to be promised anything. That's what a lot of people miss . . . [A]ll the Hmong wanted to do was to stay there, and they wanted their freedom, they wouldn't want anybody to bother 'em, they wanted their own country . . . That's what they were fighting for . . . They never dreamed of going to the U.S. . . . [Vang Pao said to me,] "We have to fight the Communists or we have to leave," that's it . . . It's not like a lot of people are saying now, that they volunteered to fight for the U.S. . . . That's not true.

But saying the CIA was simply trying to help the Hmong is a bit disingenuous. As Tim Castle has observed, "The Hmong felt no allegiance to a country controlled by lowlanders. Therefore, as the CIA case officers and their PARU interpreters/assistants moved from village to village, their message to the tribesmen was simple: 'The Vietnamese will soon come to take your land. We [the United States] will give you the means to fight and defend your homes.'"[41]

"I agreed," says Vang Pao, "because I read it like this: World War I, World War II, the Americans won. The Vietnamese wouldn't be much of a match for them . . . I felt encouraged, so I agreed. 'Don't be afraid. We have to do it, because they need us.' That's what I believed."

Once Vang Pao accepted aid from the CIA, a place had to be found to train the first of Vang Pao's recruits. "I asked him," says Lair,

"We've got to have a place where we can drop these weapons in and then give some training to [your men], so is there any place that we can go so we'd have some time? 'Cause [the Communists] are going to see the parachutes . . . and they're going to send troops up there." "Oh, yes, I know the place," he said. So I said, "And how long would we have before they get up there?" And he said, "Three days." And I believe that anybody in the U.S. Army would say, "You can't train anybody in three days," but I didn't say that. I just turned to Pranet, who was . . . the commander of the PARU, and I said, "Look, we better sit down and come up with our three-day training program." But it worked. You'd be amazed what you can do in three days.

Vang Pao had selected the remote mountain site of Pa Dong, which became the first military base for the Hmong resistance. There, Lair and the PARU commenced their intense training:

The first day we trained everybody on their personal weapons . . . A lot of them had old flintlock rifles, or they had crossbows . . . So they knew [or] had an instinct of how to shoot a weapon . . . [T]he second day, we would go into some . . . very small

unit tactics. And we also . . . had some light machine guns and some 60 mm mortars, so we also trained on that . . . And then the third day we just taught the ambush. We didn't try to go to any other tactic except ambush . . . And they did pretty good . . . [A]bout three days later, there [the enemy] came up the trail. So . . . those first three companies we trained . . . went out and set up an ambush, and . . . they just mowed 'em down. I remember when it was all over, they were jumping around and laughing; they were so happy. I've never seen anything like the Hmong because . . . nobody got hurt. And that's what you need the first operation, you need something that's a great success; it gives them more confidence that they can do this . . . [E]ven little kids would be shooting crossbows and all that sort of stuff. And of course, the big thing they already had was the ability to move through that area, that terrain . . . [E]very step they ever took was either up or down, so they were extremely mobile . . . [A]nd the first thing I did was get VP to give me twenty guys to start radio training, 'cause when the Hmong started moving and they could contact us—I mean, you would think they had helicopters. They could move through the mountains like nobody else could. They were perfect.

3 | "a very definite moral commitment"

On January 19, 1961, one day before he left office, President Eisenhower met with President-elect John F. Kennedy. With their respective advisors, they discussed the situation in Southeast Asia. Often seen as a watershed in the history of the war in Laos, this meeting is itself a subject of historical debate. According to Kennedy biographer Arthur Schlesinger, Eisenhower advised bracing for a possible war in Laos, "the key to all Southeast Asia." A Communist victory there would place "unbelievable pressure" on the rest of the region. Schlesinger quoted a classified memorandum prepared by longtime Democratic advisor Clark Clifford. In his memoirs, published thirty years later, Clifford also commented, "The way that Eisenhower discussed the issue . . . made an important, and unfortunate, contribution to the development of American policy in Indochina. The tone of the old soldier . . . had a powerful effect." In 1990, secretary of defense Robert McNamara's notes from the meeting were found during a routine process of declassification. They read, "President Eisenhower advised *against* unilateral action by the United States in . . . Laos" (emphasis added). It was eventually discovered that seven people from the meeting later reported on it in some fashion—including Kennedy. Of the other six, three stated Eisenhower warned against intervention in Laos, while the other three said he supported it. Individual agendas and perspectives brought *to* the meeting were more influential than the words spoken *in* it.[1]

So what chance do historians have of understanding not only the White House meeting on Laos but the war that still haunts Laos today? Soldiers might recall battles they should have won, leaders who let them down, or an enemy who was victorious only through treachery or help from a powerful outsider. Any number of people who lost family members, significant property, or social or political power may look for scapegoats to blame for their misfortune. They might unconsciously rearrange the events of the past in order to make more sense, tell a better story, or paint themselves and their friends as heroes. "History" becomes propaganda, foregone conclusions designed to sway an audience in a calculated, self-serving direction. One must always keep this dynamic in mind. The history of the war in Southeast Asia, and the role of the Hmong people in that war, is rife with the potential for confusion, misinterpretation, or manipulation.

Take, for example, the story told by Lieutenant Colonel Gao Moua: "The CIA contacted the Hmong . . . because . . . the North Vietnamese used the Ho Chi Minh Trail on the border of northern Laos to come to southern Laos . . . [T]he Americans thought, 'If we don't find people to watch this area, when our planes pass they will be shot down and we would have no way to rescue our people.'" Moua's account is problematic. First, there were not yet American pilots to rescue or, as others assert, U.S. radar guidance installations to guard when the meeting between Lair and Vang Pao took place. Second, if one consults a map of Laos during the war (see page vi), one sees the Ho Chi Minh Trail ran far south of Military Region 2, the area of Vang Pao's command. Hearing Americans speak repeatedly about the Ho Chi Minh Trail, it is likely the Hmong confused it with Colonial Route 7, where indeed they attacked numerous enemy convoys and served as spotters for attack planes.* Colonel Xai Dang Xiong makes this conflation apparent: "Once I became part of the CIA army . . . I was given command of *Route 7, on the Ho Chi Minh Road,* from . . . Nong Het to the Plain of Jars."†[2]

Xiong's reference to the "CIA army" points to another area of confusion: for whom were the Hmong fighting? First, one should understand there were a large number of Hmong outside Military Region 2 who fought in the Royal Lao Army, not under the authority of General Vang Pao. But even within MR 2, some create a false dichotomy in which Hmong soldiers fought only for themselves, the Lao government, or U.S. and Thai interests. They were fighting, of course, for all of the above. U.S. money paid for Thai teams to equip and train Hmong soldiers, but Vang Pao was under the authority of the Lao prime minister; his troops fought in the name of the king of Laos, not the United States or the CIA; and Hmong children learned Lao, not English, if they attended schools set up with U.S. assistance. One should not, of course, minimize the influence of American money, firepower, and humanitar-

---

* Numerous knowledgeable individuals, including former CIA chief of station for Laos Hugh Tovar, state categorically, "the Hmong didn't fight in the Ho Chi Minh Trail . . . [T]he trail itself essentially plugged into Laos further south . . . They didn't contribute there at all."

† Not until 1968, "with the creation of ethnic Lao guerrilla battalions in the Laotian Panhandle," did ground forces begin to contest Hanoi's use of the Ho Chi Minh Trail, explains Thomas Ahern.

ian aid; neither should one lose sight of the clear intention Vang Pao and other Hmong leaders had to become active citizens in a united Laos.

According to Richard Secord, who by 1966 was chief of tactical air operations for the Secret War, the Hmong "present[ed] . . . a strategic threat to the homeland of North Vietnam . . . [T]hey tied down . . . regular NVA [North Vietnamese Army] forces that could have been used elsewhere [i.e., against U.S. troops in South Vietnam] . . . They were also a buffer between [Vietnam] and the capital." But these roles went largely unacknowledged until former CIA director William Colby testified before Congress in April 1994. It was the Hmong, said Colby, who held General Vo Nguyen Giap's North Vietnamese Army, including several of his best divisions, to approximately the same battle lines from 1962 to 1972, despite the fact that Giap's forces grew during that period from seven thousand to seventy thousand. Numerous Secret War veterans find fault with Colby's numbers. Hugh Tovar, CIA station chief in Laos from 1970 to 1973, says the Vietnamese had the 312th and 316th divisions in northern Laos—probably between twenty and twenty-four thousand men total—and three independent brigades numbering no more than forty-five hundred. While forces under Vang Pao's command fought what Tovar calls "really tough, excellent troops, as good as ours," Colby's oft-cited figures seem out of line. And the degree to which one believes the Hmong held the same battle lines depends on how wide that line is drawn.[3]

But did the Hmong do it all alone, save for some logistical and material aid from the United States? One often reads that the Hmong were the only reliable fighters in Laos, that ethnic Lao soldiers in particular would regularly abandon their posts or even refuse to fight. Nothing angers Ernie Kuhn, who spent ten years in Southeast Asia working for the U.S. Agency for International Development (USAID), more than stories like these.

I disagree with that completely. There were entire SGU [Special Guerrilla Unit] battalions comprised solely of various [Khmu] ethnic groups. There were T'ai Daeng groups amongst them. The officers were almost uniformly Meo, but of the first four SGU units . . . at least two were predominantly if not fully [Khmu]. Later on, SGU 9 was a completely Lao battalion recruited from Savannakhet and brought up to the north . . . [T]he Lao get very short shrift when it comes to being fighters . . . Lao troops, when properly led, were as good a fighter as anyone else and probably could fight just as well as the Meo if not better . . . Colonel Khongsavan, commander of BV

*[Volunteer Battalion] 24 in Xieng Khouang, and Colonel Douangtha Norasing, com-
mander of BV 27 in the north, . . . were outstanding local commanders. Of course,
one of the most tragic things . . . was when Colonel Thong Vongrasamy died from
wounds trying to rescue an American pilot. Colonel Thong was a charismatic leader
who got the best out of his men . . . So the Lao put up one hell of a fight . . . made an
awful lot of sacrifices . . . and don't get much credit for it.*[4]

It would be unfortunate to use misunderstandings and disagree-
ments such as these to minimize the important role the Hmong played
in the defense of northern Laos. But in affording that recognition, one
should not ignore others' significant contributions. This much is certain: between 1961 and 1973, the CIA and USAID, in partnership with
the governments of Laos and Thailand, worked closely with ethnic Lao
as well as Hmong, Khmu (Lao Theung), Mien (Yao), and other ethnic
minorities in Laos to develop conventional and guerrilla forces capable of defending the Royal Lao government. The North Vietnamese,
with support from the People's Republic of China and the Soviet Union
and working closely with the Pathet Lao, fought persistently to overthrow that same government. The outcome of this conflict would not
only determine control of Laos but also lead tens of thousands of people who fought on the losing side to flee for their lives.

THE "SECRET" WAR

Lee Yia was worried. He had begun his first term in high school in Xieng
Khouang when the civil war broke out. "I was so sad that [school] had
to close. All of our French teachers were running for their lives . . . [W]e
were also . . . because my father was in the right-wing police force and
the invading force was the Neutralist force of Kong Le. We woke up one
morning on the first of January [1961], and *boom*, we heard these big
artillery guns . . . [coming] closer and closer." Lee Yia's father, Nor Lue
Lee, had left the family weeks before; the only news they had came
from their radio. "[T]hey were saying, 'The Russians are ferrying materials and supplies for Kong Le.' By that time Kong Le was in the Plain of
Jars, advancing on Xieng Khouang town." Lee Yia and his family frequently hid in the forest: "We were very hopeful that the town would be
recaptured and we could go back, but we stayed in [a cave] . . . for about
two weeks." Lee Yia's father sent a man to rescue them. "We were really scared of meeting enemy soldiers . . . but . . . no one saw us . . . [O]n

the third day, my father came to meet us . . . dressed in a green military uniform—not the yellow khaki police officer uniform anymore—and he had a gun with him . . . He said he is now a soldier in the army and not a police officer anymore. He was . . . gathering information on the enemy lines . . . He took us all the way from there to Pa Dong."

By early 1961, Pa Dong had become the stronghold of the pro-royalist Hmong. Like the majority of Hmong soldiers throughout the war, Nor Lue Lee brought his wife and children with him. Lee Yia was put in charge of the family packhorse. Pa Dong was

full of soldiers, the big airstrip, and the planes overhead nearly all hours of the day dropping military supplies and big bags of rice . . . There were stories about people being hit by things dropping from the sky, like ammunition boxes or bags of rice. People were pointing out, "Oh! One person died here! One person died there!" So as a young boy of about twelve, it really scared [me] . . . I was grazing the horse near a river next to the airstrip, and these planes came to drop supplies . . . [W]hen you look up, it looks like the thing with the parachute is going to fall right on you! So I and my younger brother . . . were running around all day . . . forgetting about the horses and all . . . I came to some soldiers that we knew . . . "How do you people manage without running? You seem to just stay where you are or walk around without a care!" [They answered], "No, it just looks like it's falling on you, but it doesn't actually . . . It falls a long distance away, because it's very high up" . . . So that was something that I remember to be both funny and also very scary.

As if war wasn't frightening enough for children—and their parents—they also worried about the sky falling on their heads. Years later, Lee Yia renewed his education, first in Vientiane and then in Australia, becoming a world-renowned scholar of Hmong history and culture. But today, Dr. Gary Yia Lee still recalls Pa Dong with a mixture of humor and horror.

Xai Xue Yang, a shaman now living in Australia, trained at Pa Dong when he was a young man. "[I]f I'm a Yang, I tend to join a Yang commander group . . . because you trust each other better . . . [I]f you have some disagreement, it's easier to talk things through." Yang was given a World War II–issue rifle, set in front of a tarp, and told to disassemble his weapon.* "They mixed all the parts everywhere . . . [and] wanted you to put it back together . . . over and over until you knew how . . .

---

* M1 carbine and M1 Garand rifles, semiautomatic weapons used during World War II, were most commonly issued during this early period. The carbine was smaller and easier for Hmong—especially those with no modern firearms experience—to use.

Next you learn to crawl . . . to twist your body on the ground. And then
. . . you shoot at the target . . . Then they taught us to aim and to fire
the mortar."

Looking back now, Jer Xiong Yang from Queensland, Australia, believes the training they received was good, but "[using] the Thai and
American strategies, we would all die if the enemy base was on top of a
mountain. In our country, it would be impossible." Yang excelled at
marksmanship but is now philosophical about his prowess. "[O]nly
twenty-nine soldiers . . . hit the target . . . The soldiers who failed were
not allowed to carry the bigger weapons [like a Browning Automatic
Rifle] . . . [I]f I was smart, I wouldn't have shot at the paper; I should
have missed on purpose . . . I still ache today and my hearing is not so
good from carrying that big gun."[5]

Pa Dong was not the only training base. PARU teams aided or led by
CIA case officers and U.S. Special Forces set up remote sites and sent
roving patrols in search of friendly villages and recruits. The CIA also
took Vang Pao up in small planes, scouting more distant villages. "Supported by Air America aircraft," writes Tim Castle, "Vang Pao relocated
some two hundred Hmong villages to seven pre-selected sites in the
mountains ringing the Plain of Jars." These locations, as well as other
allied villages, became landing or "Lima" sites. Heinie Aderholt, who
helped train Air America pilots, remembers flying with Vang Pao and
Bill Lair

to [learn about] the whole concept of Lima sites . . . [Vang Pao] would go over and
[point out a particular village] . . . "We could put an airstrip down there." I said,
"How do you go about it?" He said, "We drop 'em a note and tell 'em what we want
them to do. We drop in . . . shovels and stuff like that" . . . They told them, "If you
will open the site, we'll drop you rice or guns or whatever" . . . They built some of
them by tearing down the villages . . . [T]he only flat place in miles around was the
village, so I guess Vang Pao paid them . . . and they moved and built another village.[6]

The pilots who flew for Air America, Bird & Sons, and Continental
had to fly in and out of airstrips even Aderholt describes as "the worst
strips in the world! If I'd been the boss of the whole thing, I doubt that
I would have approved most of 'em." According to one participant,
"Regulations required that the [air]strips . . . be at least five hundred
feet long. Often, this was impossible . . . so we built the strips on steep
slopes, and the pilot landed uphill and took off downhill . . . [W]e flew
out of strips as short as 250 feet. Freak winds in the rough terrain,

Lima Site 50, Phou Kum, 4,300 feet above sea level, was but one of over two hundred sites into which pilots contracted by the U.S. government would fly. Note runway at far right.

fog, smoke, low cloud ceilings, thunderstorms, torrential rains, a complete lack of navigational aids, as well as enemy ground fire—all made flying a nerve-chilling, hair-raising experience." "We had guys like Ron Sutphin, Fred Walker, and Joe [Kittinger]—all the Helio pilots," says Aderholt. "They made the thing work." Whether supporting the CIA's paramilitary operations, USAID's humanitarian efforts, or some other U.S. government venture, air companies were paid for every flight they made. Ernie Kuhn remembers, "Every year there were meetings whereby the cost sharing of all the aircraft was determined . . . [T]he requirements office . . . handled logistics and support to Lao forces . . . USAID did all kinds of things, and then there was the CIA. Each one of those organizations had a different cut of the aircraft budget, based upon their usage, so pilots would have to keep logs of what they were doing." As awkward and unworkable as the system may sound, to a person those interviewed for this book say it was the most effective operation they had ever seen.[7]

There were a few bumps in the road, including use of U.S. Special Forces (SF), who had been in Laos since 1959. In April 1961, smarting from the Bay of Pigs fiasco and apparently wanting to show a stronger stance against Communism, President Kennedy authorized SF advisors to wear uniforms with rank and insignia. Renamed "White Star," they trained regular army units and guerrilla forces. They were essentially doing the PARU's job, but with far less cultural competence, especially since no White Star member stayed in Laos for more than six months.[8]

In addition, the presence of foreign advisors inevitably attracted enemy attention. In April and May 1961, two sites—San Tiau and Ban Na—fell to Communist offensives. By late April, Pa Dong itself was under attack. One early CIA recruit, chosen by Bill Lair for his facility with local languages, worked with Joe Hudachek, an army munitions expert on loan to the CIA. "Increasingly larger convoys of North Vietnamese were coming in," he recalls. "We planned to . . . string different kinds of explosives and warheads, shells . . . along the highway, and then when that went off, [our guns]would work on them . . . We had about 350 men [a huge force for an ambush] . . . who walked or were choppered in [at night] . . . [W]e hadn't even had time to get up the mountain with all of our people when the North Vietnamese [attacked]." For two nights and three days, the enemy tried to blow them off the top of the mountain. "They . . . didn't want to follow us straight up, because they would have taken . . . a lot of losses." Instead they set off about three hundred rounds of artillery, but with the difficult trajectory, much of it exploded before reaching their target or sailed over it. But the Vietnamese wiped out a supporting Lao battalion below.

"Most of our casualties were from Hmong . . . setting up booby traps on the road . . . [who] didn't tell the other guys. There were [a few] horrific casualties." Running out of supplies, they retreated in small groups toward Pa Dong. Along the way, their radio stopped working.

The Vietnamese threw a line behind us, so we were cut off . . . [W]e had to go back through their lines . . . The Vietnamese found out through their Pathet Lao friends . . . that we had these Hmong, so they sent messages . . . through villages they controlled, and they would shout back and forth, "We know who you are. You're with the bloody Americans here. You'd better go home or we'll have all your women and children" . . . So the [Hmong soldiers] split off as much as they could . . . to see what they could save. The mission was a total disaster. We buried . . . [the] stuff that we couldn't carry . . . Joe and I . . . one Thai PARU and several Hmong boys headed off back in the direction of Pa Dong . . . [W]e had help from Hmong farmers who would tip us off.

He fortified himself with shots of sweetened condensed milk, but "it was tough going, and Joe was not a young guy . . . VP's guys were looking for us . . . and we finally made it back and had this fifty-five-hundred-foot climb back up to Pa Dong."

On May 17 and 18, in the midst of the escalating pressure on Pa Dong, U.S. embassy political officer George B. Roberts came to visit. In a message sent to the State Department, Roberts praised Vang Pao and the "Meo" for their hospitality and fervent anti-Communism. It was clear to him that

> there exists a very definite moral commitment between the Meo and the United States. As members of the Lao Army we have armed them and helped them fight the Communists, which means that in any settlement which would give the Bloc a preponderant voice in Lao affairs, the Meo would be in a very dangerous position. They are aware of this, as the state of their morale testifies, and the continued declarations made to us that they depend entirely on the United States were obviously meant to be taken as requests that we do not leave them in the lurch . . .
>
> Without American support they would have to flee or come to some sort of accommodation, but the loyal support they have given the West . . . clearly entitles them to a more favorable fate.[9]

On June 6, a force composed primarily of North Vietnamese troops led what became the final assault on Pa Dong. Vang Pao was evacuated in a helicopter, a stream of refugees and a PARU and Hmong rear guard following in his wake. A new base was established eight miles to the southwest, at Pha Khao. Gary Yia Lee's family had been in Pa Dong only a week when the final push began: "Again we had to flee for our lives." Finding their way through the forbidding terrain was no easy task, even for mountain people. When they reached Pha Khao, "we saw soldiers running away from the battle, coming to join their families—not a lot of them, just the odd ones who managed to escape. We saw people crying because they had lost their father or brother or husband in the battle." With the attack on Pa Dong, remembers Nao Her Vang, Hmong people in the region finally "realized that the war was real and the Communists were there to fight with us."[10]

As the siege on Pa Dong escalated, negotiations were under way for another meeting in Geneva. The monarchs of Laos and Cambodia had both lost faith in the United States' avowed anti-Communism. Phoumi Nosavan "concluded that when the chips were down the Americans appeared unwilling to fight to defend the territory of Laos. What had stimulated them to take precautionary military moves in 1961, he noticed, was the threat to Thailand and South Vietnam." When Phoumi failed to stall the proceedings at Geneva, he attempted to reassert control over Nam Tha, a strategic town along the Chinese border in Houa Khong province. But the campaign ended in disaster and humiliation. His troops, despite an almost two-to-one advantage, failed to hold their position.[11]

U.S. officials railed against the Lao army (known as FAR, *Forces Armee Royale,* by September 1961) but created a Military Assistance Command in Thailand (MACTHAI). In Laos, their attention focused on ethnic guerrilla forces with proven ability. The CIA brought in more staff—whether or not Bill Lair wanted them—to run their operation. Lloyd "Pat" Landry, Lair's classmate at Texas A&M, was fond of carrying a "swagger stick" wherever he went. His fellow officers "used words like 'nasty,' 'rough,' and 'sarcastic' to describe him," but he and Lair had always gotten along. Landry "realized that the PARU were far better field instructors than he . . . [so he] came back to the office to be Lair's deputy. It was the right niche for him. He played tough cop to Lair's nice cop. Blunt and hard-driving, Landry worked fiendishly long hours piecing together intelligence reports, arranging logistics, doing whatever needed to be done." Lair was Landry's superior, but "Bill was very careful . . . to make sure they stayed friends," says Richard Secord. "It wasn't a 'boss-subordinate' relationship."[12]

Anthony Poshepny, aka "Tony Poe," arrived in Laos with two PARU detachments. An ex-Marine and CIA officer since 1952, Poe laid claim to an extensive paramilitary background well suited to further train and deploy guerrilla forces. Many of Poe's old compatriots talk about his growing drinking problem, but "a lot of the critical stuff you'll hear about Tony related to his later years," says Mike Lynch. "At his best, he was really something. No one could ever question his bravery. Here's a guy who was wounded five times, Iwo Jima right through to Laos and Thailand . . . Tony was very close to the Thai PARU. Although they undoubtedly respected each other, Tony and Vang Pao were not close . . . Tony once rescued a wounded Thai soldier while under heavy enemy fire. The Thais honored his bravery and cut him a lot of slack as a result."[13]

Perhaps owing to his father's service in the OSS, the CIA recruited James Vinton "Vint" Lawrence right out of Princeton in the spring of 1961, even though he was an art history major. After extensive intelligence and paramilitary training, Lawrence believed he was going to

North India to aid "what was left of the Tibetan resistance." In February 1962, he discovered his destination was Laos: "I knew nothing about Laos . . . I was twenty-two. I spoke some French, I was not married . . . and so I . . . was sent up country to talk to the French-speaking Hmong."

While the CIA and PARU trained guerrillas in the field, White Star was setting up a training base at the small village of Sam Thong. Recruiting continued in earnest.[14]

Chay Heu, a teacher in a village near Vang Vieng, had no idea why Vang Pao was amassing an army, but in March 1961, Hmong and Thai soldiers accompanied by an "Anglo CIA named Tony" came into their village to recruit them. Though they made no promises, guns and ammunition from Vang Pao's forces were dropped in only a few days later. The Pathet Lao now assumed they were on Vang Pao's side, so they had no choice but to join in the fight. In those early days, remembers Heu, "the Hmong were foot soldiers with weapons . . . The advisor and the commanders were Thai. They lived daily with the Hmong people. Maybe once a week or so, there would be an American advisor who came to support the Thai commanders." Over time, the CIA handed control of paramilitary operations over to the Hmong. First, choosing a representative sample of educated Hmong from all Xieng Khouang clans, they established twelve-man Special Operations Teams (SOT) modeled after the PARU. The first group of 120, including Shong Leng Xiong, was sent to Hua Hin, Thailand, for training in August 1961: "After six months of military training, including parachuting, some were told to stay and instruct the next group of Hmong. Others were sent back to do reconnaissance of the areas where they would be working . . . This group . . . was [also] instructed to build more airfields and recruit more men." A second SOT group of 160 was sent in February 1962.[15]

Next came Special Guerrilla Units (SGU), intended to serve a primarily offensive purpose. Five hundred SGU recruits were sent to Hua Hin in May for four weeks of guerrilla and parachute training. "Unlike the 12-man SOTs," writes Conboy, "these Hmong went through the cycle as five companies under the overall command of Youa Vang Ly, the former Hmong NCO in the French Union Army and long-time colleague of Vang Pao."[16]

Even as Vint Lawrence arrived in Pha Khao, he learned the guerrilla force was looking for a new home. Pha Khao, he recalls, "was like the interior of an old volcano, and the landing strip in the village sat up at about seven thousand feet . . . [There were] great big karst ridges going up on either side, and you're on the shoulder of Phu Bia, which is the tallest mountain in Laos, at just under ten thousand feet . . . [But] clouds would just come in and sit on top of it. So its weather was pretty iffy." Pilot Ron Sutphin and Bill Lair's young recruit had scouted a new location they thought would fit the bill nicely. It was called Long Tieng.[17]

Until early 1962, Long Tieng was a sleepy, isolated Khmu village. By the time Vang Pao came to inspect it in mid-August, it was already claimed by Edgar "Pop" Buell, USAID's refugee coordinator. Buell, a farmer from Indiana who never went to high school, was widowed in his late forties. Disconsolate, he sold his farm to his son, made sure his daughter and her husband were secure, and went overseas to teach modern agricultural techniques. International Voluntary Service (IVS) assigned him to Xieng Khouang province in 1959. The next year, he met Hmong people for the first time on the southern edge of the Plain of Jars. "[Pop] soon realized that they weren't greatly different from himself," wrote one colleague. "Conservative, independent, shrewd, and with strong family ties, they . . . experienced the same problems he had known on his own farm." Choua Thao was just fourteen when she first met Buell. "I said, 'What an old man—drinks coffee all day long and smoke and coffee, smoke and coffee' . . . He started to love the people that he worked with . . . and he always called me 'daughter.' So I called him father, the traditional way . . . He became my godfather."[18]

Eventually Buell, forty-seven, met Vang Pao, who was twenty-eight. When seventy thousand Hmong fled from their villages in the wake of Kong Le's coup, Buell "mobilized the forces they needed to survive— particularly rice and medicines. By merely being the man on the spot, he became the American representative." Buell hoped to use Long Tieng as a permanent settlement for some six thousand displaced Hmong.[19]

As Buell and the CIA wrangled over Long Tieng, an agreement was signed at Geneva. Thailand grudgingly acceded to a coalition government in Laos led by Souvanna Phouma. Phoumi Nosavan and Souphanouvong were "vice premiers." The agreement stipulated that all foreign combatants, including military advisors, should be out of Laos by October 7, 1962. Another International Control Commission was established to monitor the situation and report violations. In short, all the flaws of the 1954 agreement were once again in place.

White Star wound down its operations. No new weapons were issued to the Hmong after June 27; ammunition drops were suspended on July 21. The last Special Operations Team finished training at Sam Thong on August 6, and by mid-September the last White Star advisor left Laos. The CIA paid Pop Buell to move his refugee operations into the old White Star base at Sam Thong, and Long Tieng became the new headquarters for Vang Pao's army.[20]

When most politicians or press came to cover the war in Laos, they were taken to Sam Thong, also known as Lima Site 20, the center of the USAID operation in Military Region 2.

"The Thais still believed," writes Sutayut Osornprasop, "that the North Vietnamese would not be withdrawn from Laos, nor would the ICC be effective." They were right. "Whereas all American troops . . . as well as Filipino technicians . . . were withdrawn from Laos by the 7 October deadline . . . [o]nly forty North Vietnamese 'technicians' had checked out of Laos." As many as eight thousand North Vietnamese troops in Laos seemed to have every intention of staying put and passing themselves off as Pathet Lao. By November 1962, "Hanoi . . . introduced more troops into Laos at a rate of 500 men or more per month . . . [T]he North Vietnamese intention to infiltrate its men into Laos was not simply to take over Laos, but to serve a more ambitious purpose—the reunification of Vietnam and the domination of neighbouring countries."[21]

The United States and Thailand followed suit. The U.S. Military Assistance Advisory Group simply moved across the Mekong to Udorn Thani, as did Bill Lair's CIA operation, though they still reported to the station chief in Laos. The military requirements office was embedded in USAID and coordinated logistical support for FAR. Tony Poe and Vint Lawrence stayed at Long Tieng with the Hmong, in violation of the Geneva agreement. The Thai government "welcomed the United States into Thailand . . . [and] order[ed] roughly a hundred PARUs to remain in Laos."[22]

Almost two years before Lyndon Johnson used an incident in the Tonkin Gulf to send American troops into Vietnam, a "secret war" was already brewing in neighboring Laos. The rules of the conflict were simple: as long as everyone pretended that only residents of Laos were involved, Vietnam, China, the U.S.S.R., Thailand, and the United States could provide "aid" with impunity. American military and CIA personnel in Laos were "sheep-dipped," resigning their commissions, removing all military dress and insignia, adopting civilian clothing and "cover identity." The Vietnamese claimed they were only providing advisors and material support for the Pathet Lao. A Hmong in Laos who fought for the Pathet Lao insists, "In the beginning, [we] . . . were like children and the Vietnamese were more like the leaders. But by 1965, the Pathet Lao 'grew up' . . . [T]he Vietnamese mainly supplied the ammunition and weapons we needed." This view is discredited by North Vietnam's own records. According to Chau Huy Ngoc, who closely consulted those records, "Without North Vietnam, the Pathet Lao could not do anything." Instead of rising Pathet Lao independence, the post-1965 era witnessed "a tremendous increase of NVA troops into Laos." By October 1973, the North Vietnamese had "one division, nine regiments, four battalions: 43,000 personnel, not including hidden mobile forces stationed close to the Lao-Vietnam border, compared to the Pathet Lao's 18,500 troops."[23]

The stage was set for a war whose only acknowledged combatants fought with training, weapons, support, and money that didn't officially exist. When the war was over, the denial continued. Those on the losing side would find their former allies inexplicably absent and appallingly silent. Maintaining the laughable facade of neutrality was more important than helping those who had tied their futures to a partnership with the United States and Thailand.

the americans

Vint Lawrence was twenty-three to Tony Poe's forty-nine in October 1962. Poe outranked Lawrence, but as Bill Lair remembers it, the younger man was in charge. "[He] had to be able to give Vang Pao advice, in many cases without appearing to do so . . . Vang Pao . . . treated Vint like he was his son. One to one, Vint could talk VP into doing this and the other thing, but he was very careful not to overstep that. You've got to influence those guys *in* command to do what they should do without them believing you're running it." If Vang Pao had any idea he was being manipulated by Lair, Lawrence, Tiao Saykham, or anyone else, he doesn't remember or admit it now. "They brought airplanes, they brought clothes, they brought weapons, they gave everything to me, and I did anything I wanted with those things. I was the one who did all the planning, and all the training of our people. I organized everything."

"I ate, slept, and worked for four years with Vang Pao," says Lawrence. "I knew the man; I knew the people . . . [O]nce I learned Lao, he would speak to me in Lao . . . [and] use French for the words [I] didn't know . . . I think he was impressed by my willingness to hunker down and live his life . . . I didn't have any American friends . . . Tony [Poe] didn't like me particularly. I was a young upstart; I did all the writing. I was not a warrior; Tony was." Mike Lynch, the first American into Laos after the Geneva agreement, quickly noticed "Vint had dinner every night with Vang Pao while Tony hung out with the Thais."

"I would be uneasy saying I could tell Vang Pao to do this, this, and this, and he'd do it," says Lawrence. "[I]t was much more subtle . . . He would propose; we would discuss. I would check with Bill or Pat [Landry]. I would come back with suggestions. We would discuss again, and he would propose, [but] I would leave the final implementation of how he wanted to do a particular thing up to him . . . In those discussions, was I able to shape his plan? I suspect I might have, on the margins."

While military operations developed in Long Tieng, the humanitarian side of the effort was only three miles away by air in Sam Thong. USAID had a significant organizational hierarchy—mission director, assistant directors, and area coordinators—but its day-to-day, in-the-field operations were essentially the responsibility of Pop Buell and Dr. Charles "Jiggs" Weldon. Weldon and his wife and fellow MD Pat McCreedy spent two years in American Samoa before arriving in Laos with their three children in 1963. (Before accepting the post, neither was sure where Laos was.) At the time, about thirty Americans worked for USAID Laos. The organization's only medical services were provided through Operation Brotherhood, a Filipino group that set up emergency dispensaries for wartime refugees in Vietnam.

Three weeks into Weldon's new assignment as USAID public health director, Buell showed up to introduce himself. "Despite his nondescript appearance, brusque manner, and atrocious grammar," wrote Weldon, "it was clear . . . he was a man of consequence and intelligence." Weldon agreed to visit Sam Thong the next day. When he arrived at "a dusty dirt strip in the middle of . . . a bowl-shaped depression surrounded by mountains," Weldon was escorted to a building entrance marked "Villa Pop." Buell emerged "unshaven and dressed in military fatigues." Weldon met Buell's diverse, polyglot staff, toured the spartan but efficient facilities, and visited refugee villages with clean, well-run, but poorly supplied dispensaries. In those villages, "food, clean water, and environmental sanitation would probably make a greater impact on health than medicine." On his third day, Weldon was taken to Long Tieng to meet Vang Pao, the PARU commander, Tony Poe, and Vint Lawrence. "The trip had been a revelation—and my mind was filled with ideas of how to make a contribution to the work VP and Pop were doing . . . I wanted to start immediately."[24]

Buell, however, remained suspicious of those he called "educated fools." When Joe Westermeyer came to Laos as Weldon's deputy in 1966, Buell "tabbed right away that I grew up in Chicago . . . He made it clear he didn't like people from cities. . . [and] he didn't like people who were very educated or professional . . . Even though [Weldon] was . . . from [Louisiana] and grew up in a rural area and had [a] life probably a whole lot tougher than Pop, he had to prove himself . . . I think you started out with Pop on the basis that he basically didn't like you. And then you had to prove yourself." Indeed, every person interviewed who worked for Buell had a story about how shortly after they arrived, they were sent off into the middle of nowhere and presented with some challenge for which they were completely unprepared. Pop, it seemed, just wanted to see how they'd do. But once they earned his trust, they never lost it.

University of Texas graduate Tom Ward joined USAID, trained at University of California, Berkeley, and was the only American working with Buell for a couple of years. "If [Pop had] been back in southern Indiana, he'd be just kind of an ordinary guy at the coffee shop. But in northern Laos, he was a real leader."

"There are very few places in the developing world where an outsider can go in and . . . be accepted, be trusted the way Pop was," says Paul White, who arrived in Sam Thong in 1966. "[W]hen there was something *really* difficult . . . he'd bring *all* the different Hmong in . . . and he would listen to what *everybody* said, and then he would make a decision, and they all treated him like he was the *naikong* of *naikongs* . . . He would consult with General Vang Pao on activities that were *way* beyond his scope." Buell's rapport "didn't come from language ability . . . I think Pop was a very simple person, and the Hmong were very simple people . . . [T]hey saw him as someone who could provide . . . rice and [medicine]. When something happened, the first people on the scene were the refugee people. So the Hmong saw him as someone who could really make things happen."

Tom Ward, interviewed alongside White, added, "I don't know that he could have had that same effect . . . if this was a Lao village . . . [H]is nature . . . was tailor-made for the Hmong."

"Among other things," replied White, "he was a farmer; they were farmers. He always played that up . . . even though he didn't know a hill of beans about most Hmong agriculture. But he did know corn, and they grew corn."

"And they *drank* corn, and *he* drank corn," added Ward, both men laughing heartily.

Buell was more flamboyant and more visible, living in Sam Thong, traveling to villages, and keeping his pockets filled with candy and balloons for children, but in many ways, says Ernie Kuhn, Weldon was the unappreciated hero.

[In] accounts of Laos and of the refugee program . . . [Buell's] name is the only one that ever appears . . . [W]hen I got there . . . in September of 1965 — Pop . . . stayed at Sam Thong or Vientiane 95 percent of the time, in my opinion . . . His reputation was that he could go down to Vientiane and pound on the director's door or the ambassador's door or whomever and get something done. I think in reality it was Jiggs Weldon in many cases who quietly, behind the scenes, was getting things done . . . Pop got the credit. And occasionally, Jiggs would show some frustration, I think, about "Goddamn Pop has no idea how many times I've saved his ass in Vientiane."

If so, Weldon portrayed Buell cordially and generously in his memoir.

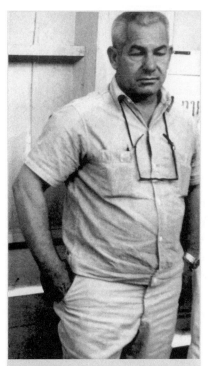

Dr. Charles Weldon, director of USAID's
public health division

Weldon "was a real innova-
tor," remembers Win McKeithen,
who came to Laos with IVS in
1962:

*[H]e hired several ex–Special Forces
medics like Steve Schofield and Don
Dugan . . . and some Thai ex–military
medics . . . [B]ecause of his strong military background, he could deal with
the military folks on their terms and
they trusted him instinctively. He was
a pilot . . . so the pilots bent over backwards for [him] . . . [H]e quickly figured out in Laos what was needed in
two completely different settings: the
urban hospital environment for which
he . . . expanded the Operation Brotherhood Filipino medical system . . .
And in the rural areas, he created this
dispensary system which was really
brilliant.*

"When I first got up there,"
remembers Tom Ward,

*they didn't have any medical care as far as I could see. There were no towns around,
no roads where you could get to a hospital . . . [I]f you didn't get on a plane, you just
didn't go to a hospital or a medical clinic unless you were about to die . . . and a lot of
people never got that opportunity . . . [Then] Dr. Weldon started his program. And
fortunately, we had aircraft that could deliver medical supplies . . . He built the hospital at Sam Thong . . . [where] the sickest people were brought . . . [H]e built a number of what he used to call "bamboo dispensaries" in . . . places where there just
weren't any type of medical facilities at all.*

These dispensaries, says McKeithen, "provided basic health interven-
tions for both civilian and military, a simple list of essential things like
soap and anti-malarials and disinfectants and bandages." Roy Wehrle,
who visited these local dispensaries, was impressed. "The medic's . . .
primary function was to deal with the diarrhea and the bloating of the
abdomen . . . because of worms and bacteria . . . and dehydration . . .
[and] with the women who hemorrhaged at childbirth and who previously, through the inability to staunch that hemorrhaging, would die."

USAID's influence didn't end with food and medicine. "Refugee leaders, as well as Pop and myself," wrote Weldon, "put high priority on establishing schools . . . [The Lao government] required that all teachers be certified and all schools be accredited by the Ministry of Education. But . . . there was no hope of schools or personnel being available for the refugees for many years—and the government had little interest in the refugees, anyway, particularly if they were from ethnic minorities." Without authorization, Buell and Weldon helped villagers build their own schools: "We recruited anyone who could read and write and made them the teacher." Weldon paid them out of his own budget, "and we scrounged money for school books and other supplies from friends in the international community." Early in the program, U.S. contract pilots provided "three quarters of all the supplies that went into the refugee schools." The USAID chief called them "Buell's clandestine schools and bootleg teachers," but through them, says Paul White, many Hmong entered "the modern world." Some joined Buell's staff. The school also served as a proving ground for USAID staff to develop their language skills and see if they really had the "right stuff" to take on more difficult assignments.[25]

USAID's Rural Development Division (RDD) provided much of the service to those living in outlying areas. At least three programs operated under the RDD umbrella. The Village Cluster program provided community development services like agriculture, roads, bridges, and public health to a cluster of villages. USAID, says McKeithen, who did this kind of work in Houei Khong, was trying "to increase affinity for the government side by producing tangible development results—schools and so forth . . . [T]he public health program that Jiggs Weldon set up was an official U.S. government program, and we IVS volunteers helped to carry it out."*

"The second major office in RDD," says Kuhn, "was the Forward Area program. These . . . were either AID or IVS people who lived in one village which was in an area of general intermittent fighting . . . hence the term, *forward area*." The third section, the Refugee Relief program, "got all the raised eyebrows in Vientiane . . . In fact, people would say to our face, 'You people are all CIA agents and not AID people' . . . [B]y 1966, [refugee relief] was almost driving the AID program . . . [It] included the

---

* USAID contracted out work in these programs to IVS volunteers throughout the war.

whole school system, the medical system, and, of course, the relief part
. . . But the refugee relief work was the most dangerous . . . [I]n the
north at any given time we probably had upward to two hundred thousand or more people . . . mostly served by air."*

In addition to the multitude of governmental agencies, there were
numerous missionaries in Laos. Some came primarily to evangelize,
but others, like Father Lucien Bouchard, cared as much about people's
immediate physical needs as they did their eternal souls. Bouchard
spent nearly eighteen years walking through the hills of northern Laos,
ministering to the region's tribes, including lepers abandoned by their
own people. As a result, he was also an unofficial intelligence gatherer
and supply runner.

A humble, plainspoken man, Bouchard "was a wonderful humanitarian and . . . an amazing specimen," says Ward. "[H]e would walk those
hills just like the Hmong . . . [But] he would steal airplanes. He would
coax us to send him somewhere. . . and then he said, 'Would you pick
me up five days later at such and such a place?' And he'd walk from that
village over to [the other] village . . . [Sometimes] the person he told . . .
forgot to pick him up."

"Every once in a while," says White, "you were with a pilot . . . [and he
would] say . . . 'I have to pick up Father Bouchard.' And that wasn't on
any flight plan that *you* had developed as a customer!" Bouchard confesses, "I would always go visit the wounded and the sick at the hospital
in Sam Thong . . . waiting for a plane to go into an area I was wanting to
help out." Asked if he ever got static from pilots or other staff for his
religion or his dependence on their airplanes, Bouchard replied, "There
was *no* problem at all—oh, never with me . . . [And] I didn't even think
of asking somebody, 'Are you Catholic? Are you Protestant?'"

But one former CIA officer recalls Bouchard approaching an air operations man named Tiny, asking "for an airplane to take him to some
leper colony or something, and he said, 'Father, what did you do before
we came up here?' He said, 'I used to walk.' [Tiny] said, 'Well then get

---

* "People don't really give much credit to Continental," added Kuhn, "because the popular per-
ception is that Air America was the CIA airline and did all the work. But . . . a major part of the
work was done by Continental Air Services. Bob Six, the owner of Continental Airlines, had
started up this subsidiary to get a piece of the pie. Bob Six and his wife, Audrey Meadows, who
played the wife of Jackie Gleason on *The Honeymooners,* took a personal interest in the program. In fact, they would themselves come over to Sam Thong and even donated a jeep to Pop
back in the days when AID was not giving him any support."

your ass out of here and start walking . . . Bouchard put his backpack on and started walking, and he got about halfway down there, and Tiny picks up the phone and tells one of the Air America pilots, 'Pick that guy up and take him wherever the hell he wants to go.'"

But despite occasional tensions, everyone in every area of operation "got caught up in the feeling that we were on the right side and that this was all a noble effort and that we were doing the right thing," says McKeithen. "It was easy in Laos to feel that way because a higher percentage of the Lao population was killed and wounded than the Vietnamese population. Moreover, there were at any one time about eight hundred thousand refugees internally displaced in Laos. That's a huge percentage . . . We calculated from hospital records and from death benefit payments that [Vang Pao's] military and paramilitary forces lost 10 percent per year.* That's totally unsustainable; it's a *catastrophe*. So from our perspective, the Vietnamese were bad guys."

A partnership of sorts had been forged in the highlands of Laos. In Bill Lair's view, it was based on the United States helping people like the Hmong do what they would have done without American support. Success hinged on it remaining a small, efficient, low-tech guerrilla operation. But "from the very beginning, I believed the U.S. would probably pull out of this thing before it reached its end," says Lair. "[A]s soon as we started arming a lot of people . . . I tried to get VP to move quite a number of people to Sayaboury province, on the other side of the Mekong . . . [I]f worse came to worst, he could take all his people . . . to Sayaboury and hold it. It backs up to a really rugged mountain range against the Thai border that the Thais paid no attention to at that time." Vang Pao agreed, says Lair, but believed his partnership with the United States all but guaranteed him victory: "He never took it seriously." As time passed, the number of North Vietnamese troops entering Laos to fight the Hmong escalated; the scale of the war and the lethality of weapons and tactics used to fight it ratcheted upward; the CIA pressured the Hmong to fight a more conventional war for which they were not equipped. And Sayaboury looked increasingly appealing—and necessary.

---

* These figures may not have been 100 percent reliable. Several Hmong veterans suggest that troop numbers were sometimes inflated and deaths sometimes falsified in order to receive more money.

vang pao

With the establishment of Long Tieng, Vang Pao put out a call for troops. They arrived in a number of ways and for different reasons. As Nao Her Vang remembers, a "mandate went out to take at least one male [from each family] to serve in General Vang Pao's army. I was among the first to be trained [at Long Tieng] for the war . . . [W]e were broken up into battalions of about five hundred, and the Thai soldiers trained us . . . Then we were put into the front, and after we got our first taste of battle, we were sent back to an area near Vientiane for additional training."

A man who became an officer in Vang Pao's army remembers going into town and being confronted by followers of Kong Le, including men from his village.

They said, "Why don't you join our movement?" but I refused. It was a good thing; when I went back to my village, there was a helicopter. Vang Pao's men had come to recruit. They said in two days Vang Pao would come to help us, so we needed to build a runway for his plane to land. We worked very hard and got the airstrip ready, but then the plane did not come! We waited and waited and finally decided to leave our village. As we were walking away, we heard a noise and looked up to see an airplane flying toward our village, pitching back and forth as though the pilot was crazy! This was done to avoid possible enemy fire. When it landed . . . Vang Pao came out and told us that soon a plane would come bringing weapons and men to train us.

Once again the people waited and waited before deciding to abandon their village. Once again the plane finally arrived. The men were trained, and the food and supplies they needed were dropped from the air.

Pa Seng Thao knew nothing about the war. He was about twenty-one when "the Vietnamese troops started to attack our villages. As we took casualties, the people started to take sides . . . The Vietnamese came and lived among us, and they killed older brother Chong Koua in his house. Chong Koua was a good, moral person, and if the Vietnamese could kill someone decent like him, then they wouldn't spare us . . . Once we took action against the Vietnamese, there was no going back. We . . . took the long dangerous road to [Long Tieng]."

Long Tieng became the seat of Vang Pao's growing power and influence—not only with Hmong in the region but in Lao political and military circles as well. As commander of Military Region 2, Vang Pao had authority over two provinces—Xieng Khouang and Sam Neua—and numerous strategic sites, including Bouam Long (Site 32) and Na

The center of military operations for Military Region 2, Long Tieng was off-limits to all but those directly involved with the war. By the time General John Vessey arrived in 1972, it "was a bustling community . . . And Vang Pao was sort of the general in charge and local emperor."

Khang (Site 36). Bouam Long, commanded by Vang Pao's father-in-law, Cher Pao Moua, was a 5,000-foot-high observation post and staging and supply point for operations in enemy territory. Na Khang, an important launching site for search and rescue missions and combat support, sat at between 3,000 and 3,500 feet.[26]

Vang Pao, writes Thomas Ahern, bound "the Hmong resistance into a cohesive and responsive whole . . . [H]is dynamism and charisma meant that, so long as he remained on the scene, just one man would be in charge." But that authority was dependent on U.S. aid, which "had to continue if he was to 'demonstrate to all Meos that their only salvation' was to follow him." Even so, says Vint Lawrence, "Vang Pao and the Hmong *always*, no matter how high you were, had a very democratic way of dealing with each other. There was nobody . . . above being berated by some farmer who just was pissed off . . . [T]hat was one

of the . . . nice things about the Hmong. They didn't care who you were
. . . If they had a gripe, they'd come after you."[27]

"I learned a lot from watching [Vang Pao] in action," says Mike Lynch.

*I thought that he had a tough job . . . [T]hings were much more complicated than
they appeared on the surface . . . Sometimes there were things that he could not do,
and we couldn't understand . . . Sometimes an airplane would land at Long Tieng
and there'd be cases of soda pop or other merchant goods on board. Usually such private cargo was prohibited. Apparently some well-connected merchant had . . . [man-
aged] to get his stuff on the plane. Vang Pao tried to control things like this but often had to bend to the influence of powerful families. He had to be careful and to
consider the political ramifications of his actions.*

Vang Pao did not seem to consider the potential benefit of using
Hmong veterans of the French wars. "Vang Pao was very bad in his ap-
proach," says Nor Lue Lee. "None of the Hmong military leaders who
fought against the Vietnamese from the beginning were retained by
him. He only had new recruits, and then promoted them. Those who
had the experience or genuine interest just retired and watched."

Vang Pao *was* concerned by a growing rivalry between himself and
Touby Lyfoung. "There was some feeling," says a former CIA officer,
"that [Touby] was not being given due respect . . . and all the glory was
being carried by Vang Pao's clan rather than his." It was widely rumored
that Vang Pao helped ease the tension by allowing Touby to trade in
anything he wanted, including opium. The CIA was not going to tolerate Vang Pao's participation in the drug trade, and by most accounts he
allowed its use only by the aged as a painkiller. Despite the allegations
made by Alfred McCoy and a cartoonish depiction of Vang Pao in the
movie *Air America,* there is little evidence to support either the existence of a heroin refinery in Long Tieng or Vang Pao's use of the drug
trade to finance his military operations.* The United States, until very
late in the war, provided Vang Pao with all the money he needed. The
social welfare he dispensed to needy Hmong who begged at his door
was amassed by skimming off a portion of his soldiers' wages.[28]

---

* McCoy does not accuse the CIA of drug trafficking but of turning a blind eye to those who did,
including Lao and ethnic military leaders and Air America pilots. While the Hmong continued
to cultivate opium in Long Tieng, and no doubt individual villagers carried opium in small
amounts while being transported on Air America planes, the evidence pointing to a scale of cultivation, a level of opium quality, or a capacity for refinement that would have significantly contributed to the massive drug supply in the Golden Triangle is still somewhat dubious, though
certainly not discredited.

Another potential rival was an increasingly influential Hmong prophet, Shong Lue Yang. In 1959, Yang was farming in North Vietnam when, his followers say, he learned in a vision that he was one of God's angels sent to earth for the Hmong. Despite his lack of education, Yang created a Hmong writing system and taught a code of ethics stressing adherence to Hmong tradition. Yang attracted followers in North Vietnam, as well as growing suspicion from local officials who tried to arrest him.* His followers sheltered him, appealing to Vang Pao for help. Impressed with what he heard about Shong Lue Yang, Vang Pao sent a unit of soldiers into Vietnam to get him. When he arrived in Laos, he immediately began preaching his message and sharing his writing system with the Hmong in Long Tieng, winning a number of converts, including some of Vang Pao's soldiers. While Shong Lue acknowledged Vang Pao's political and military leadership of the Hmong people, he also clearly believed that he and not Vang Pao would provide the religious and moral leadership that would bring them into an age of unparalleled accomplishment and contentment. These expectations may have posed a challenge to Vang Pao, or to members of his inner circle, who disliked the idea of an outsider having such sway over the Hmong people.

Vang Pao, after all, had become far more than just a military commander, and he assumed this new, sweeping civilian authority with gusto. His broad reach was facilitated in part, says Jim Chamberlain, because the Hmong are "the only ethnic group in Laos that has an organization above the village level . . . It starts with subclans and goes up. If something really important . . . happens, they all come together . . . [I]t puts them in an advantageous position . . . But it also has detrimental effects on the other ethnic groups that they tend to ride roughshod over. So we can't be too romantic about it."

"Every year [Vang Pao] had an open meeting at Long Tieng where anybody . . . could come and raise questions," remembers Win McKeithen. "He was like Solomon deciding. I'll never forget one episode . . . Some guy got up and said, '. . . What are you going to do about all the ducks dying?' And VP's immediate response was 'The goddamn Chinese and . . . the fallout from their nuclear testing is responsible for this!' . . . He could improvise and maintain an aura of wisdom and

---

* Yang also created a written language for the Khmu. Some say that Yang served as a spy for Vang Pao while he was in North Vietnam.

knowledge." He was also fond of throwing parties for his friends and allies. "You'd have to get up and dance with the local young ladies," remembers Lynch. "There would be an announcement like, 'Mr. Mike, the first dance for you.' And you'd have to get up in front of all the people . . . You can't be too pompous in a situation like that." As CIA station chief Hugh Tovar recalls, "[W]hen [Vang Pao] had a big military review . . . he gave full attention and recognition to the other Laotian people who were there . . . He wasn't just a Hmong . . . He considered himself a Laotian." McKeithen planned to learn Hmong by the time he came to Sam Thong, but when he arrived, "Vang Pao said explicitly, 'Don't speak Hmong. This is Laos . . . Lao is going to be the medium of discourse. And it's what we're going to teach in the schools, and that's it.' So that was the end of my attempt to . . . get any fluency in Hmong."

In Long Tieng, Vang Pao ordered the construction of a Buddhist temple, not for the Hmong, who were animists, but for the king. They also built him a summer home, which he never used. When, after intense U.S. pressure, Vang Pao was promoted to brigadier general in late 1963, the king visited Long Tieng. Vint Lawrence stood in the background taking photographs. "It would be hard for even such a phlegmatic individual as the king, who seemed . . . absolutely expressionless the entire time, [to remain unimpressed] . . . [T]o have . . . a long

On at least three occasions, the king of Laos came to Sam Thong to award medals to various Hmong and U.S. staff. Here he clasps hands with superintendent Moua Lia, one of the unsung heroes who made MR 2's school system a success.

runway . . . lined with kids waving Laotian flags—on their knees." The king handed out promotions, met with village chiefs, reviewed a modest parade, and participated in a baci string-tying ceremony before eating lunch and departing. In Lawrence's opinion, the visit contributed to Vang Pao's credibility within the Lao military establishment.[29]

Another CIA attempt to include and unite ethnic minorities in the Royal Lao war effort was the "Union of Lao Races" radio broadcast. It was an excellent idea, remembers Lawrence:

> I was in a tiny village . . . close to North Vietnam as I ever wanted to be, with a road watch intel team I was sending out into North Vietnam . . . I was in a little hut, and all the Hmong were sleeping around me, and at about nine o'clock three of them came racing up, all with their radios, saying, "Your president has been killed." I was about as far from civilization as you're going to get out there, and they all were in radio contact of some station . . . So the idea of connecting these people via radio made sense . . . both to give the people in the north a sense that they belonged to a larger entity, and . . . for Vang Pao to make it clear he wasn't just doing stuff for the Hmong.

Vang Pao "knew how to do lots of different things," says Lynch, "and wanted to be involved in everything . . . [O]ne time we tried to show a movie, and the projector broke. He immediately proceeded to try to fix it. He liked to analyze things and wanted to teach others. I believe that, in a way, he considered himself responsible for almost everything. He was naturally curious. Some of the pilots would invite him to 'fly' their planes when he was a passenger." Joua Bee Vang, one of the small number of Hmong trained as pilots later in the war, was flying Vang Pao in a Beechcraft Baron, a plane with dual controls so either the navigator or the pilot could fly the plane. "The general loved to fly once in a while, but the CIA wouldn't allow it . . . I was flying with the general, and . . . he just [took over] . . . Pat [Landry] was on the ground. He shouted, 'Who flew this plane?' I said, 'Well, the general did.' So Pat took his stick and hit him! And then the general said, 'Why did you tell him that I flew? I'm not supposed to fly!' . . . They . . . wouldn't let him do anything like that, but the general had an itch to fly."*

---

*Despite his exposure to modern weapons of war, Vang Pao remained firmly rooted in his traditional Hmong worldview. As Mike Lynch recalls, "Once when we were all ready for an attack . . . with everything planned and the air force ready to support us, Vang Pao said 'We can't go tomorrow.' And I'd said 'Why?' He was kind of evasive and said something to the effect that it was not the right day for the attack. Well it would turn out because he talked to some shaman person who would throw the bones and say that this was not the right day, etc. . . . Another time he said that a particular day was not right because . . . the rice at the bottom of the bowl was red or something like that. Not an auspicious sign, I guess."

Not all Hmong were as comfortable with modern technology and ideas. Intelligence was not the issue. A significant number became well educated, but despite abilities Bill Lair and others saw as almost superhuman, many more had never been exposed to the technologies and ideas Westerners took for granted. "Sometimes the Hmong would stand on the drop zone waiting for the rice [which was dropped without parachutes], and they'd get hit with a rice sack, which would kill them," says Steve Schofield, who worked for USAID from 1969 to 1973. "When we would land, the villagers would all charge up to the airplane, trying to be the first in line to get a ride somewhere . . . [T]hey'd walk into the aircraft props . . . [Y]ou can't see 'em when they spinning, and the pilots wouldn't usually shut down . . . When I'd land, the first thing I did was jump out of the airplane and make sure they didn't run into the prop or rear rotor."

Mike Lynch spent years in the field with Hmong soldiers. "One night prior to the first Apollo moon landing, I was sitting on a mountain ridge somewhere in Sam Neua province with a small group of Hmong." These men believed that a lunar eclipse was actually a huge frog trying to eat the moon. They would fire their guns, believing that when the eclipse was over, they had succeeded in hitting the frog and scaring it away. As they gazed at a nearly full moon, Lynch announced that Americans would one day ride a spaceship there.

After a lot of talk . . . one guy who spoke French came over and said, "Well, no big deal" . . . He mentioned the Pilatus Porter aircraft . . . and said, "If you could carry enough fuel, it should be easy . . . [The moon is] right there. You just fly straight and level. It's big and well lighted, and you can't miss it. We shoot at the moon with our rifles, and if you have a powerful enough gun you can hit it from here . . . [But] when you tell us that you're going to fly back to the United States, that's hard to understand, because that means going somewhere on the bottom side of the world."

On another occasion, Lynch and a team of Hmong soldiers were recovering plane wreckage. They spent almost a week dismantling the plane and helping helicopters lift pieces out, so food and supplies were air-dropped in. "We saw monkeys running and climbing the trees. The Hmong . . . asked me to shoot one . . . so they could eat it." Lynch obliged them; they skinned and roasted it.

I opened a can of Spam from the airdrop. "OK, guys . . . now, I'm going to show you [what] we Americans eat." I cut up the Spam and put it on sticks so we could roast it on our fire, just as we had done with the monkey . . . [N]one of them would touch it. They said, "What kind of animal is this?" I said, "It's pig." They love pigs. "When did it die?" "I don't know." "Who killed it? Was it sick? How do you know it wasn't sick? . . . [W]e wouldn't just eat a monkey that we found lying on the side of the road. And if it had been acting strange, we wouldn't eat him. We only had you kill that monkey and we ate him because he was healthy. And you don't know what kind of pig this is or if it was sick or what killed it—they could have just taken any dead pig and put it in there." You know, I've never touched a can of Spam since.

GUERRILLA WAR

By early 1963, the Pathet Lao had failed to convince Kong Le, now a major general and commander of Neutralist forces, to ally with them. They attacked, sending his troops fleeing from their stronghold of Khang Khay. Since the signing of the 1962 Geneva agreement, the United States had suspended ammunition deliveries to the Hmong. Pop Buell had been instructed to cut food drops to the Hmong "to [the] point his conscience permitted," largely because, as one official put it, "There is nobody in [the] Lao government who is willing to stand up and publicly say that these supply flights are being flown [on its] behalf." But on May 12, the U.S. State Department decided to supply Kong Le's troops, hoping they would side with the Royal Lao government. While the relationship remained uneasy, Vang Pao and Kong Le joined forces to keep Communist troops from overrunning the strategic Plain of Jars.[30]

Jer Xiong Yang was one of the soldiers sent near the town of Phonsavan:

That battle must have lasted all day. The big heavy guns started shooting at 8:00 AM and didn't stop until 5:00 PM . . . In all my twenty years of fighting, the place I saw the most deaths was in Phonsavan. So many soldiers and citizens died during that battle. They shot at us so heavily that we retreated, and the Vietnamese captured sixteen of our vehicles . . . Blood was everywhere and bodies were everywhere . . . Some were [soldiers], but most were innocent civilians . . . [who] didn't know where to hide . . . [T]he Vietnamese seemed to be all around us . . . It was a heavy fight, and I remember just digging holes to hide.

Yang and his men managed to escape, but were ordered into battle at Phu Khay. Reinforcements were sent, but "they were pretty loud gambling and carrying on . . . [T]he Vietnamese loaded their heavy guns and aimed at their base . . . All we saw was the ground and dirt flying. Some

The Plain of Jars, a vast area in northeastern Laos, is where much of the Secret War's heaviest fighting occurred. Many jars were damaged or destroyed during the bombing; in other areas of the country, unexploded ordnance still lies underground.

of the survivors came running and were covered in blood. We were ordered to go search the place, and it wasn't a pretty sight." Next Yang and his comrades went to Bong Hai, near Pa Dong, to "fight the Vietnamese since we knew of a base there. When we . . . started shooting, they shot at us with their long-range heavy guns, and we literally had nowhere to hide. We found a nearby swamp and hid there. We would hear the heavy gun bullets hit the swamp water like *plumb, plumb*. We fought there for three days. These three battles were intense . . . Talking about this makes one not want to live."

By mid-July, the combined forces of Vang Pao and Kong Le had retaken all the outposts lost to Communist forces over the previous fourteen months. Vang Pao wanted to push toward the northeast and retake Nong Het, where so many of his kinsmen lived, but there were doubts about the loyalty of Hmong from that area, which Lo Faydang and his allies had controlled for so long. It was decided that putting guns into their hands was too risky. Vang Pao instead sent medical and relief supplies for this desperately poor area, hoping to demonstrate his good will and capacity to confer material benefits.[31]

As the conflict escalated, wrote former CIA director Richard Helms, strong NVA forces "assumed more of the combat burden, and the Pathet Lao were relegated to the role of service troops." The Hmong needed more help. On September 23, 1963, Souvanna Phouma visited the White House. Given recent successes in the field, he asked for "secret assistance" for the Hmong. (As if there weren't enough layers of secrecy in this conflict already, here was another: Souvanna Phouma wanted aid from the United States, but only if he could deny to his own parliament that he had asked for it.) "President Kennedy then made the CIA the executive agent for the paramilitary program in Laos . . . Appropriate members of the Congress had full knowledge of Kennedy's action and were thoroughly briefed." Though the CIA ran the program, it operated under the authority of the U.S. ambassador's office in Vientiane.[32]

By early 1964, about two-thirds of the Hmong army was organized into local platoons and companies assigned local tasks; one-third was the primarily offensive Special Guerrilla Units. Ironically, the SGU were in the same position in Laos as the Viet Cong were in South Vietnam, where, says Richard Secord, "the enemy, which were mainly guerilla . . . were out in the jungle, and the U.S. and allied forces and South Vietnamese forces were very much road-bound. In the northern part of Laos, it was the opposite. The *enemy* was road-bound."[33]

Hmong forces served a number of important functions. Whenever possible, they launched quick attacks against moving convoys or fixed locations and then disappeared under cover of darkness. On other occasions, they placed and detonated cratering charges on strategic roads or explosives on bridges to stop the advance of troops and supplies. It was the best way to avoid significant losses. There were not, after all, vast numbers of Hmong, and every loss was dear.

Other soldiers collected intelligence or worked out of forward observation bases, trying to detect enemy movement. Intelligence was gathered by soldiers in S-2 or the Second Bureau. Nor Lue Lee served in the Second Bureau at Pak Kha beginning in 1964. "I was responsible for handing out news for the battalion and also getting information for them. Most of the soldiers were new recruits from the area and didn't know anything about war or the army, including [those who were well educated] . . . So I had to report to them on enemy movements."

Nhia Lor Vang was a soldier serving in a forward observation base near Phon Khou, in the north:

These bases contained about twenty-five to thirty men . . . [Anything larger] usu-
ally drew mortar and howitzer fire . . . During the monsoon season [June to Octo-
ber], the rising water cut off most of the Vietnamese routes . . . They were usually
on the defensive and could be easily defeated [with the help of U.S. air power]. Dur-
ing the dry seasons, they could move about and hide their trails. They tended to be
on the offensive and usually won, since they outnumbered us. During the monsoon
seasons, we took patrols out about five or six kilometers around our bases to look for
signs of the enemy, which were easily noticeable in the mud. In the dry season . . .
they could hide their tracks on the hard ground . . . [and] surprise us more easily.

If enemy attack was likely, Vang

took three crates of grenades . . . and made it into one big crate of ninety-six grenades
. . . We weren't allowed to use our guns, because the flash of the muzzle would give
our position away . . . They would . . . fire a B-40 [anti-tank weapon] to take us out.
Those who did fire back at the Vietnamese . . . were usually taken out in a matter of
seconds . . . Most experienced soldiers used grenades instead. This is one of the rea-
sons it was hard for them to overrun us. We also put dried tree branches along with
dried leaves all around the perimeter of our bases. Whenever enemies tried to sneak
up on us, they would make noise . . . [and] we would toss a grenade in the direction
of the noise. If we saw the enemy shooting at us . . . we would toss a grenade in that
area. These two methods were very effective . . . The Vietnamese would usually fire
red and green flares before advancing on our bases. This was a sign for their troops,
but it was also a good warning sign for us to prepare.

By 1967, in particularly intense battles involving larger numbers of
troops,

the U.S. usually sent in airplanes called "Spookies" [C-130 gunships] to parachute in
flares so we could see where the enemies were. The Vietnamese usually hid them-
selves when the flares were dropped. The planes had weapons such as M60 machine
guns. They asked us to use a 60 mm mortar smoke round to shoot into the area
where the enemies were . . . They would also send in some propeller airplanes called
"Skyraiders" . . . When they were running out of ammunition and flares, there were
more airplanes to take their place.

Other soldiers served on road watch teams that reported the movements of enemy convoys and called in air strikes or directed guerrilla
ground assaults. Though the teams were effective, it was often difficult
to recruit men for this duty, since the mortality rate was high. Colonel
Xai Dang Xiong began his career in 1961 watching Route 7. "There were
two control airplanes that were always flying overhead. Whenever we
wanted to drop bombs on the enemy, we would contact them, and they

would always relay the message to the U.S. bombers and fighters." Vietnamese and Pathet Lao troops often stood ready to fire at these planes. "There were a lot of heavy machine guns . . . [like the] 12.7 caliber . . . but there was also a heavy anti-aircraft cannon, and from time to time anti-aircraft missiles, and American pilots were really afraid of the missiles."[34]

When pilots were shot down, allies in the area tried to rescue them. Bill Lair says the Hmong played an important role in rescuing downed pilots in the early years of the war. "I would guess [this happened] maybe thirty [times], but . . . [y]ou might be looking at more than that. As time went on . . . they could pick up those pilots pretty darn quick before the Hmong would even get there because they all had communications and stuff . . . Back when . . . you didn't have all this capability, the Hmong played a big role."[35]

"The U.S. planes that came during the night hardly received fire," says Nhia Lor Vang, "because the Vietnamese lacked radar. The planes usually turned off all their lights . . . The planes that got shot down were usually the day fighter/bombers. There were no planes that went down near us, but one time a Hmong pilot who flew a T-28 propeller fighter plane was hit and he was captured. Because of the intense bombing by other planes, he escaped."[36]

Xai Dang Xiong helped rescue two pilots—one American, one Thai—in 1965 and American jet pilots in 1967 and 1968. In 1971, he was a part of an eight-man rescue team that saved two Americans flying an OV-1 Mohawk who crashed northeast of the Plain of Jars, on the Vietnamese side of the border:

> Their names were Robert Curry and Jim Edison . . . Over 260 of my men, two companies of Hmong soldiers, rushed in . . . There were roughly sixty North Vietnamese soldiers patrolling the border and 260 of us . . . and we got into a firefight. Three of my soldiers were killed; eight were wounded. It took us thirty minutes to rush in and grab the pilots. We called a helicopter, and [it] came and picked up the soldiers right inside Vietnam . . . Robert wasn't injured, but Jim['s] . . . leg was injured . . . [E]very type of airplane you can imagine was there swarming around the area . . . [T]he helicopter didn't pick us up, so we had to drag all our dead and wounded back to the base. We finally commandeered a helicopter from there.

Curry, interviewed by St. Paul reporter Jim Ragsdale in 2005, corroborates Xiong's story. "They fought the NVA . . . until the helicopters came in . . . I owe them my life . . . The Hmong would sacrifice themselves to save the Americans" When asked why the Hmong went to such lengths to rescue downed pilots, Xiong replied, "They were considered kings. They were very important to us, and we were happy to trade [our] lives for these Americans."[37]

As the war grew and more sophisticated weapons were employed, more Hmong were asked to help operate or support them. Moua Chong, code name "Tallman" became a forward air guide, directing air strikes from the ground by radio.* In a more static situation, planes could simply bomb fixed targets identified through good intelligence. But for "tactical targets on a rapidly changing battlefield, or in the case of close support for friendly forces on the ground," says Lynch, more was required. "Tallman would spot targets on the road and report them with his HF radio to [Na Khang], a distance of approximately twenty to forty miles. We would report the target activity to the B-26 base at Nakorn Phanom, Thailand." Inbound aircraft "contacted [us] for a briefing and to get directions to Tallman's position." When they got in range of his VHF radio signal, Tallman guided them in and later provided bomb damage assessment.

Long Yang had started his military career as a boy doing domestic work for CIA personnel in Long Tieng. After helping with "logistical supply" at the airstrip, he accepted assignment with a Thai unit in 1965 and was sent to Thailand for training as a radio operator, learning Morse code and message encryption. In May 1966, he returned to Thailand to learn radio repair. By this time, Hmong operators were not only sending coded messages but also trying to intercept and record enemy transmissions so they could be decoded: "I go set up a radio recorder to record the messages and send the tapes . . . to Thailand to interpret, and Vietnamese version to Laotian version." Phoumee Xiong helped with this

* The forward air guide (FAG) designation was created by Lynch and Jerry Daniels to identify those doing essentially the same job but lacking the specific air force training that went with the title of forward air controller (FAC). Sadly, Tallman was killed in 1966, but not by the enemy. "'Officially,' he was mistakenly shot in the back at night," says Lynch. "Tallman was so respected by the USAF that they 'broke the rules' to bring him back as if he was one of their own. They provided two Jolly Green choppers for the mission. This was the first time they had used them for anything other than a USAF rescue and also the first time that they had flown across Route 6 to land in the Sam Neua area. I accompanied the mission to recover the body. We never did find out who killed Tallman or why, and Vang Pao never fully explained what had happened. It may well have had to do with family politics and with Tallman getting too much attention. Later, in appreciation of his services, the U.S. Air Force flew a missing man formation over Long Tieng at his funeral and awarded him a silver star or similar decoration . . . If he would have survived the war, he could have been a real leader."

operation: "[W]e would listen to all the conversations from the field troops back to Hanoi regarding which logistical supplies were in demand. We would record the radio messages and translate them in Udorn, Thailand. The [South] Vietnamese there would translate these messages into Laotian and English. We would relay this vital information back to our bases in Laos that the Vietnamese planned to attack. In this way, our troops were well prepared."

Though Hmong soldiers have received most of scholars' attention, "The backbone of the partisan base was the women," wrote Charles Weldon. "The men were on one side of the mountain fighting a bloody little war, and the women were on the other side trying to scratch out a living and hold the family together. It was a total effort by every man, woman, and child." School was dismissed if an attack was imminent. "[G]irls helped their mothers in the fields and with the livestock, or helped prepare the food which they took to the fighting men. The boys carried ammunition or supplies to their fathers and older brothers, and slept in the outposts to help listen and watch for the enemy. They went on patrol and also acted as messengers to maintain contact with headquarters. Small, barefoot, and inconspicuous, they slipped through the jungle quickly and silently.[38]

But this kind of effort took its toll. "Before the war, life was good," says Chai Her. "There wasn't a lot of hardship . . . [During the war,] if you didn't have a son or a husband in the military, it was very hard for you. Only those with registered names were allowed any aid from the Americans . . . [They] did drop rice to the village. We lived like that for about six or seven years." As Khu Thao recalls, "During the war, we were very poor and scared. We moved place to place and never had time to watch our corn and rice fields grow. Right when it started to grow, we would have to move or run away to a different place already."

Those caught in the middle of this conflict sometimes benefitted from less formal types of "relief." "Mhor Dang" grew up in Huai Han, a Thai village only two hours' walk from the Lao border. He had cousins in Laos who sided with General Vang Pao. "When I was eighteen years old, in 1965, I started attending a Lao school . . . jointly operated by the Lao government and the French . . . Because it was on the border, the school was taught in . . . Lao, French, and Thai . . . In Thailand, General Thanom [Kittikachorn] was prime minister. He . . . treated [protesting]

Thai students cruelly. So a lot of the Thai students fled or escaped to the Lao side. I was one of them. [But in 1967,] Thai soldiers came and opened fire on my village." Mhor Dang hurried back to find his village destroyed. Though his parents were hiding in the jungle, he could not find them. Eventually he went back to Laos, but his school had closed because of the war. "The Pathet Lao who traveled with me said, 'If you would like to continue your studies, we will send you to China.'" Like many others, Mhor Dang's choice had little to do with politics, but it ultimately determined the role he would play. When he returned home two years later, he supported the Communist Party of Thailand.

Though USAID's goal was to return refugees to a life of self-sufficiency and stability, the growing number of people fleeing from their homes made this task increasingly impractical. Between 1963 and 1973, claimed Doc Weldon, "the Vietnamese and Pathet Lao displaced approximately one million people [out of a total population of 3.5 million] from their homes at least once. In the . . . provinces of Xieng Khouang, Luang Prabang, Sam Neua, and Nam Tha . . . five hundred thousand people were displaced several times—and in some instances, six times or more." While these numbers are difficult to substantiate, the scale of the refugee crisis was indeed massive. The trouble usually began at night when the enemy overran a village or group of villages: "People would flee, panic-stricken, through the jungle, often leaving . . . with nothing but a few rags on their backs." They ran for as long as it took to find a secure resting place—two, three days, maybe a week. "[T]hey would try to get to another village, or any place that had a STOL [short take-off and landing] strip or at least a chopper pad." Failing that, the exhausted refugees hacked a strip and/or a drop zone out of the forest, and USAID personnel would find them. Tending to the ill, wounded, and starving, USAID staff compiled a refugee list organized by clan and home village. "No matter how many times they were displaced," wrote Weldon, the Hmong "continued to identify with their home village. This refugee list was important for planning and administrative reasons, but also . . . as a symbolic gesture that the refugee leaders were starting to function again. After the list . . . was made, morale always started to improve."[39]

"[For] the normal, 'run-of-the-mill' kind of refugee program," remembers Ernie Kuhn,

I'd always have a Hmong naikong with me . . . If there were troops with them, they would tell us what the signal was going to be. You were never supposed to land unless there was a prearranged signal . . . If it was secure enough . . . the first thing I would do was call back for food . . . [T]he Meo naikong . . . would start getting a list of people . . . [I]f it was a location where . . . they were going to be perfectly safe, . . . we would give some hoes . . . hand tools . . . and seed and try to get them back on their feet again . . . The next thing, if it were really going to be a permanent place, [was] a school . . . Jiggs would usually try to get a medic up to any new refugee group . . . The intent, in every case, was . . . to get those people thinking as a unit again and . . . interacting again as a village . . . [T]hat wasn't very practical in most cases because nobody was going to stay in these areas long enough . . . [I]f . . . it was not going to be safe . . . then I would have to call down to Sam Thong . . . [where] we had government offices for both Xieng Khouang and Sam Neua . . . You get permission . . . to move them . . . as soon as possible . . . [The new location] would hopefully be a place where there might be some reasonable chance of them being able to plant some crops.

Critically wounded or injured patients were sent to the hospital at Sam Thong—probably the closest thing to a M*A*S*H unit in Laos. "We had to make major decisions without X-rays, relying on the ability to use your stethoscope or palpate or osculate—lost skills, you might say," remembers Joe Westermeyer.

We did a lot of major surgery with spinal anesthesia and nerve blocks, literally hundreds of amputations . . . , abdominal procedures, sometimes head procedures . . . We never opened a chest . . . They just didn't live. I remember the first time that I opened a skull. A guy had a piece of shrapnel that went through an artery . . . [He] had a bleed inside of his head and wasn't going to live unless we let the blood out, and there were no drills. I remembered seeing a carpenter. I asked one of the medics if they could go and borrow that guy's hand drill. We sterilized the bit, and one of the nurses then turned the drill while I held onto the bit with a hemostat. We pulled the guy through, and everything worked out just fine. So you had to be creative.[40]

Demands on the medical staff would continue to increase as the war grew larger and bloodier.

On February 19, 1966, Pathet Lao and North Vietnamese troops attacked Lima Site 36, Na Khang. Vang Pao ordered troops, including Fay Chia Lee's Battalion 24, to reinforce the Lao soldiers defending it:

I clung on to my spirits at times . . . The Vietnamese didn't seem to have a retreat plan, but kept pushing forward even if their comrades had fallen . . . [N]ot all of the soldiers had guns. In a squad of five, only two would carry rifles; the others would either carry grenades or other things . . . If the soldiers were marching forward and . . . one with a rifle suddenly got shot . . . automatically one of the soldiers without a gun picks it up . . . [F]or us, if we know there is no other way, we have to retreat.

Once we retreat, we can call for more backup or plot different strategies. No retreat for the Vietnamese soldiers.

Fortunately, Na Khang was also supported by overwhelming air power. "This was . . . probably the first post–Geneva Accords example of friendly forces in Laos under attack . . . [receiving] USAF assistance . . . [in] a very effective real-time response," says Mike Lynch, who was there during the battle. "We had a couple of Americans on the ground with a radio, as well as personnel in Udorn and Vientiane who . . . stuck their necks out to pull out all the stops . . . to allow the first use of napalm . . . I assure you, we were very grateful."

During a lull, Vang Pao came to visit his troops. As he was standing on the runway near a helicopter, he was hit by a bullet that nicked his throat and shattered his upper arm. Vang Pao walked back to a more protected position, where he was evacuated by another helicopter. He was eventually flown to a hospital in Korat, Thailand. In response to Pathet Lao rumors that he had died, Vang Pao recorded a message in Lao, Hmong, and French that was broadcast for three days over government radio to assure his followers that he was very much alive and would return.[41]

Lynch had been standing next to Vang Pao when he was shot. He and his colleague Jerry Daniels were ordered to leave the area by nightfall:

Jerry and I pleaded our case with the embassy, but to no avail . . . The enemy did attack again that night, but it was a weaker effort than their first attempt. This time the friendly forces were well prepared, alert, and very well armed, as planeloads of supplies had arrived that afternoon from Long Tieng . . . Site 36 remained in friendly hands overnight and suffered minimal casualties. As the enemy was retreating to the northeast the next morning, the remaining friendly forces abandoned Site 36, heading west to Moung Heim [Site 48A]. The fact that the Americans had withdrawn was probably the key factor in their decision to leave.

Lynch joined Vang Pao in Hawaii, where the general received further treatment for his wounds and took some time to recover. Soon he was back to his old self, sending tapes to his men in Laos and giving Lynch and others unsolicited advice.

Vang Pao also noted that nurses—women—were providing much of his day-to-day care. He had regularly opposed Pop Buell and Jiggs Weldon's suggestion to train Hmong women to become nurses at Sam Thong, but now he was warming to the idea. He didn't know that his two friends from USAID had long ago commenced a nurse training program.

Edgar "Pop" Buell and Diana "Dee" Dick, whom Buell and Charles Weldon managed to steal away from IVS to help start a nursing program at Sam Thong

Choua Thao, the first Hmong nurse at Sam Thong, was Dee Dick's primary assistant and supervised the other nurses trained there.

It began in earnest with the arrival of Diana "Dee" Dick, an IVS nurse whom Weldon and Buell had transferred to Sam Thong. "If she was ever scared or nervous, she never showed it," wrote Weldon. "She worked seven days a week from dawn until late at night." To assist Dick, Buell recruited his "goddaughter," Choua Thao, who went to school in Vientiane and received nurse's training through Operation Brotherhood.[42]

"Pop . . . found me and [said], 'Daughter, you go with me,'" remembers Thao. "'Work in the hospital [at Sam Thong].' I was twenty-two years old," had been married for six years, and had four children. She began by making rounds with the doctor on duty and serving as a teaching translator for Dee Dick. She then translated Dick's entire course into Laotian to make things work more smoothly. Thao also visited village medics who had trained at Sam Thong but needed follow-up.

Weldon called the first class of nurses the Magnificent Seven. They were finishing up their training when Ernie Kuhn arrived in Sam Thong. Some girls had come from remote parts of Laos and were living alone for the first time. "Unfortunately, the first couple of groups—pregnancy was a big problem. I mean, these girls had no supervision.

Dee Dick . . . used to just go crazy trying to chase the soldiers out of the nurses' quarters every night. And some nights there'd be a patient at the hospital that'd die: a nurse had fallen asleep or forgotten to go in and change his IV or something. But these girls six months before had had no training of any kind . . . So it was a tremendous advance."

Recruitment of nursing candidates became intense, remembers Ly Vang:

[C]lan leaders would go around the community . . . [S]ometime it's pressure, just like they recruit a soldier: "OK, in this province you have to have two or three people" . . . [D]uring the war, we had a very limited [number] of nurses . . . It's not like you have time to really go to school for three months before you practice . . . [T]he first day you enter the field . . . [y]ou go to school in the daytime; at nighttime you have patient care. So you don't know what to do, what you will do right, what you will do wrong . . . [I]t's a lot of struggle, and some nurses who have been there longer [are] too busy [to help you] . . . so you're on your own a lot.

But despite initial challenges, and with the addition of two doctors sent by the Lao army, the Sam Thong hospital provided excellent care for its patients.

The growth of operations and populations in Sam Thong and Long Tieng may have been seen as a sign of success, but they also indicated at least two significant concerns. More people in and around Long Tieng meant that fewer areas of the country were safe. And ever-increasing levels of military and humanitarian activities showed the scale of the war—a conflict Bill Lair had hoped to keep small and homegrown—was becoming larger and increasingly reliant on U.S. and Thai support.

THE CHICKEN OR THE EGG?

Why did the Secret War continue to grow? Which side is responsible for provoking the other? The answer, of course, depends on whom one asks. Already in 1963, U.S. ambassador Leonard Unger feared significant Lao military success would elicit overwhelming enemy response. Indeed, after a major Hmong operation in August 1963 rendered several stretches of Route 7 impassable, NVA/Pathet Lao retaliation in September led to thirty-six separate engagements with Hmong guerrillas.*

---

* Before a failed coup attempt in February 1965 that led to his exile in Thailand, there were also concerns that Phoumi Nosavan might reenter the conflict, insert troops permanently along Route 7, and use the Hmong "as a 'cat's paw for breaking [the] situation wide open . . . claiming he has to become involved because American-sponsored Meo started it.'"

As the war in Laos grew and—perhaps more importantly—as the Vietnam War became increasingly unpopular in the United States, there was greater pressure for larger, grander schemes in Laos that might take some of the heat off U.S. forces in Vietnam. To many, Laos seemed expendable.[43]

That impression was reinforced for some by the firearms Hmong were given, which often lacked the range or effectiveness of their enemies' weapons. "We were providing [them with] old World War II equipment," says Joe Westermeyer. "They'd throw a grenade, it wouldn't explode." AK-47s used by the Vietnamese, says Mike Lynch, were fully automatic weapons holding thirty rounds and could be loaded quickly. Some Hmong carried older, heavier, eight-round M1 rifles, but because of their small stature, "most of Vang Pao's troops were issued with M1 carbines, which were smaller and lighter than the M1 rifles. They were semi-automatic, held fifteen rounds, and could be quickly reloaded."

"I remember numerous times where . . . my gun jammed from shooting it so much," says Jer Xiong Yang. "The AKs . . . were more durable," says Ong (Adam) Lee. "The American artillery didn't have as long a range as the Chinese and Russian ones did . . . The only . . . advantage for us was air support and supplies, whereas [the enemy] carried everything on their backs. [Even so,] if we were as determined as the Vietnamese were, we might have won."

Toward the end of 1965, CIA Far East chief William Colby came to visit Long Tieng and forbade Vint Lawrence to stay in Laos for a third tour.* Apart from removing a competent and experienced man from a highly specialized position, Colby's decision may have significantly changed the relationship between the CIA and Vang Pao. Since Lair had moved to Thailand in 1962, Lawrence was the person who saw Vang Pao the most. Now more experienced and independent minded, Vang Pao might be less inclined to listen to a newcomer, even one handpicked by Lair, and become more ambitious.[44]

Not long after Lawrence's departure in February 1966, a new CIA station chief, Theodore Shackley, arrived, announcing to Lair and Pat Landry that the operation in Laos had to keep pace with the growing

---

* Colby, who had come to admire Lawrence's work, was concerned that he might be killed or might come to identify with the Hmong people with whom he'd spent so much time such that he would "go native," taking on the cultural traits of and becoming more loyal to them than the United States. Lawrence went to work for Colby in DC but left the agency shortly thereafter.

war in Vietnam. As Lair saw it, "The north Laos war was going reasonably well, but . . . in the southern panhandle . . . [t]he outfit hadn't been
able to damage the enemy's supply lines into South Vietnam. [T]he situation in South Vietnam was getting desperate . . . Shackley was . . .
sent to wring whatever could be wrung out of Laos, not for Laos's sake
but to help the war in Vietnam." Shackley essentially corroborated this
assessment in his 2005 autobiography: "[M]ore had to be done from
Laos to contribute to winning the war in Vietnam while helping cut
American manpower losses . . . Lair and Landry did not like much about
the inevitable expansion of the effort in Laos . . . [P]erhaps they anticipated the damage it would do to the Hmong people. Still, both clearly
understood that the sole factor driving this change was U.S. national
interest."[45]

Shackley's ability to understand or implement the national interest
was dubious, since the U.S. embassy in Laos, the Joint Chiefs of Staff,
the U.S. Air Force, and the CIA all seemed to have different opinions
about what should be done and who should be in charge. Ambassador
William Sullivan, who inherited his role as "field marshal" of the Secret
War from Leonard Unger, sought to keep all U.S.–sponsored actions
subordinate to him. While some saw this as a function of his own hubris,
others believed it was the only way "to keep [General William] West-
moreland's paws off Laos."* Sullivan, says Vint Lawrence, "didn't want
to see northern Laos become an adjunct of . . . the [U.S.] military in
Saigon." But Shackley likely tipped the scales against Sullivan, contributing to a more aggressive posture against the North Vietnamese.[46]

Still, Shackley and the military were not the only ones to blame. As
discussed in the introduction, Bill Lair succeeded in getting select
Hmong into the "Water Pump" pilot training program. In January 1967,
Lee Lue and Vang Toua were poised to graduate. In their final exercise,
they would fly bombing runs. Lair sent Secord down to ride in the backseat with Lee Lue. Lair says Secord reported back, "'I'm an instructor
pilot in the air force. I have never seen better bombing runs.' That en-
abled us to get the others into the program." When the exercise was

---

* This tension between veterans of the State Department, the CIA, and the military persists. Ask
military personnel connected with the Secret War and they will tell you the war was lost by a
controlling ambassador and a group of "cowboy types" in the CIA paramilitary who clearly didn't
know how to run a war. Ask CIA or State alumni, and they are likely to blame the military for
running roughshod over established protocols and upsetting a delicately balanced situation.

complete, recalls Secord, Vang Pao was thrilled. "He had his own damned air force . . . But on the other hand, people much more senior than me were concerned about fragmenting the political situation [in Laos]. The big wheels . . . in Vientiane didn't exactly like Vang Pao . . . [I]n some of their minds, he represented a threat, 'cause he had a lot of military power, . . . a good chunk of geography under his control, and the ear of the Americans . . . It was a delicate thing that they were doing."

Hmong pilots were, according to Pa Cha Kong, "a source of joy" for their people. But only a few, like Captain Joua Bee Vang, survived the war. After serving as a radio operator in Long Tieng, Vang began pilot training in 1969. "If you were tall and educated, you were told, 'Be a pilot' . . . [T]he Americans had . . . jets over [Laos], but they were too fast; they couldn't pinpoint specific targets. Hmong . . . [and] Laotian [pilots] knew where the Vietnamese were; they could see the difference between Vietnamese troops and our troops . . . Because of the lower speed of our propeller airplanes, we became more effective close-support fighter pilots." To the best of his recollection, after his training he flew with an instructor only six times before going into combat.

"The Lao all had education, high degrees before they could become pilots; the Hmong had no experience. In that sense, it was easier to train us, because we wouldn't go against the instructor." The situation changed once the Hmong were actually in combat:

The Americans always wanted us to use the same tactics . . . But if we used the same maneuver, the Vietnamese knew exactly where we were coming from, so all they had to do was point their machine gun and just fire away . . . [W]e developed different tactics. If there were several of us and we saw any guns . . . shooting at us, we let the two best pilots circle above. If the Vietnamese started shooting, the other pilots either shot back or . . . used their machine guns to suppress fire and keep everybody down. Then another pilot would come down and use his bombs on the enemy anti-aircraft artilleries. Almost every time we used this tactic on the Vietnamese, none of their guns fired again.

Most of my missions were . . . really close [to Long Tieng] . . . [T]here was always fear about combat missions, because the Vietnamese used . . . the 12.7 mm machine guns, the 14.5 mm machine gun, the 23 mm cannon, and the 37 mm. The two smaller ones were for lower-altitude range, so as soon as you see those smaller machine gun flashes, you instinctively fly higher . . . [I]t's a really slow process for . . . the two larger caliber weapons to rotate, so you go down low and fast . . . It was never a matter of "I can't do it;" it was always "you have to do it." You have to complete the mission no matter what.

Bill Lair hoped Hmong pilots would provide more security and support for ground offensives, but their training and skill also sent more North Vietnamese forces into Laos to counteract them. Even more provocative, from the NVA perspective, were attempts to take the war closer and closer to the Vietnamese border—even beyond it. The two primary examples of this ill-fated strategy, which many say helped turn the tide of the war, were Phu Pha Thi and Nam Bac.

Phu Pha Thi,* aka Lima Site 85, was a fifty-five-hundred-foot mountain less than twenty miles from the North Vietnam border, only 160 miles from Hanoi. The airstrip there was used by CIA contract pilots to recover Hmong reconnaissance teams from Communist-controlled areas. Pha Thi was also one of four sites equipped with a tactical air navigation system (TACAN) to guide bombing planes to their targets.[47]

Ambassador Sullivan vehemently opposed the placement of a TACAN so close to the Vietnamese border. Such brazen violation of the 1962 accords seemed unwise. But on February 27, 1967, in keeping with President Johnson's order for an expanded air war in Laos, CINCPAC admiral U. S. Grant Sharp asked the Joint Chiefs of Staff to approve a more sophisticated guidance system at Pha Thi. He and others predicted it would save American lives and improve bombing effectiveness. Sullivan responded with full-throated dissent; Lair and even Shackley opposed the plan. The Hmong expected to guard it, said Shackley, could provide warning and a brief shield but "could not be expected to hold it indefinitely." In April, the Joint Chiefs recommended the plan to Secretary of Defense McNamara. Sullivan was ordered to propose the plan to Souvanna Phouma, who allowed it only with the understanding that if the installation was discovered, he would deny any knowledge of it.

The "TSQ-81" at Pha Thi commenced operation on November 1, 1967. In its first month, it guided seventeen missions involving 130 sorties into North Vietnam. Over seventy of those sorties were considered effective. With a few operational adjustments, the system was declared a success.[48]

In late 1967, encouraged by various military attachés, Shackley had decided to "bloody the nose of the North Vietnamese" by creating "an iron arc of bases in northern central Laos" to deny the enemy use of

---

* *Phu* is the Lao word for "mountain."

their traditional invasion routes. One intended point on this arc was Nam Bac, a small outpost in a valley sixty miles north of Luang Prabang and forty miles southwest of Vietnam. Lao irregular units had already taken the lightly defended site, so why not keep it? Shackley asked Lair what he thought of the idea.[49]

Lair recalls, "I said, 'It's a terrible mistake . . . [Y]ou're creating a target close to the North Vietnamese border.'" Nam Bac was in a valley. "I said, 'They're going to come in there and take the high ground around that airfield.'" There was no way the Lao army could provide ongoing support to a force there. Too many soldiers had pilfered army stock. Once ammunition was used up, Lao positions would break and disaster would surely follow. But a few weeks later, Lao troops secured Nam Bac. Shortly thereafter, North Vietnamese troops began moving in their direction. Shackley told Lair to ask Vang Pao for help, but he already knew what the general's answer would be. "The lowland generals should never have allowed themselves to be trapped in . . . Nam Bac . . . [H]is people were already under great pressure. No SGUs could be spared."*[50]

In early January 1968, North Vietnam began firing mortars into Nam Bac. It was not their only target. On January 11, a Soviet-built MiG jet flew over Phu Pha Thi, apparently taking pictures. The next day in the early afternoon, two North Vietnamese biplanes approached the mountain, strafing and dropping 120 mm mortar rounds converted into bombs. One was chased by an Air America helicopter pilot, whose flight mechanic shot it down with a borrowed AK-47. The other crashed, apparently brought down by ground fire. The TSQ-81 site was undamaged, as were the U.S. embassy's expectations that the Vietnamese would leave Phu Pha Thi unmolested. Since the attack was a disaster, they reasoned, surely it would not be attempted again.

On January 13, North Vietnam launched a full-scale assault on Nam Bac. Within a day Lao forces were routed, abandoning $1.125 million in weapons, ammunition, and communications equipment. Less than half of the original Lao army was recovered; some joined the Pathet Lao. Vang Pao and the Hmong had been spared the disaster at Nam Bac, but the same imperatives would fall on their heads. In one CIA officer's opinion, "There was a very conscious decision to turn this

---

* Vang Pao did send troops in the late stages of the battle, trying to relieve pressure off Nam Bac, but it was a token gesture.

very effective . . . guerrilla organization into something far more conventional that . . . [tied] down more and more NVA soldiers in Laos . . .
In order to keep the program from going over to the [U.S.] military, [the
CIA] juiced up the Hmong to fight in the more conventional manner,
and it would be a total disaster for the Hmong."[51]

It didn't take long for the operation at Pha Thi to go south, either.
Already in December, only its second month of operation, almost half
of the missions guided by Site 85 were in Laos, not Vietnam. By February, the crew at Pha Thi directed nearly half of its 417 Lao sorties at
troops heading right toward them. On February 25, the CIA issued a
report predicting the North Vietnamese would launch a "final assault"
on Site 85 within two weeks. Instead of evacuating, the 7th Air Force
increased the number of personnel there. By the time they arrived, they
were able to launch only three more attacks against Vietnam before the
site came under a well-coordinated and executed siege on March 10
that silenced it once and for all. No personnel had been evacuated prior
to the attack, in part because advancing Vietnamese forces provided
too appealing a target for USAF command to ignore. Eight guerrillas
were killed and thirty-three wounded while defending Pha Thi. Eighteen were missing. Of the nineteen Americans at the site, nine were
dead, seven rescued, and three missing but presumed dead. Later evidence from the Vietnamese suggested that at least one had been taken
prisoner. Adding insult to injury, U.S. attempts to destroy Site 85 after
the attack failed, leaving the technology in enemy hands.[52]

North Vietnamese mortar and gunfire were now audible from Sam
Thong. Pop Buell reported, "The situation as a whole can be listed as
critical, the people themselves and the troops are more worried and
morale at the lowest I have seen it in five years . . . As he has many times
when there are big problems, [VP] comes to me to pour his troubles
out. He is again in the mood where he asks, 'When it happens, are you
going to North Thailand with me? How long do you think my people
can stand it? How much longer will they have confidence in me?"
Hmong soldiers later retook some of the territory they had lost, eas-
ing the minds of people in the short term, but Buell observed, "We are
now back to where we were four years ago. The difference between now
and then: over 25 percent of our fighting men have been killed, others
captured, and everyone worn out and tired of war."

Between the enlarging of the war, the build-up of American air power, both to support guerrilla efforts in the north and to attack the Ho Chi Minh Trail in the south, and the devastating losses at Nam Bac and Phu Pha Thi, Bill Lair had seen enough. After seven long years, he requested a transfer, having "lost his war . . . to his own government as much as he had to the North Vietnamese." Pat Landry, far less subtle but still effective, would take his place.[53]

DESPERATE MEASURES

Vang Pao went on a vacation to the United States in September 1968. One stop was Colonial Williamsburg, where he saw that Americans were once people who forged their own tools by hand, used iron plows to till the soil, and cooked their meals over open fires. He came back to Laos on October 20 with the belief that his people could put themselves on the same path toward modernity as the Americans had. But while Vang Pao returned well rested and inspired, his army, which "in the preceding year . . . had been the most active military force in the [Royal Lao Government]'s arsenal, accounting for 71 percent of enemy troops killed," was all but spent. With the rainy season coming to an end, Communist forces already had their strongest foothold ever in Military Region 2. Vang Pao drew up an ambitious—some said foolhardy—offensive plan for November which included the retaking of Phu Pha Thi. Years later he confessed he wanted to make a good impression on his American patrons by recovering the bodies of U.S. Air Force personnel who had died there.[54]

Vang Pao "was not averse to getting out on a limb and hoping that . . . the CIA would back him up," says Win McKeithen. "[T]rying to retake Phu Pha Thi was just madness." But try Vang Pao did. A protracted seesaw battle ended in stalemate by January 1969, despite the USAF's use of napalm and air-to-ground "Bullpup" missiles normally deemed too unreliable for use near friendly forces. Hundreds of North Vietnamese soldiers had been killed, but Hmong losses—two hundred casualties among three battalions—would be difficult to replace.[55]

As Vang Pao's forces retreated, enemy troops recaptured the long-contested base at Na Khang, killing the Lao commander who was also the provincial governor. The circumstances of the defeat did not bode well. The Hmong had repelled the first Communist attack with relative ease. But rather than waiting for another assault, they fled. "Their compatriots at other sites in northern Xieng Khouang had done likewise in [an earlier battle]," writes Ahern, "and CIA officers . . . heard that, in one case, the defenders left their post in the hands of recruits as young as twelve. These had driven off two communist assaults before being over-run . . . [T]heir heroism provoked CIA people . . . to say . . . if you now wanted the Hmong to fight, you had to count on children to do it."[56]

Bouam Long was now the northernmost base in friendly hands. Having overrun the Plain of Jars, NVA detachments were only six miles from Sam Thong and Long Tieng. Their patrols lurked even closer. Every civilian male old enough to carry a gun was now a soldier; fearing a night attack, women, children, and the elderly slept in the woods.[57]

To restore his credibility and his people's sense of safety, Vang Pao planned a massive assault on the Plain of Jars. The new chief of station, Larry Devlin, forbade the operation, so Vang Pao turned to Souvanna Phouma and the king, who at least did not openly oppose him. After ha-ranguing the United States and Thailand, Vang Pao finally got the green light. Souvanna Phouma lifted longstanding restrictions on bombing in the eastern Plain of Jars—restrictions that had helped Communists take over the region in the first place. Beginning March 17, 1969, the USAF commenced "Operation Rain Dance," launching eighty strikes a day while Vang Pao's forces approached the Plain of Jars from the south. Lee Lue, the sole surviving Hmong pilot, harassed the enemy from the sky with his Lao compatriots; Hmong scouts on the ground communi-cated to their "backseat" translators in single-engine, propeller-driven aircraft flown by American "Ravens," who guided fast-moving jet bombers to their targets.* The Lao government had even sent one of its best battalions, the 103rd, to fight in Military Region 2. After Rain Dance expired on April 7, Vang Pao was still guaranteed fifty air strikes a day, allowing him to continue his push into the Plain of Jars.[58]

In late April, Vang Pao's troops briefly seized Xieng Khouang city before an NVA counterattack sent them into the hills. There they re-turned to their guerrilla roots, harassing the enemy for a month or so. American planes tried to cut off North Vietnamese supply routes into the Plain of Jars, but the NVA remained on the offensive even as the

---

* Ravens—forward air controllers in small, single-engine planes—were a link between the man on the ground, a forward air guide, and the jets ("fast movers") in the air, ensuring that enemy targets were hit without causing injury to friendly forces. Ravens were first brought in from Vietnam after the disasters at Nam Bac and Phu Pha Thi.

rains of 1969 began to fall. In June they captured Muong Soui. From there, they could launch an attack on the road connecting Vientiane and Luang Prabang, the old royal capital last threatened by the Vietnamese in 1953. The capture of Muong Soui also enhanced Communist capabilities during the rainy season. Previously limited to small-scale probes and defensive actions, Hanoi now "felt itself capable of not only holding virtually all of Sam Neua province, but also pushing deep into Xieng Khouang."[59]

Vang Pao had some reason for hope. A new group of Hmong T-28 pilots had graduated. With their help, perhaps the next campaign, "Operation Off-Balance," could recapture Muong Soui and reverse the tide of the war. On July 11, much of that hope died, along with the supposedly invincible Lee Lue. Jer Xiong Yang, a part of the Off-Balance force, saw it happen. "Lee Lue went low, and they had guns that were high on the mountains . . . There were four of them that shot him . . . [His plane] dropped straight down to ground and just shattered. There was a Hmong Vang person with him in there too, and they both died. The plane caught on fire . . . We only picked pieces [of their bodies] here and there for the funeral." Vang Pao was overcome with grief for the man who had, in many ways, been the embodiment of his own power on the battlefield. He wept openly at Lee Lue's funeral.

Yet only a few days later, Vang Pao was making plans for a "hit and run" assault against battle-hardened NVA troops. "The decision to use Hmong against such a large, conventional force," writes Tim Castle, "was controversial, and several CIA veterans openly questioned the wisdom and morality of such an undertaking. Nevertheless, the operation went forward . . . supported by some two hundred daily USAF sorties." Aided by Bouam Long forces attacking from behind enemy lines, lowland Lao from Savannakhet led by U.S. paramilitary officer Will Green, and some of the heaviest bombing of the war, Vang Pao's forces swept across the Plain of Jars, retaking Xieng Khouang on September 12 and Muong Soui on September 28. Communist forces were completely unprepared for such a ferocious assault. So, too, were the area's civilians, who after years of Communist domination were considered guilty by association. Hmong soldiers shunted many of them down to the Vientiane valley. "Some of . . . the traditional Hmong leadership," remembers McKeithen, "stole all the cattle from the Lao on the [Plain of Jars].

There was a huge . . . buffalo rustle, which we . . . reported in great detail." Even so, Vang Pao was once again the hero of the Hmong people and the anti-Communist effort in Laos. But it wouldn't last. By January 1970, the Vietnamese recaptured the Plain of Jars. Only Muong Soui, on the western perimeter, remained standing.[60]

In late October 1969, former ambassador William Sullivan testified before a secret meeting of a Senate Foreign Relations subcommittee cosponsored by Missouri senator Stuart Symington. Symington had visited Laos on several occasions, met with Bill Lair and Vang Pao, supported the effort, and grown chummy with those running it. Then he realized it was easier to get reelected if he adopted an antiwar stance. When the Secret War became public knowledge in 1970, Symington feigned ignorance of and outrage over the whole affair.

Back in 1961, Stuart Methven had blanched at Vang Pao's suggestion that the United States might be just like the French. "When we make a commitment," he remembered saying, "we keep it." Sullivan sat before members of the U.S. Senate and told them their country had no written, verbal, moral, or other commitments to anyone in Laos. Committee counsel Roland Paul pressed Sullivan on the issue of General Vang Pao and the Hmong:

Paul: *Another aspect that could be considered a moral commitment is . . . urging [Vang Pao] to continue the effort that he has made. Do you see any obligation . . . for the safety and well-being of General Vang Pao and his people?*
Sullivan: *No formal obligation upon the United States, no.*
Paul: *You . . . [urged] General Vang Pao to continue the effort when he was willing, perhaps, to move his people away from the frontlines to avoid the high attrition rate . . . As a result of this urging . . . we do not owe him any obligation?*
Sullivan: *. . . [The Hmong] are hill people, and I think that General Vang Pao's decisions and the Meo people's decisions about where they will remain and where they will defend and where they will sustain, are decisions that they are going to make themselves.*

After seeking them out, training them, paying them, deploying them in the field, contributing to a buildup that made less and less of their land safe, increasing their dependence on food drops and combat air support, the United States of America, said William Sullivan, owed the Hmong nothing.[61]

THE END

In February 1970, NVA sappers briefly penetrated the defenses of Long Tieng. Vang Pao pled with the Lao government for reinforcements. They sent only ethnic Mien troops accompanied by a much-diminished Tony Poe. When tensions flared between the Hmong and the Mien, Poe simply took them back home. Thailand, however, sent a five-hundred-man regional combat team to help shore up defenses, and soon, with Souvanna Phouma's blessing, sent three more.

In desperation, Vang Pao flew to see the prime minister, insisting that it was time to evacuate his people to Sayaboury. No one took him seriously. Even if they had, there was no way the task could have been accomplished. There was little but the Hmong standing between the North Vietnamese and Vientiane. "If the Thai had trusted the Hmong and the Lao king could have given up his teak forests, settling Hmong along the [Thai] border would have made sense," says Ernie Kuhn. "But the timing was off, and by the time the move was needed it was too late and the numbers to move too great."

The ethnic Lao, including Tiao Saykham, were leaving Sam Thong. For years, says Kuhn, Saykham castigated CIA staff. "'You've spoiled everybody. [The Hmong can't] do anything without . . . [using] an airplane. If they want something, all they do is get on the radio and scream and a plane comes and drops it to them . . . [Y]ou should have made them walk.' That's an oversimplification, but . . . I think there is some truth to it." The dream of ethnic unity was dead. Hmong families slipped into the jungles, sometimes joined by Hmong soldiers who had decided to quit fighting.[62]

Carol Mills had been Pop Buell's secretary in Sam Thong since 1965. When she first arrived, rats well fed on the rice stored nearby scurried along the rafters above her bed. Even worse were male colleagues who simply ignored her. But Mills won over even the most sexist among them, selflessly staffing the radios at all hours, managing much-needed supplies, and baking scrumptious cookies. She left in 1967, but in 1969 "Pop asked me to come back." By early 1970, it was clear Sam Thong would fall. Vang Pao didn't have the troops to defend it and Long Tieng. A new site southwest of Long Tieng, Ban Xon, had already been scouted. "Every night," says Mills, "it was 'they're fifteen miles away; they're ten

The staff at Sam Thong, ca. 1966. Front: [unknown,] Ly Seng, Vang Chou, Nao Tou, [unknown]. Back: Blia Vue, Carol Mills, Zeukeu, Boun Mee, Pop Buell, Ly Choi

miles away.'" Morale hit rock bottom when the USAID director stopped allowing U.S. staff to remain there overnight.

The evening of March 16, "we heard a lot of gunfire—I mean a *lot*. The next morning they . . . said, 'We're going to evacuate. You can take one suitcase' . . . [T]hat whole day—planes rushing in, and we were *mobbed* with people who wanted to go out. It was *really* sad. They evacuated people from the hospital . . . We left on the last plane," the pilot helping Mills find a box for her two Siamese cats.

We flew out to Vientiane that evening, and I worked with Pop and Doc Weldon . . . typing memos . . . [and] sending them in. The next morning at dawn, Pop and Doc . . . were out on airplanes looking for our staff . . . I could never believe we didn't take them, but there wasn't room . . . Two weeks later, they took Sam Thong back, and some of the guys went to my house. They said it was destroyed. They had cut up all my clothing; they had opened canned food and dumped it on everything. They brought back my Bible. It was really an emotional time.

"Pop had established his headquarters in Sam Thong in 1961," remembered Weldon. "[I]t had provided the only support for approxi-

mately 800,000 refugees displaced by the Vietnamese and Pathet Lao
. . . [and] primary education for more than 150,000 children in tribal
groups that had never seen schools before. In later years, its normal
school graduated more than three hundred teachers. Over eight hundred medical auxiliaries were trained at Sam Thong, 100,000 patients
were hospitalized, and 450,000 outpatients were treated. The medical
dispensaries throughout the countryside . . . had more than ten million
patient visits." It was a tough loss, especially knowing that nothing now
stood between Long Tieng and the enemy. Vang Pao and his forces
would wage heroic efforts in 1971 and 1972 to beat back the North Vietnamese, but in both cases their victories were subsequently erased.[63]

It is hard to imagine how, in the midst of all this turmoil, families
could cope and children could somehow grow up with any sense of security or normalcy. But even in Long Tieng, Lee Pao Xiong and others
were not only surviving but managing to enjoy some semblance of
childhood. Xiong's mother lived in the nearby village of Phou San, but
he stayed with his soldier father so he could attend school in Long
Tieng. "We would garden or go hunting . . . Whenever I eat green beans,
I remember that experience with my dad." When his father was in battle, he would buy *pho* at the local market or stay with his mother. When
his father participated in one of the offensives to retake the Plain of
Jars, "[U]sually in the evening or early in the morning . . . [my mother]
would be carrying my brother on her back, and we would go to the
highest point, and she would call into the field and talk to my dad . . .
That's pretty romantic!"

When he wasn't in school, Xiong played with his friends and
scrounged the area for treasure, "mostly parachutes and Styrofoam . . .
[T]hey shipped bullets and all of that stuff in Styrofoam . . . [W]e would
[cut] model airplanes out of it." They fashioned knives out of the metal
bands wrapped around wooden crates and scavenged rope that tied rice
bags together. "Bullet casings . . . [and] batteries were also very, very
popular . . . Those were our toys . . . American soldiers would land helicopters in the soccer fields . . . next to the airstrip . . . And we would
go, and they would give us gum—and *chocolate!*"

But despite their times of fun and adventure, children also endured
the traumas of war. "I remember the two times that Communists infil-
trated [Long Tieng]," says Xiong.

Right in front of our house we had . . . a bomb shelter . . . and whenever we'd get attacked, we would run and hide there . . . [I]t's all covered and dark and dirty . . . We would be sleeping, and my parents would come in, "Wake up! Wake up! Let's go! Let's go!" . . . and we would rush out of there and go down to the bomb shelter and stay there . . . [M]y wife accuses me of having PTSD . . . *I told her, "In the middle of the night . . . wake me up slowly; don't wake me with a loud noise" . . . because automatically I go back to that . . . I remember one time we were attacked the evening before, and I woke up the next day really early in the morning, going out there searching for parachutes . . . [from] flares . . . I walked all the way to the airfield, and I saw . . . the dead enemies.*

Xiong also witnessed numerous accidents on the runway, including a C-47 "Dakota" whose pilot likely forgot to remove his control locks from the tail of the plane before takeoff. "[T]hey crashed at the end of the runway . . . I was there, and I could smell the jet fuel; I could hear the people screaming for help; I could see the bloody bodies that were pulled from the airplane . . . As a young kid, you are curious . . . You see body bags being unloaded from helicopters and from airplanes, and decomposed bodies—and I was there, and I saw all of these things."

Body bags laid out on the runway of Long Tieng was an all-too-common sight, especially in the later years of the war. The 1972 documentary *The Meo* concludes with a heartrending scene in which a dead soldier is mourned by his family on the runway at Ban Xon. The man is encased in a body bag unzipped to reveal only his lifeless face; a young woman waves flies away as his older brother sings, tears streaming down his face:

My little brother, what can I do? I will never be able to forget you . . . If only I had foreseen your death . . . I would have forced you to stay with me always . . . Why were you not born a girl? Then you could not have gone away to war . . . [Y]our body decays and melts forever into the earth. The country is troubled and rotten . . . I am left an orphan on this painful earth. I have no younger brother to help me when I am in need. Our soldiers are only . . . a fence to protect people of other races. Fighting has overrun the country. We have no homes left and my little brother is dead . . . We have entered the way of misery.[64]

As each side competed to conscript young men, Vang Pao started awarding military rank to or otherwise promoting men who brought in the most "recruits." Nao Cha Yang from Stevens Point, Wisconsin, was just a boy in 1970:

[B]ecause of heavy fighting . . . because men died every day, they forced you to become a soldier—no questions if you wanted to or not . . . A Hmong leader [from your clan] comes to your home: "I encourage you to come with me to become a soldier . . . If you don't want to go, it's up to you, but I will report that you don't want to go to the higher level." At that point, if they ignore you, you're lucky. But if they don't ignore you, they will have someone get you. And you think about that. They say, "We'll let you decide," [but you know] it's better to just go! I could fight at that time, but some of those still younger than myself were becoming soldiers—for example, age twelve.

Yang's unit had only a few young boys, who did the cooking and various chores. "Some of the younger fought, but [with others we] said, 'Oh, this guy is still young. Let him stay back.'"

Numerous American veterans of the Secret War remember seeing in uniform boys barely as tall as the rifles they were supposed to carry— "carbine soldiers." While it was often difficult for Westerners to accurately gauge the age of Hmong soldiers, one might fairly ask why even sixteen- or seventeen-year-olds were expected to fight. One factor most Westerners don't consider is that Hmong culture does not recognize adolescence. According to Leng Wong, himself a soldier at a young age, "Back home in Laos, when a child turns ten, eleven years old, they are treated like an adult. They are asked to learn to act properly, to do things in the right manner. They have to respect the elderly and have to take responsibility for their actions." While it is doubtful that anyone at the beginning of the war expected to enlist twelve- or thirteen-year-olds— and there are still credible sources who insist this was rare—their recruitment would not have been seen in quite as appalling a light as in Western countries. One might also note that while practices employed by the Hmong were indeed harsh and traumatizing, they were no worse than those used elsewhere in the region. The Lao, for example, were known to surround movie theaters and drag off young men. And, of course, antiwar sentiment in the United States was tied significantly to the draft.[65]

More troubling (though also consistent with their peers and enemies) was the Hmong predilection for torturing and killing prisoners of war. One former soldier remembers,

The CIA selected ten or eleven of us and sent us to Thailand. We trained for three months . . . Before we interrogated a prisoner, we knew what unit he was from, where he was located, and we used this to see if he was telling the truth . . . [T]he CIA didn't give us general guidelines of how to [interrogate] but let us use our own methods . . . [I]f the prisoner tried to withhold information, we were allowed to . . . beat up the prisoners to give out . . . whatever secrets they had . . . [O]ne method was to wrap wires around their arms . . . [and] shock the prisoners into submitting and telling the truth.

Hugh Tovar, who replaced Larry Devlin as station chief in 1970, remembers, "[W]hen they got a Vietnamese, the first thing they wanted to do was hose them down with an M16. They didn't believe in this prisoner-taking. I sat in a jeep for two hours with this guy, guarding him while the Hmong soldiers walk up and down, clicking the hammers of their guns . . . [T]here was tremendous hatred up there, and Vang Pao shared it." Chay Heu, now a Christian minister in Kansas, bemoans the tactics of the old days. "Lots of times . . . we would kill people senselessly, without any court, without any justification. They're the enemy, so we kill them."

Vang Pao also had a reputation for executing his own men. "I believe that this was a rare event and usually associated with a murderer or traitor," says Mike Lynch. But an officer in charge of POWs remembers an occasion where young Hmong who were forced into service but refused to fight were put to death. "I tried to convince the colonel in charge not to do it, to understand that these were just sheltered, frightened boys who should be forgiven for not measuring up to a warrior's standard." But his entreaties were ignored. "I felt great sorrow seeing Hmong killing Hmong."

There is no doubt that Vang Pao was a controversial, mercurial leader who engaged in tactics no one would wholeheartedly endorse. At the same time, he was in an increasingly unenviable position. Beginning the war believing the United States would sufficiently support and equip him and his people, Vang Pao slowly learned that support was conditional and subject to expiration. He was surrounded by driven, sometimes corrupt, sometimes inept subordinates who cared more about their personal ambitions than about prosecuting the war, as well as powerful clan leaders who freely expressed their displeasure. Vang Pao had excellent commanders in the field, most notably Soua Yang and Youa Vang Lee, but Chia Deng Lor believes too many were busy fighting for a leadership position. "[O]nce they became a leader . . . they thought they could just sit home and order people around . . . [S]ome military leaders . . . became corrupt . . . And that's how we lost the war, because they want to have a good life, get paid well, get a good house, and have a high rank."

Vang Pao in the field directing the fire of a 105 mm howitzer, ca. 1966, perhaps to the displeasure of a Khmu soldier

Vang Pao also had to worry about his tenuous standing in the Lao military bureaucracy. As he once told Vint Lawrence, "he was fighting a war on two fronts. The lowland Lao . . . sought to undermine him. Yet at the same time they wanted him to be their hunting dog against the Pathet Lao and the North Vietnamese." Vang Pao was "more easygoing and flexible in the beginning because he was less encumbered by outside responsibilities and political maneuvering," says Mike Lynch. But by the time they returned from his convalescence in Hawaii, Vang Pao seemed paranoid. When they stopped in Hong Kong, he didn't want to disembark. "[H]e said, 'Well, the Red Chinese supply the water to Hong Kong, and they might have poisoned the water' . . . [He] later told me he was afraid that someone was going to try to assassinate him when we landed in Thailand. Perhaps one of the Lao generals would use one of his Thai cousins to eliminate him."[66]

At least in part because of this tension, says Win McKeithen, Vang Pao gave the order to eliminate Shong Lue Yang, the prophet and creator of the Pahawh Hmong writing system. Always looking for a way to discredit Vang Pao, some of the Lao generals began spreading allegations first voiced by corrupt Hmong officers exposed by Shong Lue. When his predictions about enemy movements came true, they charged that he could only have such knowledge if he were a Communist himself. They insisted his writing system was based on Russian, part of a broader Communist plan to brainwash the Hmong people. After he was imprisoned for three years in Pha Khao, Shong Lue's followers arranged for his release in November 1970 and tried to keep him hidden, but assassins found and killed him and his wife in mid-February 1971. Others, including at least one of Shong Lue's former disciples, insist that Vang Pao gets the blame but someone in his inner circle was responsible, trying to gain power for himself.[67]

Vang Pao must have also realized that by the time he seriously considered evacuating his people to Sayaboury province, no one was interested in helping him do it. Perhaps they thought this desire came only during his bouts of despair. Perhaps no one wanted to contemplate putting the interests of the Hmong people above the strategic imperatives of the war and U.S. national interest. As early as January 1965, Vang Pao met with Vint Lawrence. He was grateful for what the United States had done for the Hmong, but too many of his good leaders had died. It might be best for him "to leave, or die. Maybe he should resign from the army." He was concerned for his people and felt responsible for getting them entangled in the war. Maybe it was time, he said, to go to Sayaboury. But Lawrence's job was not to save the Hmong people; it was to prosecute the war. By the next day, "Vang Pao was already a little more relaxed, more his normal self."[68]

By the time North Vietnam rolled back the gains of Vang Pao's 1971 rainy season offensive, President Richard Nixon had sent Henry Kissinger to meet with Mao Zedong. The so-called "Symington Ceiling" strictly limited U.S. spending in Laos. For a year, Nixon did a financial end run around Congress, classifying fourteen Thai battalions as "local forces" and paying for their training and deployment into Laos. Five interdicted the Ho Chi Minh Trail, four patrolled the Thai border, and five helped defend Long Tieng. But the Lao government feared "Thai imperialism," the press discovered Nixon's accounting tactics, and Thai recruits became harder and harder to find. The clock was ticking, and anti-Communist forces in Laos knew they were losing their chief ally, supplier, and—some might say—instigator.[69]

"After the collapse up there in December '71," says Hugh Tovar,

[Vang Pao] disappeared... I got ahold of Pat Landry, and... we got in a helicopter, and we landed here and there... looking for him. We finally found him on a little mountaintop, way the heck to the east... [H]e looked like hell. He was sitting there

wearing a big overcoat that somebody gave him. It was cold up there, too, and it was nasty weather. He was sitting in front of a fire . . . [M]ost of his officers were around him there. They weren't saying anything. He didn't speak. He got up and looked at us, "Oh" . . . [Finally] he said, "War all over. America has no give us help. We cannot fight. We go to Sayaboury." . . . And we just sat down, and he tore into us. I mean me as the target. He pounded the table and stomped his foot, and everybody else was sitting there quietly. And I just let him beat up on me . . . He needed to get something out of his system. He was crushed. He had been defeated up there, and he was sick on top of it . . . And finally after an hour or two of this, he quieted down. "OK, General. We've got to take you back to Udorn. You're sick and have to go to the hospital. And we'll talk more about this war afterward." So by that time, he said, "OK. We go." So we got in the helicopter, and we flew back, and we got back to Vientiane, and I left him with Pat . . . [T]hey put him in a hospital there, and he had pneumonia . . . He was having something that could have been a nervous breakdown, except that he was a terribly tough guy. And he snapped out of it.

Bill Lair says he tried to get Vang Pao to send most of his people to Sayaboury province early in the war. Was this wishful thinking looking back years later, trying to find a way that the war could have been won or Hmong now in the West could have stayed in Laos? At what point did this plan lose its feasibility? It is interesting that U.S. personnel thought Vang Pao was "not himself" whenever he talked about going to Sayaboury. Sayaboury suggested failure was just around the corner. In this context especially, it is difficult to argue that the United States had no obligation to the Hmong and its other allies. On their own, the Hmong would never have stayed involved in the war for so long or become so deeply mired in it.

By 1972, even the CIA was keeping Vang Pao from waging what it saw as another foolhardy and bloody offensive. That summer, Hugh Tovar was back in the United States on leave but joined General Vang Pao in Washington, DC, for a meeting with Henry Kissinger.

Kissinger started talking in French . . . "Now, what's holding you up, General? . . . [It's] the wet season. It's your time for an offensive" . . . [T]he general was stunned because we had been putting the heat on him . . . not to move . . . I said we've been holding him back. He wanted to go . . . [Kissinger] said, "No, that doesn't count now. Go forward." Well, you can say who the hell is Kissinger to say this? But as far as we're concerned, Kissinger was the voice of Richard Nixon . . . I went back out there with my marching orders in my hand and Vang Pao . . . was tickled to death.

Why Vang Pao was excited is hard to say now. But it could not have been because he and his soldiers were executing another small chess move in Kissinger's ongoing gambit with the North Vietnamese.

On September 22, 1972, as the United States and North Vietnam moved toward an agreement in Paris, the Pathet Lao made overtures with no preconditions for peace talks with the Lao government. Souvanna Phouma accepted. But before the talks even began, the prime minister knew he was in a far weaker negotiating position than he had been in 1954 or 1962. The United States was eager to withdraw from the region. "There was little indication that America would ever again commit its military power and national prestige to protect the Lao kingdom's avowed quest for neutrality." Whether intentionally or not, Richard Nixon and Henry Kissinger undermined the Lao government's negotiating position from the beginning. It seemed the cease-fire and the Lao Provisional Government of National Unity that followed were mere facades, a fig leaf of legitimacy giving the United States just enough justification to pull out and leave its former allies to fend for themselves.[70]

4 | "YOU ARE GOING TO STAY WITH THE PATHET LAO. JUST SIGN."

Breakdown

D espite the loss of U.S. military support, the signing of a tooth-less cease-fire, and the formation of a coalition government with an uncertain future, both CIA chief of station Hugh Tovar and General John W. Vessey, deputy chief, Joint U.S. Military Advisory Group, Thailand, who had arrived in Laos in 1972, believed they were leaving their allies—and the country of Laos—at the appropriate time. "The Pathet Lao," says Vessey, "was a militarily insignificant outfit. Souvanna Phouma seemed to be in pretty good shape and . . . the Chinese were still in the far north building their road. We thought that there was reasonably good hope for Laos being at least as much of a country as it had been before and perhaps more."

Vang Pao was busying himself with not only Long Tieng's continued defense but also its commercial development. USAID advisor Xuwicha Hiranprueck, whose father owned a Thai mining business, was under contract from Vang Pao to explore the areas around Long Tieng for exploitable natural resources. His father, a friend of Dan Arnold, Hugh Tovar's successor, established a modest "geology school" in February 1974 to train Hmong civilians to locate and mine iron ore and other resources. Vang Pao also continued to encourage others to staff and equip as many schools as possible.

Tony Zola, who grew up on a dairy farm near Akron, New York, was serving as a USAID agricultural development officer. Nearly sent home after the coalition government was established, Zola accepted an assignment in Xieng Khouang: "I was given every Hmong that graduated from Dong Dok University, whether they made it in agriculture or not. I was told to train them as agriculture extension officers." Zola and his new recruits helped local farmers set up chicken and pig operations: "My job was just training those guys, . . . get the farmers involved, get some income in their pockets. I basically moved . . . [to] Long Tieng, because that's where the Hmong capital was . . . The idea was to wean them off the American food, the maize and the wheat . . . and the rice . . . and then to get it on their own basis."

Despite the immediate disbanding of eighteen thousand Hmong troops after the Vientiane Accords were signed in February 1973, "the general was very optimistic during that time," remembers Joua Bee Vang. "Every side was saying, 'We're sick and tired of the war, we want peace, we want to come together,' so he felt that even if the Americans were gone, he could somehow create a unified Laos. When he went to the politicians, however, with the generals that met up with them, a lot of them didn't really care about their duties . . . [W]hen they came together, they never agreed on anything."

With the cease-fire in place, Captain Joua Bee spent time flying General Vang Pao to various meetings, including one with a Vietnamese general at the Soviet embassy in Vientiane he remembers vividly:

It was the hot season of 1973, because the windows were left open and I could hear the conversation. General Vang Pao said to the Vietnamese general, "[L]et's put down our military ranks and talk like brothers. Since you are older than I am, I will treat you like an older brother . . ." The Vietnamese general said, "We have military rank, so we will talk to each other by our ranks." General Vang Pao said, "Then tell me, why did you send your troops to come and fight us here?" And the Vietnamese general said, "I haven't sent any troops. They're all Laotian troops." And General Vang Pao got so angry, he struck the table. I could hear all the papers flying everywhere . . . "You're lying! There are [forty-five] thousand Vietnamese troops in Laos right now fighting against my people. And every time I capture them and I prove it to you, you claim they are just Vietnamese merchants" . . . As soon as the Vietnamese general was cornered, his aide-de-camp came and said to him, ". . . It's getting late. We'll meet another time." And so they took off.

The Vietnamese and the Pathet Lao were emboldened to drag their heels and deny their none-too-subtle maneuvering because of the Nixon administration's eagerness to withdraw from Southeast Asia.

After earning his PhD in social sciences from the University of Paris, Yang Dao returned to Laos, serving in the Ministry of Plans. He became one of forty-two citizens appointed by the king to a national political council composed of sixteen Communists, sixteen Rightists, and ten Neutralists. "In February 1973, Dr. Kissinger came to visit Laos . . . And then two weeks or one week after, the Lao government and the Pathet Lao signed the Vientiane Accords . . . And I heard that Mr. Ngone Sananikone, who was the minister of finance . . . signed the political agreement . . . 'with tears.'" These tears were elicited in part because the agreement only blamed the United States and Thailand for the destruction wrought by the war. No mention was made of China, the Soviet Union, or North Vietnam: "The U.S.A. [wanted] to wash their hands. Kissinger came . . . to meet with the prime minister in the beginning of February 1973 . . . Prince Souvanna Phouma asked Mr.

Ngone to come to report about the negotiations to Dr. Kissinger. And [Kissinger] said, 'Mr. Ngone, why do the negotiations . . . last too long? Why do you not sign?' And Mr. Ngone said, 'Because of these many, many obstacles' . . . And Mr. Kissinger said, 'Mr. Ngone, sooner or later, you are going to stay with the Pathet Lao. Just sign.'" Hugh Tovar concurs with Yang Dao: "Kissinger . . . [and his staff] had just come back from Hanoi . . . and they were trying to . . . keep the heat on Souvanna Phouma to accept this, because they knew they had their problems in Saigon . . . And we were, in effect, ramming this thing down Souvanna's throat."

Though the official cease-fire persisted, tensions over disputed territories—and access to them—grew worse. "[T]here was no place to go in Xieng Khouang and MR 2," remembers Ernie Kuhn, "because it was all Pathet Lao controlled, and the Pathet Lao [even] contested the government's right to [fly] into Bouam Long, because everything around Bouam Long was Pathet Lao held."

USAID staff grew concerned about the future of their programs and the people they served. "AID had sent somebody around in '73, '74," remembers Kuhn, "saying [they were] going to eventually do away with many of the foreign service personnel . . . So all of a sudden there was an unease among a lot of people . . . [A]re we going to leave here and suddenly find that everything's been abolished, that there is no more USAID, that there's no more foreign service people coming around? . . . [T]hose of us who had been there long enough knew how much territory the government controlled ten years previous and what we controlled now . . . Was it really logical to think that . . . there was going to be a good outcome to this? . . . A lot of people started moving their families out as early as January [1975]."

The coalition government seemed to function reasonably well for several months. The cease-fire held as Royal Lao and Pathet Lao forces jointly but warily guarded Vientiane and Luang Prabang. But the balance of power had already shifted. Tong Vang, fresh out of army training, was one of a company of Hmong soldiers sent to guard Wattay Airport in late 1973 or early '74. Communist soldiers stood on the other side of a narrow chain-link fence. "I knew that if . . . the Vietnamese attacked, we would all be killed. We requested more ammunition and more equipment; they said, 'No, we don't have any more,' because . . . America had withdrawn everything, so we had *no* equipment . . . They had brand-new AK-47s and a B-40 [bazooka] . . . new uniforms, ammunition, *everything* . . . [I]t was the one thing that told me that we already lost."

The tentative peace was upset when Prime Minister Souvanna Phouma suffered a heart attack in July 1974 and flew to Paris to convalesce. In his absence, numerous strikes began to roil the fragile country. Walk outs by municipal workers, hospital orderlies, and staff at an electrical plant spread from one town to the next, joined by students who protested against their schools, the presence of foreign instructors, and the visit of a Thai dignitary. Communists accused Rightist politicians of incompetence and corruption, an often-justified charge. Attempts by conservatives to make new allies through bribery and influence peddling had left them open to attack and put the government in a horrendous state of deficit spending. The committee assigned to investigate corruption, however, did nothing. Souvanna Phouma's return in November did little to quell the turmoil. He ultimately chose to rest quietly in Luang Prabang.

The Pathet Lao convinced the King's council to dissolve the national assembly, blocking all attempts to hold new elections, and intensified their drive toward unilateral power. Hmong soldiers resisted pressure to merge into the Royal Lao Army, remaining one of the few forces available to check the Pathet Lao's spread. But they were a shadow of their former selves. Lacking American funding and supplies, Lao government sanction, and support from the Thai, Hmong soldiers now made 10 percent of their former salary. Where forty battalions had once stood, there were now only fourteen.[1]

The Pathet Lao and NVA finally abandoned all pretense of a ceasefire in October 1974 when they marched on Sala Phou Khoun, attempting to seize control of the strategic intersection of Routes 7 and 13. Hmong and Thai forces beat them back—and did so again in February and April 1975. On this last occasion, most non-Communist politicians, including Souvanna Phouma, were north in Luang Prabang celebrating the Lao New Year. If Communists controlled the intersection, their return to Vientiane could have easily been prevented or ambushed. But Souvanna Phouma, convinced Vietnam would recognize Laos's sovereignty, responded to Vang Pao's April assault with fury rather than thanks.

On May 6, Vang Pao rushed to Vientiane in his full dress uniform to see the prime minister. Souvanna Phouma tore into the long-beleaguered general, dismissing the threat posed by Communist forces and insisting Vang Pao had no business violating the cease-fire. Of course, Vang Pao was concerned not only with the defense of Sala Phou Khoun; he knew Long Tieng would be one of the enemies' next targets. Perceiving the prime minister's indifference, he removed the medals from his uniform, handed them to Souvanna Phouma, and stormed out.[2]

Meanwhile, Dwight D. Eisenhower's dreaded "domino theory," echoed by every subsequent president as the reason for America's presence in Southeast Asia, seemed to be coming to fruition. On April 17, 1975, Khmer Rouge units entered the Cambodian capital of Phnom Penh. U.S. embassy staff had been evacuated five days earlier. Though ambassador John Gunther Dean offered asylum to officials of the Khmer Republic, most declined, choosing to share the fate of their people. Most were ruthlessly executed. Less than two weeks later, as the largest helicopter evacuation in history was being completed, the People's Army of Vietnam seized Saigon, bringing all of Vietnam under its control. Encouraged by their counterparts' success, the Pathet Lao forced the resignations of key Rightist leaders: seven generals, as well as the ministers of defense, foreign affairs, finance, health, and public works.[3]

"I [was] worried and scared because the Pathet Lao troops are coming down the road towards the capital city," remembered Tou Geu Lyfoung, Touby's brother, who served in the ministry of justice:

The ministry that takes care of all the bulldozers, all the trucks, is now headed by a Pathet Lao general. When he orders all the bulldozers and heavy equipment to go help the Pathet Lao troops at Muang Kasi [on the way to Long Tieng], still Souvanna does not say anything critical to the Pathet Lao . . . If the Pathet Lao troops and tanks are coming from Sala Phou Khoun to Muang Kasi, it is because it is important for them to show us that . . . the Communist North Vietnamese have won the war in Vietnam and now only the Communist Pathet Lao and North Vietnamese have power in Laos.[4]

A FATEFUL DECISION

Vang Pao returned to Long Tieng seething, humiliated, and spoiling for a fight—but also aware that the NVA controlling the surrounding mountainsides had him in easy artillery range. Any battle would cost countless civilian lives. Only one American, CIA advisor Jerry Daniels, remained in Long Tieng. Daniels was, by most accounts, the best American friend the Hmong ever had. "I think his greatest contribution," remembers a colleague, "was to let them know that there was nothing that they did that he wouldn't do, and there was nothing that he did that they couldn't do."

"On the surface, he often played the role of a tobacco-munching Montana cowboy with minimal social skills and education," says Mike Lynch.

In reality, he was very smart and had been the junior chess champion of Montana in addition to being a rodeo competitor . . . Jerry was the kind of guy that could go out all night on the town in Vientiane, catch an 8:00 AM airplane back up country, and then work straight for another month. He was tireless and dedicated to the mission . . . When I told Jerry what Pop [Buell] had said to me, that the Americans would someday quit Laos and abandon the people, Jerry said that he was not leaving until the job was done. As it turned out, he stayed involved . . . until he died in Bangkok while working on Laos refugee programs in [1982].*

In early May 1975, Daniels coordinated an effort to evacuate Vang Pao and other military personnel from Long Tieng.

Yang Dao was part of an eight-man delegation touring five Communist countries. He returned to Long Tieng with bad news. In Moscow, President Nikolai Podgorny had made his thoughts on Laos clear: "If the Rightists don't want to follow the rules [makes a slashing motion across his neck]—like this." That same day, Long Tieng learned another massive NVA offensive against Sala Phou Khoun had driven Hmong soldiers from their positions. They ran all night to escape death or capture. It was a terrible blow. In addition, numerous Hmong had only recently arrived in Long Tieng. The prevailing sentiment was that many of these newcomers were Communist spies sent to prepare the way for Vietnamese invaders. "We were not certain who among us were now informants, reporting to Communists our names and our plans," remembered school superintendent Moua Lia. "Everyone was scared. We [believed] that the enemy considered everyone in Long Tieng to be CIA—whether we had worked with the CIA or not."[5]

Yang Dao returned home, where his wife handed him an urgent message from "my *best* Lao friend" to come and see him as soon as possible. His friend informed him that Communist troops were planning

---

* Daniels's mother recognized his close ties with the Hmong and had his funeral conducted according to Hmong custom.

Long Yang (left) with friends, including Jerry Daniels (right). Yang was a radio operator and repairman and later worked in military intelligence. Daniels, the last CIA advisor in Long Tieng, counseled General Vang Pao to leave Laos and helped facilitate the massive airlift that followed.

to attack Long Tieng. Yang Dao called Souvanna Phouma's secretary and asked to see him the next day. "May 11, 1975, at 11 o'clock . . . I explained the whole situation to the prime minister . . . 'I am coming to ask you to do whatever you can to avoid a bloodbath.'" Souvanna Phouma tried to call the vice prime minister, who was a Communist— "*twice,* two times, in front of me. The telephone didn't work. So the prime minister said to me, '[I'm] the prime minister, and the telephone doesn't work!'"

Souvanna Phouma sent Yang Dao to see the vice prime minister:

It was twenty past noon . . . "I came here to ask you to do whatever you could to avoid a bloodbath in Long Tieng." After [discussing this] with him for forty-five minutes . . . his first answer: . . . "[I]f Vang Pao would like to fight, we are ready to fight for ten years, for thirty years!" . . . I said to him, ". . . General Vang Pao is a military official of the Lao National Army. He is under your leadership." [He didn't know Vang Pao had resigned.] "I don't see any wrongdoing from [him]" . . . [F]inally after forty-five minutes of discussion, Mr. Phoumi Vongvichit, the vice prime minister said . . . "[I]f General Vang Pao implements the Vientiane Accords of February 1973, nothing will happen in Long Tieng." So I left his office to go . . . to Long Tieng.

As Yang Dao ferried back and forth between Vientiane and Long Tieng, Jerry Daniels was making preparations for some of his Hmong comrades. Long Yang, who had served as a radio repairman in the army, learned English, and later operated a gas station in Long Tieng, remembers his friend Yang See (code name "Glassman") picking him up in a jeep to see Daniels on May 9. "Jerry said, 'You should leave this country.' I said, 'I don't know. I don't have skills to go to [an]other country and to raise my family.' He said . . . 'You have the skill to fix the radio, to learn a skill, fix TVs . . . You'll still be able to make a living.' I told Jerry, 'But I [will] miss my family.' He said, 'You can take your family with you' . . . I said, 'In the Hmong culture the family is mother, father, brother, sister, wife—*all* this is family . . . I have about a hundred people.' He said, 'No . . . [the] American way is you and your wife and your children. That's what we call family . . . You have to make [a] commitment.'" Yang spoke with his wife, mother, and mother-in-law, and after tearful consideration, his mother gave her blessing, believing her son would be killed if the Communists took over Long Tieng.

"After Vietnam fell apart on April 30," says Long Yang,

[T]he general made plans to defend, to stay. Jerry called him on, I think, May 7, to talk . . . [A]t that time I was in there, too . . . General Vang Pao said, "I'm going to defend my Hmong people." Jerry said, "You tell me how long you're going to be defending." He said ["For as long as possible"]. Jerry said, "How much ammunition you have in here?" He said, "Ammunition and the guns I have . . . [should be] able to defend me for three to five years." Jerry said, "Who's going to supply you with additional ammunition?" He said he didn't know. And then Jerry began to say, ". . . The time that we give you guns, ammunition, directions, and provide planes for bombing, so on, is over. The treaty [is] already signed. We cannot come back. Not only that, Gerald Ford is not elected by the people, he is appointed . . . and he has no power . . . So right now, if [you] defend here, good luck [to] you, but I don't think you can make success." And then General Vang Pao got upset and said, "I'm going to leave my officers and everything behind and go myself? I want to die with these people! I don't want to just escape myself and then [become a] scapegoat." So then Jerry asked, "How many families you want to take with you?" That's when the list began.

"The list" remains one of the great controversies among history-conscious Hmong. Where did the idea of the list come from? Who had control over it? Who placed limits on it? Did General Vang Pao try to have *everyone* evacuated from Long Tieng? The answers to these and other questions fluctuate from person to person. While Long Yang insists that Jerry Daniels set the terms for inclusion on this list, Yang See told Gayle Morrison, "Vang Pao makes that list himself . . . Whoever Vang Pao says should go, Jerry will allow them to go." Ultimately, says Long Yang, the list contained the names of ninety-eight Hmong officers and their family members—about 2,000 to 2,500 people.[6]

For many Hmong old enough to remember the evacuation of Long Tieng but young enough to have gone to school and succeeded professionally in Western countries, the list continues to haunt and anger them. "When you really think about it," says Lee Pao Xiong, director of the Center for Hmong Studies at Concordia University,

our military leaders abandoned us . . . Today when I hear General Vang Pao say, "I brought you here," I think, "you didn't bring us here" . . . It was the refugee program that brought us here; our sponsors brought us here . . . The Hmong people were used! So I question . . . did the general know that the Hmong were being used? And if he knew . . . and he proceeded on with the war, then he was looking out for his own interests . . . not the interests of his people. But if he didn't know, and he fought . . . then he's OK . . . But people like my dad, like my uncle who died, and many countless people out there who died fighting the war . . . they were fighting to protect their homeland. I give them great respect. But for the military leaders [who left] . . . during the time when all hell broke loose, they only looked out for themselves.

But what if both Jerry Daniels and General Vang Pao had less power than many suppose? In the estimation of Captain Jack Knotts, a Bird Air (and former Air America) helicopter pilot who flew Daniels and Vang Pao out of Long Tieng,

[T]he evacuation was solely as a cover to get VP and Jerry safely out of Long Tieng, and there was no intention of taking thousands and thousands of Hmong out of Laos . . . But here's the duplicity of the whole thing: they led the whole Hmong group to think that this evacuation was going to go on for days more and maybe they were all going to be taken out . . . Then when the thing got started that morning, VP drug his feet . . . After all, this was a very traumatic thing for him, and it was for Jerry, too, to be truthful about it . . . If he had done what the plan was and gone right away . . . there wouldn't have been very many refugees—which is what the embassy and the Americans wanted, I believe. Maybe VP did it on purpose—I don't know . . . By dragging his feet during the evacuation, there were quite a number of flights. So a lot of people got out.[7]

By Gayle Morrison's reckoning, General Vang Pao began making preparations to evacuate his immediate family, including his six wives, on May 6. Those closest to Vang Pao knew what was happening. Yang See remembered seeing VP's private plane flying back and forth. "Jerry himself is involved in moving Vang Pao's family to Udorn and trying to get security for his family to stay there . . . Vang Pao does not want the junior officers to know what he is doing."[8]

Despite efforts to maintain secrecy, rumors were flying between the servicemen and their families at Long Tieng. Tong Vang, who'd returned to Long Tieng after his stint at Wattay Airport, remembers,

There's a lot of things, guys talking on the radio and in the Vientiane Times *and the news from South Vietnam . . . But [we were] not officially told what to do . . . [On] May 10 . . . the colonel who was commander of that area came out and said, "Find a couple of guys to watch guard, and then I can tell you something." Then he said, ". . . We lost everything, so tomorrow, if you want to come into work, fine. You don't want to go to work, you want to go back home, fine. Our general and our higher-ranking officers will be leaving the country, to Thailand . . . So if any of you want to go just quickly and prepare yourself—because maybe some airplane might take some, but some might not . . . So after we heard that, everybody went home . . . In the morning, everybody was gone.*

Many soldiers walked to nearby villages to find their families and tell them the news. They hoped they would somehow be included among those flown to safety. It took Tong Vang two days to walk home, one to discuss the situation with his family, and two more to walk back. By then, it was already too late.

Yang See had seen enough. Since 1970, he had worked for Jerry Daniels as a community liaison officer, saving money to take Daniels up on his offer of a college education in Montana. He had helped Daniels spend the balance of the $1 million in "postwar economic development money" the CIA had left behind. But now it was all coming to an end. "Every time Jerry got out of his office, drove outside, and saw thousands of people waiting in the runway, when he came back into the office he always sighed and kept saying, 'Jesus Christ! Somebody's got to tell these people to go back to their homes . . . The United States of America has no program or policy to take them to Thailand.'" On May 8 and again on May 9, Yang told Daniels he wanted to resign, fly to Thailand, and see if he could set up a refugee camp for Hmong people fleeing Laos. Immediately voicing his strong objection, Daniels continued, "You may be able to help people cross to Thailand, but where can you get food, shelter, and other immediate needs for them? Did you think about that? What about people who will die of hunger and from various other sicknesses? The United States should not be blamed for that. You

alone will be blamed for that." Daniels made Yang promise that if he actually went to Thailand, he would never speak to a member of the press
or any governmental agency and speak ill of the United States.

The next morning, Yang "made a speedy oral resignation." Daniels
once again warned him of the "strong potential risks" and forbade him
from openly criticizing "his agency" but ultimately wished him luck,
promising to airlift Yang's wife and son out of Long Tieng. At 9:00 AM,
Yang See left Long Tieng for good. He only hoped he could reach Nong
Khai and convince the governor that he should be allowed to establish
a place of refuge for some of the Hmong people who were sure to follow him.[9]

Yang Dao returned to Long Tieng on May 11. By then Vang Pao was
living in isolation, trying to avoid assassination or a last-minute coup
d'état. "I went to meet with General Vang Pao. I reported [my] two conversations with the prime minister and the vice prime minister . . .
General Vang Pao was really *upset* [about] the situation . . . I could not
sleep the whole night. And then the following day, I went to General
Vang Pao's house." It was 8:00 AM, and the general was already in a
meeting. Yang Dao was asked to wait. "I could not sit down. I walk up
and down the hallway. It was too stressful. And then the door opened,
and suddenly I saw a major who just left the meeting, shake hands with
me, and he didn't say anything . . . Ten minutes [later] I saw a colonel
come out from the meeting—and then General Vang Pao came out . . .
[He said,] 'I have decided to bomb Vientiane.'"

Clearly Vang Pao was mortified at the thought of leaving his country in defeat. Despite his alliance with a seemingly inexhaustible and
invulnerable power, his efforts to integrate his people into Lao society,
and his remarkable attempts to forestall the enemy and safeguard Long
Tieng, he had failed—though the failure was hardly of his own making.
As Yang Dao remembers it, Vang Pao was determined to go out in a
blaze of glory, in a way that would be recorded in the annals of history
for generations to come. In the end, he came to believe that saving the
lives of thousands of soldiers and civilians was more important than
glorious defeat.

(The relationship between Vang Pao and Yang Dao became almost
star-crossed in the years that followed—so much so that it is almost impossible to separate truth from fiction where stories about Yang Dao are
concerned. Vang Pao "loyalists" would say in later years that Yang Dao

had betrayed the Hmong; had kept Vang Pao waiting as he attempted to arrange Yang Dao's evacuation; had attempted to establish himself as the new leader of the Hmong people in Laos once he knew Vang Pao was leaving; had tried to dupe the Hmong people into staying in Laos even though he knew they were no longer safe there. While these stories should not be casually dismissed, there is at their heart one glaring flaw: when Yang Dao relocated to the United States from France in 1983, General Vang Pao didn't shun him or attack him as a turncoat. In fact, a year earlier he had invited Yang Dao to join Neo Hom, a group vowing to overthrow the Communist government in Laos.)

It is easy—and far from wrong—to blame Laos's fall on the machinations of the North Vietnamese and their Lao counterparts with support from China and the Soviet Union. But many Americans who worked closely with the Hmong don't want to let their own country off the hook. After he retired from the CIA, Bill Lair spent many lonely nights driving trucks cross country, pondering the consequences of America's partnership with the Hmong. "[W]hen we decided it was politically necessary to pull out because of Vietnam and the resistance in the U.S., . . . we basically turned it over to the Communists," says Lair. "The Hmong could not survive there . . . [A]nd I led them down the garden path . . . There was a little cosmetic thing of a coalition government, but if you look at history, the Communists never worked in any coalition government. That's just one step before they take over . . . I think when [the United States] signed that treaty with the Communists and everything . . . that basically abandoned the Hmong."

"There's a lot of things we should have done before we got to the Hmong," laments General Harry Aderholt.

But . . . we had no policy ourselves. If we'd had a policy, the Hmong would not have been left behind. Whatever it took, we would have had a war plan to bring the airplanes in and kick the shit out of whoever was there—or even if we had to threaten an atomic bomb and bring them out. But what about the Montagnards? What about the Tibetans? What about all of the others? . . . [E]very country in Southeast Asia, we've deserted, we've betrayed . . . Americans that knew the situation over there wanted to win that war, wanted to see that the Hmong were not left behind.

Whether the United States could have ever been truly victorious in Southeast Asia is a debatable point. There is little doubt, however, that it could have done more to safeguard its former allies.

As Hmong who hoped to escape rushed into the area, the population of Long Tieng reached as high as fifty thousand. But not everyone was fighting for a spot on an airplane. Some who agreed with leaders like Touby Lyfoung and LyTeck Lynhiavu expected the Communists would keep their word and integrate the Hmong into the new "people's state." Many of them were later moved from Long Tieng to Phonsavan, near the Plain of Jars, where they returned to a life of farming. Others were determined to stay and fight for what they believed was their country. They fled Long Tieng, but instead of crossing the Mekong River into Thailand they eventually settled near the forbidding mountain of Phu Bia. There they formed several resistance movements that came to be known collectively as the *Chao Fa*. Some hoped for the return of Tswb Tchoj, the Hmong messiah king, while others reformed old military hierarchies and set to ambushing government troops.

Most who had served in the military and were loyal to Vang Pao could never feel secure living in a Communist-controlled country. They risked life and limb to board one of the airplanes that promised to take them to safety. But no one knew how long the airlift would last, how many planes would ultimately arrive, and just how many people could squeeze into each one without significantly increasing the likelihood of its crashing into the side of a mountain.

THE AIRLIFT

Heinie Aderholt, it seemed, was not done with his duties in Southeast Asia. After retiring as a colonel in December 1972, he was recalled to active duty in October 1973 and sent to Bangkok as deputy commander of the American Military Assistance Command in Thailand (MACTHAI). In May 1974 he was promoted to brigadier general, and later was made MACTHAI commander. His was the thankless job of closing out the U.S. air presence in the region. On the morning of May 13, the phone rang. The man on the other end of the line would not identify himself but said the United States was "abandoning" the Hmong: "I need airplanes." Aderholt replied, "'How many you need?' He says, 'I don't know. All I can get.' I said, 'All right. Let's start with one' . . . I called a four-star general, George Brown." After explaining the situation to Brown, Aderholt received permission—practically carte blanche—to commandeer any planes he could locate. Aderholt started with Bill Bird of Bird Air, but he had no pilots. He next tried Howard Hartley, who ran Bird Air at U

Taphao Airport. There were two C-130s waiting in Thailand to be returned to Clark Air Force Base in the Philippines, but only one pilot remained. He was waiting at Don Muang airport in Bangkok to board a
KLM flight to meet his wife in Amsterdam. Aderholt would need to convince the pilot—Matt Hoff—to postpone his long-awaited reunion and
volunteer for a last-minute rescue mission.[10]

Aderholt contacted the commander at Don Muang and asked for a
favor:

*"I want you to get an officer, or you yourself go up to KLM departure and grab this guy.
Put him under arrest if you have to, and bring him down to your office." So it went
about thirty minutes, and they find him, and they bring him down. He is so pissed off
at [me]. I knew him. I knew his wife. My wife knew his wife. I said, "Look, how much
is it going to take to change your mind?" He said, "You don't have a right to do this."
I said, "I got a right now. You can refuse or you can go." He said, "All right. I'll go."*

Aderholt and Hoff agreed that each member of the crew Hoff assembled would receive five thousand dollars for their trouble.

Meanwhile, Les Strouse and Al Rich were receiving orders to join the
hastily assembled evacuation team. "I was in Bangkok," remembers
Strouse. "I had brought Pop [Buell] down on the tenth, and the C-46s
were parked down here. I was called and told, 'We're going to have to do
an evacuation out of Laos'—no details, didn't say Long Tieng. They said,
'Take your C-46 up to Udorn.' So . . . on the eleventh, we took two C-46s
up to Udorn . . . We briefed with the Thai base commander so that we
didn't get intercepted, and we stayed well away from the Lao . . . [W]e
started the evacuation out of Long Tieng [on the twelfth]."

Though Strouse and his compatriots commenced the American
phase of the airlift, Morrison interviewed several Hmong pilots who
say they started the evacuation on May 10 using a Lao C-47. "[T]he C-
47 loads slowly," remembered pilot Ly Teng, "because we follow the list
set for the colonels and their families. When the American planes
come, they load faster than us because they don't check the list. They
take whoever is waiting, so everybody just runs to the planes . . . The
families all fight to get on the plane." Xiong Moua, a mechanic also
trained as a pilot, concurred: "The leaders put their families in there
first . . . If all the leaders leave and only the soldiers are left, what will
the soldiers think? . . . 'Who cares about us?' . . . [I]f they had prepared
themselves for this situation, they would say, 'Just get in line. First
come, first go. It doesn't matter what rank you are.' Then the people will

A C-130 readies for takeoff during the evacuation of Long Tieng. Note the long line of people awaiting the next plane.

follow the evacuation plan . . . No one will panic. But that is not what happens." "People wanted to get on the planes," recalls Joua Bee Vang. "[T]hey were scared . . . so when you were flying you could hear them wailing and crying throughout the whole Long Tieng area."[11]

U.S. planes may have loaded quickly and without deference to or awareness of the list, but they carried as many people as they could. "We determined on the C-46 the most we could carry was forty people," says Strouse. "We ended up with sixty-five . . . We had seats that folded up inside the airplane. We tied ropes across the airplane, everybody sitting, straddling the guy in front. The ropes were for them to hold on to so they wouldn't slide to the back on take-off. And it was *hot*, and they were pushing to get in the airplane. And the worst situation— first one in is the last one out. The guys who were lucky were the ones who were the last ones in, 'cause they were the first out" Strouse and Rich spent the first part of their day flying Hmong from Long Tieng to Udorn, later shuttling refugees from Udorn to Nam Phong, a Thai base formerly used as an air wing of the U.S. Marine Corps.

"There were refugees coming across the river," remembers Strouse, "and they were being picked up by buses and trucks in Nong Khai and

brought down and stashed in a hangar at Udorn. Then we started shuttling *them* down . . . [A]s soon as it got daylight again, then we'd go to
Long Tieng. The second day [the thirteenth], we did pretty good up until the afternoon. Then we started having problems . . . [Things] just lost
control."

Lee Pao Xiong was nine when news of the evacuation began coursing through Long Tieng. He ran with his father to a nearby village to
retrieve his family.

*[M]y grandma and my grandpa . . . didn't want to come . . . We decided, "OK, if . . .
[they] don't want to come, then they can stay." We went halfway, then came back
. . . and forced them in the car . . . [W]e also brought some of our ducks and chickens.
And when we got to Long Tieng, it was pretty much an abandoned town . . . People
were all at the air base waiting for the evacuation. So we stayed there; we quickly
. . . butchered a chicken, butchered two ducks, and we ate some of the food and took
what was left and went to the airfield.*

The mad scramble for airplanes reserved for higher-ranking military
personnel led to a cat-and-mouse game between the soldiers guarding
the planes and Hmong civilians trying to board them. "They're always
tricking us," remembers Xiong. "They said, 'Get back, get back! Those
planes are *enemy* airplanes!' . . . They would land, and they would just
[taxi] down by General Vang Pao's house, and then all these colonels
would . . . jump in . . . and abandon the people . . . And suddenly we realized that they were playing games, so we went down there." But first,
Xiong's father slipped into a nearby cave, removed his uniform, and
changed into civilian clothes. He kept his M16 until he arrived in Nam
Phong. As one plane arrived, Xiong's father heard a soldier announce,
"This is Colonel Xai Dang Xiong's airplane." Though not a blood relative,
he was from the same clan and close to their family. Lee Pao's father
replied, "What are we waiting for? Let's go!"

"So I got in, my mom got in, a couple of my brothers got in. I remember how tightly packed we were in that C-46 . . . And you have to
climb—the stairs are pretty steep, so you have to climb up there in order to get in. And my dad was pushing us in." But despite his efforts
Xiong's father, one or two of his brothers, and other family members
were left behind. Miraculously, they managed to squeeze onto Matt
Hoff's C-130 later that day. After waiting all day with his mother at a
holding facility, Xiong was finally reunited with the rest of his family.

Many families were separated or left behind once the airlift was over.

But failing to board a plane was not the worst fate endured during those frightful days. Major Chong Ge Yang, stationed at Phou Pha Sai, was trying to enforce the cease-fire, knowing the Vietnamese were coming toward him. He visited Long Tieng on May 13 and saw that most of the officers were already gone: "A lot of the soldiers complain to the general about why can't our families go too?" After conferring with a colonel from his clan, Yang met his family at Pha Khae. He was told the general was sending a C-130 there. But even as he was preparing to leave, he saw a C-130 make two runs in and out of Long Tieng. By the time he reunited with his family, he was told the information he'd received was false. Yang's family took only their most important possessions and left even before they'd finished their meal, eighteen of them packed into one jeep. On the way, at about 8:00 PM, they were hit by M16 fire. Three of Yang's children were killed. The shots, they discovered, came from nervous Hmong soldiers. "Emotionally I am paralyzed from losing three children in one night, in five minutes," remembered Yang. "[M]y mind keeps asking, 'Why? Why? Why?'—over and over again." In a matter of only a few hours the family had to find caskets, conduct a hasty funeral ceremony, bury the three children side by side, ride in a bloodstained jeep back to pick up Yang's brother and sister, and race to the airport. They flew to Thailand the next morning, leaving their children's graves behind.[12]

Early on the morning of May 14, pilots Dave Kouba and Jack Knotts, charged with evacuating Vang Pao and Jerry Daniels, were eating their last breakfast at Long Tieng. They had just watched Matt Hoff fly out with his first load of the day. When he returned in ninety minutes to two hours, they hoped to use his plane and the attention it would draw to make their escape. Only two days before, Kouba had heard a friend remark, "one message . . . he sends to Udorn says, 'I'll never leave my people.' The next message you read is, 'Well, I'd better go to Tango Zero Eight [Udorn]' . . . What is VP really going to do?" Daniels, cool as a cucumber, was dealing with an angry Hmong soldier demanding that he and his family be loaded into the next plane and threatening murder if he wasn't appeased.

Knotts evacuated VP, left him at a safe location, then returned to pick up Daniels. Knotts and Kouba planned to depart together and rendezvous at the strip where VP was waiting. From there, Kouba would fly Vang Pao and Daniels to Udorn. Knotts waited by the house Vang

Pao had built for the king, engines running, for Daniels to show. "Hog" finally emerged, but he seemed to find more reasons to delay.

[H]e started talking on the radio, and he messed around, messed around—finally— and this was a very bad thing to Jerry, he'd been there so long—he saluted . . . [H]e came to attention, and just like he was saluting the jeep. But he was really saluting . . . years of hard work that turned into nothing . . . He saluted . . . and turned around and walked over and got in the chopper . . . [A]nd there were a whole gaggle of sol- diers walking . . . up around the hill, and just as we lifted off and we were just sort of hanging there in the air . . . two of these soldiers dropped their M16s off their shoul- ders . . . and threw a round into the chamber. And my heart jumped in my mouth. I thought they were going to let us have it. And we just edged off and sort of went around a corner of the hill, and they never fired. And then I saw [Kouba], picked [him] up, and we followed [him] on out.[13]

As Knotts and Kouba were departing, they saw C-46s piloted by Strouse and Rich flying toward them. The aircraft tried to raise each other on radio, but something or someone interfered with their com- munication. The incoming pilots were told to abort their mission but never heard the message. What they encountered on the ground was absolute mayhem. With Daniels gone, all semblance of order had van- ished. "Someone on the ground knew there was a serious problem," re- members Strouse. "[A] mob of people there . . . tried to throw the kicker out of the airplane. I had to blow them off the ladder just by putting so much power on the engine . . . and said, 'Sorry, that's it . . . We're going to lose the airplane and the crew. We have to stop.'" With that, the Long Tieng airlift was over. Strouse and Rich spent the rest of their day shuttling Hmong from Udorn to Nam Phong. "We'd made three trips," remembers Strouse, "and then we stopped to refuel, and they washed the airplane out, because so many people had thrown up . . . [W]e stayed in the cockpit, and we never got out of it."[14]

When Joua Bee Vang landed in Nam Phong, the general was in Udorn conferring with Pat Landry. Vang Pao ordered him to fly to Udorn. When he arrived and reported to the general, Vang Pao said,

"I saw your plane fly overhead! I thought you might go back to Long Tieng and you might get captured, so that's why I called you here. I didn't want you to go back!" And the general started expressing his sorrow. He was heartbroken. The general was saying that he felt so devastated that so many soldiers and so many families were left behind . . . and he didn't know what was going to happen to them. And he was in such a low, depressed state that he was saying to his officers there that he just

Captain Joua Bee Vang, seen here in front of his T-28, became General Vang Pao's personal pilot after the cease-fire was declared.

wanted to take a poison pill and kill himself. And we knew that the general was very emotionally distressed, so we didn't say anything. But then all of a sudden the general went into this . . . optimistic mood, and he said, "You know, maybe God wanted me to be here so I could help the Hmong. If I kill myself, I don't want to come back in another lifetime to do this all over again. Might as well just finish it right now, and help the Hmong as much as I can so that in my next life, if I do come back, I want to be someone simple so I can just roam the world peacefully." That's what the general said.

FIRST THe Cia, THen usaid

As the situation in Laos continued to deteriorate, USAID came under siege. On May 10, Les Strouse flew Pop Buell, the patron saint of USAID, out of Laos. Strouse told Dave Kouba, "He had three suitcases—small ones. Said that's all he owned. He was just about to break down in tears, I guess. Really, really didn't want to go, but he knew he had to . . . All the way to Bangkok he just . . . stared straight ahead, and Les said he didn't dare say anything to him, 'cause he knew he'd break down if he did."

On May 21, Lao students sympathetic to the Pathet Lao occupied the expansive USAID compound in Vientiane. Their actions took most of the embassy staff off guard, says Steve Schofield, a USAID public health advisor. "[W]hile we were gone [on vacation], Vietnam fell. And then we got back, and Cambodia went . . . We had a party at my place . . . probably three weeks before everything went to hell . . . [T]hey had the embassy political officer there . . . and he got up and made a little speech . . . 'We're going to be here forever. This doesn't mean anything.' Well, you know how quick it happened—I never got the bill for that party."

Ernie Kuhn received a phone call telling him to stay away from the compound and the protesters. He would receive notice when it was time to leave the country.

The decision had been made then to evacuate all the Americans in what's called Kilometer 6, which was six kilometers outside of town. It was where most of the Americans lived. And there was a question about whether or not the demonstrators would seal off Kilometer 6 and refuse to allow [about fifteen hundred] people to leave. Or would they cut off electricity or would they shut off the water somehow? There was a lot of concern that those people could be trapped out there and held for ransom. But in the meantime . . . we were supposed to stay behind and help close out the mission.

"It was a strange situation because there was no invasion of Vientiane in the spring of '75," explains Win McKeithen. "Rather, there were spontaneous demonstrations before each ministry . . . and the government just sort of fell apart in pieces. And the problem that the AID bureaucracy faced, the embassy faced . . . was abandoning millions of dollars of AID assets in the face of what? No overt hostilities like the fall of Saigon. So we had to stay there . . . [O]ur group of twenty-odd Lao speakers helped to negotiate the release of the families during April, May '75."

Tony Zola, who had left Long Tieng for Vientiane only a few days before the airlift, seemed to have jumped from the frying pan into the fire. The one consolation was that his agricultural program had offices outside the compound, near the ministry of finance.

I actually went to the office that day, and then we were told . . . that we should go home and not come to the office anymore because it was too dangerous . . . I didn't live inside the American housing compound . . . I had a house just outside the gate . . . [and] a nice little French car with a French flag on it, so I could scamper all over the city . . . [But] there were a lot of Americans who had houses outside who then left the country, went across the river to Nong Khai, got on the train, and went to Bangkok.

I stayed outside for as long as I could; I think until about the twenty-fourth. And then . . . [that] morning . . . I got up and there was a [Lao military] guard standing outside my gate . . . at which point I realized that I had been discovered.

Zola called in, reported his situation, and was told, "You'd better come in." He gave most of his possessions to his housekeeper and gardener, convinced a friend to safeguard his treasured French horn, and drove to the front gate of the compound. "We were told, 'Once you go in, you can't come out' . . . I went in, and nothing was confiscated. I . . . went to the gymnasium, signed in, and said, 'Here I am. Another American.'"

With little to do but wait, staff were assigned various tasks to prepare for departure and deny the Lao valuable assets. Zola was given the keys to most of the 128 houses in the compound and instructed to open all of the liquor cabinets—by force, if necessary—and dump all of the liquor down the toilet: "The last thing you want is an armed Pathet Lao soldier, drunk on the best whiskeys and brandies . . . from the PX, mingling about with a number of Americans . . . I consumed a considerable amount myself during the day." Schofield's job led to even more drinking. He and his friend Don Dugan, who had both chosen—against orders—to retain their firearms, were told to kill all pets in the compound to prevent their abuse or consumption.

The largely unarmed USAID staff uneasily patrolled their side of the fence, stared down by Pathet Lao with AK-47s and SKSs. Chaos grew as Lao protesters, anticipating the Americans' evacuation, cut through the fence and looted houses on the periphery. Even so, observes Zola, "it was totally calm compared to what happened in Phnom Penh, what happened in Saigon." Beginning on May 24, the Americans were allowed an "orderly departure"—women and children first. On May 28, the last group from Kilometer 6 left Vientiane.* "We found out from people in the ministry of public health," explains McKeithen,

that the negotiating track of the Pathet Lao was to physically assemble all of the jeeps and the bottles of aspirin and the tin roofing sheets and every single commodity . . . that had ever been brought into the country, and compare the physical inventory with the paper inventory, and then see how much we had stolen, and then to put us on trial for having stolen the people's property, and then to begin negotiations on war reparations. So when we found out . . . we were able to convince Washington that there was no future dealing with that government, that they were not interested in development.

By June 26, USAID Laos would be shut down and its assets liquidated. In the intervening days, Mac Thompson, a seasoned USAID veteran, was in charge of collecting furniture and effects from houses formerly occupied by USAID staff. Every house had a rental contract listing items in the home. Negotiating with Pathet Lao lawyers and students, Thompson determined which items belonged to the owner of the house and which had been rented. The latter were confiscated in the name of the new government. Anything not on the list was assumed to be personal property of the Americans who'd lived there. The Pathet Lao captain who traveled with him supported his reclamation of these items, says Thompson.

That was sort of my daily job for several weeks. And one . . . hot day, we're just taking a break . . . and a couple leftist lawyers were pulling my chain. "Hey, how much money do you think . . . USAID is leaving here in Laos?" [W]e had heard this at a staff meeting: $100 million worth of warehouses and vehicles and heavy equipment and . . . food in the warehouse out at Kilometer 9 . . . And they said, "Don't you feel pretty bad about that?" And we said, "Well, a little bit. But we look at the bright side of it." "What's the bright side?" We said, "You know what the USAID budget was just for next year? It was $65 million . . . for Laos" . . . "[T]hat sounds good—$65 million." Thompson replied, "Well, how much of it do you think you're going to get [now]?"

Havoc

In Laos, May and June 1975 brought far more than the demise of US-AID. Tens of thousands of people were forced to make harrowing decisions that would determine the course and quality of the remainder of their lives.

---

* Steve Schofield says the last group numbered twenty-six; Tony Zola remembers fifty-four.

Fungchatou Lo actually enjoyed the weeks leading up to Long Tieng's fall. In March, "The announcement came out of the loudspeaker throughout the whole school saying, 'Tomorrow, don't come to school.' As students, we were happy! . . . No school after a week; no school after two weeks." But as time passed, a sense of menace began to infiltrate his community. "Pretty soon, we started seeing strange soldiers walking around our town. And that's when everything went to chaos."

Lo's brother and other relatives lived in Long Tieng, supporting the war effort.

Suddenly my brother just said, "Our aunt is moving to Thailand" . . . [P]eople were just moving all over the place . . . and all this chaos just happened overnight . . . [T]hen we saw these strange soldiers walking around town. And my father said, "Those are the Communist soldiers." But actually they're Hmong! . . . [A]ll of these relatives that we hadn't seen for twenty or thirty years suddenly show up . . . And my father said, "Yeah, we are relatives, but be very careful with them. They're Communists" . . . I would imagine that at that time most of the houses in the village would have some kind of hiding place. And all the men suddenly became very agitated, because the Communists were searching for them. My father . . . was a very peaceful man, a farmer most of his life, and had a business on the side . . . [He] believed that he would not be in danger . . . [S]ome people on the mountain moved down to the valley, to the city; some people in the city moved up to the mountains. And no one knows which direction will be safe! But my father knew that he didn't want to go to Thailand . . . He knows that he will be safe because he was not active in the military, so they have no record of what he was doing. But at the same time, he [fears] the Communists, so he chose not to surrender . . . [T]he only option is to hide in the jungle.

If Fungchatou Lo's father feared the Communists, one can imagine how former soldiers felt.* Thousands of those still in Long Tieng after the evacuation gathered their families and the possessions they could carry and began walking toward Vientiane and the Mekong River. The column of people stretched for miles. Wang Her was among the throng.

---

* Those feelings were indeed well founded. Since Chao Monivong, General Vang Pao's replacement in Military Region 2, was also a personal friend, the changeover was amicable. There was, therefore, no reason to destroy the CIA's detailed files on all the Hmong personnel they had employed. But when Monivong heard he would not be allowed to retain his position without first visiting a reeducation camp, he fled to Thailand, leaving the files behind—and intact. Upon arriving in Long Tieng, Pathet Lao troops broke into the cabinets containing the files. They were eventually transferred to the interior ministry, where, according to Arthur Dommen, "they were to serve the new authorities as a who's who of Vang Pao's secret army and of their 'crimes against the people' for years to come."

Converted to Christianity in 1949, Her served in Vang Pao's army but returned to farming in 1970. When his family learned of the general's departure, they planned to leave right after the rice harvest, which was late that year, affording them little to eat.

We went to Nasu, but the main road was closed off. The Pathet Lao soldiers were guarding the roads... [But] daughters from the Her and Kong clans decided to break down the roadblock... [T]he soldiers did not know how to stop these girls. If our sons had done it, they would have been shot. We did not tell the girls to do it; they decided to risk it on their own. Then everybody... followed these young girls out, and the guards could not prevent our escape. The Pathet Lao decided to put up another roadblock at Hin Heup... It took us about seven or eight days to reach it.[15]

Now an author and businessman living in Sydney, Australia, Pao Lee was a young, newly married man attending teachers college and trying to build a bright future for his family when Long Tieng fell. His parents wasted little time: "If our leaders have fled to Thailand, we must go there, too." Lee's extended family walked through a checkpoint at Ban Xon and on to Hin Heup, where they built a hut along the side of the road and waited three days before deciding on their next move.

Rumors circulated about the prospects for crossing the bridge. Some walked back to Long Tieng, believing Vang Pao was sending more planes. Others claimed the Communists wouldn't allow any vehicles through but would permit those on foot to pass. Most Hmong had spent their whole life walking. Only a few more steps, some believed, would ensure their freedom.

Sao Lee, Pao's "cousin,"* was traveling in the opposite direction. A student at Dong Dok University in Vientiane, Sao went in search of his mother in Pha Khao. Sao's parents had been divorced since 1963, when his father unexpectedly brought home a second wife. His mother "still had her small shop where she sold Hmong groceries, lolly [candy], biscuit, some small things . . . I told my mother, 'You'd better go with me, because the country will fall to the Communists now' . . . [S]he said . . . 'No way! I still have all these things! What am I going to do with my shop?' I said, 'Forget about your shop! . . . Your life is worth more than your shop.' And she said, 'No, I don't want to lose this. I'm not going to go with you.'" Accepting his mother's decision, Sao Lee returned to Vi-

---

* In Hmong culture, of course, almost everyone with the same clan name is a "cousin." Pao Lee and Sao Lee had a common great-grandfather. Their fathers were first cousins.

entiane. Soon the roads between Vientiane and Pha Khao were dotted with checkpoints, all controlled by Vietnamese, Pathet Lao, and Neutralist soldiers.

Sao finally decided he had to return for his mother, no matter the risk. He concocted a story of an imaginary brother who was killed and required a funeral ceremony. "I need my mother," he claimed, "because she knows the old traditional ways, and I do not." On May 27 he convinced a Communist officer to sign a two-day pass, recruited the assistance of his brother-in-law who owned a jeep, and negotiated himself through several checkpoints along the way. His next stop was the bridge at Hin Heup. "The bridge there was very long and the river very deep. There was no way to cross but through the checkpoint . . . [O]n the side from Vientiane, it's Lao Communists. On the other side is the neutral Lao, but they are as bad as the Communists now . . . [W]hen we arrived on the first end of the bridge . . . to my surprise, some of the soldiers there were actually Hmong—but Hmong Communists." Sao Lee again convinced the sentries to allow him passage. "And all the way from the bridge to Ban Xon, Hmong were everywhere!" He called out, asking if anyone knew or had seen his mother, but to no avail.

About six to ten miles from Hin Heup, as the two men rode through a small village, a man suddenly appeared on the road, brandishing an M16 rifle. He insisted they turn back. Sao persisted:

"Look, we have the paper here. We got the stamp, everything." And he said, "No, I'm not interested about that. You have to go back." And then my brother-in-law said, "No, we are not going back" . . . Then [the man] put the gun on my brother-in-law's head . . . I said, "Please, don't do that!" And I just . . . tried to talk very nice, softly, and I just begged him that I needed to go to see my mother, because I had problems in Vientiane with my young brother . . . [H]e thought for awhile, and then he just said, "OK, you can go."

On May 28, the Hmong assembled at Hin Heup bridge seemed ready to surge across toward Vientiane. Wang Her remembers a Vietnamese captain coming to speak to the crowd:

"Brother Hmong, stay with us. Where are you going? Do you have any cigarettes? Please give me one." One of us had some and gave him one. He took it and said, "Look here, you do not want to stay with us, but here in Laos you could ask your neighbors and they will gladly give you what you need . . . Once you are out of Laos, people will not even give you a single cigarette if you ask for one" . . . Even after the Vietnamese captain's speech, we decided to move out of Laos. We were not satisfied with the con-

dition in Laos at that time . . . The guards pulled out their guns and were ready to shoot us. They asked us if we wanted to go see [our old leaders] Touby Lyfoung and Ly Teng. We decided to go see them . . . I was one of the six that was chosen . . . We did not meet Touby, but we met Ly Teng. [He] was a political figure who used to work for General Vang Pao but switched sides. Ly Teng told us that we could not leave. We agreed with him, since he was a man with authority. We slept in his house for the night.

In the early morning hours of May 29, remembers Pao Lee, "[the people] said, 'OK, now, today, we have to march across the bridge.' And then we started moving to the bridge, and they started shooting . . . You could hear the rifles—*bam-bam-bam-bam-bam*—everywhere! And you could see people fall down in front of you."

Wang Her and others were buying food at the morning market nearby.

[S]ounds of gunfire could be heard back at the roadblock . . . The Hmong had only small arms and were massacred. The Hmong retreated back into the hills. There were dead bodies everywhere on one side of the bridge. Most of them were Hmong. I saw one who lay dying on the foot of the bridge. There was another moaning on one side of the road. At the site of the roadblock, there was a lady sprawled dead on the road; one side of her face was missing. After we passed her by, there was a child crying for its parents from the side of the road . . . There were lots of belongings dropped on the road as the Hmong fled back . . . [W]e heard that many of the bodies were thrown by the Communist troops into the river below . . . There were so many belongings left behind on the road. Even valuable items were discarded.

"[T]hey were chasing us," says Pao Lee, "maybe half a day—until we got to the next village . . . And then we stopped there, and all the soldiers . . . stopped shooting behind us . . . [T]hey said, 'OK, now, anybody who cannot run, come to the truck, and we'll take you back [to Ban Xon].' I [went] back there to the road, the junction from 'to Vientiane and Luang Prabang' and 'to Ban Xon' . . . I stopped in there, and then we started to think, 'Oh, where are we going to go now? Are we going to go back or what?'"

That same day Sao Lee and his brother-in-law were heading back toward Hin Heup. Not only had they failed to find his mother, but the car had broken down at a Neutralist checkpoint. The brother-in-law had been forced to run into the jungle when someone pointed to him and exclaimed, "This is a Vang Pao man!" But their luck was changing. Sao found a man who could make the repairs, and as he drove down the road, his brother-in-law emerged from the jungle and jumped in the jeep. At least they could get back home in one piece. But Sao was also worried. What had happened to his mother? Would he ever see her again? To make matters worse, their pass was expiring, and they needed to be back in Vientiane as soon as possible. If Sao Lee chose to escape to Thailand, Vientiane was as good a departure point as any.

[W]e came . . . about five kilometers from the bridge. Then we saw these Hmong refugees running, running from the bridge, and we didn't know what happened . . . [A]nd when we passed these people, we started seeing these Lao Communist soldiers with . . . AK-47s, the rocket propeller, chasing these Hmong . . . Then one Hmong guy shouted to us . . ."They killed our people on the bridge! We will go back home and we will get our guns and we will kill them!" . . . We were very scared. Then the soldiers were waving to us to stop the car. And luckily they didn't make any trouble. They just said, "You take us back to the bridge" . . . Maybe they would have kept chasing our people if they had not seen us . . . We came about two kilometers from the main group, and we found a very old lady. I felt very sad for her . . . She was alone because she told us she couldn't run after her family, and she was dropped behind . . . She didn't know where to go. She was just sort of dazed. And then we didn't say a word because we were so scared of these soldiers, too! They had all the guns.

When they arrived at the bridge, the soldiers got out of the jeep and walked to their quarters, situated on the banks overlooking the river. Sao Lee saw at least three or four people lying on the bridge, wounded or dying, with their belongings still at their sides.

One captain was sitting eating food on the shore . . . [W]hen I took my paper, my traveling document . . . he was still talking to his soldier, who was standing up with his M16. He said, "How do you feel?" . . . I pretended that I wasn't listening to anything. I just put the paper in front of him and stood there with my head bowed. And then the soldier told the captain, "Oh, this is the first time I killed people. I am really shaken" . . . I pretended I didn't hear anything, and I just said, "Sir, can you sign my paper? I have to go to that side. I am a student. I came from Vientiane, but now I have to go back to study." And then he just had a look, and then he signed it—luckily . . . I took my paper, and I just ran.

It is difficult to know the number of Hmong killed at Hin Heup. Grant Evans has written that five were killed and about thirty wounded. While others insist the numbers are significantly higher, there can be no doubt that the incident "proved" to many pro-Western Hmong that the new government was out to exterminate them. But it was not the only evidence that led them to this conclusion. As Yang Dao observed,

Soviet president Nikolai Podgorny had expressed open hostility toward the royalists. The opinions of at least one Lao official had also been published in several newspapers: "It is necessary to extirpate, to the root, the 'Hmong minority.'" This phrase not only reverberated throughout Laos but has resounded in Hmong newspapers, films, websites, and chat rooms to the present day. It is the Hmong political equivalent of "waving the bloody shirt." Any time someone tries to reasonably address the problems associated with Hmong still hiding in Laos or stuck in camps or prisons in Thailand, this quote is thrown in his or her face. Even the existence of some three hundred thousand Hmong in Laos, the vast majority of whom live in peace, if not in freedom by Western standards, cannot dissuade right-wing Hmong from asserting that the government of Laos has engaged in unrestrained, wholesale genocide against their people.[16]

But to many former soldiers looking for some indication of how the new Lao government might treat them, the most damning evidence came in the wake of Pathet Lao takeovers of Hmong territory, most no-

The Lao PDR distributed this photograph of Hmong Pathet Lao women being taught to defend their villages with crossbows.

tably Long Tieng. As Shue Long Yang of Melbourne, Australia, remembers, his father, a village leader, was originally open-minded about the new government. But then, "they called my father, to study—they call it the 'seminar' . . . First, they take the *naiban* and *tasseng* to seminar. For many, they stay in their own village. But they take the soldiers [to] reeducation camps away from [their] village . . . Some never come back." Indeed, concurs Pang Her Vang. Anyone proven to be a soldier was taken, though the focus was on high-ranking officials: "Those who were below the official rank of captain were allowed to come back if they followed orders."

"Following orders" involved some form of forcible "repentance," sometimes extracted punitively. Shue Long Yang's father came back from seminar observing, "'Oh, [the Vietnamese] brains [are] different . . . They want to control all the Lao and [are] kicking other people out' . . . They say, '[The] old agreement—nothing. Now, we use the bullet mixed with sugar.' They lied [to the] government to sign the agreement. 'Now we won. So we hold the power.' [My father] said, 'I'm old, but you [are] young, and you [will] not be able to stay here. Better [that] you go.'" Refusing to depart without his father, Shue Long Yang's family nonetheless began making plans to leave the country.

Nao Her Vang, a soldier forced to flee the Pathet Lao's last attack at Sala Phou Khoun in 1975, initially managed to escape the clutches of his enemies. "As soon as the general and all of the high-ranking officers left," he recalls,

without anybody's command . . . we soldiers donned our civilian clothing and hid all of our weapons in the hillsides. And at first there was no hostile threat from the Vietnamese. But there were some of our Hmong who weren't too comfortable having the Vietnamese all over the place, so they grabbed their weapons and fought the Vietnamese with guerilla tactics. Then these Hmong drew the Vietnamese into our villages, and we had to fight . . . [O]ur families had to run into the jungle. We were using the weapons and the ammunition we were issued from the Americans. We had to be conservative with their use. At first when we started fighting, it was just the local Laotian Communists, but then the Vietnamese forces started coming in to hunt us. There were groups of Hmong who made it to Thailand, but our group did not.

After witnessing the results of the shootings at Hin Heup, Wang Her also chose to fight. He and his kin ran back to their villages, found their old weapons, and hid in the jungles, attacking Vietnamese and Lao convoys. "We fought guerrilla warfare for two to three years. We fled to Phu

Bia, and the Vietnamese attacked us there. We then decided to give ourselves up, and the Vietnamese took us back to Trau Yia [Straight Moun-
tain]. We planted and harvested rice there for that season."

Nao Her Vang's group also surrendered. They were taken to an area
near Long Tieng, where they too returned to a life of farming. "[T]here
weren't a lot of Vietnamese [there]," says Vang. "The majority were Laotian Communist troops. They forced all the Hmong in the surrounding areas to come to live near the bigger cities, because they wanted
better control of us."

After one year, Wang Her's family heard a government radio broadcast that seemed too good to be true. "[They] said we were free to do
whatever we wanted if we filled out some papers in the town square.
We ask[ed] for farmland near the Thai border, and when we were allowed to move there, we escaped quietly into Thailand." Nao Her Vang
was not nearly so lucky. After the first harvest, he and eight others
from his village were arrested and put into a stone building Vang Pao
had once used to hold POWs. Two months later, they were transferred
to Luang Prabang. Their families tried to follow them but were ultimately shipped to Nong Het, along the Vietnam border. After a period
of interrogation, seven of the men were released. Only Vang and his
"brother," Xai Vang remained. For five years, Nao Her Vang was kept in
a stockade with manacles around his wrists. Xai Vang died during the
third year.

Vang and his fellow prisoners were fed two meals a day, consisting
of an egg-sized ball of rice and a small cup of water. He was in the most
secure area of the prison. "During the daytime, you had to put your
handcuffs on and you could walk around in your building; at night, they
had to put you in the stockade." When he had to relieve himself, his
only choice was often to urinate into a bamboo tube that the guards
placed in front of him.

*In other areas, the prisoners were allowed to go out during the day to work out in
the fields. There was usually about one guard per three prisoners . . . [E]very morning the guards would cook rice for us. The top, the best portions, were given to the
prisoners that worked out in the fields, so [the rest of us] got what was crusty on the
bottom. A lot of this rice was surplus from the war, and it had a lot of sand and grit
in it. I developed ulcers and stomach problems. The rice was given on banana leaves,
and whoever was fortunate enough to serve actually had a chance to eat the banana
leaves, too. Pretty much anything that was green that we could reach we ate.*

For five years, interrogators grilled Vang about his life. He stuck to his carefully crafted lie: he was an orphan who simply followed the Hmong leaders from his community wherever they went. He did nothing more than farm and tend cattle. Most of this questioning occurred under the supervision of a high-ranking Lao officer. Guards would not mistreat him in front of their superior officer, but when they had him alone, they would put a pistol to his head and say, "Tell the truth, or I'll shoot you right now." Vang remembers another night when the prisoner in charge of supervising inmates was inspecting bunks and told them, "Whatever noise you hear, just stay down." As Vang recalls, "I was sleeping . . . My left foot was stuck in the stockade, while the other foot was just bent, and then the guards started shooting on one side of the building—through the building! It looked like termites were eating the whole building, there were so many bullet holes. One of the bullets ricocheted and hit me on the knee, and another grazed the back of my head."

After five years of abuse and neglect, Nao Her Vang was released from prison and reported to Phonsavan, near the Plain of Jars. He and other former detainees were put to work cleaning and grooming a local official's property. Owing to his weakened condition, Vang could do little more than pick up trash and lawn clippings. Every six months, he and his peers were forced at gunpoint to visit a reeducation camp. "We had to write an essay of what we learned, about how we could become good citizens . . . And if we wrote anything that might hint that we might do something wrong, we would be punished."

Vang was eventually transferred to work in the fields of Xieng Khouang. Some of his relatives discovered his whereabouts and came to claim him. Finally reunited with his wife and children, he settled south of Phonsavan: "We harvested one season of rice there. Just before we were about to harvest the second season, we decided to make an escape to Thailand." Vang and his family arrived ten years after Vang Pao and his officers. He had no illusions of returning to Laos. Unlike many other Hmong, he wanted to leave for the United States as soon as possible.

The treatment of Nao Her Vang and his fellow Hmong was clearly inhumane. But from the perspective of the Pathet Lao, he and the other inmates were no longer prisoners of war. The United States had ceased its support of anti-Communist forces and had signed a treaty relinquishing its claims to influence over the region. Vang Pao and his officers had fled the country. The "people's revolution" had won. The war was over, and the Hmong who stayed to fight were no longer rivals but revolutionaries committing treason against the Lao People's Democratic Republic (LPDR).

This argument falls apart, however, when applied to the widespread removal of Hmong leaders like Touby Lyfoung, who were friendly to the new Lao government, and the disappearance of village leaders and numerous soldiers who had already laid down their arms. In March 1977 the new government even imprisoned King Savang Vatthana, whom they had forced to abdicate in December 1975. It seemed any former enemy or critic of the new government was deemed a potential saboteur or subversive. Though Lao prime minister Kaysone Phomvihane "announced" the king's death in 1989, most sources say he died of starvation in "Camp 01," the reeducation camp designated for the new government's most prominent prisoners.

TERROR IN THE JUNGLE

For Hmong who fled, as well as those who chose to stay and fight, the years following the Long Tieng airlift were ones of terror and tribulation. Both groups, whether armed or not, were seen as enemies of the state, either fleeing the country to escape punishment or hiding in the jungles to arm, mobilize, and attack government positions and convoys.

Some of those who stayed behind simply chose to trust that the new government would treat them fairly—or at least no less poorly than any other ethnic minority in the country. Many had family members who sided with the Pathet Lao who no doubt helped facilitate their surrender. A small number, like one couple still living in Laos, became educated in Lao universities. Their story is particularly fascinating. The wife's family moved several times during her childhood, from Luang Prabang to Sayaboury and finally to Vientiane in 1967, where they enrolled her in school. The husband, several years her senior, had left his home in northeastern Xieng Khouang to study in Vientiane in 1966. In the early 1970s, her family moved back to Sayaboury, leaving her and her younger brother in school. But before they left, he sent emissaries to ask for her hand in marriage. They would wait to wed until after she completed school.

Both of their families supported General Vang Pao. In May 1975, not long after the evacuation of Long Tieng, her family fled into Thailand's Nan province. She and her younger brother remained in school in Vientiane. "We were too young to understand the politics at the time," she says. The husband also had many family members who fled Laos and who today live in the United States. But at the time, staying and completing his education seemed more important.

Her father tried but failed to return to Vientiane for his two children, but an uncle still living in Thailand managed to bring them. But her betrothed crossed the Mekong, found her, convinced her parents that she would be safe, and brought her back to Vientiane. Though the intervening years were certainly not easy, both now have successful careers.

Though there are other such Hmong, including those with positions in the Lao government, their stories are by far the exception. The vast majority who surrendered returned to a life of relative isolation and poverty. They farmed in areas scarred by bombing and riddled with unexploded ordnance. Whether because of their desire to return to a life apart from mainstream society or the new Lao government's desire to marginalize them, they enjoyed far fewer educational and economic opportunities than most ethnic Lao. Nonetheless, they escaped the extreme harshness suffered by those who remained in hiding and instead put themselves in a position to work within the new government to improve their lot in life.

But for many others, surrender was intolerable and flight inconceivable. Many lived in the surrounding countryside, often organizing into groups the new Lao government called *Chao Fa* or "the army of heaven." Though this phrase has been used collectively to refer to all resistance fighters, it refers properly to those who followed any of a number of charismatic and/or spiritualistic leaders. Some were followers of slain messianic leader Shong Lue Yang who avoided assassinations that claimed him and his successor, Yong Lee Yang. Before the evacuation of Long Tieng, Shong Lue's followers worked underground, bringing in a few people at a time, teaching the Hmong script, and passing on his teachings. After Long Tieng fell, says a member of the Lee clan, Hmong Communists came to see them. "They said, 'Don't leave the country . . . We will love you the same as General Vang Pao loved you. At least stay with us for a year, and if you don't feel like we love you enough, then we will let you go.'" Many came out of hiding, says Mr. Lee, but once they did, they were invited to learn "our new policies and rules of conduct. You are used to the American way, General Vang Pao's way." Many of those who went, says Mr. Lee, "disappeared" on the way. Then news came that Touby LyFoung had been arrested; even the king had gone to "seminar." In August 1976, two men who had gone to seminar at Muong Vieng Sai returned to Lee's village. They told us, "'So many of Vang Pao's former soldiers came that they ran out of room. So they started killing ten of us every morning. One morning it was our turn, and God helped us, so we escaped. Don't wait for the others from Muong Vieng Sai,' they said, 'they're not coming back.'" Lee and others started making their way toward Phu Bia, where they heard others were already forming a resistance.

Some leaders, like Chai Her, believed that during a battle, one virgin girl would stay behind in a temple while another would accompany the men into battle. She would have the power, says Fong Lor, to swat bullets away with her apron or *sev*. Others, like Xai Shoua Yang, had no real religious beliefs but wanted to participate in the broader movement. They were called *pattikan* (reactionaries). Another, Zong Zoua Her, had been a more secular follower of Shong Lue but had earned rank in Vang Pao's army by providing him with a thousand soldiers late in the war. When the movement began to gain steam, he reemerged to claim a leadership role.

The Chao Fa became a force to reckon with, in part because at first the new Lao government didn't take it very seriously. "Our leaders left," says Pa Xe Vang, "and all we knew how to do was pray, so we prayed to the sky. They called us the crazy Chao Fa . . . It was meant to be negative, those who followed the sky instead of the real world, but we accepted that name. It inspired us, so it kind of backfired on them." Mr. Lee had been fighting since the days of the French, but his faith inspired him. Wherever he and his men went, says Lee, "We would get a feeling in our gut that soldiers were coming this way or that way. We would be ready for them. We had very limited ammunition; we made sure each bullet killed one person. When we fought for the Americans, we made a lot of noise to scare our enemy away without killing anyone. Now we had nothing to waste, so each bullet had to kill someone without giving away our location. Each time you heard a shot, a soldier would fall."

More and more villages turned to the Chao Fa as they grew more successful. But most failed to consider the implications of the war many of them had just finished fighting and losing. Vang Pao and his forces, once armed and trained by the Thai PARU and the American CIA, had enjoyed successes in their early battles as well. But these triumphs only served to redouble Hanoi's determination. As North Vietnam's resolve increased, America's waned, and the Hmong were caught in the middle. In this instance, too, well-trained, well-equipped, and lethally determined Vietnamese troops would be called in to put down the rebellion. And there was little hope that the United States, Thailand, France, or anyone else was going to come to the rescue.

escape

For those who escaped in the first few weeks, the situation was not nearly as grim. The Pathet Lao and Vietnamese had not yet placed patrols along the Mekong River or sent soldiers into the forest. "My wife and I still had sons in Vientiane," recalls Pa Cha Kong, "so we decided to go there [instead of Long Tieng]. I owned a taxi, so it was easier for me to drive around. I was one of the earliest to leave the country, so it only cost me fifteen thousand kip [ten dollars] to rent a boat. I rented three . . . for my family and my relatives." Kong was clearly not panic-stricken, staying behind long enough to donate his taxi to a Lao pastor married to a Hmong woman. "I told him, 'if I come back to Laos someday, then this taxi is still mine, but if I don't come back, you can have it to do God's work.' And then I left."

Sao Lee, returned to Vientiane safe and sound after a harrowing and unsuccessful search for his mother, couldn't leave Laos without her but couldn't risk another journey to Pha Khao. Then one day, seemingly out of the blue, she showed up on his doorstep with his brother Ying, his sister-in-law, and a baby that was little more than two weeks old. "They were very clever!" exclaims Lee. Getting to Ying's house was easy enough, but when they tried to travel to Vientiane, the road was blocked. "So they turned . . . to Sayaboury. Then they came back to Luang Prabang [and] just came by plane straight to Vientiane . . . I just felt very happy that suddenly everybody was there in Vientiane!" Sao Lee appealed to the same Lao police captain who had helped him obtain his travel pass through Hin Heup. "[H]e organized a rowing boat—up to ten, fifteen people could fit in that big, long boat . . . Then at nighttime . . . he brought . . . a Lao, who . . . watched, and when the [patrol] boat passed, he said, 'Quick,

As a young man Sao Lee, shown here at age twelve, would undertake a harrowing journey to find his mother and be caught in the aftermath of the shootings at Hin Heup bridge.

quick, quick!'" Lee and his family jumped in the boat, and their Lao boatman noiselessly rowed them to Thailand.

Sao Lee and his family were fortunate. His older brother, Yia Lee, had completed his master's in social work from the University of New South Wales in Sydney, Australia, in late 1974. He had submitted his thesis but decided to wait for his graduation in May 1975.

And then even before I had the graduation and got my degree, [the Communists took Laos], and my family's in Thailand. And I said, "Oh, wow! What am I going to do now?" There was no point for me to go back to Laos. I've got no one there. If they're all in Thailand, it would be a danger for me if I went to Laos. We didn't know what the Pathet Lao would do. Everybody was so scared . . . All the Western countries were very sympathetic . . . [so] I applied to the Australian government to stay on as an asylum seeker. It took them quite awhile to make a decision. It took them about maybe five, six months. So in the meantime, I was just working away in the factory, supporting myself.

Yia Lee, eventually granted asylum, worked with his fellow Hmong students to petition the Australian Committee on Foreign Affairs and Defense to investigate the refugee crisis in Thailand and allow their family members to migrate to Australia. In time, Sao Lee and his family joined Yia Lee "down under."

But for every tale of good luck, reunion, and ultimate safety that provides a redemptive finale to a story filled with the suffering and deprivation of war, the abandonment at Long Tieng, and the fear of being stalked by starvation and enemy soldiers, there are probably many more that still haunt those who tell them.

Jer Xiong Yang had seen death, mayhem, and unspeakable misery on the battlefield, but "we suffered the most," he says, "when we were in the jungles." There were perils almost too numerous to mention for those who crept quietly southward toward the Mekong River. Most immediate was the fear of running out of food. For many Hmong, starvation had set in even before their journey began. While some brought along as much rice as they could carry, it almost inevitably ran out too soon. Those who brought livestock ended up slaughtering them quickly and sharing the meat with others or simply leaving the animals behind. Fungchatou Lo's family had been hiding in a mountain village when, just before the harvest season of 1977, they heard Communist soldiers were heading their way:

That was the practice of the Communists. By attacking the people who resisted them, at the time that the crop was about to be harvested so that they don't have food to eat, they would [force their enemy to] surrender or starve to death . . . [W]e had to eat just about anything we could find. The best food that you could find at that time, if you were very lucky, was a yam—and corn. Not rice. Rice would be like steak now . . . And after yams and corn were gone, then we started eating roots . . . and tubers, and anything that was soft that would keep your body moving.

But many of the foods foraged from the jungle contained toxins that could sicken, immobilize, or even kill those who ate them. "[C]ertain roots you have to be very careful and wash over and over and over and over, until the poison was diluted. [The water where one washed these roots] actually turned black. So when you walked into a town, the first thing you looked at was the water. If there were colors in the water, then you knew that this town was starving for food . . . [If] there was a village where the water was clean, clear, you said, 'For some reason they can find food here. We'll stay here for a little while.'"

By the time Lo's group reached the Mekong, their food was gone; many of the young children were crying from hunger.

We knew the Communists were near, because their military base was right along the Mekong River. And so the best thing you could [do to] keep the children quiet was to [give them] opium . . . to go to sleep and keep them quiet. [But] without knowing the . . . amount of opium you [should] give, you could destroy a life. So my young sister . . . was crying, and my mother put a little bit of the opium . . . into a spoon of water and then forced it down my sister's throat. And then, thirty minutes later, she didn't move! And so what do you do? . . . [N]ot only my sister but all the children were being poisoned by opium. But one of the fortunate things was they went into a deep sleep, but no one died.

Many others were not so lucky. Fear of detection led to an unknown number of unintentional homicides, as well as outright abandonment or murder for the sake of the greater good. One Hmong woman is still haunted today by the memory of her little brother. He was slowing down everyone else and wouldn't stay quiet, so she took him to a secluded spot in the forest, gave him something to play with, told him she would be back, and then left him behind.

The Mekong itself posed another grave danger. As mountain people, many Hmong had never learned to swim. Family members all too often drowned while trying to cross—or watched helplessly as others did.

Of all those interviewed for this book, perhaps no one experienced more misfortune and lived to tell the tale than Chia Xiong. Already twice widowed by the time of the Long Tieng evacuation, Xiong had borne five children, but only two survived. The oldest was already in Thailand, leaving her with her youngest, Chia Cher Yang. Almost constantly on the run, Xiong and her extended family eventually surrendered to "the Vietnamese" at Muong Oun.* They lived there only a short time, she says, before the area was overrun and they were forced to flee once again. "We kept moving and hiding in the forest, but finally we couldn't survive any longer, so . . . we moved back and surrendered ourselves once again." At that point, Xiong made a decision she would later regret. She sent her young son, barely more than ten years old, to Thailand. He would be better off, she thought, with his brother. Like Sao Lee's mother, Xiong was loath to leave her possessions—and the only way of life she'd ever known—behind. "I didn't even have much of anything, but I still worried and treasured all those things . . . So I stayed behind . . . After he left, I missed him so much that I couldn't see myself staying any longer." Her son felt the same way. Now in his forties, Chia Cher, who lives with his mother, her third husband, Jer Xiong Yang, and his own family, strained to control his emotions as he told the story of parting from his mother. Two of his cousins, accompanied by several other relatives, were soon back to retrieve her. They stayed for about a month, carefully planning their journey and how to cover their tracks before they departed.

When she left her village, Xiong traveled in a party of about one hundred people. But when they reached the village of Na Pha, approximately two hundred others, representing a number of different clans,

* Elder Hmong often say "Vietnamese" when referring to any enemy.

joined them. They approached a small river north of the Mekong and stopped to gather food. Encountering a Lao man and fearing he would betray them to nearby soldiers, they asked nothing of him and retreated northward. Hiding for a time, they cautiously made their way back south.

The Laotian must have tipped the soldiers . . . When we returned to the river . . . some people were . . . drinking water. Just then gunshots came from everywhere. Many people lost their lives . . . [T]he nephew who led the group had a wife carrying a three-month-old baby on her back. During an ambush, they were afraid that the baby's crying would give them away, so he took the baby from her back and tossed the baby into the water . . . But the Communists shot and killed his wife and his mother right on the spot, along with another child. [P]eople were running, drowning, and dying everywhere.

Devastated and panic-stricken, separated from her nephews, Xiong retreated northward once again. When she regrouped with other survivors, she learned that one of her nephews had been killed, along with two of his children. Her other nephew adopted the surviving children into his family and then led those with him to Pa Xang, where they surrendered. It would take months for her nephews' wives back in Thailand to discover what happened and hire Thai "coyotes" to rescue them. Chia provided her guide with her silver necklace as a first installment, knowing her family would help finance the balance of her debt when she arrived at Nong Khai refugee camp. But she knew others had already paid a steep price for her indecision.

Even in Thailand, Chia Xiong's luck did not change. She was transferred to Ban Vinai while her youngest son, Chia Cher, remained behind at Nong Khai.

Despite her many trials, Chia Xiong was ultimately reunited with her son. But again, for every story of reunion, there is one of parting. Vue Yang's parents willingly gave him up so he could enjoy a brighter future. Only a small boy in 1977, Yang had spent two years hiding in the jungle with his family, about two thousand others, and a "shaman lady" who told them when danger was imminent and they needed to move. When their food finally ran out, the women and children went ahead to surrender. If the Communists knew they had control of the women and children, it was thought they would accept the men's surrender more easily. "All the kids were just scared and crying that if they ever go to . . . a Communist school, they will be gone until they are grown up, and

Both Jer Xiong Yang (left) and Chia Xiong suffered terrible losses in Laos. They met and married in Ban Vinai refugee camp and now live in Australia.

if they are lucky, they might return back to see their family. If they are not lucky . . . they would disappear without knowing about their family." One night Vue was playing outside when he heard his father calling him. Expecting he had chores to perform, he told his friends he would return as soon as he completed them. In a hushed tone, Vue's father asked him what kind of education he wanted. "I was concerned. I said, 'Why are you asking me that?' . . . 'We're thinking about getting an education for you, but it's up to you.'" Vue made it clear he wanted no part of a plan that sent him far away to study under a Vietnamese system. He had no idea what he was setting in motion.

"At that [time] there were [Hmong] guerilla groups returning back from Thailand. They were messengers sent by General Vang Pao to relocate their family members or relatives or to see how the movement was organized and so forth. There was one gentleman who was close to my father . . . So [my parents] decided to send me out along with him so I could be . . . in a different country to live a better life or to educate myself properly rather than going under Communist education."

That same night, Vue's parents packed a small bundle for him; his father said, "Follow me." Frightened by the darkness and the furtive nature of their journey, Vue protested, but his father replied, "Son, quiet. I'll take you to get a good education. No talking . . . if anybody hears about us, then we will be killed." His father's words only amplified his fears. They traveled to Vue's uncle's guerilla camp, and there his father simply said, "You stay with your uncle here, and he will take you to get a better education. Don't be concerned about us. I will follow you shortly." His father then turned and disappeared into the darkness. Yang, left in the care of a strange uncle, began a long, hushed journey through the wild. He was only a boy in the company of well-armed men. His uncle spurned all of his many questions, simply telling Vue to stay close and keep quiet. "Whenever you get sore legs or you cannot follow us, let me know. I will take your hand . . . Just stay with me, and I'll try to protect you as much as possible."

After what seemed like several days of nonstop walking, the group reached the top of a high mountain. Finally, his uncle said, " 'Son, look at the blinking lights over there—it's like stars over there. That's where we're heading . . . Those blinking lights are in Thailand. They're in a totally different country.' That's what he told me only. So we just followed by instinct, and there was no guarantee of safety." After walking even more cautiously toward the Mekong River, the rest of the men vanished into the night. Vue was told he would be swimming across, riding on an inflatable "water balloon" tied with a simple string to his uncle's backpack. He was to make sure the string remained tight. If it became slack, he was separated from his uncle, and "I needed to whisper 'Uncle! I am lost!'"

With that, his uncle slid into the water. "In a second, I tried to grab back on my string. And I did not feel my string at all, so I whispered back to my uncle, 'I'm lost, I'm lost!' And suddenly . . . I saw him appear back. Then he said, 'Hand me your string.' So I handed him my string . . . And at that time he put me into a secure position, so the string was never loose again. And then he kept pulling me, and we were going in the river until early morning, like 2:00 AM." They reached the other side after what surely must have seemed like an eternity to a young boy. "[My uncle] said . . . 'We are lucky that we are safe here . . . [I]n the border here, the Communists are patrolling . . . and we could be located or targeted, too.' So we took a rest along the shore there for a few hours, until the daylight was on, and we could hear the rooster crowing from the other side of the river . . . [A]t that time I felt sad . . . I knew right away that I would never see my parents again." But Vue (now Edward) Yang never forgot his parents' sacrifice for the sake of his education. He is now a teacher at Achieve Academy in St. Paul, Minnesota.

an uncertain future

As refugees from Laos, Cambodia, and Vietnam began pouring into Thailand, the office of the United Nations High Commissioner for Refugees (UNHCR) sent registration teams into the makeshift camps that dotted the Thai side of the Mekong River. They gathered refugee families together, recorded their names, took down their stories, assigned them to a camp, and gave them a card providing access to food. Family profiles were presented to countries most likely to accept them as immigrants. If, for example, a Hmong family already had a relative in France or Australia, their form would be taken to that country's embassy.*

Escaping to Thailand after abandoning one's home, crossing through hostile territory, and suffering from hunger, exposure to the elements, potential betrayal, accidental poisoning, gunshots, and a host of other dangers left most refugees in a state of shock. For most, their experiences cemented forever a view of the Pathet Lao and the Vietnamese as butchers, barbarians, and bullies. One need not be a former soldier to hold such opinions. Having spent most of the war farming and raising livestock, Pa Seng Thao expected to remain in Laos. He had joined Vang Pao at Pa Dong in 1960 but had fought for only one year. "Since I wasn't an important person who was paid by the Americans, I didn't feel like I had to run," says Thao. "I was well off, and I had enough to live on. I felt that I would become one of their citizens and life would just go on. But when the Communists came and saw my livestock, they asked me why I had so many . . . I told them that I only had a couple cattle at first and after a long time they reproduced and became numerous. I told them I didn't buy these livestock from anyone."

The Communists, Thao says, insisted that he had bought the cattle and could only have done so if he had been paid by the former gov-

* Despite their relatively minimal role in the Southeast Asian wars, Australia and Canada were, per capita, two of the most helpful countries in accepting refugees.

ernment. Otherwise he certainly must have stolen them. In any event, he was obviously too rich to respect and obey authorities from the new government. Thao decided to take his family and flee from his village, leaving behind almost everything he owned. They went first to Phu Bia, the center of the Chao Fa resistance. "There were Vietnamese everywhere, and there was no place to hide."

Everywhere they went, Thao's family seemed to find soldiers looking for him or people willing to betray him. Others who respected him as a leader wanted to be with him, making it harder to keep his family safe. When they reached Pa Khe, they again tried to hide, but would-be followers gave away their position. Though most of the males had hidden in the jungle, soldiers captured all of the women and girls. As he told his daughter, Nao Thao, "It was a scary time and your mother was crying terribly. [The men and boys] went into the jungle while the women and children stayed out in the open. The Vietnamese troops picked up the women and children. Your brother was killed. He was a good person who was an able leader . . . He would have made us proud if he was alive today. I cannot go into detail because it's too emotional, and I'm heartbroken by his death."

Though Thao was eventually reunited with his family and made it safely to Thailand, he remained permanently embittered toward the Lao government. While they robbed him of his livelihood, he was far more upset about the loss of his son. "I couldn't forgive myself for leaving him behind. He took my burden and died in Laos for me while I brought everyone else over . . . Why didn't I leave when he was still alive? I . . . could not forgive myself. This was the reason why I did not want to come to America. I stayed behind while others came because I couldn't bear the guilt of leaving my son behind."

Grief and trauma plagued or paralyzed many Hmong who made it into refugee camps. But finding haven in Thailand only initiated a new set of questions and challenges. How long would the government allow them to stay? Would they be safe? Would they ever be able to go home? If not, where would their new home be? Children would be born and others would die, but life had to continue, even in uncertain times and places.

5 | "HELPED THE LEAST AND DESERVED HELP THE MOST"

refugees

Being an immigrant—changing your home country—is hard enough under the best of circumstances. But refugees—forced to flee from their home countries—endure not only a major relocation but a situation so dire and need so great that circumstances are almost by definition the worst possible. Far too often refugees flee to a new country that doesn't want them, live in an environment fraught with adversity, danger, and crushing boredom, and face a disturbingly uncertain future—all after experiencing trauma that would leave most in need of serious therapy.

A ten-year veteran of the International Rescue Committee (IRC), Jim Anderson is still haunted by memories of life he saw in Thai refugee camps:

It was probably the most boring existence you can possibly imagine, because they weren't allowed to do anything. Folks, particularly young folks, would clamor to come and work for agencies that set up programs in the camp . . . [Many] enrolled in child and adult education programs, but there wasn't anything to do. It was just enforced idleness. It was so unnatural—kids growing up and spending fifteen years never seeing dad or mom work . . . Nobody was starving to death, everybody had housing, everybody had access to medical care . . . but it was just a totally empty experience . . . It was painful to hear kids talk about, "Yeah, I know where rice comes from. It comes from the back of the UN [United Nations] truck" . . . It was amazing to me that there weren't more interfamilial conflicts.

While Thai attitudes toward refugees differed from person to person and changed as the situation intensified, the relationship between reluctant host and desperate guest was always tenuous. Stoicism became an important asset: "I was content," says Xai Thao, "because they did not kill us."

Many young Hmong professionals in Western countries today were born or grew up in one or more of these refugee camps. Most had little idea what their parents were enduring, and passed their time playing games, going to ad hoc schools, or standing in line for the food and supplies trucked into the camps. Vang Chou Xiong remembers, "[M]y grandfather found [an old] rubber ball . . . We kind of treasured it. That must have been our only toy." Most games were simple, like tag, or involved sticks, stones, and castoffs from nearby merchants, like rubber bands.

But despite their horrendous environment, most Hmong were in no hurry to seek new homes in the West. For fifteen years, Dennis Grace worked for the IRC, coordinating the network of private organizations that helped bring half a million Southeast Asian refugees to the United States:

In the other camps, people were already ... wanting to vacuum up language or clothing, style of places that they would ultimately go ... [But] you'd go to the Hmong camps, and they may as well have been ... inside Laos. People dressed the same ... It looked like every attempt was to preserve ... where they'd come from ... The only leaders in the other camps were temporary figures that were not really leaders in any sense ... [I]n the Hmong camps ... [w]hen ... leaders spoke, everyone listened—and acted accordingly.

The Hmong, says Grace, "were helped the least and deserved help the most—and never asked for help ... I always used to think ... [they were] the most deserving refugee population ... from our perspective and the one that wanted to come the least. A great irony. Most people are *dying* to come to America ... The Hmong did whatever they could to *not* come to America, and that says a lot."

SeaTS on THe TRain

As evacuees from Long Tieng were flown to Nam Phong in May 1975, Heinie Aderholt, who'd already arranged for a C-130 to help with the airlift, received a call from Bill Lair, who was back in Thailand, working out of the CIA station chief's office. "He called me and he said, 'I need a favor ... I need one hundred beds ...Vang Pao is going to move down south of Bangkok to [Nam Phong].'" Aderholt sent them posthaste.

"Nobody knew what to do," remembers Lair, "[T]hey were *pouring* in ... [USAID] suggested that perhaps we could find some sort of a shelter for the Hmong and let them have kitchen gardens, and then they could help them under the USAID agricultural program ... [Then] I went to my [Thai] brother-in-law, who was the head of the national security council ... [H]e saw the prime minister every day ... He helped me to find the land to build the temporary shelters [for] the Hmong." With that, an aid program was born.[1]

While airlift evacuees were kept at Nam Phong, most refugees who came to Thailand on foot were given shelter at Nong Khai, which sat directly across the Mekong from Vientiane. By 1977 it held twenty-two thousand Lao, Hmong, and Lao-Vietnamese, earning it the nickname "Little Vientiane." On the outskirts of Nong Khai city was a Buddhist temple or wat called Samakkhi, where Yang See had set up a small refugee camp for his people. After leaving Long Tieng on May 10 and taking a taxi from Vientiane to Nong Khai, he first asked the leaders of a Tai Dem camp if they would accept Hmong refugees and was refused. The next day, without an appointment, he visited the office of Nong Khai's governor. After two days of waiting, the governor's secretary took pity on him and scheduled a meeting for the following day. Thrilled at the chance but fearful of rejection, Yang See returned on May 13 for his ten-minute meeting. Instead of feigned interest or outright hostility, the governor "understood well the plight of the Lao-Hmong refugees . . . He called in an aide and told [him] . . . to take me around to find a place of my choice and he would approve it." Yang chose Wat Samakkhi and made preparations for the onslaught of refugees he knew was coming. He also made arrangements for the safe evacuation of several members of his clan, including Dr. Yang Dao and his family. When he contacted Jerry Daniels by radio on the thirteenth, Daniels told him, "Everything is finished in Long Tieng." Though they would now be working independently from each other, Daniels pledged, "If you run into trouble, let me know. I will try to help you as much as I can—personally, but not officially."[2]

By May 18, Wat Samakkhi was already suffering from overcrowding. Yang See had spent a considerable amount of his college savings on taxis, boatmen, food, and medicine. Nam Phong, Yang heard, had not reached capacity, so he contacted Daniels to see if his people and other nearby refugees could be taken in. "That was only a request from a powerless man who had no way out of huge and complex refugee problems," says Yang. Over the next several days, Daniels sent Yang money, including his last pay from Long Tieng, and, unbeknownst to Yang, "tirelessly spent much time on the phone talking and writing cablegram memos . . . to officials in Washington, DC, requesting again and again for authorization and the dollar amounts necessary to feed each individual living in Nam Phong camp." In the process, he expanded the population of Nam Phong, sending dozens of buses to pick up refugees in outlying areas. Yang See was once again working with Jerry Daniels, this time as a refugee advisor.

Mai Lee Yang and her mother, separated from father and husband for ten years, had been forced to adjust to the shattering news that he had a new wife and other children. By the time her extended family fled for Thailand, Mai Lee was carrying a little sister on her back. As she stepped into a canoe waiting to take her family across the Mekong, the boat tipped, sending her into the water. Yang could not swim; even if she could, her sister's weight pulled her under the water. "I couldn't breathe . . . I couldn't do anything—just *BOOM!*—darkness. I had long hair . . . [and] my father grabbed my hair, and he pulled me up . . . [T]hat's how I'm still alive."

When her family reached Nong Khai, they could hardly believe their eyes. "[T]here were *so* many people, refugees, who had come to Thailand from Laos already . . . [I]t's all full, *everywhere!* People were sleeping *everywhere!* . . . I just saw *so* many people: children crying, mean people—and I can see only the mosquito netting—white everywhere, under the Thai's houses. And I just asked my mother, 'Where did they come from? . . . I thought we were the first!' . . . And my mother and father said, 'This is incredible! These Hmong were so quick!'"

Mai Lee's family stayed in Nong Khai for three or four days before a bus took them to Nam Phong. There were old barracks to sleep in; each quarter of the camp sent family representatives to a large kitchen where they prepared meals. Because of the scale of the operation and the size of the pots and cooking utensils, men cooked the food while the women washed and prepared it.

In Nam Phong, Mai Lee's family was once again split in two. "[M]e, my brother and sister, my mother, had to live outside . . . in the tent. My father lived inside, and his [other] wife and children." When it was her family's turn to help with the cooking, Mai Lee was sent:

[T]hey would call your name: "This house number—who? Is it Mai Lee?" "Yeah, it's me." [Shouting] "You?! You're too small; you're too young! You can't cook!" . . . I remember that really pissed me off when he said [that] . . . I said, "Oh, my parents are in separate houses, [and] my mother's got young children, she can't come" . . . [H]e said, [Yelling] "What can you do for me? Tell me!" I cried; I was scared [because] he was crabby with me . . . I wasn't that young—I was thirteen and a half, fourteen. But it was very hot and dirty in there . . . and they didn't want any young children [hurt] . . . So he took me outside and there was a big table . . . [where] women . . . chopped the pumpkin and the vegetables. And he said, [Loudly] "Can you do this?" I said, "Yes, I can do that." And he left me there.

Unfortunately, this method of food preparation led to widespread food poisoning, so people were given their own raw meat and vegetables to cook in their homes. "I started cooking for my family since then . . . [M]y mother . . . had my younger sister now, so she couldn't do anything much."

Paul Herr (*née* Pao Her), who now works in Washington, DC, for the Department of Homeland Security, was seventeen when his family came to Nam Phong. He remembers being concerned about how and where the dead would be buried:

People died in [a space] not even one square mile—over twelve thousand people . . . [T]hey just buried left and right, anywhere, as long as the Thai government said, "Yeah, you can bury in this area, temporarily." I remember they said temporary, not permanent . . . We didn't know where we were going to end up. One day you . . . hear, "Yeah, we're going to stay in Thailand permanently." The next day . . . , "[W]e are too close to the border of Laos, and this place may not be secure for us." The next day you hear, "The French are going to come and interview and accept five hundred . . . or one thousand people." The next day, "[The] U.S. is going to resettle us in Argentina."

Hmong veterans and their families had found temporary shelter at Nam Phong. Thousands of civilians dislocated by the war were at nearby Nong Khai. But their clandestine operations in Laos were all but unknown to decision makers at the State Department and Immigration and Naturalization Services (INS), many of whom felt the Hmong were too backward to ever qualify for resettlement. According to one former refugee worker, a "senior USAID management-type" issued a cable stating "that they were far too primitive to ever be considered for settlement in the U.S. because they were straight out of the trees." Without formal recognition, the Hmong were in limbo, stuck in Thailand with no other recourse.

No matter their fate, Hmong refugees were soon parted from their longtime leader, General Vang Pao. Living in the old commandant's headquarters at Nam Phong and continuing his practice of holding nightly dinners for his officers, he raised the ire of Thai generals by acting like a "big shot military commander rather than a guest," frequently leaving the camp to check on the thousands of Hmong who crossed the Mekong. They saw his departures from Nam Phong as an attempt to mobilize his forces, assess his best point of reentry into Laos, and reignite "his" war. The U.S. embassy bowed to Thai pressure and, with the help of the CIA, arranged for Vang Pao and his family to leave—on tourist visas—in June. They settled on a farm near Missoula, Montana, the home of his longtime advisor and friend, Jerry Daniels. Over the ensuing years, Vang Pao tried to maintain influence in refugee camps through hand-picked "leaders," with limited success.[3]

Both Vang Pao and Yang Dao often tell stories of their central roles in gaining recognition for their people. "I talked to President Ford," says Vang Pao, "and I told him that Laos, Vietnam, and Cambodia were in the same boat, fighting against the same enemy . . . 'Why do you let the South Vietnamese and Cambodians come to the United States, but not the Hmong and the Lao? You are not being fair.' He said, 'Don't be upset, General. I will include you in the [refugee resettlement] program.' It's only since then that we could come." It is rare indeed when Vang Pao is in front of any significant group of people and does not say that all Hmong people in the United States owe their new home and their new opportunities to him. Even an otherwise cutting exposé in the Minneapolis *Star Tribune* asserted, "Because of Vang Pao, tens of thousands of Hmong were able to immigrate to the United States after the war."[4]

Dr. Yang Dao met with and sent letters to a number of important individuals, including the French and U.S. ambassadors, the king of Thailand, the presidents of Brazil and Argentina, and the prime minister of Australia. He also frequently mentions a trip he made to Bangkok in August 1975, accompanied by Dr. Shur Vang. There he met with ambassador Charles Whitehouse, CIA station chief Hugh Tovar, and an "immigration officer" at the U.S. embassy, precipitating the October visit to Nam Phong of a U.S. State Department delegation that ultimately permitted the Hmong to migrate to the United States.

Reasoning deductively, and spurred by a sometimes white-hot rivalry that developed in the United States, both men have concluded that their roles were essential: "I advocated for X; X came to pass; therefore I am responsible for X." But the author found no evidence to suggest that the Oval Office initiated or approved policy regarding the status of Hmong refugees, with or without the urging of Vang Pao, or that visits by U.S. representatives to Nam Phong or policies forged as a result of those visits were a direct result of Yang Dao's initiatives.* But it is indeed clear that two visits to Nam Phong in the fall of 1975 opened the doors of greater possibility for Hmong refugees.

---

* It is important to note that I am speaking only about the case of Hmong migration to the United States and not other countries (e.g., France or French Guiana), where figures like Yang Dao may have played a more significant role.

In the beginning, only Jerry Daniels and Mac Thompson, stationed at Udorn, regularly visited Nam Phong. John Tucker, a former USAID Laos worker, joined them in October. All three had little idea what might happen to the Hmong. "My understanding," says Thompson, "is that decisions had been made that the Hmong . . . were not eligible for U.S. resettlement, no real need to send them to the U.S. And that was sort of blanket for all hill tribes."

But in late September, the INS district director from Hong Kong, Sam Feldman, a man with authority to approve requests for immigration, was visiting Udorn. "We were talking about all the . . . groups in Udorn and other places in Thailand," remembers Thompson.

Sam . . . decided he wanted to see what a Hmong was. So Jerry set this up with the Hmong . . . down at Nam Phong . . . [H]ere's a line of Hmong . . . [Imagine talking] with Yang Dao, and [he] says, "Parlez-vous Français?" Sam asked, "Who's this?" "Well," they said, "he's the only PhD Hmong we've got in the world." "Oh, well, he doesn't speak English. Don't need to talk to him." And then there's USAID medic this and then there's major that and captain this and, oh, nurse this—everybody's speaking decent English to fantastic English, down the line for fifty or a hundred people. We were back at Udorn that evening, and Sam's on the phone at the consulate calling back to central office, saying, "I will personally pick twelve hundred Hmong for the U.S. program."

INS central office approved Feldman's proposal. The first Hmong person listed in INS records, Yang Ge, and almost five hundred others, were processed for resettlement on October 1. "At that time," Thompson recalls, "we had no idea there would be any future programs."[5]

Later in October, another visitor came to Nam Phong. Lionel Rosenblatt had spent 1967 to 1969 in Vietnam as a member of the foreign service. In 1970 he was assigned to help reassess old areas of military engagement in the region, including the highlands. "[I]t became very clear how absolutely instrumental the Montagnards were in Vietnam. We'd heard distant stories about the Meo—they were always known as the Meo then—in Laos, and the fact that they were playing a major role in the war, but nothing more than that." Even so, suggests Thompson, that knowledge of "under-the-radar" activity put Rosenblatt in a unique position to seek out people like the Hmong.

While serving on an inter-agency task force (IATF) to investigate the refugee situation in Southeast Asia, Rosenblatt discovered, "By the time the evacuation dust had settled . . . about eleven thousand evacuation admission slots remained unused." Rosenblatt got IATF head Julia Taft's blessing to survey the refugee population in Thailand. The last stop in his survey brought him almost accidentally to the Hmong in Nam Phong. Rosenblatt had no clear idea of how many Hmong refugees there were or what their role had been. His visit left him aghast:

[T]hey had pretty good English, and . . . these American call signs in so many instances—Snowball, Hammer, Bison, Worm, Glassman—people who had clearly worked very closely with the U.S., and played a very heroic role, and seemed as bright and as interested in the outside world as any refugees . . . I got a lot of mileage out of Yang Dao, being able to say, "Hey, here's a guy who has a PhD, and who is just as intellectually competent as any of the best you can see from any of the other Indochinese refugee streams." And they were amazed. Nobody knew there was such a thing as a Hmong PhD . . . We brought his book back to Washington and got it translated, so we began to have an idea of the history of the Hmong—written by a Hmong! And that impressed people . . . I found no reason why they should have to be consigned to the "it's OK to fight and die for the Americans, but you don't want to resettle them" category, which seemed to be where they were. Nobody from the embassy was actually saying that . . . but that was certainly their philosophy. What I saw really just stunned me, in terms of the caseload that was very, very important to take care of.

Perhaps Daniels and Thompson expected some kind of "separate track" for the Hmong, says Rosenblatt, given their special relationship with the United States, but "it was pretty clear to me . . . that there was only this one train leaving the station, and if we were going to start to get a caseload on the agenda, the thing to do was to do it right away."

There was a way to get the Hmong a few seats on the departing train if he could secure the eleven thousand unused evacuation admission slots. To do so, his field report had to be forwarded from the embassy to the IATF in Washington. "The embassy was not enthused," remembers Rosenblatt. "Among others, Ken Quinn, then of the NSC [National Security Council], persuaded the embassy to send the report out." When Rosenblatt returned to Washington, Julia Taft supported his recommendation. "To paraphrase her, history would not look kindly on us if we turned away from the refugees in Thailand when we had money and authorities to help. This was no easy decision given the widespread view in Washington that the evacuation ended the Indochinese problem." This transition from evacuation to refugee program was one of the most important turning points in the saga of the Indochinese refugee crisis.

By December 1975, Rosenblatt secured the eleven thousand unclaimed spots for ethnic refugees in Thailand. There was just one catch: all applicants for migration had to be processed and ready to leave in six months. Rosenblatt, Daniels, Thompson, Tucker, and a number of other instrumental staff, including Rich Kocher, Charlene Day, and Carol Leviton, raced against the clock. While they hastily interviewed and assembled lists of candidates for resettlement, Shep Lowman, an assistant secretary in the bureau of refugee programs, ensured that the proper authorizations were in order.

Lowman, who'd already fled the embassy in Saigon months before, spent the summer of 1975 making a new home for his Vietnamese wife and her family. He returned to Washington "heartsick, of course, as most of us were . . . I wasn't really looking to get involved in the big resettlement effort." When Rosenblatt arrived in the fall to plead his case with Congress, Lowman listened sympathetically but told Rosenblatt flatly, "Unless you go out there yourself and take this on, it's probably not going to happen." As Rosenblatt remembers, Lowman added, "'If you . . . do this . . . you're going to need somebody back here in the State Department to run interference,' and I said, 'More than that, really . . . to be in charge.' And he said, 'Well, who will that be?' And I said, 'It's got to be you, Shep, nobody else.'" The two men shook hands, and the deal was done.

"We were still concerned that the program could be torpedoed by one big gun going against us," says Rosenblatt,

but we had no time to waste. We began to field teams and go through every camp to interview people and pick the eleven thousand most closely associated with [the U.S. government]. At that point, to explain all this to the Hmong, we sat down and said, "We want to hear from you. What are your aspirations?" . . . [I]f you went down the list of their choices, it was first to go back to Laos together, armed . . . [T]hey had a list of arms they presented to us, which we refused to look at . . . [S]econd, to be armed and staying in Thailand to protect themselves against the local Communists and forays from Laos; third, to go somewhere (preferably in the United States, if they had to go to another country) like an Indian reservation or an Eskimo area, and then finally, the choice we gave them, which was not on their list, which was to go to the United States and be resettled, but to be dispersed across the country to individual sponsors.

Harold "Hal" Meinheit, originally assigned to Bangkok in 1974 as a political officer in the U.S embassy, was pulled literally overnight from his responsibilities in counterinsurgency and counter-narcotics to work with refugees.

[T]he U.S. was not prepared to respond to the growing refugee crisis . . . As refugees continued to come to the embassy seeking support, there was nothing we could do but report on the problem and ask for authority to move people to the U.S. . . . [Our] position at that time was that any refugee arriving in Thailand was the responsibility of the Thai government and the United Nations. The Thai government viewed this as a U.S. problem, and the . . . UNHCR . . . office in Bangkok was not prepared to deal effectively with the problem at this early stage.

One way to simplify matters for refugees who demonstrated a clear connection to the United States and its military objectives in Southeast Asia was to expand the U.S. attorney general's "parole authority," waiving the normal requirements and procedures for immigration. "There were three categories eligible for parole: (1) family reunification cases; (2) former U.S. [government] employees; and (3) high-risk refugees. With parole authority, our work became somewhat more regular, determining which refugees met the conditions for parole."[6]

The Hmong, says Rosenblatt, were kept as part of the larger "ex-Lao" category of refugees to avoid the attention of those who opposed Hmong resettlement. "There was . . . the group that said they were . . . qualified to fight for us [but] were too primitive in one way or another to . . . live with us; or they had a good chance of just fading happily ever after into the Thai woodwork (which we thought was total hogwash) or that they didn't want to go anyway. And once we had pierced those various arguments, and left it up to individual families, then it was pretty easy."

Next, Rosenblatt's team "developed this rather intricate but fair and workable point system. We gave points for . . . everything from length of service to whether somebody had been wounded to the kind of service they performed, and the Hmong in the north still came out ahead of most of the Lao and most of the Cambodians." In thirty minutes "an experienced officer . . . could quickly 'point up' a case and say, 'We're going to assign eighteen points to this case'—and the cut line . . . is going to be, let's say sixteen—and present them to INS."

Hmong were interviewed by ethnic affairs officers (EAOs), usually Daniels, Tucker, Thompson, or someone working for them, before being sent on for prescreening. "From '75 on to at least '80 or '81," says

Thompson, "our EAOs . . . would select which cases were going to be presented to INS. And for the most part, [we] interviewed every family in the camps to, [to] some extent, verify their stories."

"Jerry was the most knowledgeable about what individual Hmong had done," says Rosenblatt, "and ferreting out people who were misrepresenting, which you always have in any caseload . . . [E]very family that was interested in going had to be interviewed from scratch, and records kept." There would be times, says Tucker, when Daniels "would throw his hands up and say, 'There is no way in hell these people could be related by blood.' And he would sense that somebody was trying to pull over a second wife in the family at the same time . . . [But] with so many adult males killed during the war years . . . [many] minor kids who were incorporated into the family unit were legitimate cases because they *were* nephews of the head of the family or nieces." Daniels would have to sort out the legitimate cases from the frauds trying to buy their way in.

While Dennis Grace has no recollection of the practice, most other refugee workers of this period remember being assigned the task of determining which Hmong in the camps had been allies of the United States. As one recounts,

I usually started out with basic things: "Which unit did you belong to, and who was your battalion commander, and which company were you in?" and all this sort of thing. The higher-ranking officers [were] much easier. In the vast majority of cases, there weren't many problems . . . Geography was the next test: did they really know the area they claimed to come from, and was it logical that they would have gone into this or that [unit]? . . . This was a learning experience for me . . . I used a lot of the old guard to educate me about who was who and doing what and going where.

Boua Long, who now lives outside Melbourne, Australia, recalls being shown photos of grenade launchers, rifles, and other military equipment—sometimes from the side, other times from the front or the top—and asked to identify them, "just to make sure I was a soldier." Even so, says Tucker, at least a few refugees spent days peering through the latticework dividers

to see what was going on and try to overhear the interviews to get a jump on them. In fact, there were little schools . . . like "You, too, can be an SGU." At night, after we would all leave the camp, there would be training sessions . . . primarily [for] young kids . . . to give them some basic military training or learn how to answer the questions, to . . . come up with a fake military history kind of thing . . . [E]ven [strong

*candidates] would bring letters to prove that they had relatives in the States . . .
[W]e'd have our interpreters read [them] to us, and there would be things like "This
is what you say when Tucker comes to interview you." So we had to contend with attempts like that to get into the program.*

Tucker was the EAO for ethnic Lao refugees, though he also worked
with the Hmong when caseloads were especially heavy or Daniels was
on leave. As he recalls, the records collected for applicants were
painstakingly kept, verified, and double- or even triple-checked. If
there was any discrepancy—if, for example, a brother who had already
gone to America did not mention this particular person in his own
file—the application would be sent back for more information.

In 1977, Shep Lowman watched from Washington as the refugee
crisis across Southeast Asia grew more critical. One day Judy
Chavchavadze, a civil servant in his office, commented to him, "'You
know, Shep, you just aren't going to be able to do this unless you get
some help outside this building . . .' That thought stuck in my head."
Lowman eventually turned to Leo Cherne, chairman of the International Rescue Committee, describing the unfolding situation. "Leo
asked, 'Why are you telling me this?' And I said, 'I don't really know. I
just am frustrated and worried and thought you might have some
thoughts.' And he said, 'Well, yes, I do.'" Cherne organized a citizens'
committee, including a broad cross-section of volunteer members, who
paid their own way to visit refugee areas and investigate the situation.
As a result of their recommendations, "the IRC provided Bob DeVecchi,
who . . . went out as a staffer and became the first Joint Voluntary
Agency [JVA] director."

JVA was a unit within an existing American refugee resettlement
NGO. Each country hosting refugees had one JVA. The first, in Thailand,
was run by the IRC. Each JVA coordinated an intensive refugee interview
process, carefully prepared files for INS interviews, supervised the Intergovernmental Committee for European Migration*—the agency that
conducted medical screening and transportation of refugees approved

---

* ICEM, the Intergovernmental Committee for European Migration, "would interface with the
Thai government in getting the refugees medically cleared and moving them to Bangkok," says
John Tucker. "We had holding areas in Bangkok where they came from the camps once they
were sponsored and then moved out to the airport for the flights on to the States." ICEM was led
by Albert Corcos, a seasoned veteran of work with refugees. "He kept trying to retire from ICEM
and go and play golf and boat in France," says Shep Lowman. "We kept drafting him back." ICEM
is now called IOM—the International Organization for Migration.

for resettlement—and sent reports both specific and general to the offices of agencies who provided all manner of services in the camps.

The Hmong and other refugees were aided by a small number of key individuals who could have ignored what they saw or in some cases even received commendation from those wanting to discourage refugee relocation. Instead, they followed their convictions, whether they had a history with the Hmong people or not. Through their efforts, the Hmong were given opportunities many had initially opposed.

CHANGES AND MORE CHANGES

Nam Phong had provided the Hmong with a stable environment for six months. Unlike other places the Hmong would stay, it was comparatively uncrowded, and people enjoyed more freedom of movement. Lee Pao Xiong remembers Nam Phong through a child's eyes: "There was a pond with lots of crocodiles, and also a tank there. I remember us climbing that tank . . . [L]ife there was good." But by late 1975, as plans to resettle Hmong in the United States were being finalized, Nam Phong, never intended to serve as a long-term holding area for refugees, was closed. Four years later, authorities also closed the Hmong section of Nong Khai. Residents of both these camps were moved into an area that became home—whether for months or for many years—to most Hmong who now live in Western countries: Ban Vinai.*

Paul Herr had studied in Vientiane and could speak and write Thai. To avoid cooking duties at Nam Phong, he became an assistant to Thai administrators. "The Thai government actually came in saying '[Nam Phong] is only a temporary holding place . . . We will find a permanent place for you.' So I think they went to many different locations, and none of them were accepted." Indeed, says Yang See, the Thai government initially wanted to send the Hmong in Nam Phong "to a location in an inner province far from the . . . Lao border."† Clearly the Thai saw a Hmong presence so close to Laos as unnecessarily provocative. At last, says Paul Herr, all parties agreed on "a place up in a flat area . . .

* Ban is a Thai word meaning "village." Many simply call it "Vinai."

† Yang See says the Hmong representatives on these exploratory trips were "Colonel Ly Tou Pao, the new president of Nam Phong refugee camp, his second deputy, Colonel Tou Long Yang, and Colonel Shoua Yang."

surrounded by mountains, very close to the Mekong River outside Pak Chom district. [They] called [it] Ban Vinai . . . They said, 'This is a good place for you to stay,' because no one else wanted it." The camp leaders at Nam Phong agreed to visit the proposed site. "I didn't go, but I was actually typing the names, the documents, everything . . . They came back, and they said, 'OK. That's a good place for us to go' . . . [M]y quarter [of the camp] volunteered to go first. So I ended up doing all the paperwork, typing days and nights and then listing all the people going, [bus manifests], etc."

The Hmong brought to Vinai often built their own homes. Cy Thao, now a Minnesota state representative, remembers making the move from Nong Khai to Ban Vinai as a boy of about five. Even at that tender age, he and a few of his friends were put to work digging postholes. "They kind of hired us . . . Five years old, trying to dig a hole and make some money!" says Thao, laughing.

"Ban Vinai was basically just forest," remembers Paul Herr. "We ended up cutting all the trees and building the playground, school, church—everything was done by the refugees." Long houses, each with ten rooms, were built; each room was meant to hold about ten people. "So if your family only has three [people in it], then you have three families living in one room . . . At first, they contracted with local Thai to come and build those houses. So [what] we called section one was pretty much built by the Thai. After that . . . the Hmong people . . . really knew how to build, so the Thai actually contracted us to build houses. Many houses in section numbers two, three, four, five . . . were built by us, even myself." But Thai middlemen, who held the government building contracts, made most of the money: "They probably got paid like a hundred baht a day, whereas they paid Hmong thirty-five baht a day."

"I remember that the houses were wooden houses, and they were all on stilts, 'cause [Vinai] is on a hill," says Lee Pao Xiong.

[A]nd they would put us in these temporary houses . . . There wasn't any place for a kitchen, so . . . the Hmong men went and cut down some of the grass and started big cooking houses . . . And at that time in 1975, '76, people could still go to places. There was no fenced area. People were allowed to go and forage for food. That's one of the things [I remember]—foraging for mushrooms after a rain. We would go and pick mushrooms and bamboo shoots, and also go and fish. There was a little creek that meandered through—but the leeches were terrible! . . . [W]e would also go and ask

The rhythms of life in the camps included regular visits from United Nations trucks supplying food and water. When their arrival was expected, children, who often had little else to do, fought to hold a place in line for their families.

Thai farmers if we could work as laborers, as migrant workers, and work in their fields. So I can understand some of the Hispanic migrant workers here [in the United States] . . . Maybe that's where my advocacy . . . comes from!

Minnesota state senator Mee Moua's father was a medic during the war. Her family was also transferred to Ban Vinai in 1975, first living in a temporary camp. She remembers attending one of the schools established there, instructed by Hmong who were teachers in Laos:

In addition to the notebook and pencils that you were supposed to take with you, each parent was supposed to bring a really long bamboo . . . [W]e were contributing . . . so that they could . . . build another school hall.

I remember standing in line for the mess hall to go get food . . . I had these little girl-friends, because the parents didn't want to come and stand in line . . . [W]e would have our legs and our arms out like this [stretches them out as far as she can reach], and that was to reserve that space for when our parents showed up . . . [W]hen we went to the permanent camp, I remember that I used to go stand in line to get wa-ter, 'cause there was one well in the camp, and I would go stand in line to get water . . . I would bring my tin water carrier with a strap on it, and I would put water in it, and I would put it on my back. But I didn't know how to do it . . . [B]y the time I got home I would get a really good bath and there was not much water left—until I got a little bit older, and I carried two tins on a stick.

While hundreds of Hmong families settled once again into an unfamiliar environment for an unspecified period of time, they were unaware that the Thai government, often viewed as an oppressor, was reeling from the repercussions of accepting refugees from Vietnam,

Laos, and Cambodia. Karen refugees from Burma would also arrive in 1984. "Thailand was besieged," remembers Jim Anderson,

and their initial reaction was the same as any country to a large wave of what they considered to be undocumented illegal immigrants—and that is, "No, you can't come in here." But [this attitude] was also in the context of a very dicey situation . . . [By early 1979] Cambodian refugees were being chased to the border . . . by Vietnamese troops, so the dreaded Vietnamese army was literally at their doorstep, and there was very little doubt that if the Vietnamese had wanted . . . they could march right in to Thailand . . . It was definitely a national security situation, and they were able to parlay the refugee crisis into a ton of international agreements for their own national security's sake: agreements with the United States . . . [and] China, who was backing the Khmer Rouge [in Cambodia and] was seeking Thai access to be able to supply [them].

The Chinese and Vietnamese were also exerting pressure from within, providing material and logistical assistance to the Communist Party of Thailand (CPT). The struggle all but completed in Laos by 1975 was still at high pitch in Thailand. The situation deteriorated further in 1976 when, on October 4, students at Thammasat University protested the return of exiled former dictator Thanom Kittikachorn—a man whose departure in 1973 was largely a result of student activism. At least two newspapers covering the protests the next day included a doctored photo of figures burning in effigy, including one made to closely resemble the crown prince. On October 6, about four thousand soldiers and vigilantes, egged on by the photo, attacked the campus, shooting, beating, lynching, even raping indiscriminately. After the carnage was over, a military junta seized power while many students fled to the jungles controlled by the CPT, breathing new life into the resistance.[7]

The upsurge in strife between the left and right could only hurt the pro-royalist Hmong in Thailand's refugee camps. Despite training and support from the Thai government and Thai "volunteers" during the war, they could now be associated with Communist Thai Hmong. In addition to the secrecy surrounding their activities in Laos, the Hmong were buried under the widespread media coverage of the Vietnamese boat people and the Cambodian killing fields.

To make matters worse, economic conditions in Laos, especially a drought in 1977 followed by floods in 1978, encouraged many ethnic Lao, Hmong, and Vietnamese to seek better prospects elsewhere. The Thai government and the UNHCR began to suspect people were being

"pulled" across the border by news that their countrymen were resettling in more prosperous and stable countries. Thai citizens who lived
near camps grew increasingly angry as they saw UN trucks bringing food
and supplies to refugees. Most of this resentment, says Dennis Grace,
was along the Thai-Cambodian border,

*where people had been impoverished for a long, long time . . . Suddenly, you'd see cars
flashing by and relatively well-dressed people moving by and a lot of money being
spent and restaurants mushrooming to feed the foreigners . . . The average Thai was
little affected by [the refugee influx], financially or otherwise. It didn't bring war to
his doorstep; it didn't bring great wealth . . . It was an annoyance for them, more than
a great, great burden. And it's important that people understand that it was not because of refugee outflow that Thailand got on its feet . . . Thais were already disposed
through four hundred years of very effective diplomacy and enlightened monarchs to
. . . get along in a way that benefited Thailand as much as the other side.*

Of greater concern to the Thai government was the apparent waning
interest of Western countries. The United States saw a backlash against
immigration, sparked in part by the post-Vietnam economic and political crises it was experiencing and in part because eight hundred thousand immigrants—more than all immigrants to all other countries in
the world—came to America in 1980. Congress passed the Refugee Act
of 1980. While it created an office of refugee resettlement to coordinate
efforts with nongovernmental agencies willing to help with the effort, it
also empowered INS officers to determine on a case-by-case basis
whether an individual or a family unit qualified for refugee status. Prior
to this act, INS officers presumed that if "you had gotten off that boat
or you had come across from Laos, you were a refugee," says Grace. "If
you are a Hmong, and you've been in a reeducation camp . . . [or y]our
brother was in it . . . you have a well-founded fear of persecution." But as
the years went by, cases became less clear. "If those who had suffered in
a certain village come out in the first year and then later people hear
about it and they come out, and later people hear that those who heard
about it are off now in America in Minnesota or Santa Ana, 'maybe we
should go, too.' It starts to get more complicated. But the Refugee Act
of 1980 really had INS focus on the responsibilities that the law had
given it . . . And that stopped everything in its tracks as far as the pre-
sumption of refugee status." It also created a new and difficult unofficial responsibility for numerous refugee workers who had become well-
acquainted with the communities they were serving.[8]

"INS would come in and make the final determination as to who was going and who was not," remembers Anderson. "And unlike for the Hmong, for a lot of the Cambodian refugees and Vietnamese refugees it was very difficult . . . The INS came in with a 'border defense' mentality, and it was their job not to provide easy access to the United States . . . [They] had a very, very strict constructionist view of their role there, and basically it was to keep the stop sign up . . . So we found ourselves pretty dramatically opposed to what INS was doing."

"Most of the people on the JVA side . . . [had]a real interest in seeing these people get out of the camps," says Grace. "[F]or INS, some of them came out of the enforcement side . . . They're bound to follow the law . . . They're going to look at it with a longer view, less open to emotion." As a result, the refugee camps of Thailand became a testing ground for the Refugee Act of 1980. JVA workers did everything in their power to advocate for refugees, while INS officers did their best to interpret the law as they understood it and to remind JVA staff that, by law, the final decision rested with INS.

"We naturally thought that a lot of the INS decisions were arbitrary," says Win McKeithen, a USAID Laos staffer who worked for the State Department's Office of Refugee Affairs from 1979 to 1981, "but they could be appealed. The head of INS was Jack Fortner—a very capable guy . . . He had some cowboys under him. And so we were often able to take a case to Jack and get it reversed or get another hearing."

"It certainly didn't shake out where the good guys were JVA and the bad guys were INS," says Grace. "One might feel it's a gatekeeper on one side, an advocate on the other. At times, it felt like that, but over the long run, it was truly a cooperative effort."

Mac Thompson and Jim Anderson remember INS staff less charitably. Anderson recalls a particular officer who kept a length of two-by-four at his side. Any time he heard an answer he didn't like, he slammed it on the table, terrifying his interviewees. It also became "official" policy, says Anderson, to force families, even the aged and infirm, to stand during their entire interview. "In general," says Thompson, "the INS people I worked with were a bunch of cretins, Neanderthals . . . [T]hey were too glorified in their authority, in approving and rejecting people . . . Jerry and John and I probably rejected more people than INS did . . . But many of the INS people sat there just happily rejecting people—and, god, it still bothers the shit out of me."

In 1981, in an effort to stop the influx of refugees, Thailand instituted a policy of "humane deterrence"—providing the barest minimum
of services and food rations to refugee camps and offering no hope for
resettlement to third countries. Hmong and others who were actually
fleeing reeducation or jungle resistance camps fought the increasing
suspicion that they were economic opportunists rather than political
refugees. More and more were robbed by angry Thai citizens as they
reached the Thai side of the Mekong River. More and more Thai police
officers sent back to Laos the Hmong they intercepted. And the pro-
cessing centers where Hmong waited to make application to the UN became infamous for their squalor. Kao Kalia Yang vividly recalls one such
place in her memoir, *The Latehomecomer:*

> [T]he UN people told the family they would be taken in a bus to So Kow Toe [Sob
> Tuang, in Nan province], a place where refugees were temporarily placed until fur-
> ther arrangements could be made . . . So Kow Toe . . . was also fenced in, this time not
> with barbed wires but high aluminum walls. The dominant feature of the camp was
> the stench of feces. There were toilets, but they were all flooded. There were no trees
> . . . Twice a day . . . [e]ach Hmong person could only get one ladle of soup, and peo-
> ple had to share cups and bowls and plates and various containers, anything they
> could find that might hold food.[9]

Wa Yang, whose family was forced to spend two months or more in
Sob Tuang, remembers it with revulsion: "That is the worst place I have
ever lived in my life." Because of the aluminum fence, "you could only
see ground and sky." The rest of the outside world was completely oblit-
erated from view. For people who were extremely shy and private, it
was deeply humiliating to urinate or defecate in the open. And though
they struggled to keep even a small area clean, people slept "only ten,
twenty feet away" from piles of human waste.

According to Anderson, Thailand periodically would announce, "All
right, that's it! We're closing the border!. . . We're going to let the U.S.
embassy come up here, and they're going to interview you for resettlement. If you don't take it this time, this is your last chance' . . . And the
Hmong, for their own reasons, would take that with a grain of salt, and
then six months later they would get their next 'last' warning. And that
went on every year." At the same time that Thai officials kept threatening to close access to third countries, elders connected to the resistance kept delaying their family's departure. It was a dangerous game
to be playing with the lives of so many people, but the Thais had made

Seexeng Lee (the second-youngest child) and his brothers pose for a picture in Ban Vinai refugee camp.

threats so often, says Anderson, that the Hmong "absolutely stopped believing it entirely. And so when the Thais, in the early nineties, finally moved to actually start closing camps, they didn't believe it then either, until it was too late."

"By the early eighties," says Grace,

the number of camps in Thailand was at least a dozen. And it became, from the Thai perspective, . . . a magnet that created an ongoing problem [continued influx and support for the resistance in Laos] . . . [T]hey wanted to be cooperative to the U.S. and other countries that were still interested in resettling people, but that meant to consolidate the populations, make it easier and to understand that those who were in a refugee camp are there because they want to resettle elsewhere . . . A lot of those people actually wanted what was not available, and that was local integration . . . Thais wanted them to either go home or resettle: "You're not going to stay here . . ." So it started with closing Chiang Khong, Chiang Kham, Nan, consolidate inside Ban Vinai. And that lasted five or six years or so inside Ban Vinai. And then, "OK, we've got to close Ban Vinai."

By 1992, Ban Vinai had closed. Options were dwindling for Hmong who wanted to stay in Thailand and wait for conditions to improve in Laos. One place of refuge was a Buddhist temple or wat called Tham Krabok, which offered a treatment program for opium addicts. As time passed and other options evaporated, a community of Hmong began to settle near the wat, protected by its abbot, who had significant pull with the Thai government. For those who still refused to resettle in a Western country, Wat Tham Krabok provided one last hope that they could stay in Thailand long enough to walk back into a "liberated" Laos.

CHOICES

There were essentially three options for Hmong accepted into a refugee camp: apply for migration to a third country, stay in camp for an indeterminate period of time, or secretly return to Laos to fight against the new government and the Vietnamese soldiers who by 1977 were mobilized to fight against the Chao Fa. The last two options were often inextricably linked and probably had some impact on Ban Vinai's organization and appearance. "Ban Vinai looked very rough compared to some of the other camps, less orderly, just not as well kept or provided for," says Grace. Unlike the ethnic Lao camps, "the Hmong wanted to go home . . . Very little Lao [was] spoken in the Hmong camp . . . And Ban Vinai stayed the same, pretty much, until it closed . . . [T]hey never lost the heightened interest in returning to [Laos]."

Anyone considering migration wrestled with numerous considerations. First, could Australia, France, the United States, or some other country really ever be home? Informing the head of a Hmong household of his options, recalls Thompson, usually started with a few jarring facts. He might ask, "'How many Hmong are there in [the city where I'm going]?' 'Well, zero.' 'Who's there?' 'Well, a lot of Americans.' 'How many of those people speak Hmong?' And this guy had been a USAID bulldozer operator. He didn't speak English . . . 'Zero.' 'Oh, well, I'm not sure if I really want to go.'"

One might assume that many Hmong were too angry toward the United States to ever think of migrating there, but Anderson observed surprisingly little rancor:

Some of these folks had been actively fighting since they were twelve years old, and now were grandparents—young grandparents . . . Very rarely did I ever encounter

anybody that blamed the U.S. Most ... insist[ed] that they were grateful for the as-
sistance that the U.S. provided to them, but really what they were doing was fight-
ing for their own cause ... [T]hose in the know ... who had really been through a
lot ... with some of these folks, were much more adamant ... that we basically
turned our back on them ... But I rarely heard that from the Hmong themselves.

Polygamy, a part of Hmong culture and society for centuries, posed another thorny obstacle to migration. Given the United States' own struggles with plural marriage during the days of Joseph Smith and Brigham Young, there was no room for interpretation in American law. "Our policy," says Thompson, "was [that] the head of family would choose ... his wife that he'd apply for the U.S. program with ... And then if he had one or two or three others, we said, 'OK. They and their children have to come up with a resettlement solution on their own before we will process the original head of family' ... And whether that ... is going to France, going to the U.S. on their own, remarriage in camp, or whatever, if that took one or two or five years, that was the rule."

"With INS, you wanted to be sure that it wasn't just a charade for the purposes of an interview," observes Grace. "[Y]ou'd say, 'OK, look ... you must understand U.S. law does not permit one man to enter the country with two wives *or* for a man to live in the U.S. with two wives ... [Y]ou're going to have to have one wife on your family tree and stand a certain test of time—six months or twelve months ... [I]f we do this charade and you go off to wherever—California, Montana, wherever— you get into problems there, and you can end up in jail.'" But the question remained: would polygamous Hmong families stay separate once they migrated to Western countries, or would some reunite, living together as "in-laws" or "relatives" without ever revealing their secret?

Ambivalence about leaving Thailand was further magnified by uncertainty about the political future of Laos, concern about family members unaccounted for, and many other unanswered questions. Might General Vang Pao return and invade Laos? Might the stories of an impending revolution in the jungles actually be true, and might that revolution succeed? These concerns, as well as a desire to help each other maintain their way of life and defend themselves against exploiters and predators, kept many Hmong in the camps for years. Captain Joua Bee Vang, for example, could have left for the United States almost immediately in 1975, but stayed in Thailand until 1988.

Pao Lee, whose family had survived the shootings at Hin Heup, suggests that many Hmong stayed in camp because of numerous rumors, perhaps the result of news from a Western country that was blown out of proportion or intentional misinformation spread by those seeking to preserve a Hmong beachhead in Thailand in case a military opportunity opened up back in Laos.

At that time, it was darkness from four corners. You see nothing . . . A lot of people . . . went to America, and they sent news back saying, "[I]t's not that hard. You can survive, you can find a job, and there are people over there that look after you," so when we heard that news, it made us a little bit happy . . . But . . . [others] went to Argentina, and those people sent news back, saying, . . . "[I]t's not good at all . . . They just put us to the farm working as slaves." [S]o they stopped interviewing to go there . . . [and] the people from there started to move to French Guiana . . . [T]here was so much news going around, and some of the news made you very scared; you don't want to go anywhere. And that's why . . . some people that now still live in Thailand . . . were scared, because they said, "Oh, you cannot trust the people that go overseas. Some of them lie" . . . [T]hey don't want the people in the camp there to move anyway, because . . . [they] thought—if people there moved into a third country and then they have no people to . . . [help them] go back to Laos. So they tried to make news to make people scared, so people would not go.

The Hmong, less eager than others to move to America, often stayed in the camps for months, even years, during which they strove to maintain their cultural practices. In a ceremony shown here, the shaman "rides the bench" while blindfolded, seeking contact with the spirit world.

Whatever the reason might have been, remembers Anderson,

Most still had the dream of recapturing an independent lifestyle in the hills of Laos
. . . and they knew that life would be so much different in the United States than . . .
they were prepared for . . . [Many] felt it was probably a good idea at least to have a
file [with the UN], but . . . after they got approved, and the buses would arrive in camp,
they simply wouldn't show up. And these were interview approvals that started back
in 1978, '79. When we were interviewing them in '81, '82, '83, they were coming
back and we [asked], "Why didn't you go the last time?" . . . and they'd say, "Well, we
were told by our parents or grandparents back in Laos that our cousin was coming
out, and we needed to stay and wait for them." In one [case] . . . the family said, "We
were ready to go . . . and we were walking from our house down to . . . where the buses
were, and a snake crossed the path, and it stopped in the middle of the path.* We tried
to shoo it away, and it wouldn't move. So we knew then that it wasn't just a snake:
it was the spirit of our grandparents telling us that we weren't allowed to go yet,
that we had a cousin who had not yet come out, and that it was our obligation to
wait for him." So I asked them, "Well, what happens this time if a snake crosses the
path?" and they said, "Well, then it's just a snake, because our cousin is already here."
So there were lots of reasons, but for most, either the father or grandfather was a
former soldier who still felt a military obligation to be available to carry on the fight
. . . and recapture what they had lost.

One of the things that constantly amazed me was we'd have these very, very
bright, young interpreters, often married with children of their own, who weren't
applying for resettlement. I'd say, "It seems like you would do extraordinarily well
in the United States," and they would say, "My father or grandfather says no, we're
not going." There wasn't any sense of, "I have the right to question that in any way"
. . . The rule of the family leader was absolute.

The high rate of Hmong no-shows led to frustration in some circles. "[L]ots of our American people and the Thai were really upset," remembers Thompson.

And on the American side, "Oh, look at all this wasted money, the wasted resources;
only one-third of the people that came up for prescreening have gone." And my atti-
tude was "We are not running a forced U.S. resettlement program . . . I'm not going
to go up there and dynamite them out of their hooches to get on the bloody bus . . .
They'll be around later—if there's a continual program" . . . I was never a real strong
proponent for U.S. resettlement of the Lao or the Hmong or the Yao or the other
highlanders. My [greater] concern was . . . that people who fled Laos for decent rea-
sons should be allowed a first asylum in Thailand . . . [R]esettlement in Thailand
was really the best solution [for most]—common language, no snow like Min-
neapolis . . . [B]ut to ensure first asylum in Thailand, a certain number of people had

---

* Hmong have traditionally believed that a snake crossing one's path signals danger.

Uncertainty was the rule: a Hmong girl looks away as her family is interviewed for relocation to a new country.

to leave Thailand. You know, keep the Thai government, their embassy, their ministry of interior happy. To allow an influx of the five thousand, one thousand had to leave, sort of showing the flag.

For those who remained in a refugee camp, life seemed to stand still. Most who lived in the camps as adults have little to say about their experiences. It was a time of drudgery, inactivity, and death. Funeral drums reverberated throughout the camp almost every night. And in some areas, at some times, Thai guards were looking for easy prey. "In Vinai," says Pa Sher Yang,

we were afraid of the Thai . . . As I see it, since we ran from a war, first they wanted to get girlfriends; that was the main reason. The second reason was wanting to rape

young women, and the third was to steal money. But though we didn't have
weapons, we were well prepared . . . At nighttime we rounded up the young boys to
keep watch . . . I taught signal noises to everyone . . . By doing that we were able to
help each other . . . [T]he Thai came, but when the noise was made, everyone rose
together so Thai couldn't do anything bad to us.

Other Hmong say the Thai guards, while tough and sometimes
mean, were not predatory. "The Thai authorities were nice because
they were paid by the United Nations," asserts Pa Seng Thao. "They
weren't too strict unless we tried to sneak out of the camp perimeter.
The Thai told us that they couldn't help us if we were kidnapped or hurt
by bandits outside of the camps. Those who traveled outside of the
camps had to have written permission. The Thais were pretty fair unless the crowd became rowdy; then they beat everyone. They were fair,
and that's all there was to it."

The few opportunities available to work or simply be active were
highly coveted. "From the main road into Ban Vinai and that section
right before that," remembers Paul Herr,

the older people built a blacksmith [shop]. They made their own knives and their
own things to help themselves. You'd see twenty, thirty people—it doesn't matter
how hot it was . . . and you could hear all the noises. And next to that there was a
hospital, and that's where my first son was born . . . We had many volunteers. We
had many nurses and even a few doctors at the time . . . [T]he Hmong taught them-
selves how to improve, to be nurses, and they taught a lot of the younger generation
of people, who didn't have anything to do, to become nurses.

Indeed, remembers Chuck Whitney, director of Ban Vinai hospital
for several years,

We had an outpatient facility where we could see a hundred to two hundred outpa-
tients a day . . . [and an] inpatient facility with five wards . . . And that's where the
students that I originally trained worked, as nursing assistants on those wards . . .
I had a classroom; I taught in English [with a] translator . . . The classroom was
jammed . . . [T]hey were so eager to learn that the ones who weren't in the class stood
outside the windows studying, too . . . [T]hey ended up being very, very good nurs-
ing assistants. We gave them expanded duties so they could give injections, they
could start IVs, they could do stuff like that.

Eagerness to escape boredom and purposelessness, says Nhia Lor
Vang, was one reason resistance activities flourished in Vinai. "We were
herded like pigs in there. There was really nothing to do . . . and no way
to educate yourself, to progress. So it was easy for people to come up

with some great ideas and have a huge following." When Americans started showing up in the camp, it seemed to indicate they might be supporting resistance activity somehow. By 1984, Vang went into Laos on several occasions with two men he assumed were CIA, though their behavior suggests otherwise: "They didn't look like the type of men who were in the field at all . . . They would take pictures with us, but they would wear . . . something like a military uniform . . . When they were done, they'd just take that shirt off and put it back in the bag . . . and wear their civilian clothes." It is doubtful that anyone from the CIA would have wanted to be photographed.

One of the only ways to stay busy and earn money in the refugee camps—for men as well as women—was to engage in the Hmong handicraft of paj ntaub, or needlework.

Hmong who were children in Vinai often remember it more fondly than do their parents. Despite the hardship they and their families endured, Vinai was the last place Hmong people got to "be Hmong" in a way that was similar to their lives in Laos. For the children of Vinai, these experiences and memories were the closest thing to "the old country" they would ever know. It bound them to their elders and their heritage in ways that would be broken once Hmong children were raised in Western countries. "I remember being [in the United States] and reading . . . the story of the Three Little Pigs—the brick home lasted the longest," says Kao Kalia Yang. "And to know that my home was never meant to last . . . [and] that when the seasons changed that these things would fall down and they would never rise again, it's powerful stuff . . . I'm a refugee from Southeast Asia; somebody else [who] grew up in a tent in Africa says "I'm a refugee, too." And we share the fact that our homes were never meant to last, and there's this need to remember . . . It's a part of my identity."

Chou (now Peter) Vang spent his early childhood in Ban Vinai, along with about thirty family members. His father, Nhia Lor Vang,

went across the border to fight the Communists in Laos. I guess by that time they were considered Chao Fa, because they weren't really supported by the U.S. government anymore. But I know that he got paid for doing that, and then he also . . . worked at this butcher shop in the refugee camp. So he usually brought home scraps of food . . . So I was kind of spoiled compared to the standard, because my dad . . . would find enough money to usually buy me little treats . . . [M]y parents said that we usually didn't have a lot to eat, but as a little kid I don't remember being starved or anything like that . . . I'm pretty sure it was hard for them, but I don't remember any hardship.

Still, Chou managed to create hardship of his own. As he recalls, a Thai merchant used to come into camp to collect scrap metal. He used a little siren to attract children. If they brought him old tin cans or other items, he would give them a few pieces of hard candy. One day, Chou heard the siren but didn't find anything he could use, so he looked through the kitchen: "I took a bunch of my mother's nice pots, and I took it to the guy . . . I think those were my mom's prized pots, and it was really expensive to get those, especially when you were a refugee . . . I remember the guy looking at me kind of funny, but he took it. So he gave me six or seven candies for it. When my mom got home and found out what happened, I got a good beating. And I think those candy were the *best* candy I ever had!"

Mai Lee Yang's family moved from Nam Phong to Ban Vinai, where they finally lived under one roof. Having established a reasonable semblance of peace, they settled into the everyday routines of a refugee family. But there was no doubt in Mai Lee's mind: if her father left for America, he would take his second wife, not her mother, with him. One day her father and stepmother were outside of the camp working for Thai farmers. As they boarded a bus to return to Vinai, her stepmother saw a cousin who had studied abroad on a scholarship and earned a

Even in the camps there were bustling markets, blacksmith shops, and other familiar institutions that helped bring a sense of normalcy to refugees of the Secret War.

master's degree. He was returning to conduct research for his PhD, accompanied by a Thai guide. Mai Lee, tending to her hospitalized younger sister, returned home at dusk. Her father and their new guests had departed, but their luggage was in her room. "My stepmother just told me, 'Tonight we have an uncle who came from overseas . . . I have no room . . . so they will sleep with you.'" The men returned after she had gone to bed. In her sleep, Mai Lee pulled the blanket off her sister, who began to cry. When the "uncle" got up to investigate, he saw a blanketed figure he assumed to be an old woman in need of warmth and a young child with no covers. He surrendered his own blanket, shivering through the rest of the night under a mosquito net.

Mai Lee was up early in the morning to do her chores. She was about to return to the hospital when her stepmother asked her to fetch water for their guests. "I opened the door, and the two of them were up already . . . I said, 'Mom told me to take this water to you to wash your face.' They were just staring at me . . . And [the guide asked my uncle], 'Who is that?' He said, 'I don't know!' And after they washed their faces and dried them, I just grabbed my basket and went straight to the hospital."

Unbeknownst to Mai Lee, her "uncle" had come to Vinai to marry. After bringing his own extended family to Australia in 1976, his mother brought him the picture of a Hmong girl. She wanted to come to Australia but had no blood relatives in the country. Perhaps, his mother suggested, he could marry her. In Vinai, he sought her out. After they got to know each other better, he asked her to marry him, but to his surprise she said no. After all his time and effort, growing attracted to her and thinking he was rescuing her from the camp, both the girl and her mother said no. "After I tried twice, I just thought 'maybe they don't like me.'"

During the courtship, he stayed with Mai Lee's family.

Then I found out that [Mai Lee's father] had a first wife . . . who was stuck in enemy territory . . . [H]e came out as a soldier of Vang Pao to Long Tieng and then married my cousin, and all that time never told us about this wife that was left behind.

So after that other girl said no to me, [my] Thai friend . . . said, "You should marry this girl [Mai Lee], not that one! This is the one for you." And I started looking at her in a different way . . . I was very attracted to her, but . . . she was only fifteen—and very shy . . . I only had a year in Thailand, and I had to go back to work. And I wanted my wife to go with me to the Hmong village there so I had somebody to cook and keep me company.

One day, Mai Lee was babysitting her sister and brother when her uncle appeared. Courtship was the last thing on her mind. "I didn't have any boyfriends because I was too young. I did have some young men [who] liked me, but it was only like puppy love." She invited her uncle to come and sit with them. "[H]e just asked me questions: 'How's your mom? How are you? How are your parents? What are your parents doing?' I just answered one by one. And soon my stepmother came from the other house to that place where we were sitting down, and I just got up and took my brother and sister out. And [he] said, 'Oh, you're nasty! I come and talk to you, but you run away from me!'"

Having failed at his first attempt, the "uncle" consulted his relatives. "I said, 'Look, maybe I want to marry this girl . . . but I can't get a word out of her . . . Maybe the only option is the Hmong way of asking her parents.' So they said, 'Yeah, if you like her, we'll do it for you.'" It was time for the Hmong New Year celebration, so there would be ample opportunity for wedding negotiations. "My mother dressed me," remembers Mai Lee, "and I went with [another] uncle, my brother, and my two friends . . . We went to the festival, and he came to our house, but we met each other at the rice field."

"She was playing [the] ball game in the football field," he remembers, "and they all went there to have a look at her . . . [T]hey all came back and said, 'Oh, yes, she is good.' And I went around asking people what she is like, her personality, if she is hardworking, if she is nice . . . And they all had very, very *good* things to say about her . . . My relatives went to ask [Mai Lee's] parents for her hand."

Her father replied that she was too young to be married.

"[Our] leader in [Vinai]," says Mai Lee, "was Vang Pao's relative, Vang Fong . . . [W]e left all of our [Yang clan] behind, and . . . crossed the Mekong to Thailand with the Vang family . . . And on that day, [the wedding negotiators] went to Vang Fong's house . . . [T]hey told Vang Fong's second wife and my cousin to come and get me from the festival."

Mai Lee was literally dragged kicking and screaming to Vang Fong's and escorted into a carport filled with men, her suitor among them. His family, sitting on the floor on their haunches in the Hmong way, made their intentions clear.

In Hmong culture, if you've got a daughter and somebody likes her, and there's nothing wrong with him, you can't say no . . . I'm crying louder and louder, and Vang Fong said [Shouting], "Don't cry! Whatever you say, even if you cry until you're dead, I'll still give you to Lee Yia"—at that time his name was Lee Yia. And I said, "No! I don't want to marry him!" He said, "Don't say anything! You just marry him! You are only a young girl! . . . He's studied high, he can feed you, he can clothe you, he can take you to another country." They say anything they can . . . but I still don't want to go!

Beyond the shock of marrying this man she saw more as an elder than as a peer, Mai Lee was terrified of being parted from her mother after all the years in which they had been each other's primary source of emotional support.

[M]y mother was very quiet. She was caught. I didn't think she could interview to go to America, because my father didn't want to be a head man for her. I wanted to be a head for her, and take her and my brother and sister to America. I wanted to be like that for her . . . [T]hat's the one thing that got me crying so much. . . I would have to leave my mother and my family behind. I had to go start my life, but what about my family? They can't go anywhere.

But Vang Fong was unrelenting. Mai Lee had been selected by a bright, promising, and therefore powerful man. "So they just made a

Mai Lee Yang in Ban Vinai refugee camp not long before her stepmother's cousin, Lee Yia, came to visit. Lee Yia courted and wed Mai Lee—a choice she initially (and strenuously) opposed. In time, however, the marriage became a happy and successful one and allowed Yang to bring her mother and siblings out of Ban Vinai.

wedding . . . [O]n the wedding day, I went and hid myself in my auntie's house and covered . . . my head. I wouldn't eat . . . I had to go with him to his family's house, stayed with him for two days, and then he took me to Chiang Mai, in northern Thailand, because of his research with the Hmong in northern Thailand."

Mai Lee had essentially been given away to a stranger, taken from everyone she knew, and plunged into a situation more uncertain than the one she had left behind. "It was very hard . . . [T]he person . . . [is] like a stranger, [but] you are married to him . . . [Y]ou don't love him, you don't like him—I mean, he's a very nice person, but he's too much different to you." But despite all of the travails she endured, Mai Lee's life began to change for the better. Ask her now, and she will admit, "He spoiled me. Why did I stay with him? Because of his [candy]! Now he says that right to my children! . . . I didn't want to speak to him, but I wanted to eat his [candy]."

Her husband also gave her more money to spend than she had ever seen and quickly showed that he was not the loud, angry man her father could be. "I used to do everything: wash clothes, cook, carry water, start fires, get firewood by myself. But . . . he didn't let me do anything like that . . . He'd take me out, and he bought clothes, such nice clothes — shoes. He'd dress me up, you know; he was very nice. And I got to know him each day . . . Each day I thought, 'Maybe today he'll just pretend he's nice. I'll have to see tomorrow.' And then tomorrow he's the same. He never changed."

Mai Lee and her husband, Dr. Gary Yia Lee, eventually settled in Australia. And as a result of her marriage, Mai Lee was able to be a "head" for her mother and siblings, eventually bringing them all to live with her in Australia.

Like many of the two thousand or so Hmong who now live in Australia, Mai Lee is content. She has no aspirations of living in the United States and doesn't feel she has missed out on anything by living in a country with so few Hmong. "[T]here are less people, but there are less problems . . . I really want to come [to America] and visit during the holidays, but I don't want to stay. I . . . like America, but I'm just not used to it, and I'm not used to the Hmong people [there]. Too many people, too many problems. I think I'm better off staying in Australia . . . That's my home."

no QUARTeR

There is no doubt that many Hmong stayed in Thai camps, or even risked returning to Laos, in the hopes that they could re-create the lives they had known in the mountains of Laos. But as early as 1978 there were serious obstacles to that hope ever coming to pass. Vietnamese troops called in by the Lao PDR to help subdue Hmong resistance groups had been all too effective. Several former Chao Fa members interviewed for this book recounted stories of leaving their encampments in the Phu Bia area to find food for their families, only to return and find their families slaughtered. As the reprisals against Chao Fa attacks grew harsher, many Hmong decided to flee across the border. With them came stories about a horrifying new weapon being unleashed against an unsuspecting enemy: "yellow rain."[10]

No issue related to the Secret War seems to more thoroughly divide the scientific community, as well as former USAID and CIA personnel, than whether yellow rain (trichothecene mycotoxins, poisonous compounds produced by fungal molds that infect grain) was actually used against the Hmong in the jungles of Laos (as early as 1976), as well as in Cambodia (1978) and Afghanistan (1979). Hmong entering Thailand in the late seventies and early eighties told of planes and helicopters spraying a liquid (most often identified as yellow in color) that smelled like gunpowder and left a sticky residue on leaves, rocks, and rooftops. Those who inhaled or ingested it in significant amounts suffered from heavy bleeding of the nose and gums, blindness, tremors, seizures, other neurological symptoms, and even death. Arguments began to develop over whether yellow rain actually existed. In 1981, the U.S. government obtained a sample of yellow rain taken from an alleged attack site in Cambodia. It was sent to the laboratory of Chester Mirocha, a plant pathologist at the University of Minnesota. Mirocha concluded that the sample tested positive for three separate forms of trichothecene mycotoxins, whereas none of the substances were found in a control sample away from the attack site. The strange combination of toxins did not occur naturally in Southeast Asia, he asserted, meaning they had to be formulated by humans. In addition, U.S. intelligence learned that the consumption of trichothecene-contaminated grain had long been a serious public health problem in the Soviet Union. Since that country had invested substantially in research on the poison, it seemed natural to conclude that Soviet scientists had found a way to weaponize trichothecenes. In September 1981, secretary of state Alexander Haig announced that the United States had sufficient proof to accuse the Soviet Union of producing and supplying its allies with a dangerous chemical toxin.

But in early 1982, a British scientist examined his own sample of yellow rain and noted it consisted mostly of pollen. His findings were confirmed by the U.S. Army Chemical and Research Center, which had its own collection of samples. At first it was suggested that the pollen served as a sort of "carrier" for the toxin, but Matthew Meselson, a professor of biochemistry from Harvard University, was unconvinced. Using samples obtained by ABC News and U.S., Canadian, and Australian sources, engaging in further studies, attending conferences, and consulting with Thomas Seeley, a Yale entomologist, and Joan Nowicke, a pollen expert at the Smithsonian Institution, Meselson announced a stunning conclusion. "Yellow rain" was not a deadly man-made toxin; it was bee dung. Seeley, in fact, "recalled a phenomenon he had ob-

served in which tens of thousands of Southeast Asian honey-bees, flying high above the ground, defecated *en masse* to create showers of
pollen-rich feces." The debate had been joined. A number of questions
and inconsistencies lingered. The bees in question, for example, were
indigenous to Laos and Cambodia but not Afghanistan. It was also difficult to determine which samples came from actual attack sites and
which were provided by individuals eager to please or make a buck.[11]

In 2005, Rebecca Katz, a scientist with a background in infectious
disease epidemiology, defended her dissertation, written at the Wood-
row Wilson School of Public and International Affairs. Having received
seven boxes of unanalyzed data on yellow rain from a mentor at the
Defense Intelligence Agency, Katz declassified the documents she had
inherited and filed Freedom of Information Act requests for more
records, compiling "8,529 pages of declassified material . . . [along] with
. . . over eight hundred open-source documents, and then interviewed
about fifty people, and then [studied] the toxicology analysis . . . The
point wasn't to prove or disprove what had happened, but rather to
look at how you investigate allegations of chemical and biological
weapons use, and what can you learn about theories of evidence." Approaching the problem from a different perspective than Meselson and
his colleagues, Katz arrived at a different conclusion. While yellow rain
skeptics had proven that the bee dung phenomenon existed, they had
done little or nothing to explain the symptoms manifested by numerous Hmong, Khmer, and other victims.[12]

Meselson and coauthor Julian Perry Robinson had already asserted
that "Symptoms ascribed to alleged chemical attack were repeatedly
judged by experienced physicians on the scene to be of altogether different origin. In March 1981, for example, the U.S. Embassy's Regional
Medical Officer examined purported Cambodian and Hmong victims,
but he found no clear evidence to support CBW [chemical/biological
weapons] allegations." Katz, on the other hand, had declassified numer-
.ous pictures of victims with rashes they claimed were caused by yellow
rain: "I sent them, without any background, to the dermatology faculty
at Stanford [and asked] 'Is this something that you would find normally?'" The answer, though obviously based on limited data, was a resounding "No." Katz also created a database of symptoms and ran them
through "differential diagnosis software," trying to determine if they
could have been caused by natural phenomena like malaria. She then tri-

angulated the reports of illness with declassified reports of military over-flights and other intelligence data at her disposal. Katz, whose study focused more on the methods used than the conclusions drawn, believes it is extremely difficult to explain what happened to the Hmong and other victims using only natural phenomena. "I think that a lot of people got sick, and a lot of people within the Hmong community can list off who died. And something—*something* had to have accounted for that."[13]

The issue is complicated further because patients with possible yellow rain–associated illnesses did not always come running to doctors. Chuck Whitney remembers, "We had a doctor [at Ban Vinai] who insisted we had a TB problem. So he wanted to start a TB clinic . . . [W]e treated everybody and tracked them in the camp for a half a year, and they didn't get better. So they didn't have TB. So then we started asking more questions, doing a better patient history, and they all had the common story of being gassed in Laos."

To this day, even former CIA and refugee workers hold divergent opinions on yellow rain. Mac Thompson remains unconvinced:

Lionel [Rosenblatt] and I and another guy did what may be the first official U.S. government reports on the yellow rain, and that was in August of '78. Jerry [Daniels] was up in Nong Khai, and he set up several interviews for us . . . [We] spent the day interviewing Hmong with interpreters about what they'd seen, what they experienced, and came back to Bangkok, and Lionel wrote a two-page cable about yellow rain. A few months later, Reagan's in, Al Haig's in—you know, the great anti-Communists are in government. So we're really down on Russia and the yellow rain . . . [But] the Commie Lao are no better secret keepers . . . than the old Royal Lao government people were. There's got to be a hand grenade, a rocket, an artillery shell. Even if an artillery shell weighs forty pounds, you can pull just the head out of it or the guts out of it and bring it out in a bag. The CIA put money into that search. The State Department put money into it, a consulate up in Udorn. [The] Defense Intelligence Agency . . . had a lieutenant colonel working on it quite extensively . . . And as far as I knew, absolutely zero came out of that except Matt Meselson's bee shit theory.

Merle L. Pribbenow, a retired CIA operations officer and Vietnamese language expert stationed in Vietnam from 1981 to 1983, insists that science and intelligence have proven that yellow rain was not man-made. For example, in all of the interviews he conducted with deserters from the Vietnamese army, some of whom knew a great deal about the organization and activities of Vietnamese in the region, none

seemed aware of yellow rain. Some had even served in areas where attacks were said to have occurred. Pribbenow and his colleagues also received (or purchased) numerous samples of yellow rain allegedly stolen
from Vietnamese chemical weapon stocks. But despite the CIA's desire
to prove the Soviet Union's and Vietnam's perfidy, "We never received
any feedback on the results of these tests, nor did we learn the test results for any . . . samples we sent in over this two-year span." In short,
in-the-field CIA agents proved long ago that yellow rain was no Soviet
toxin, but their bosses didn't like their answer.[14]

But other veterans of the Secret War don't want to see the issue
fade away. One former refugee worker remembers the horror of seeing
Hmong coming across the river and hearing their stories about yellow
rain:

*People that came out [were] really dying; famished, emaciated children, babies. And
whoever was shooting on the other side of the river . . . were shooting babies on the
backs of Hmong mothers who were swimming or holding on to a raft . . . [T]here
would be as many as two thousand people in the little Thai police station sleeping
on the ground. And these were villagers, their clothes soiled, and spontaneously the
first thing they talked about often was the chemical attacks and how people had
died, and their animals had died, and they were very ill from that . . . [T]hey only
had one set of clothes, and they would wash those clothes, so I think it would be very,
very difficult at that time to get chemical proof, because no one was really thinking
in those terms until quite a bit later . . .*

*[There were] eleven thousand kids [at] the Ban Vinai Primary School. Kids
would also talk a lot when they had just arrived . . . because this was a horrific experience they'd gone through. [T]hey just wanted to get it out. And . . . kids would
draw in the school, pictures of planes or helicopters spraying things coming down on
the ground. And one time I picked up one of those kids' drawings off the desk, just
while I was walking though the school, and I saved that. But to me, that's as good a
proof as having a chemical analysis and all of that.*

Another refugee program veteran says there is no doubt in his mind
that yellow rain was real. "While spray may have been released from
planes originally," he says, "it was probably most often delivered in B-
40 shells. The gas might not kill a healthy adult but would kill children
and animals." On one occasion, this man was called in to investigate a
case of two men who had arrived in Nong Khai. Both had at least a couple red, swollen limbs. The reddened areas were riddled with small holes.
A doctor originally diagnosed these holes as shrapnel wounds, but X-

rays revealed no shrapnel. Over the two years or so, the affliction never went away. The swelling subsided, but a kind of fungal infection or inflammation with these red spots migrated to different parts of the body.

On another occasion, this same individual accompanied a colleague on a mission to purchase a "cartridge" of yellow rain that a group of Hmong rebels claimed to have. He saw the cartridge. On one end was a kind of nipple that his colleague tried to pry off, causing everyone else to leap out of the car in which they were sitting. The colleague, who'd been given more than enough money to purchase the cartridge, claimed it was fake and refused to buy it, thereby frustrating efforts to prove the existence of yellow rain. "I find the bee dung theory preposterous," he says. "I think it's an insult to the Hmong, who knew bees and harvested honey, to think they didn't know the difference between bee shit and a chemical attack."

Katz also questions whether studies on yellow rain were as immediate or thorough as Pribbenow believes:

There were often delays of months to even years in the analysis of samples collected . . . Once the sample arrived in a laboratory, be it government or private, the sample could either be examined right away, or left waiting for months or even years.

The delays between collection and analysis are important because the ability to detect trichothecenes in a sample greatly diminishes over time, particularly if the sample is not properly stored. The samples degrade and the trichothecenes are metabolized . . . Samples that tested positive by [Chester] Mirocha soon after collection were negative when reanalyzed after several years . . . [D]ue to the pace of degradation, it would be surprising to find any trichothecene mycotoxins in a sample older than one year. Some even argue that mycotoxins metabolize so quickly through the body that they would be surprised to find any toxins in a blood or urine sample analyzed just weeks after an attack.[15]

While controversy still rages within Western circles, one would be hard-pressed to find a Hmong American who questions the existence of yellow rain. The status of this discussion is unlikely to change until scientists spend less time debating over the chemical composition of old samples and more time explaining what caused the numerous maladies and deaths suffered in the forests of Laos.

A JVA representative announces the names of people who will be interviewed for resettlement. A list was later posted to show who was accepted for migration to another country.

MOVING ON

By 1981, writes Lynellyn Long, 93 percent of the refugees in Thai camps had been approved for resettlement in a third country. "Humane deterrence" was discouraging, though certainly not halting, further immigration.[16]

Individuals from every refugee community can share horror stories about living in a camp, making application, being at the mercy of individuals who had almost absolute power over their destiny, waiting for a decision on their disposition, and then ultimately being told yes or no.

Hmong refugees with military service connected to the CIA operation in Laos had an advantage over other Lao, Vietnamese, or Cambodian refugees, but even so, a green light for migration to America or elsewhere created more problems. Given their large and close-knit definition of family, moving out of the refugee camps almost always meant leaving someone important behind, either in the camps or back in Laos.

Pa Sher Yang had two brothers who were bachelors. In 1978,

they transported young men with no parents, so we signed them up . . . to come to [the United States]. I'll always remember how the fact that the family wasn't separated gave you peace. Being separated makes you heartbroken because . . . no one had been here [yet]. All we knew was that it went past the horizon. We didn't know if there were people or demons on the other side. But if you stayed, you had no idea how to find food or how your life would end. So when separated we never thought to see each other again, because the person who left would never come back and you would never be able to visit them. In truth, you missed them more, your heart hurt and burned more, than if the person died. When they're dead, you see that their body is decaying, but when they leave and are still alive, you miss them more.

The Hmong could, if they wished, come to the United States. But in doing so, their losses continued to mount. Already bereft of their former homes, their property, their way of life, members of their family, and any sense of independence they had once enjoyed, their ages-old kinship structure would also be sundered as families were sent to different communities across the United States and around the world.

6 | "WHERE IS LAOS, AND WHO ARE HMONG?"

GOING TO a naTion OF immiGRanTS

The United States has always been a nation of immigrants. Even Native Americans have forebears who crossed an Aleutian ice bridge before settling in various parts of the Americas. The first Africans came to the United States in 1619, a year before the *Mayflower*. Though the importation of slaves directly from Africa was outlawed in 1808, many others were brought in through the Caribbean. (As a result, most African Americans have significantly longer lineages in this country than European Americans.)

But in the 1880s, when immigration became a source of widespread controversy, it was the relative newcomers—whites, who viewed "Indians" and "Negroes" as inferior—who sounded the alarm. They feared the sheer number of these new immigrants (twenty million between 1880 and 1914), but also their countries of origin. While the majority of previous immigrants had come from northern and western Europe, the old patterns shifted in the late nineteenth century. As Philip Martin observes, these newcomers "created the image of immigrants to America that endures to this day. Poor southern and eastern European peasants and laborers arrived in New York—in some years over 2,800 per day—and most of them crowded into urban labor markets in the Northeast and Midwest. Sometimes racist language was used to argue for immigration restrictions."[1]

"Racist?" one might ask. "But most of these immigrants were European." Indeed. But in the age of Social Darwinism and eugenics, many still believed in a hierarchy of races that created distinctions between and even within the races. While those of English, French, Germanic, and Scandinavian origin were considered "white," the peoples of Italy (the crucible of Western civilization) and Ireland (somehow Ireland wasn't in Western Europe), the Mediterranean, and all of Eastern Europe were not—in large part because most were Catholic or Jewish instead of Protestant. These immigrants, as well as Chinese and Japanese Americans already in the United States for decades, often became the targets of discrimination, harassment, vandalism, assault, and, in times of severe economic distress or antilabor/anti-Communist hysteria, even forced deportation.

Immigrants responded to these crises in a number of important ways. Forced to occupy the poorest neighborhoods owing to their low-skill, low-paying jobs, they often lived two or three families to a unit or accepted renters to gain extra income. They developed mutual aid societies that provided payments to the families of disabled workers or offered money to bury the dead. They developed businesses that catered to their own kind, providing a means to create wealth and support in the community. They used their places of worship not only to sustain their faith but to preserve their customs and language—and to debate whether they should hold on to the old ways, embrace the new, or try to straddle a line between the two. Suspicious Americans often criticized these communities for being too clannish, for failing to learn English quickly enough or sufficiently demonstrate their gratitude and loyalty to their new country.

The jobs that barely paid the bills also kept parents from their children and from each other. Family members clung to each other for support but also endured heightened tensions that often led to strife, domestic abuse, neglect, youth alienation and crime, and other ills. The age of industrial revolution, after all, was also the age of the juvenile court, settlement house, camping, and playground movements, which sought to help immigrant families and forestall delinquency.

While the experience of every immigrant is unique and each immigrant community should be studied and appreciated in its own context, there remain a number of commonalities in the immigrant experience. But as the children of immigrants and refugees grow up, become educated and successful, shed parts of their former identity and language, move into more prosperous neighborhoods, and become a part of the "American Dream," they often forget their own family history. Rather than regarding newer immigrant communities with a sense of kinship, they sometimes view them with the same suspicion or fear visited on their own forebears. "For some, it's a matter of many generations," observes world-renowned immigration historian Rudolph Vecoli. "For some of us, like myself—I'm the second generation. It's my parents who emigrated from Italy. So it's an experience that, for many of us, is still relevant in our own biographies."

The Hmong who came to the United States had little or no sense of where they were going or what their lives would be like. They only knew they would not have to live in a forest or a refugee camp; they would not be killed by Communists; and their children would receive an education that could provide them with opportunities beyond their imagination. But with those opportunities came unforeseen challenges as well—challenges that have defined the immigrant experience for generations. Though the Hmong people and their customs may seem strange to others, Americans with deeper roots in this country can still find a common bond with them and with other more recent immigrants if they just look over their shoulder far enough. "We should have the capacity for empathy, for compassion, for understanding," says Vecoli, "based on our own history."

THE JOURNEY

The journey from refugee camp to a new home in a Western country was taken in uncertain steps. "[T]here was a time where my father had to go take a test," remembers Cy Thao. "[T]hen eventually . . . his name showed up on the list of people who could come to the U.S. . . . [W]e had to go to get our pictures taken, and then we were given a date when we were going . . . to America. So the days before us actually leaving, we had a big going-away party and killed half of the livestock that we had

For tens of thousands of Hmong, camps like Ban Vinai had been home for many years. Pursuing the greater opportunities offered in Western countries almost always meant leaving part of one's family behind. Bittersweet scenes played out on a regular basis.

acquired and then gave half of them away and gave almost all of our possessions to people."

Of course, many Hmong wasted little time giving their possessions away, since they had few or none to begin with. Mai Lee Thao, fifty-five when she left Ban Vinai in 1980, remembers "When we were about to leave, we were uneasy, so we just bought two chickens to use for soul-calling ceremonies [to ask for protection on the journey] and then just left. There was really nothing to bring. We just brought ourselves and our bodies. There were not even [extra] clothes to wear."

"Tons of people came to the market . . . inside the camp . . . to say good-bye," continues Cy Thao, "and then they took us to another camp . . . [T]hey were showing films of what to expect, and they were putting the parents through some kind of education of what to expect when they came to the U.S. . . . [T]here were . . . Cambodian and Lao, other people who were there as well."

Many Hmong refugees were processed for resettlement at Phanat Nikhom. There they were given orientations on life in America—how to use a toilet, to say "hello" and "thank you," and so forth. These sessions were designed for adults but left out children and the elderly. "My grandmother would say years later that in Phanat Nikhom she stopped being a woman and was turned into a child," writes Kao Kalia Yang. "'Ban Vinai Refugee Camp was not so bad for an old woman like me. We had feet so we could walk. In Phanat Nikhom, my children became busy, and there was no walking for me to do. It was a place to practice being in America . . . where if you are old and you don't have a car, you are like a man or a woman in a wheelchair with weak arms. You wait for others to push or pull, a child who does not have the face of youth.'"[2]

Ready or not, Hmong families who completed orientation were sent on to a point of embarkation, like Hong Kong, where they awaited transportation to their new homes. Choua Thao's family was taken to a hotel in Hong Kong. "The refugees were so scared of the elevator! [There] were eight people in the family. They put me and the two girls in one room in the fourth floor at the hotel. And they put my husband and his little girl and the two boys in the ninth floor." The family was together in the hotel restaurant but then went off to their separate rooms. A door opened, family members got out, and those who remained wondered if they would ever see them again. "We think the [doors] close, [and if] you don't get through, they will cut you." Choua Thao laughs heartily now, but she and many other families spent at least one distraught evening fearing the worst.

Mee Moua's family was quarantined in Bangkok before being sent on to the United States via Hong Kong:

[T]he garbage dump . . . was our playground . . . I remember the distinct smell . . . Sometimes we were searching for Coca-Cola bottle caps . . . [to] trade them with each other, or sell them to the adults, and they would use them for checkers . . . [T]he food was really bad . . . [W]hen we lived in the refugee camp we didn't have a lot of food, but at least we ate clear liquid food that Hmong people eat. When we were quarantined, we were being fed potato curries . . . We couldn't eat a lot of that.

After arriving in Hong Kong, Moua's family stayed overnight in a hotel before catching their connecting flight to the United States. "[W]e didn't know that you were supposed to separate the blankets and sleep underneath, and so we were looking for blankets, and we couldn't find blankets, and we were really cold, and we were really scared . . . [W]e didn't even go into the bathroom . . . [or] turn on the shower. We were so scared when we came in we huddled together, and when they came in to get us we left."

While many Hmong had been transported in airplanes or helicopters during the war, air travel was a completely new experience for others. "[I]t was my first time . . . riding [an] airplane," remembers Mai Lee Thao. "When I was inside it, I just [sat] in it; I didn't know what the air-

plane would do! On the way to [the United States], the waters were so big! What were we going to do to go back?" Wa Yang, only a small boy at the time of his flight, was even more surprised. "I remember we got off of the bus, and then we went [up] this stair. And we did not know that it was a plane, because it was so big! We walk into it . . . [W]e are in the center section, so we do not see the plane take off or land . . . [W]e sit down . . . for a long time, and then they say, "OK, you guys can leave now." And when we come out, it's a totally different place . . . and we are all confused!"

Peter Vang's father had grown tired of his forays into Laos. The Americans who accompanied him seemed more interested in potential American POWs than in helping the Hmong. He finally gave up and chose to come to America in 1987. On the plane, Peter remembers, "I was sitting with this American man in a business suit . . . [The] flight attendant . . . asked him what he wanted, and he said, 'Coffee' . . . I saw it was black, and I thought it was Coca-Cola. So I just pointed, and she gave me one. I was so thirsty, and I wanted to sip it down . . . [I]t burned my whole throat, but I was too embarrassed to yell or scream because my parents weren't there . . . [M]y throat was burnt the whole way."

Left to right: Chou (now Peter) Vang as a young boy preparing to leave Ban Vinai for the United States in 1987; with his father, Nhia Lor Vang, in 2006; and as a model for the angel Gabriel in a Hmong version of the Annunciation

Myriad challenges faced the Hmong who came to live in Western countries. Most of their new hosts had no idea what kinds of food they ate. "Back in your homeland," remembers Mai Lee Thao, "when you eat and make food, the smell of food is sweet . . . [H]ere . . . the smells are like bark! You wonder how you're going to adjust to eating these things . . . When living here longer and longer, you no longer smell that smell." American families who sponsored immigrant families bought five or ten pounds of rice and thought it would last a week or generously but ignorantly prepared foods so foreign that many Hmong couldn't eat them.

"When we first landed, it was like looking into the sky," remembers Gao Moua. "We couldn't understand the language. The fortunate thing for us Hmong was that we had relatives who came before. It was harder for the ones who came first, but because of them it became easier for the ones who came afterwards." Choua Thao, former Sam Thong nurse, came to Minneapolis in 1976 and made it her responsibility to help Hmong who came after her. In 1979, under the auspices of Lutheran Social Services, "I created the orientation for sponsors and for churches. And I said, 'Families, you must have *one hundred pounds* of rice—from the beginning! *Leave them alone!* Maybe you can visit them three times a day only, but not everybody knock at the door every fifteen minutes, because they are so tired—they're sleeping, because [of jet lag]."

But the most crushing, isolating obstacle for most Hmong was the language. "Not knowing English is like being a pig," remembers Mai Lee Thao. "When they talk to you, you don't know; then you have to have someone to translate for you . . . It was so hard that I thought, 'how could my children ever know?' . . . I wanted to learn English. But when I was taught so many times, I still did not know it. You come home and go the next day, and you don't even remember."

Sao Lee, who was brought out of Thailand along with his extended family by his older brother Gary Yia Lee, spoke Hmong, Lao, French, and some Thai, but none of those languages got him anywhere in Australia.

[V]ery few people speak French here, so . . . it was very hard to communicate with anyone . . . In the sense of food, clothing, transport, everything, it's very good. But [you're] mentally very sick, because you miss your relatives . . . I missed all of my sisters, because we used to live together in the camp, and suddenly we just never saw each other again, and I just felt very bad. And then the language was the main problem . . . because to go to the doctor or do a bit of shopping or anything at all was just so difficult. You don't know what to say when you need something. And we were

among the very first Hmong to come here to Australia, so there were only a few Hmong students, but they are not with us, they were at school . . . [T]he most diffi-cult is when you go to see a doctor and you are sick . . . [I]f I have a bad headache, I point my finger to my head, and the doctor thinks I might have had a big fall or I hurt my head somewhere, and they start pressing their fingers on to my head, starts turning my neck to see if any bones are broken, and it's just so hard. Not just hard for us, but I think very hard for the doctor or the teacher.

Different opportunities were presented to the Hmong who settled in different countries. France, for example, does not recognize or cate-gorize people by race or ethnicity. "French officials in the refugee camps in Thailand," writes Khou Xiong, "were instructed to accept discrimi-nately persons who demonstrated a minimal knowledge of the French language and/or who had served under the French military or civil service in Indochina." Great emphasis was placed on ensuring that Hmong refugees in France would assimilate as quickly as possible. They were accepted "if they had family already living in France, or if they could prove that they were fleeing persecution."[3]

Yang Dao came to France in July 1976 after learning his son had contracted polio.

[R]efugees . . . had a kind of orientation for one week, and then the French sent them to regional refugee centers scattered across the country. They stayed there for six months . . . learning the French language, the French social system, how to find a job . . . [A]fter four months of orientation . . . they sent . . . those who were able to un-derstand the French language . . . to work in the factories. After six months, every-body had to leave the center . . . The authorities helped the Hmong to find a kind of public housing. All health care is provided by the government . . . and if you had chil-dren, they sent . . . family allocations . . . [u]ntil the time the kids reach the age of eighteen. That's a very big difference . . . So the social system is better in France than in the United States . . . But it was difficult to find a job for many people, and they didn't have an opportunity to finish their education . . . [T]he French say that if you go to a French university, you have to speak French very well. You have to write the French language very well . . . [There were] no accommodations like the United States . . . [M]y younger brother . . . finished his tenth grade in the French high school in Laos . . . [H]e spent two years in the refugee camps. Then when he arrived in France, they said that he was too old. He was nineteen years old! . . . They sent him to professional education training for two years . . . [H]e became an auto mechanic.

After nine years in France, "he came to [the United States]; he learned English for six months; he passed the examination, so he was allowed to go to the university in Washington State, and . . . he received his bachelor's degree in computer science." While other differences exist among the Hmong who settled in different parts of the world, they also share in common many of the experiences discussed below.

FINDING A WAY

When the Vietnam War ended and Saigon became Ho Chi Minh City, Kathleen Vellenga was in St. Paul, Minnesota, recovering from surgery. "I was having every need attended to . . . and I'm watching the horrific escape of Vietnam on TV, thinking 'Where are these people going to go?' By the time I'd recovered enough to look about me, I said, 'Well, some of them are going to come to Minnesota.'" She learned the International Institute of Minnesota had received money from the State Department to hire staff to assist refugee families resettling in the area. Vellenga asked members of her small church, Dayton Avenue Presbyterian, for help. Though unable to provide substantial support on their own, they forged a partnership with Macalester Plymouth United Church. "We made these commitments," she remembers, and then prepared for the arrival of a Vietnamese family. "Maybe a month or so before they arrived, we got the formal letter from the State Department that said they were Laotian. They referred to them as *Meo*. I didn't even know where Laos was—I knew where Vietnam was; I knew where Cambodia was. I had to look it up on a map. We knew nothing about the Secret War at this time."

The head of the family coming to St. Paul in February 1976 was Leng Wong. His military experience and English-language proficiency made him one of the first Hmong selected to immigrate. "When I left Thailand, the American people that interviewed us and gave us permission to come to America—actually not asked, but *told* me that because there were very few Hmong people who could speak English . . . they would pass my phone number and my address [to] other Hmong people who followed us. So I said, 'Fine.'"

"I think both sides were in a state of shock," says Vellenga.

For one thing . . . there was a different date on the State Department letter. Because of the international date line . . . they arrived a day before we planned. . . It was well below zero in February. I woke up at six o'clock in the morning when Olga Zoltai of the International Institute called me and said, "They're here!" I said, "No, that's to-

morrow," and she said, "They're here!" and we grabbed every coat and blanket we could find, and ran to the airport. They were waiting out by the baggage claim, this huddled group of people. They looked, at that point, so unusual, so out of place, and they definitely felt out of place.

"So when we arrived here," remembers Leng Wong, "they thought we were Vietnamese, so they started talking to us and asking us what part of Vietnam we were from. And I said, 'We're Hmong, and we're from Laos.' And they said, 'Where is Laos, and who are Hmong?'"

"They were flown within twenty-four hours directly to this extremely frigid place," says Vellenga.

But as soon as we started talking to them, the women were . . . nervously giggling, and Leng was being very formal and considerate. We offered them all jackets, and Khampou, Leng's younger relative, said later, "I turned you down . . . and then when I got outside, I found out what you meant by cold, and I took it back!" We drove from the airport to Liberty Plaza [subsidized housing owned at the time by Vellenga's church]; they were looking around, and Leng . . . commented on the bare trees. So I walked him through the "four seasons" concept and told him this was winter and the trees had no leaves but they had buds and they'd grow back. And years later he told me that he thought I was making up a story because I didn't want to tell him that we'd had Agent Orange sprayed over the trees.

Many Hmong still recall with gratitude the kindness shown them by members of their sponsoring congregations. Ly Vang, a nurse at Sam Thong hospital, remembers, "The Immigration [Service] had done a good job to arrange the churches to sponsor [us], so we connected to church members just like a brother and sister. They taught us what to do: go to school, to work. There was [often] a job lined up before the family arrived here . . . And we still love those families, and they are still connected with us."

Missionaries had preached Christianity throughout northern Laos, so the faith was familiar to many and had been accepted by a small number. But in gratitude for their church's kindness (or out of a sense of obligation), many more adopted Christianity in the United States. Keith Vang's family moved to Lansing, Michigan. His father, Za Thao Vang, had felt tormented by some of his shaman spirits and seemed happy to leave them behind. "I started first grade when I got to Lansing," remembers Keith, "and I started learning the catechism . . . all the way to eighth grade, and working at church as the acolyte. My pastor came and taught us Bible lessons, so my pastor and I were pretty close, because I was his only means of communication to my brothers, to my father and mother . . . until we found . . . a Hmong lay minister." As a mark of their new faith, each member of Vang's family wore a cross—Za Thao Vang a particularly large one.

As the Hmong community in Lansing grew; many who knew Za Thao Vang was a shaman came and begged him to perform the old rituals.

[M]y father was always a kind person; he decided, 'Well, maybe . . . just this once' *. . . [H]e came back and he said he didn't feel the same; he felt the shaman spirit wasn't with him anymore . . . [Then] he realized he had the cross with him . . . More people came and asked him to perform . . . And as he got into that again, every time he went he took the cross off . . .*

[I]f you perform shamanism, you have to have an altar for the spirits to communicate . . . so we had an altar built in our apartment, and when we had Bible study they would cover the altar. Later on . . . my father asked the pastor if it was OK for him to perform shamanism . . . [W]hen my pastor heard it, he asked, "Are you doing something to harm someone or is it something good?" My father replied that it was a good thing. And the pastor, without realizing what my father was doing, said, "It's OK. If it's good, it's OK." So later on when the lay minister came . . . that got across to my pastor, and then he said . . . "If I knew about this, I would have told him not to do this." They took my parents to church, and they talked to them about taking down the altar and really just being Christians, sticking to the word of God . . . (I felt he was pressured into taking down the altar.) So I got home one day and saw the pastor and the lay minister, along with my father . . . and the pastor told me, "Your father has decided that he wants to take down the altar" . . . I thought my father was happy. I was glad he wanted to do that, because like I said at the beginning, he wanted to escape that . . . So I helped him take down the altar.

Then later on, my sister-in-law came and said, "What are you doing? Do you know that if you do this the shaman spirit is going to attack [your] father?" And that reality just hit him or something. He was scared to death . . . He experienced a lot of sickness, and we didn't have the support from the church . . . [b]ecause of the language barrier . . . They didn't come to pray for him. Also he was upset at the pastor, so the pastor had . . . cut the communication between him[self] and my parents. And it was me—I would still go to church, but it was just me.

[E]ven though he . . . decided to practice shamanism again, [my father] always encouraged me to continue to go to church . . . He would not perform the shaman ritual on me, because he felt I was protected by a higher power . . . [A]s a child growing up in that sense, I never really struggled with my Christian identity or anything. I had the free will to go worship. My mother took me, even [though she] also took care of my father. And I saw that a lot of other parents were not as open. I think that my father was open [because] he understood the spiritual world. He knew that I would be different.

The transition from a life in Southeast Asia to one in the United States, Australia, France, or elsewhere was at best disorienting, at worst horrifying, even tragic. Some memories of this period of readjustment now elicit smiles and occasionally laughter. Nhia Xiong Thao, a Secret War veteran and father of Minnesota representative Cy Thao, was taken to a grocery store for the first time by one of his sponsors. "[I]t was . . . very strange. I didn't really know any English. She just pointed her finger. I didn't know what she said. I just took the whole thing! And she said, 'No, no! Just one!'"

Fungchatou Lo's family came to Minnesota in March 1980. "When we arrived, the snow was still out there, and we thought we were in hell," he recalls, laughing, "because the Hmong religion says hell is very cold . . . [M]y uncles [said], 'No, we're not in hell. This is called snow here' . . . [W]e don't have a Hmong word for snow." Vang Chou Xiong came to Chicago with his family in November when he was only five. "We never knew there was forest or jungle in this country at all, because all we saw was building after building . . . You'd see people walking all the time, and the city lights were on twenty-four hours every day." When they saw snow for the first time, "We thought someone was throwing cotton from the top story of our building."

Cy Thao's family came to the Twin Cities on March 12, 1980. He recalls,

There was a big, big snowstorm right before we got there . . . [O]ur sponsor had put a spread, a big spread of food, chicken, everything on the table . . . to welcome us. (And our sponsor was this Catholic family, the Fishers. And they lived in Brooklyn Center, and they had a lot of kids . . . so they were used to having a lot of kids in the house.) We didn't know what that was; we couldn't speak English—so we never ate it! . . . [T]hey [also] gave us pajamas. I didn't know what pajamas were. [Back in Laos or Thailand,] you went to sleep with what you had on, you get up, and you're there . . . We wear these clothes everywhere. We didn't know it was pajamas, so we had them on the whole day! So we got up in the morning, . . . we slide out the patio door, and there's all this snow—but we didn't know what snow was. [W]e had to find out. So I volunteered and ran upstairs and got a spoon and took a spoonful of snow and ate it . . . I said, "Oh, yeah, it's just ice." We knew what ice was. So that was my first morning in Minnesota, was a spoonful of dirty snow.

After living with the Fishers for about two weeks, the Thaos were placed in a new home in south Minneapolis, where many other Hmong families had settled. The following summer, they were spending a beautiful night outside: "[T]he whole family was out on the balcony. All of a sudden, there's rockets shooting, and one of them landed right on the balcony! And we freaked out! We were like, 'Oh, my god, the Communists are coming; they're amassing an attack!' You know, 'War! There's a war going on!' Then suddenly everybody ran into the house and turned off the lights and waited to see what was going on. Later on we found out it was the Fourth of July. There was a fireworks display close by."

In stories like Thao's, one is reminded that the Hmong often came to their new homes with significant emotional and psychological scars. As Fay Chia Lee recalled his war experiences, he confessed, "All my closest friends are dead, the ones I shared a plate with . . . they are all dead . . . I've seen my friends die right in front of my eyes; it's like us sitting here, and we have another one sitting over there. Before you know it, you hear gunshots or bombs, and your friend suddenly is dead." Surely no one could endure such horror without being forever changed.

"What I think a lot of people don't realize is how traumatic moving here was," says Jane Kretzmann, a resettlement worker for Lutheran Social Services in 1976. "I think one of the . . . lessons for me in all the work with refugees was how long war lasts. Once the fighting ends, the damage for people and the pain they carry all their lives is profound . . . [E]ncounters with the medical system were very traumatic, especially given certain [spiritual] beliefs about touching the head or, god forbid, having to do surgery on the head of a child. There were people who would take their child and run away."

"We come from a background where we have limited exposure to the Western medical system, other than military hospitals and [dispensaries]," says Leng Wong. "[P]eople just took care of themselves . . . with home remedies. The Western medical system was new to them, and so it took time to understand it and for our Western medical profession to understand the culture. So there is that gap that we had to live through." Indeed, as Anne Fadiman chronicled in her now-classic book, *The Spirit Catches You and You Fall Down*, there were occasions of cross-cultural misunderstanding so great that patients died or suffered profoundly and unnecessarily. By the same token, Fadiman's study describes one case at one point in time. The Hmong have, as a whole, come to understand, appreciate, and navigate through their new countries' medical systems. Dr. Patricia Walker, daughter of Air America chief pilot Fred Walker, came to Minneapolis–St. Paul from Thailand in 1987 and joined a medical clinic treating patients from around the world. "I've seen my colleagues become more patient, more understanding, and less time-pressured . . . with the Hmong community . . . [D]efinitely the Hmong community has changed a lot in terms of saying, 'Wow, we really have learned a lot about . . . the value of a lot of the things you do in Western medicine' . . . [T]he next generation of young Hmong people are now medical students, practicing physicians . . . and that's been such a relief to the Hmong community." Family physician Dr. Kathleen Culhane-Pera has extensive clinical experience with Hmong in the Twin Cities: "I fear sometimes when people read [Fadiman's] book that they'll come away and say, 'Oh, Hmong culture is barbaric or wrong . . . [T]hey really need to learn the American way.' This is really damaging." Not only should people develop a respect for Hmong traditional healing, she suggests, but they also should recognize their ability to adapt to Western medicine.

Unfortunately, cultural practices that clashed with those in the West, along with the inability of most Hmong to immediately speak English, were often uncharitably interpreted by casual or callous observers. Says Tom Kosel, who served for many years as director of refugee services for Catholic Charities in St. Paul,

The general community has an impression that if people can't speak English, then they must not be very smart — or you treat them like children, because they're small of stature . . . You have to understand that these are adults who have had life experiences far more severe and critical than many of us . . . One of the major disservices [to] the Hmong community . . . in the early days [was] the attitude that said, "You can't work if you don't speak English." Many . . . ended up being sent to English class or feeling they had to go to English class and not even try to go out and work, even though they wanted to. And here we had people coming in who spoke Hmong, Lao, Thai, and in many cases also French, and for the most part had always learned those languages by immersion . . . [W]e put them in a classroom, which they had never experienced before, and expected them to learn a language our way, rather than helping them to learn it their way.

Despite the challenges they faced, many Hmong who had lived in a state of limbo in Thailand experienced at least a brief period of relief at finally arriving in a place they could call home. They had flown across an ocean and put war, harrowing escapes, and the indignities of life in refugee camps behind them. Laos, once their home, was now under Communist control; coming to America was for the best.

Tong Vang had watched the Communist troops at Wattay Airport with their new uniforms and their plentiful, modern weapons. He had been told of the evacuation of Long Tieng but missed the airlift. Laos was lost, and America was his future. Sure, he had to walk to work two miles in each direction, even in the middle of winter. Yes, he was making only $2.60 an hour as a metal assembler. But even so, "I hate Laos . . . and I love this country. I feel good. But after six months, I keep thinking about my country. It's good. It's mine. I lost my country. And you have a whole bunch of relatives left behind. Even when I went to work, my tears were running down every day. I could not tell anybody about it, but your tears keep running."

"Hmong men tend to be a proud group," observes former USAID doctor Joe Westermeyer, "and in their own place, in their own context, are the people who live on top of the mountain and are wealthier and harder working, better organized, cleverer than the people surrounding them, and so are used to being at the top of the heap, not at the bottom, so it's a big adjustment for them."

As Tong Vang remembers the depression that gripped him, he admits, "If I think about the job I had in my home country and [my first] job here, the job [in Laos] was more responsible, a higher level. You work for the government; you are an officer, and you can tell people what to do . . . [H]ere you are on the bottom of the floor. You think . . . 'If I was still in Laos, I would be a leader, a commander' . . . Here I have no authority, no power."

Perhaps the biggest blow to Hmong men was the loss of their central role in caring for—and having authority over—their families. "There is no way for us to be self-sufficient like back in Laos," laments Nao Her Vang. Having fought in a war and suffered the indignities of life first as a prisoner and then as a refugee, Her and thousands of other Hmong men found it difficult to cope with their new status. "In Laos, it didn't matter if you were educated or not. If you had the strength and will, you could farm and be successful . . . Here in the U.S., there is no farmland for those who want to work on it. You must be educated to get a good job." And for many, an education was out of reach. As former St. Paul mayor George Latimer observes, "the older men [had] deeper problems and in that regard were similar to previous immigrant waves, where you simply have too many years behind you and too few ahead of you to spend it learning about [American] culture."

These problems were further amplified because most Hmong had little or no education. Even holding a pencil was a foreign concept for some. Like so many other immigrants before them (how else would we have the ethnic neighborhoods that still exist today?), they sought to gather together for mutual support, seeking out areas not only with relatives but with job opportunities and good educational and social welfare systems. Long-separated families reunited, and elders who had little hope of learning English or finding gainful employment formed their own networks that at least partially restored the sense of community they had left behind. Hmong who initially settled in small towns where they were a curiosity sparked a second wave of cross-country migration, moving to larger Hmong communities in cities like Fresno and Santa Ana, California; Minneapolis and St. Paul, Minnesota; or Madison, Milwaukee, Wausau, and Sheboygan, Wisconsin.

While these connections undoubtedly brought much-needed comfort and stability, they also further entrenched the problems that separated Hmong elders from their children and grandchildren as well as from the broader communities in which they now lived. Jim Anderson, who moved to Chicago after his years in Thailand, eventually settled in St. Paul, where he became a refugee and immigrant planner for Ramsey County: "Those folks who had arrived here as adults . . . were still very immersed in their own culture. They were, by and large, located in specific neighborhoods . . . which allowed folks to carry on very well in their native language, and it didn't encourage a great deal of intermingling. So here were folks who had been in the United States for ten, fifteen years . . . The service needs when they first arrived were still very much intact."

While older Hmong all had difficulties adjusting to life in America, Hmong women had a slight advantage over Hmong men. Jane Kretzmann remembers Joe Westermeyer telling her,

"If I'm a man and I was a [tiger] hunter and I come here, there are no [tigers]. My value to my culture and my society is nothing. [If] I'm at home as a woman in Laos, I care for the children, I cook all the meals, I do all of these things, and I come here, and I still get to do that. And I'm still a person of value in the culture." So women had an easier time. They had the self-esteem to say, "I can go and work" . . . But the men had a very hard time.

Once a nurse at Sam Thong, Ly Vang helped form the Association for the Advancement of Hmong Women of Minnesota, seeking to address many of the tensions that developed between men and women as they made the difficult adjustment to life in America.

"The biggest adjustment for the women," avers Kathleen Vellenga, "other than just losing their whole culture, was that we have children in day care. They were just horrified that we did not let them bring the children to work. At home . . . when they farmed the land, they had the babies wherever they were. Even in the camps, they had little stores on the street, and their babies were with them all the time. So it made me realize how unnatural it was, the way we do it . . . even though I grew up in an era where mothers stayed home."

"Hmong women were struggling," remembers Ly Vang,

because our tradition and culture was different. Many women were . . . not allowed to go out of the home to go to school, to go to work. Their husbands were working . . . and they needed to go around and pick up their children from school, talk to their teacher, or have doctors' appointments. And the women were facing abuse because the husband misunderstood them [when they went] to school or doing things around . . . So we saw women . . . black and blue, and they were talking about . . . a conflict of understanding, and blaming, accusing. We saw many women who . . . couldn't go to the hospital because their husband didn't . . . let the wife see the doctor, so they have to deliver the baby at home, or if they go there it's going to be a problem because their body should not be showing . . . Hmong women always depended on the extended family and the husband, but not here . . . [Here] we were facing extremely difficult [conditions], not being able to speak English, not being able to help ourselves.

A particularly acute problem, especially for young women and girls, was the practice of bride kidnapping, which persisted in America. As one woman recalls, hers was the only Hmong family in the midwestern town where they settled in the late 1970s. In the summer after her eighth-grade year, a young man came to see her. They had met before when her family came to the Twin Cities to visit relatives; their mothers were from the same clan and had lived together in Laos. He was older than her, and, unbeknownst to her, his relatives had suggested that she might be a good wife. "They usually say, 'Oh, she's a nice girl. Why don't you go and call her? Talk to her, see if you like her?' That's what the elderly usually do."

It seemed to start innocently enough. He called and said, "'I'm in town . . . Let's meet and talk.' So we talked. The next day, he came back and said, 'I'm going to KFC. You want to go?' I said, 'OK.'" They finished eating, but he didn't want to leave. "I kept saying, 'I've got to go home. You have to take me home,' and he said, 'Oh, no, not yet . . . I'm expecting someone to come. And so we were waiting there for *hours* and hours." While they were waiting, his relatives went to her parents' house and announced their daughter was being kidnapped. Then they came to KFC. "These two men came walking over, and he went and talked to them. I thought, 'Oh, my goodness! Is this happening? Is this real?'" It was. A man she barely knew was taking her, a girl not yet in high school—but recognized by Hmong culture as a woman—and forcing her to be his bride.

"It was terrifying. And you don't know what to do, because this is a Hmong . . . cultural thing. You don't know if you should call the police, you should run, or you should demand to be taken back. And there's all these thoughts going through your mind . . . I guess I just kind of thought, 'OK, maybe this is fate.'" Her parents were frantic. Her father drove for miles hoping to find his daughter, even though he didn't know where the young man lived.

As the young man drove toward Minnesota, the two were silent. She felt a torrent of emotions:

I mean, he's probably an adult, he probably knows what he wants, he knows what he's going to do, but for me, I didn't know what I wanted. When we stopped at a rest area, I went to the restroom, and I think I stayed in there for a long time, and I was debating, "Should I call home, or should I go?" So I decided, "OK, I should just go out and see." So I go out, and I know he was kind of scared himself, because he was searching for me, so I guess I decided when I walked out.

It would be two weeks or more before her parents finally learned where she was.

Despite the trauma of her experience, she settled in to her new life with this stranger who became her husband. She started ninth grade that fall. Despite everything, she says, "I wasn't going to stop going to school." The following year, her parents moved to the Twin Cities, and when she gave birth to her son two years after her marriage, they watched over him while she finished school.

During that time, there were a lot of Hmong girls who got married early and became pregnant. There was a school for pregnant girls . . . I remember when I was pregnant, I went to see my counselor. I said, "Should I go to this other school?" She looked at my record, and she said . . . "I think you're better off staying here. You're taking algebra, and you're taking all these college prep courses, and they don't offer them." So I just stayed on . . . I had some really good teachers . . . [I]t's really funny. You are a married woman, but here you are in class, and your teacher is patting you on the head when your grade is really good. It makes you feel good, and it makes you feel childish . . . I graduated from high school, and I went on to college. I wasn't going to stop. My parents encouraged me . . . and I made a couple of friends who were still single and planned to go to college.

This story has a happy ending. The couple stayed together, had more children, and enjoy a good marriage. Many other young women were not so lucky—and even if they were, the trauma they experienced in the process could not be easily justified. Even so, more often than not, families honored tradition rather than availing themselves of American law and pressing charges against the kidnapper.

To combat kidnapping, Hmong women found ways to counsel and support Hmong girls. Jane Kretzmann recalls efforts in Minnesota by women like Choua Thao and Gaoly Yang, who led the Women's Association of Hmong and Lao in the early eighties. "Gaoly . . . [brought] Hmong grandmothers together with mainstream American women . . . [T]he Hmong women learned to knit, and the American women learned to appreciate Hmong *paj ntaub* . . . [W]hile they worked they did some real community education on a variety of subjects, including the rights of women. So the Hmong women encouraged their granddaughters not to get married at fourteen—not to get kidnapped at fourteen—to understand what an order for protection was . . . [T]hese were really groundbreaking times."

Hmong women who worked or otherwise ventured out of the home encountered problems of their own. There was, says Ly Vang, "a lot of misunderstanding, even when [a woman had] a [male] coworker . . .

[E]ven if you just talked and made a joke, it created problems . . . [I]t was very, very difficult, because if you were not doing anything, you couldn't help your husband or family, but if you stepped out, there were a lot of [problems] you had to deal with." To help Hmong families make the transition to the radically different American environment, Vang helped to establish the Association for the Advancement of Hmong Women of Minnesota (AAHWM) in 1981. This organization helped to "control the misunderstanding between the family [and] avoiding violence and domestic issues at home." Although members of some male circles viewed it as an organization bent on destroying tradition, Vang says, "The majority [of men] were supportive . . . [M]ale elders were involved in fundraising, on the board, and trying to be advisors. So then people had to accept it."

Choua Thao was recruited to work for the AAHWM and spent many hours mediating conflicts between men and women. In many cases, she says, men were angered by what they perceived as outside meddling in their personal lives. They found themselves fighting the same wars that already existed—and many say still exist—in this country.* Thao comments,

Hmong men . . . are good men, hard-working men. They should receive their recognition. But they need to know . . . how to cooperate . . . [K]ind of like you drive a car. You're going to hit that! Why don't you [swerve] a little bit and don't hit that? Hmong men don't do that! They . . . feel so bitter. "My wife has the power. Law enforcement helps my wife. Law enforcement doesn't help me." I say, "No, you're wrong! Law enforcement will help people who listen and follow the rules" . . . You say, "Hmong women are so free, they destroy the family" . . . "[Women] want to be good and you are overpower[ing them]. So they have to call for help."

Difficulties such as these should not mask the fact that the majority of Hmong couples, despite the stress of coming to a new country, managed to work through their differences without violence or threats. Many Hmong women who became successful in the United States today had fathers and mothers who encouraged them to pursue an education, to take advantage of opportunities that never would have existed for them in Laos or Thailand.

---

* One example from U.S. history: In 1904, the Ohio State Supreme Court ruled that a woman who had owned her own home before marriage had no right to bring her own mother into the house if her husband forbade it.

"I've never heard my parents say, 'You can't do that because you're a girl, and your brother can do that because he's a boy,'" says Mee Moua. "I think the birth order issue is much more influential . . . [A]s the oldest, because I graduated from high school and went to college, my siblings all graduated from high school and went to college . . . [I]t's just because my parents had defined that to be the culture for our family. The expectation is there, and the opportunities were created . . . My parents were very open, and their idea was, 'Whatever you want to do, we'll support you.'"

But young Hmong women often found—and still find—themselves defined (or confined) by their parents' traditional expectations. "There is an old Hmong proverb that says something like 'seven daughters will not match one son,'" confesses one young woman. "It's a summary of what my life, what girls' lives have been in the Hmong culture." In Laos, young men spent hours every day working in the fields, feeding livestock, hunting for food, and making, mending, or sharpening tools. In America, they had far less to do. As the apple of their parents' eye—the child who would perform the proper rituals at their funerals—sons were treated with far more indulgence than daughters. "The boys have this ego, because parents feed into it so much," says another young woman. "[Parents say,] 'Oh, we have a son! He's going to continue the family line. He's going to be the one to take care of us! You girls, we raised you, you're going to marry, you're going to take all the resources we invested in you to another family' . . . [M]y brothers . . . don't know how to do much. My older one doesn't even know how to do the laundry." Without realizing it, Hmong parents often helped determine their children's educational destiny: success for the daughters they had taught to work hard; struggle for the sons upon whom they had doted.

Generation Gap

Even families with long roots in this country understand the pain of conflicts that can develop between generations. Whether inspired by the civil rights and Vietnam War protests of the 1960s or the different ethics that have evolved in our new online culture, parents and children often find themselves alienated from each other. These problems are amplified in immigrant communities. "Immigrant parents, by and large, retain much of the values, the worldview of the country they come from," says Rudolph Vecoli. "The children embrace an American identity, and through popular culture, shared American experiences, they feel more American than their parents. But they also absorb different values, a different sense of identity. And this becomes a source of conflict—a conflict which is often painful and disruptive."

"[Our children] are different from us," said Chai Her to her nephew. "[O]ur ways and habits are different. If we follow our traditional way, then our children will not understand. But we don't understand their American ways, and we don't like them, either."

Hmong raised in the West were the first in history to experience adolescence, making their unique problems difficult to identify and address. In addition, Hmong culture relied on corporal punishment to enforce discipline on children. "It was a challenge," says Ly Vang, "because . . . the Hmong tradition is that if a child misbehaved, he got punishment from the parent, so they should not do that again. And one time learned lasts forever! But in America, there is a law that is protecting the children . . . from facing that kind of punishment. The Hmong parents were facing a lot of problems. 'If I discipline my children my way, rules and regulations here stop me . . . But for me to follow the American law here, I don't have that kind of parenting skill to do it.'" At the same time, when children ran afoul of the law, Hmong parents discovered they and not their children were legally responsible for their actions. "So that was causing a lot of anger from the parents."

"Everybody in *my* family . . . [respected] my dad," remembers Chris Her,

[But for us] it had the reverse effect, because we knew him . . . He'd tell other kids, "Hey, you guys go to school," do this and do that. [But] it's America. There's this fine line between abuse and discipline; kids can manipulate that . . . My parents might not have spoken English, but they understood American law. So we have the advantage now . . . If my dad said, "You kids go to school," sure, I'll go to school, but if I don't want to I don't have to, because you can't stop me . . . [Y]ou're calling their bluff, basically . . . I eventually started doing anything I wanted.

J. Kou Vang, a successful real estate developer in St. Paul, grew up without his father, who was killed in the war in 1972.

My mom didn't speak English, so we would translate for her at our own parent-teacher conference! It gives you a lot of power, you know? You can tell her what you want her to know! . . . [W]e'd take her to the hospital, to the clinic, and translate for her there. I remember I was in sixth grade, my aunt had a son born with fluid in his brain, and it had to get drained . . . [W]hen he was three years old, we had to go . . . to the Children's Hospital in Milwaukee for them to replace the shunt. I went down to translate that procedure to my aunt, and I was in sixth grade! I had no idea what a shunt was, I had no idea what the heck they were doing, but you kind of make do with it. We were that link for our parents.

That responsibility often put children in traditionally adult roles even as they were experiencing "American" adolescence. "I remember . . . in eighth grade, we had sex ed," says Peter Vang, "You always needed your parent's signature . . . [but] in the Hmong culture, [discussion of] sex is taboo . . . I stayed up all night trying to master my father's signature . . . because I didn't want to be the only one in my classroom who could not be there . . . I wouldn't have said to my parents, 'This is about sex. Can I join?' . . . So I signed my dad's name . . . [T]hat was a bad thing that I did." Despite this deception, Vang was an otherwise obedient son. "I was so used to translating for my parents and translating here and there looking at the bills . . . My uncle started grabbing me and taking me with him instead of his son [who] was my age, too . . . [M]y parents got irritated. 'Why don't they take their son? Why do they need you?'"

Many Hmong youth found themselves carrying heavy loads of responsibility at home in addition to their new and disorienting lives in school. "[T]he younger folks," remembers Anderson, "had learned the language fairly quickly. Many had been doing extraordinarily well in school. *All* of them had tremendous pressure placed upon them, because . . . the decision to resettle to the United States was one that [parents] made primarily . . . to give the children a chance . . . That presented a great deal of pressure for the kids growing up here . . . [T]he whole family is saying, 'It's all on you now, it's all on you. You've got to carry this forward.'"

"I think a lot of parents' expectations for their kids being in America, because of having a chance that they didn't have, kind of pushed their kid off a little bit," observes Chris Her. "[E]very parent wants their kid to become a doctor. Well, some of these kids might not *want* to be a doctor." For children, especially boys like Her, negative response to this kind of pressure, alienation from the mainstream culture in their school, bullying, and other factors led them into the gang lifestyle— though it wasn't always as glamorous or cool as some had imagined.

"Now that I look at it, there was really nothing fun about it . . . [A]ll we would do is just sit in the parking lot, smoke cigarettes . . . Sometimes we'd go cruising, just drive around. And it's not like we were looking at anything or had any significant conversations . . . We'd just basically go there to say . . . 'We can go and sit wherever we want to. You guys have to respect us.'"

Asian gangs came to Minnesota through the same route as their predecessors, says Bill Snyder, who served on the St. Paul Police's Asian gang strike force for many years:

It started out with a soccer group that called themselves the Cobras . . . [O]ppressed by other gangs . . . [they] formed together to stop the oppression and realized they had power and then began to oppress other people . . . But the two [main Cobra] leaders got into a fight over one leader's brother [who was] jumped for a baseball cap he was wearing . . . [H]e broke off and started a new gang called the TMC — Tiny Man Crew. And they became a Blood gang, so that's how the rivalry started . . . The Asian gangs [copied] . . . the West Coast gangs, the Bloods and the Crips. Bloods wore red, and Crips wore blue . . . Then other gangs came from California.

Parents who discovered their children had joined gangs sent them to relatives in another state. Instead of surrounding the child with positive influences, this tactic often served the opposite purpose: exporting gangs to new locations.

Other students responded to the same pressures in very different ways. Seexeng Lee, who spent his refugee camp years drawing pictures in the mud with a stick and listening to his father tell folktales to his friends, came to Minnesota with his family in the summer of 1984, starting third grade that fall:

Not knowing a word of English was difficult, not knowing the culture was difficult . . . So having cousins, nephews who had been in the country longer dragging you— that helped . . . It's almost like the blind leading the blind, but the good thing is, they actually know a little bit more, 'cause they have two, three years' experience . . . To watch cartoons . . . and for them to understand it and you don't, it's so cool! . . . I mean, some people look at this and say it's so tiny, but I look at it and think, "When am I going to get there? When am I going to understand these cartoons?" . . . And I think that the moment I landed here, the moment you start seeing everybody, you want to be just like them. And I think that's the pressure, the beginning of . . . everything.

Mee Moua, whose family moved from Providence, Rhode Island, to Appleton, Wisconsin, in 1978, went first to a public school where there were many other Hmong students:

I remember we used to get taken out of our regular class . . . down to this classroom where the ESL teacher tried to use flash cards to teach us. And I remember "apple" and "table" and "chair" and "banana" . . . [A]fter third grade, my uncle, who had gone to school in Vientiane . . . with the Jesuit priests . . . took my brother and sister and me to a Catholic church . . . I started fourth grade at the Catholic school . . . We were the only Hmong kids at that time. And that was the first time in my life that I had friends who were not Hmong. I still didn't speak any English, but . . . I would play tag with them, and they would come to my house, and I would go to their house. I learned a lot from my American friends. In fourth grade I joined the Girl Scouts. I also played soccer, and I was in track, and I played basketball . . . [M]y parents were very willing to allow me to do things with my non-Hmong friends and their families . . .

The first time I realized that I could speak English was in the spring of fifth grade . . . in Miss Barker's class . . . [W]e were talking about the cycle of precipitation and evaporation. The teacher always asked students to raise their hands to read the paragraphs out loud, and for some reason I remember I raised my hand. She called on me, and I read one whole paragraph that talked specifically about the sun shining on the water, and the water evaporating, going up to the clouds and becoming rain, and it came down again. And I got a little certificate with a smiley sticker on it, and I was very excited, and I took it home to my parents. I felt like that day marked the moment in my life where all the clouds cleared away and I could speak English, I could understand people.

But the educational process that opened doors of opportunity to the newest generation of Hmong also served to alienate them from their parents, even from each other. "There were . . . cultural pressures around things like dating, intermingling with mainstream Americans, particularly of the opposite sex," observes Anderson.

The parents attempted to keep very tight controls about this, and to have their kids live in this other world but hew very closely to the cultural norm of the Hmong community. That presented a whole separate set of tremendous pressures for some of these kids, and some of them reacted by rebelling, by running away from home, by being kicked out of the home. It's ironic that many of the kids who were kicked out . . . because their parents perceived that they were too American, were not really American enough to adapt to life on their own . . . so they were caught in this limbo land.

Despite the gains many were making in school, they were still not accepted by their non-Hmong classmates, who saw no difference between the various national and ethnic groups from Southeast Asia. To most of them, these new immigrants were all Vietnamese, all reminders of a war America wanted to forget.

"Walking to school . . . cars would stop by the corner when we were waiting to cross the light, and people would spit at us or throw things at us," remembers Mee Moua.

> On the playground . . . a lot of people [pulled on corner of eyes to simulate "slanted eyes"] and [called me] "gook" . . . [P]eople would do [karate moves], the Charlie Chan thing . . . [A]t school . . . people didn't pick on me, and . . . for the kids who did pick on me, I had friends who would protect me. But outside of the school environment, there was a lot of hostility from adults, from kids . . . in part not so much because I was Hmong but because we were poor. We lived in public housing . . . At the holidays, a lot of white people would come to our house with bags of food, so the neighborhood kids knew that those weren't our relatives coming to holiday dinner but the church folks bringing us food shelf food . . . [T]he neighborhood kids who didn't go to [my] Catholic school . . . would come to our house and . . . pee on our garage or they would take the mud and they would write "f—- off" and things like that on our garage. I used to have to help my dad hose down and wash down the garage . . . [M]y dad used to say that he didn't want the landlord or the neighbors to think it was his kids who did that.

Cy Thao, who attended school in Minneapolis, remembers difficult times also. "I had a lot of fistfights . . . all the way up to the end of junior high. That's when all of the bullies started to show up . . . [W]e looked different, we couldn't speak the language . . . [W]e're smaller, too, and so we were a prime target . . . [F]or a while I thought I might need those skills for the rest of my life! But as people mature, you resolve problems without fistfighting."

As if harassment from other students wasn't enough, newly arrived Hmong students often faced scorn from more established Hmong who had learned the language and immersed themselves in American culture. Born in Spencer, North Carolina, Chris Her "predominately hung around more American kids, African American kids, growing up. Then about the point of junior high and high school, I started shifting back to hang out with the Hmong kids." When his non-Hmong peers would see "these guys who didn't speak English well or—the way they dressed—they'd make fun of them . . . I'd stop and think, 'Wait a minute. Making fun of the other Hmong kids is just the same as them making fun of me' . . . So I went back and started hanging out with them." But Her had been in the United States his whole life. A part of American culture since birth, he found himself engaging in the same kind of discrimination:

> [Y]ou start categorizing Hmongs now, where you have your main core Hmong which can speak fluent English and dress right, which really understands the thug culture

... Then you have ones that just came from Thailand, Laos ... [W]e call them FOBs, fresh off the boat guys. [T]hey would walk around in their sandals, wear purple shorts ... [B]ut then ... they'd come and try to join us, but we wouldn't accept them, because [we thought] "We're better than they are, because we're cultured, we can speak English, and we're not as—" I guess ignorant.

Her's disdain extended to his parents, who saw his growing antipathy toward school and his intensifying gang associations and tried to keep him on the straight and narrow.

[My father was] always trying, every day he's trying. And it got to the point ... when I was smoking ... he said, "Go fishing with me"—early in the morning, 'cause he knows I come in at about two, three in the morning—"Go fishing with me; I'll buy you cigarettes." He tried to pull me off ... the way I was going ... [A]nd sometimes I'd give in and go fishing with him ... He says, "Just sit here and listen to the wind blow through the trees, listen to the waves, watch the river" ... and once in a while he'd go into the "why he doesn't want me to do this, why he doesn't want me to do that" stuff ... But the thing is, we know that he's not that well educated ... I thought I was smarter ... because I was street smart ... "I know the American culture better than you do ... so you can't tell me what to do, because you're still stuck in the past." I think all kids think their parents are stuck in the past. [S]ometimes I'd even say, joking, "Dad, we have cars now," "Dad, we have shoes now."

Those who found more success in school also wrestled with their identity and with their parental relationships. For Seexeng Lee, part of the problem stemmed from his parents' age. As one of their youngest children, he often felt more like a grandchild than a child.

[Y]ou're kind of embarrassed, because your parents don't fit the stereotypical parent. They don't come to your soccer games, they don't come to parent-teacher conferences, they don't tell you wonderful things, even though you bring home straight As—"That's not enough ... Make sure next time you ... continue to bring straight As" ... You keep seeing 90 percent of the people around you in terms of how their parents treat them, how they act toward their parents, and you see some of your friends who are better off than you, and you're like, "How come I'm not like that?" And it's really hard, at that age, to say, "Hey, I'm proud to be who I am."

While families like Seexeng Lee's stayed in the city and found a way to support each other and keep their children in school and out of trouble, others responded by moving out of urban areas in California, Minnesota, or Wisconsin. Though Peter Vang's family came to St. Paul, Minnesota, in 1987,

the Hmong gangs were kind of on the rise, and so my dad wanted to get away from everything, especially from Wisconsin and Minnesota ... [M]y dad has like a cousin—

he took care of her [after] her parents passed away . . . She wanted to . . . repay his kindness, and invited him to Pennsylvania to live . . . [In 1992] we moved to . . . Lancaster County . . . [I]t's a big farming area with a lot of Amish and Mennonites . . . I grew up with Americans, and I picked up the language pretty well. When I went to school, the only people that I spoke Hmong to were my cousins . . . [E]very time I came home, if there was nothing to do I usually ran over to the landlord's house to help him at the farm . . . And I was involved with the choirs, soccer, a lot of the sports . . . And so I guess that's where I started picking up the English language.

Vang escaped gang influences but lost the opportunity to learn about Hmong culture. "I have to think about it before I can do it. Let's say there's an older gentleman in the room. [My friends] automatically say, 'Oh, how are you doing, Uncle or Grandpa'—it depends on what their status is . . . [I]t's not second [nature] for me like for my friends who were born and raised . . . in heavily populated Hmong areas."

As Chris Her became more and more involved in gangs, his parents tried to move him into a Lutheran school in Eagan, a suburb south of St. Paul. But after five weeks of taking delight in shocking the relatively sheltered students, he finished the semester, enrolled in summer school to finish junior high, and went right back into the public system with his old friends. High school presented a whole new array of opportunities, coupled with teachers who were less strict, "and now you've got cars." But with this newfound freedom also came increased violence between "jocks, preps, African Americans," and others. One particularly large and violent outbreak further drove a wedge between different groups of students. "[O]ne of my friends . . . tried starting a food fight . . . in the chow hall, where he hit this African American girl. She thought it was me, and she came to me and dumped a carton of milk on my leather jacket . . . I didn't even have to throw a punch. She just got attacked." Police rushed in to the lunchroom, and Her was sequestered in an office. But after the next class, the fighting broke out again, and school staff struggled to bring the conflict under control. After school, Her's gang met outside to regroup. "[T]he [other] Hmong students saw it as, 'OK, I'm not involved in their gang, but [the African Americans] aren't going to know any better. They're just going to say, 'Oh, he's Asian. We're going after him' . . . So I think the fear that they were going to get assaulted led them to come out and join us. And then when I saw it, to me it was more like, 'Oh, power! There's something here!' "

Her attended classes so seldom and was getting into so much trouble that his father supported his decision to leave school when he was sixteen. Unfortunately, dropping out only made matters worse. Without making "appearances" with his gang, the "respect" he once thrived on was slipping away. Her wanted to marry his girlfriend: "[M]y dad said, 'You can't get married unless you finish high school, until you're able to support yourself *and* your family.'" For once, Her relented. But once he returned, he was confronted with the consequences of skipping so many classes.

I was seventeen, and I was in freshman classes . . . I know all these kids are younger than me, but I've got to be the one to ask the stupid question . . . I'm like, "Well, if I don't know it, I'll just try to wing it." So I start trying to wing stuff, and I find out that there's absolutely nothing I know . . . So I got back into my old routine of, "OK, maybe I don't like math class, so I'll just skip math class, and then go to the other classes that I like."

He reached the point where he woke up thinking, "Maybe I won't get up and go to school today. I'll just stay in and sleep today." He was supposed to drive his girlfriend to school, but soon "I was like, 'Aw, whatever. She'll find her way to school somehow if she wants to.'"

One day Her was attacked by members of his own gang:

I was really pissed off about that, and I was thinking about revenge, revenge, revenge . . . They call one night, and I said, "Come on over and hang out" . . . I set this all up, they come over, and we get into it at my house, and they all drive off . . . (I was in a car accident, so I couldn't drive my car anymore.) I call one of my friends over, he picks me up, and we go over to another friend's house. Well, we arrive, and [the gang members I'd just fought with] were there. I'm thinking, "What's going on here? Why are they here?" So I come out of the car, and I start questioning everybody . . . [T]hey all come out of the car, and the guy that—

Her paused for several moments before finally saying

—my victim . . . really didn't have anything to do with it. We grew up together . . . We were really good friends, but it just happened to be he was there with those guys, which really offended me . . . And I brought a gun . . . I didn't have nothing planned . . . but we started talking . . . and he said something . . . I can't really remember what he said, but I know that I got mad real fast . . . There was no thought—nothing, just "I need to get my respect back" . . . So after I shot him, I turned and tried shooting at the other guys, but my friends stopped me. They grabbed me, grabbed the gun . . . [T]he scary thing was, my thought wasn't "Oh man, what did I do?" My thought was of my old self coming back, saying, "OK, I've instilled my dominance again . . . I've got my respect back now, I've put my foot down."

Chris Her, interviewed in Faribault prison, became a gang member at a young age and was involved in a shooting that sent him to prison.

Her skipped town, aided by gangs in various states, but eventually came back to see his girlfriend. They hid out with one of his brothers, planning for a life on the run. But someone tipped off the police, and all three were arrested. Her's first strategy was to deny what he had done, exploiting the fact that eyewitnesses were telling the police different stories. "[I was] sitting in county jail . . . listening to all of these other idiots . . . [O]ne guy [says], 'Oh, you're only going to get twelve years, and you've got to do eight.' Here's another guy saying, 'Oh, you're going to get *life*, man!' . . . [I]t came to the point where I just said, 'I did it. I know I did it, so whatever punishment they're going to give me is what I should get.'" Her was convicted, sent to prison, and at first felt almost as if he was in the wrong place. Despite his horrible crime, he got clothes, a bed, and three meals a day. With the time he now had on his hands, "all the lectures my dad gave me started resounding in my head . . . and I'm like, 'Wait a minute! I understand where he's coming from now.'"

For years, Her tried to write a letter to his victim's family. But once he got past "I'm sorry," he froze. "My apology isn't enough . . . There's nothing else I can say to make it better, because there's nothing I can do to bring him back." Her has tried to speak to other at-risk kids, with some success, but he is amazed at how often they seem more interested in stories from his criminal youth than in learning from his mistakes.

[Y]ou watch in every movie, all the drug dealers do fine until the end of the movie . . . Either they die, or the IRS comes and locks them up . . . Kids watch it to the climax point . . . and once you reach that climax point, everything else in the movie is a blank. So I only see the parts where he'll sell drugs, make money, get all the girls, buy a big house . . . I don't see the end where his rivals might come in and kill him or the IRS or the cops might come in and bust him, 'cause kids live in the now. "I want to get money quick, I want to spend money, I want to live large." They don't understand the way of earning it. So you try to teach them: "You shouldn't be glorifying these rappers, glorifying these drug dealers, glorifying these thugs. You should be glorifying your parents, because they went to school, they earned a living, they supported you . . . Your parents get up at six in the morning, hold two jobs, work every day, come back, deal with you guys, feed you guys . . . They're the ones you ought to respect."

But hard-won insight like Her's wasn't always easy to heed, even for Hmong children who succeeded in school and stayed out of trouble. Seexeng Lee graduated from high school, went to college, earned a degree in art education, and began teaching in the Minneapolis public school system. Along the way, he had ignored many of the lessons his father Vang Lor Lee tried to pass on to him. It wasn't out of disrespect or enmity. In fact, when he graduated from college, "I painted a black-and-white picture of him, and I used his soldier photo, the small little black-and-white photo (everybody has it) . . . and gave it to him at my reception." Seexeng thanked his father for encouraging him throughout his years of schooling. "He said, 'OK,' and he handed it to one of my brothers and said, 'My home is very dirty . . . I'm going to give it to you so you can put it in your house.' That was the last I saw of it." In 2005, Vang Lor Lee died. Since coming to America, "no one in our family had passed away. So to have the first, to have the most significant anchor of your family pass away . . . was devastating, left a huge void. And all of us felt it; we didn't know how hurtful it is to lose somebody . . . [H]e died late April, and we couldn't do his funeral until June because of how busy it was [in the Hmong funeral home]." As a tribute, Lee wanted to place his father's painting near the casket. He asked his brother where

Drawing inspiration from iconic paintings that used gold leaf to denote sacredness, Seexeng Lee added this touch on the stars, epaulets, hatband, and hat insignia worn by his father, Vang Lor Lee, in a painting made before his death in 2005.

it was and learned it had been tucked away in a dusty closet.

As Seexeng thought of a fitting homage to his father, he remembered something from a college art class. Byzantine Christian artists showed the sacred nature of their iconic subjects by gilding them in gold leaf. He thought, "'What if I made [my father], or things about him, gold?' . . . If my dad is sacred to me and it's important to me, I think I have the right to use gold leaf . . . So I made the bars [on the shoulders of his uniform] gold, the stars . . . [and] crest [on his hat] gold, and it was in black and white, so the gold really just gleamed." Suddenly everyone wanted the painting that had languished in a closet for ten years. "Is it because of dad passing away? Is it because it was at the funeral? Or was it because of the gold? I think it was all of the above." Lee has kept the painting, and "every year, on the day of my father's passing, I have a light, and I will turn it on—and the day we buried him, I will turn it on, and go visit him in Oakland Cemetery."

Vang Lor Lee's death inspired his son to do more than decorate a painting in his honor.

When an elder passes away . . . that is when you see the big picture of what is a community, what is a family . . . That's when you feel like, "I've never felt so helpless." But that moment was also at the time when I felt most supported, because distant family that I heard of but never really connected [with] . . . they actually connected with us. And so that really pulled me back to where I am today, and where I am today is way more appreciative of my origin—not just mine, but the entire Hmong origin, the entire Hmong culture.

Lee has since created numerous artistic images depicting the most treasured aspects of his culture. Each one bears an embellishment of gold—the mark of its sacred nature to Seexeng and to other young Hmong who yearn to remember—or recover—the lessons their elders have tried to pass on to them.

LONGING

"Here in the U.S. we are losing our traditions and heritage," Chai Her told her nephew.

Back in Laos, we took care of each other no matter who you were . . . [Y]our brain didn't hurt like here . . . We didn't argue and have divorces . . . Even though we had less than here . . . we had great love in our community. If you killed a chicken, a pig, or an ox, you invited the whole village to come and enjoy it with you. Here in the U.S., we have lost this important value of our culture . . . I would be willing to sacrifice all [modern] comforts to go back.

Chai Her and many other Hmong joined a long line of refugees in America—a line that stretches into the present—who still longed to return to the land of their memories and imaginations. In some cases, they worked behind the scenes, forming secretive organizations to realize a dream of triumphant return. Even the casual reader of history can think of examples: the Irish Republican Army, the Zionist movement, Cuban Americans' anti-Castro activities, and most recently the Somali community's struggles with the Al-Shabaab (The Youth) organization. In the 1970s and '80s, Hmong desire to return to Laos was easy to find. It was also, writes Sanford Ungar, an impulse easily exploited by those conducting "frequent fund-raising campaigns in the Hmong community to underwrite their allegedly imminent, CIA-supported reconquest of Laos." Those who contributed had no idea how it would happen, but even if they and their families were impoverished, they sent money to Vang Pao to help realize that dream.[4]

Vang Pao initially settled in Missoula, Montana, largely because his friend Jerry Daniels lived there. Three of Vang Pao's sons, with Daniels's help, went there to study. "Montana is a bit like the Plain of Jars," says Vang Pao, "I decided to buy a farm . . . I knew that when the Hmong came here, they would need to eat, but they could not beg for food, so I decided to grow rice . . . and stand on my own two feet." It was a cataclysmic fall from commander of Military Region 2 to farmer. No huge ceremonial welcome awaited him. For almost fifteen years, he had American and Thai advisors as constant companions. Now a nominal

CIA "handler" offered occasional advice, but Vang Pao was mostly on his own and did as he saw fit.

While farming, says Vang Pao, "I was running around helping the Hmong at the same time." Indeed, as soon as Hmong began arriving in the United States and learned where Vang Pao lived, they called him collect. Bills began to mount as his role as leader of the Hmong in exile expanded. He eventually gave up the failing four-hundred-acre ranch he had purchased with the CIA's help.[5]

In late 1977, Vang Pao traveled to Santa Ana, California, where many Hmong had settled, looking for funding to engage in welfare work without bankrupting himself. The result was Lao Family Communities, Inc. (LFCI), the first Hmong-operated mutual assistance association in the United States. In 1986, well after the establishment of Lao Family, Montana court records show Vang Pao was more than $170,000 in debt. At least a portion of that figure must have resulted from trying to help his people find their way in a disorienting, frightening country. But Vang Pao had no particular knowledge of or connections in the American social welfare system. What could he do?[6]

If the image of Vang Pao in Laos is complex and controversial, it is even more so when discussing his postwar activities. While not esteemed by scholars for their accuracy, books by Jane Hamilton-Merritt and Keith Quincy still seem to be the sources to which most people turn to learn about Vang Pao. They offer two starkly different portrayals. Hamilton-Merritt's tale is of rapaciously vengeful Communist Lao and Vietnamese intent on punishing the Hmong for their ties to the United States and their ongoing attempts to break free of oppression. The United States, Thailand, the UN, and most other nations are, by this point of her story, coldhearted, callous, or unwitting conspirators with or lackeys of Hmong oppressors; ignoring evidence supporting the ongoing existence of Lao reeducation camps and the use of yellow rain in the jungles; blind to humanitarian abuses in Thai refugee camps; and passive observers as Thai soldiers and civilians traumatize the Hmong by digging up the graves of their dead. In this context, Vang Pao's efforts to help his people come under attack from "[f]ormer anti–Vietnam War activists, many of whom were now involved in the refugee resettlement business [who] reported him to the federal authorities for raising funds in the U.S. to overthrow a foreign government." Vang Pao's problems are, in this depiction, the result of his own understandable passions, desperate Hmong refugees and their relatives, liberal critics, and "[a]gents trained by Hanoi, who had entered the U.S. as refugees through a sloppy screening process [and who] trailed Vang Pao, waiting for an opportunity to strike." According to one of Hamilton-Merritt's sources, "In Fresno, I see Red Lao come here to visit, sent by the Lao government to tell the refugees propaganda. They also collect money from refugees here, saying they'll take it to their families in Laos. They are only here to make money for themselves."[7]

By contrast, Quincy's Vang Pao is the product of his own overweening ambition. Initially content to leave the fighting in Laos to the Chao Fa, he sprang into action after their widespread defeat in 1978. Vang Pao, writes Quincy, ordered Hmong militants in Laos and Thailand to stay put, amassing, by 1981, two thousand guerrillas in Laos overseen by his father-in-law, Cher Pao Moua, the former commander of Bouam Long. On June 18, Vang Pao helped form the United Lao National Liberation Front (ULNLF—also called Neo Hom), a coalition of exiled Hmong and ethnic Lao claiming the support of "the majority of the Laotian people living inside Laos." The ULNLF boasted Moua's two thousand men as well as two battalions led by former Military Region 5 commander Thonglith Chokbengbou and the son of former prince Boun Oum. But the only groups doing any real fighting in Laos, writes Quincy, were a "Lanna Division" supported by the Chinese (who were trying to check the spread of Vietnamese influence) and two resurrected Chao Fa groups led by Xai Soua Yang and self-proclaimed Hmong messiah Pa Kao Her. But the ULNLF "was a reunion of former players in the old regime, old cronies looking to revive their careers and improve their fortunes. Religious fanatics [Yang and Her] were not welcome."[8]

Quincy also makes serious allegations against Vang Pao and Neo Hom's fund-raising practices, relying heavily on the work of journalist Ruth Hammond, who in 1989 wrote a series for the *Twin Cities Reader* and an article for the *Washington Post*. Hammond first met a Hmong family in the late seventies while writing a piece on community gardening for the *Minneapolis Tribune*. When she rode her bike home from work, she would stop and introduce herself to Hmong families along the way. Volunteering to teach English, she was quickly befriended by scores of Hmong families and began writing stories to help introduce her new acquaintances to the broader Twin Cities community.

A woman Hammond met "invited me back to her apartment. Her

son-in-law, who lived with her, had been collecting money for Vang Pao. It didn't seem to be a big secret to him." Not until several years later did Hammond begin investigating Vang Pao's activities in earnest. Owing to a 1988 article making reference to Neo Hom activities, "I started getting calls from other people, saying, 'Finally someone has written about this . . . [B]ut this is just the smoking gun; there's a lot more going on.'" Hammond dug deeper, spending eight months interviewing Hmong in Minnesota, Wisconsin, California, and other states and viewing copies of Neo Hom correspondence provided by former members.

The details revealed in Hammond's articles were stunning. Vang Pao and Neo Hom were using a hierarchical, clan-based organization to raise hundreds of thousands of dollars every year from Hmong families, many of whom were on welfare: "To become members of Neo Hom, families were required to pay $100 down and then $10 a month. Those who paid $500 were given certificates [signed by Vang Pao] that they believe entitle them to return to Laos after the 'liberation,' with the understanding that their airfare will be free and they will receive a return on their investment." (While acknowledging that these sales occurred, one former member of Neo Hom insists these documents were not signed by Vang Pao but were forged or stamped with his signature.) By the mid-1980s, reported Hammond, "Neo Hom leaders began direct sales of offices in Vang Pao's future government. Refugees paid $1,000 or more to secure positions such as police chiefs, district leaders, army officers, and cabinet members. Some people are paying up to $1,000 a month to hold their positions . . . [T]he aspiring government officer asks his cousins to help him make payments, promising in turn to appoint the cousins to lesser positions." These same posts were allegedly sold at a discounted rate to Hmong in Thai refugee camps and promised to Hmong in Laos as a way of recruiting them into the resistance.

Hammond also divulged serious allegations that Neo Hom was controlling leadership positions of the numerous Lao Family chapters that sprang up in American cities with large Hmong populations, making the social services organization appear to be a front for the resistance. While Vang Pao supporters like Hamilton-Merritt insist that all the charges surrounding Vang Pao and Neo Hom are manufactured by Hmong rivals, liberals, and Communists, these practices have long been an open secret in the Hmong community.[9]

Only one example of the tragedies that befell "true believers" is a man interviewed in 2007 who fought in the Secret War, fled to Thailand, and came to the United States. In 1982, he attended a Neo Hom rally: "The general said he needed men to go back to Laos, to help start the war . . . He said he would come later with a bigger army . . . I thought we would go . . . and after some time the Americans or the French . . . or some strong country might think about us . . . We didn't know when; it depended on how big of a war we could make." He left his family, went to Thailand, and sneaked into Laos to try, along with two or three hundred other men, to incite a war with the Lao army. No reinforcements, no flow of money, food, or supplies came after him. For a year he traveled between Laos and Ban Vinai, where letters and money occasionally arrived. After several harrowing battles and the loss of many men, "I was scared a lot. I cried; I prayed to God. I promised myself, 'I will fight no more. It's too dangerous and nobody will help. The Hmong people are not being Hmong people. General Vang Pao just stays in America.'"

Having left the United States before attaining his citizenship, there was no going back for this man. The Thai military made him an offer: fight against the Communist Hmong in Thailand. The Thai didn't have much skill at mountain warfare and preferred sending others rather than losing more of their own men. So the man, his fellow guerrillas, and even some Chao Fa signed on. The Hmong swore loyalty to the king, and the Thai swore that if the Hmong succeeded, they would receive land and citizenship. The Thai armed their new Hmong recruits, pointed them toward the enemy, and sent them on their way.

"We just went behind enemy lines and up the mountains from behind," says the man. "It was our kind of terrain; we spoke the same language as the Thai Hmong, so when we went there, nobody was scared . . . That's why the Thai government sent us." Those sent on a fool's errand in Laos found a mission and—they hoped—a new home in Thailand. They persuaded Communist Hmong to come out of the mountains and surrender, defeating others in battle. But when the fighting was over, "the Hmong we fought . . . received amnesty, Thai citizenship. They got a house . . . [We] got barbed wire . . . [T]hey told us, 'Go back to the refugee camp.'" Like others who share his fate, this man who fought for Vang Pao during the Secret War and answered his call to return to Laos and be a part of the Hmong people's glorious homecoming now lives in Thailand with no status, no property, and an uncertain future. His American relatives call and send him money, members of the

Thai military who remember his service say he will be rewarded "some day," but there seems no end to the limbo in which he is caught.

It is easy to conclude that Vang Pao and his inner circle simply used the pretense of a rebellion in Laos to collect money from the Hmong people. But the story is far more complex than that.

In November 1980, ardent cold warrior Ronald Reagan was elected president in the midst of the Iran hostage crisis and the Soviet Union's war in Afghanistan. He sought to bring the "evil empire" to its knees by spending billions of dollars on defense and aiding any effort around the world to topple or prevent Soviet-supported regimes. In March 1981, CIA director William Casey wrote a memo "outlining a covert plan to roll back Communism worldwide by aiding resistance in Afghanistan, Cuba, Grenada, Iran, Libya, Nicaragua, Cambodia, and Laos. The overt and covert dimensions of what would eventually be called the 'Reagan Doctrine' became a matter of record in places like Afghanistan, Cambodia, Iran and Nicaragua." But as a U.S. Senate committee discovered in 1993, a plan for Laos had evolved as well. On July 28, 1981, a State Department meeting, including representatives from the Pentagon and the NSC, discussed the possibility of asking the ethnic Lao resistance to look for clues about missing U.S. servicemen. A post-meeting evaluation of these insurgents deemed their numbers too small and fragmented to pose any real threat to the Lao government but capable of serving U.S. interests if "strongly motivated." What began as an attempt to raise money to find American POWs and MIAs, determined John Mattes, the Senate's chief fraud investigator, developed into a fund containing over $550,000 "used to arm Laotian resistance groups in a covert network run by 'members of the NSC.'" These groups "could have served as a prototype for Lt. Col. Oliver North's later fundraising activities on behalf of the Contras [in Nicaragua]."[10]

The operation uncovered by the U.S. Senate was not unique. Numerous individuals also sought to bring the Hmong to the Reagan administration's attention. Ardent advocate Carl Bernard, a highly decorated veteran of World War II, Korea, and Vietnam, had served on a White Star team in Laos. Over those six months in 1961, Bernard developed a deep respect for Vang Pao and the Hmong people. He believed America had abandoned and betrayed its allies when it withdrew from Southeast Asia in 1973—an act so personally abhorrent that he rented an office in Alexandria, Virginia, established an informal working group to consider how best to help the Hmong, and used his many connections in the United States, France, and elsewhere to find support for Vang Pao and to inform the media of the Hmong people's plight. Bernard's old friend and fellow Korean War veteran D. L. "Pappy" Hicks was involved in deep cover operations in Laos between 1960 and '62 and spent much of the 1980s petitioning Congress to have the Hmong recognized as soldiers who fought for the United States and to give them an easier path toward citizenship. He also helped send civilian supplies to the resistance in Thailand and Laos.

In 1985, Rick Wade, a private citizen from Alaska initially following up on stories of American POWs still trapped in Southeast Asia at the behest of Senator Daniel Murkowski, met one of Vang Pao's aides, Moua Xiong. Xiong took Wade to Thailand, showing him illegal sites along the border where officials kept refugees from registering with the UN as well as small guerrilla bases from which Hmong soldiers snuck in and out of Laos. "[The Thai] would run operations with the Hmong forces and help support them," says Wade, "especially if they wanted a particular mission carried out." But they never wanted the Hmong to be so successful that they attracted too much attention. Wade thought the Thai military was waiting for a clear signal from the United States: would it support this insurgency or not? At the same time, "VP and his whole organization back in the States were raising . . . quite a bit of money. In the beginning they were getting around three hundred thousand dollars a year, at least that I knew of." Most of that money, says Wade, made it overseas, but when Thai officials found out cash was coming in, the more corrupt ones would take a significant cut.[11]

Wade says he believed the Hmong were exactly the kind of freedom fighters the United States was looking for. If he, with the help of sympathetic U.S. and Thai officials, could shepherd vulnerable Hmong through, more resources would get to men in the field: "I wasn't working for anybody. I went out there as a favor for this aide of Vang Pao's and then . . . I met with VP . . . [He] actually asked me to go for them." Wade made numerous trips to Thailand and put out feelers in the States, speaking with a staffer from UN ambassador Jeane Kirkpatrick's office, Oliver North aide Rob Owen, and others: "These guys are checking you out and seeing if you're legit and if anybody else wants to talk to you . . . [Y]ou work your way up the ladder." Wade also met with wealthy conservatives, like Ellen Garwood, who were interested in bankrolling anti-Communist efforts.* But Wade was not alone. Says Pappy Hicks, "There were a lot of different people who went over. I'll vouch for Rick Wade . . . [W]e wound up knowing each other pretty well . . . I won't give you any names, but there were others."

As Wade was making his way up the ladder, Vang Pao was trying to make something happen in Laos. It was 1985, the year he allegedly predicted the Lao government would fall. He "circulated a letter on Neo Hom stationery to every Hmong community in the U.S.," writes Keith Quincy, "claiming his guerrillas were heavily engaged with communist forces all across Laos, which they were not." Vang Pao ordered Cher Pao Moua to send a thousand guerrillas in Xieng Khouang province into battle. After several days of heavy combat with no supply lines or reinforcements, Moua's men retreated, leaving behind local villagers who had assisted them. The Vietnamese herded them into a nearby cave, blocked the entrance, and fired explosives inside. A few Hmong in the back of the cave survived to tell the tale. A subsequent attempt to send a demolitions team into Vientiane ended in disaster: Cher Pao Moua's own son, the team's leader, was killed in a premature explosion. "Vang Pao's standing in the refugee camps plummeted," writes Quincy. Thousands of refugees suddenly made application for resettlement. And after years of obscurity, Pa Kao Her's movement in the United States, Ethnic Liberation of Laos, started gaining members.[12]

Her was also gaining traction in U.S. anti-Communist circles, especially with General John Singlaub's U.S. Council for World Freedom.† A veteran of World War II, Korea, and Vietnam who wanted to help reify the Reagan doctrine, Singlaub was interested in finding leaders who might help roll back Communist victories in Southeast Asia. He knew of Vang Pao's role in Laos, and his longtime friend General Heinie Aderholt gave VP high marks. For a time Singlaub helped connect Neo Hom to potential supporters. But some of Vang Pao's former associates "cautioned that 'his reputation is getting weak now, because of com-

---

* Garwood, a Texas conservative, was known to have given $2.5 million to help bankroll Contra forces in Nicaragua.

† In 1984, Singlaub became head of the World Anti-Communist League, an organization originally founded by Taiwanese and South Korean leaders Chiang Kai-shek and Syngman Rhee in 1954. He renamed the U.S. chapter of the WACL the U.S. Council for World Freedom, wanting the organization "to stand for something positive," and other nations followed suit. It is worth noting publicly that General Singlaub was happy to discuss these details, dispelling any notion that he and his associates were trying to hide what they were doing.

plaints from some of the Hmong that they are getting bilked . . .' He
was soliciting his people and promising them that if they [financially]
supported him, he would obtain from the United States Government
recognition in the form of back pay for those who had followed him
and worked with him against the Communists in Laos. Well, that was
simply false." Singlaub says he arranged a meeting with Vang Pao in Los
Angeles to see for himself. "I was not impressed . . . [H]e gave the impression that, well, he never promised that he would get [payment for
veterans], but he would try. So I figured 'this guy is not playing it
straight' . . . [T]hat's when I said, '. . . [W]e'd better find somebody else.'"
Singlaub's friend, conservative activist and adventurer Jack Wheeler,
said he knew just the man: Chao Fa leader Pa Kao Her.* After a meeting
arranged by Wheeler, Singlaub deemed Her "a real patriot." Singlaub
brought Her into the United States through Canada to attend a world
council meeting in Dallas, Texas. Her was also showcased at a June
1985 event in Jamba, Angola. Sponsored by Wheeler, young ideologue
and future lobbyist Jack Abramoff, drugstore magnate Lewis Lehrman,
and Reagan speechwriter Dana Rohrabacher (responsible for drafting
a letter of support from the president), the "Democratic International"
brought together rebel leaders from several embattled countries fighting against "Soviet colonialism." (The word *Communism* was avoided,
since China supported rebels in Afghanistan and Laos.)[13]

Within the Hmong community and among Americans seeking to
reignite a rebellion against Communist forces in Laos, people chose
sides. It is difficult to know the extent to which one side sought to undermine the other. "I did not want to support Pa Kao Her at the expense of anyone else," says Singlaub, "[but] it was clear that he had broken with Vang Pao, and my supporting him made it clear to everybody
else that I was no longer infatuated with Vang Pao." But men like Ader-

---

* After their defeat in 1978, the Chao Fa reportedly sent Pa Kao Her to plead for help from Jerry
Daniels and Vang Pao. When neither could deliver, Her turned to the abbot of a Buddhist
monastery, Tham Krabok. Well connected in Thai political and intelligence circles, Abbot Phra
Chamroon Parnchand helped Pa Kao Her gain the ear of the Thai prime minister as well as the
Chinese. Several of Her's former followers, interviewed separately, all insist that the Chinese
offered Her a leadership position in a conquered Laos, but Her offered it to Vang Pao. They claim
the two men were supposed to meet in Bangkok and take a plane to China provided by Deng
Xiaoping. "Vang Pao promised he would show up," says one man. "Then [he] called and asked Pa
Kao to fly to Malaysia . . . and meet him at the border . . . So Pa Kao went there, and Vang Pao
didn't show up . . . [He] was still in California . . . Pa Kao drove all the way back to Bangkok but
missed the flight to China."

holt and Bernard, who had served with Vang Pao in Laos, remained steadfast.

By August 1986, Bernard and Rick Wade had found sympathetic ears in the offices of several congressmen and senators—including a member of the Senate Intelligence Committee—in the State Department, and in the Defense Intelligence Agency. Individuals from conservative groups like the Heritage Foundation, the American Freedom Foundation, GeoMiliTech Consultants Corporation, the Free Congress Foundation, and the ultra-right-wing Civilian Military Assistance (CMA) were also interested. In fact, CMA had already pledged sixty thousand dollars, contingent on Congress passing a bill for additional support.[14]

But in November, a Lebanese magazine broke the story that the U.S. government had traded arms for hostages in Iran. Soon afterward it was discovered that only $12 million of the $30 million Iran paid for those weapons had made it back to the United States. The rest had been diverted by Oliver North and his operatives to Contra rebels in Nicaragua. In the allegations, indictments, and hearings that followed, former or potential supporters disappeared, fearing congressional investigation. Vang Pao's cohorts would have to look for money elsewhere.

On February 5, 1987, with the support of Richard Fisher and Kenneth Conboy from the Heritage Foundation's Asian Studies Center, Vang Pao briefed a group of invited guests, listing crimes Vietnam perpetrated against the Lao people. They had created, he said, "a new holocaust . . . Laotian women were taken . . . for the purpose of human reproduction with North Vietnamese men so that the new generation in Laos will be purely Vietnamese." Responding to the desperate call of Lao people of all races, he said, the ULNLF had fully armed 8,611 troops, "extensively" trained almost 8,800 more, cooperated with almost 25,000 Pathet Lao, set up communications, medical, and engineering networks, "actively controlled most highway and river transportation routes," and established several "resistance zones" in the countryside. "The Laotian people," concluded Vang Pao, "are sure that with moral, political, and financial support from the world community . . . [we] will be able to drive the Hanoi invasion troops out of Laos." It is unclear how much money was raised from this speech and ensuing meetings with potential supporters. But the attention from Americans with government ties or memberships in prominent-sounding organizations may have made a greater impression on Vang Pao than any amount of money could. Perhaps he thought if he only made the right move at the right time, the United States might do for him what they were doing for the Mujahedin in Afghanistan or the Contras in Nicaragua.[15]

In 1987, Fred Caristo met Pa Kao Her for the first time. Caristo served under General Singlaub in Vietnam with SOG (Studies and Observations Group), at one time helping a group of Special Forces–trained Lao Hmong infiltrate North Vietnam by helicopter. Caristo had no further contact with the Hmong until Singlaub asked him to assist Pa Kao Her. When asked about Vang Pao's Heritage Foundation address and the forces he said were at his command, Caristo retorted, "That was simply not true. Vang Pao didn't have any support inside Laos . . . That's what impressed me about Pa Kao Her. He had the troops—I met the troops, I saw the troops." While Rick Wade admits Vang Pao's claims were exaggerated, he believes nonetheless, "None of those [other] groups held a candle to the following VP had out there. It wasn't even close . . . The Thais really recognized him [as well]."[16]

Neo Hom kept looking for their opportunity. Encouraged by the decline of the Soviet Union, protests in China at Tiananmen Square, uprisings in Burma, and the withdrawal of 35,000 of Vietnam's 45,000 troops in Laos, they declared a provisional government, claiming it was already operating in the "liberated zones" of six provinces. Shoua Xiong, interviewed by the Wall Street Journal in 1990, left Milwaukee, Wisconsin, where he had earned his U.S. citizenship, and returned to Laos to command resistance forces. "[C]ommunist rule is at the end of its century," he exclaimed. "I want democracy for my people." In addition to attacking truck convoys between Luang Prabang and Vientiane, reported the Washington Post, the resistance claimed to have "cut parts of Highway 7, the east-west road leading to Vietnam through . . . the Plain of Jars." But times had changed. Not only had the Iran-Contra scandal killed any hope of official U.S. support for an insurgency in Laos, but Thai prime minister Chatichai Choonhavan wanted to improve relations with Laos. He had no interest in indulging further Hmong intrigue. As Neo Hom's provisional government convened close to the Laotian border, "Thai officials arrived, accompanied by soldiers, to collect all U.S. passports, announcing that the Thai government would not tolerate efforts by foreign nationals to overthrow the LPDR. The officials let it be known that anyone wishing to go back to the U.S. immediately would have his passport returned." The provisional government collapsed in disgrace; Vietnamese troops returned to Laos to help wipe out the resistance.[17]

In Laos, Vang Pao had won admiration from Americans working for the CIA and USAID as well as from most of the soldiers who fought for him. But in the United States, he damaged his potential legacy—or allowed others to. He was paraded through Washington by ambitious sympathizers who arranged meetings with government representatives who may have had no intention of helping him. One former State Department official recalls, "Vang Pao . . . called on one of [our] more senior officials . . . I escorted him to the meeting and sat in . . . [O]ur general intention [was] to listen politely to what Vang Pao had to say but to avoid making any commitments to him or his supporters. This was exactly the outcome of the meeting." But Rick Wade and others suggest that politicians and policy makers have successfully buried or destroyed evidence of their genuine attempts to aid Vang Pao and rid Laos of Communist rule. Even if no one in the U.S. government intended to aid Vang Pao, nothing was done to curb Neo Hom's fund-raising activities, emboldening their efforts and perhaps further suggesting that the CIA had some kind of "under-the-table" deal with Vang Pao.[18]

In 1989, Fred Caristo went to Thailand to live with Pa Kao Her. In his opinion, Neo Hom's attempt at a so-called provisional state had really messed things up, succeeding only in inflaming the Vietnamese and alienating the Thai. Her, says Caristo, had a written agreement with the Thai "that he could move all his people into Thailand, they would be given Thai papers as legitimate refugees, but they would not fall under the [UNHCR] . . . There's a section of Laos that is west of the Mekong . . . [T]hat area was to be a free zone . . . [for] the Chao Fa." By 1994, however, logging interests jealously eyed the teak forests on the land Her and his followers occupied. The Thai government abrogated its agreement, says Caristo, and came to Her's encampment: "'[E]ither move farther inland or . . . come into Thailand, but we want you off of this border area . . .' And Pa Kao said, '. . . I have an agreement, and I'm not moving.'" Caristo says the Thai were ready to start firing artillery, so Her reluctantly moved near the Lao village of Ban Nam Mo, establishing a compound Caristo calls "Happy Mountain."

With the help of at least four others, Caristo brought in supplies to help them stay alive and defend themselves. "We built a hospital there . . . We bought [treadle] sewing machines in Thailand and backpacked

Fred Caristo with Chao Fa leader Pa Kao Her in 1992. A Vietnam veteran with brief ties to the Hmong during the war, Caristo traveled to Thailand in 1989 to assist Her and his people.

them in . . . and gave them all the . . . [supplies] to can bamboo shoots; medicines, the capability to blood type, to . . . write a prescription for eyeglasses, to do surgery." People would step on land mines," recalls Caristo, and "everybody'd stand around . . . until they bled to death . . . So I brought in vascular clamps and everything else so they could clamp off the blood, taught them stitching, sewing of wounds, communications, gave them radios where they could communicate . . . [and] broadcast all over Laos, and bring the Chao Fa message to the Hmong people . . . And the only armament in that area was not offensive . . . it was defensive." Even so, Caristo admits the traffic into and the broadcasts out of the area made Chao Fa followers the targets of Lao and Vietnamese soldiers. But "there was never anything political broadcast on that radio." Messages instead focused on cures for dysentery, which ran through villages during the rainy season when people drank polluted river water, and Hmong cultural music. "[P]eople would be told, 'if you want to come to the safe zone . . . this is who to get into contact with,' and there were contacts in each of the villages."

While Caristo and Wade both characterize their efforts as primarily defensive and humanitarian, they also insist their operations had the opportunity to successfully overthrow the government of Laos. Caristo declares that Pa Kao Her's forces could have launched a coup in 1995. While he would not provide details, he says, "There were plans to keep the North Vietnamese out of it; there was a third country that was going to help them with aerial resupplies and everything." Once again, he says, the Thais intervened. They "had Pa Kao's family in Thailand, so they pressured him not to go through with it, and it fell apart." Wade can't remember the year but recalls there was an attempt to reassert Neo Hom's provisional government through military action. Vang Pao's role was to provide $100,000, maybe $150,000 for radio communications and resupply. When it became clear he couldn't raise the money, says Wade, Vang Pao allowed the operation to go forward, dooming the men involved. "It was just sort of a Hail Mary pass," says Wade. "He knew what was going to happen to these guys, and he went ahead and allowed it to happen. After that, I started having some issues with him."

The hidden war in Laos has spawned numerous other secrets and deceptions, many of which may never be completely unraveled. It is difficult to know whose version of events—if any—should be trusted. And even those critical of the former general, including Keith Quincy and Rick Wade—who broke with Vang Pao once and for all after money lent to his son Cha Vang was not repaid—insist that he never took money himself. But he tolerated corruption all around him. Vang Pao's decisions were his to make, and he is responsible for them. But one must not ignore the potentially dizzying context in which they were made and the uncertain, often unpredictable waters through which they were navigated. Was the U.S. government encouraging, discouraging, or ignoring him? Were the Thai allies or manipulators? Did the activities of men like Wade give Thai military staff an erroneous impression about a potential tie between Vang Pao and the CIA? Were Singlaub and others abandoning Vang Pao, or were their "flirtations" with Pa Kao Her some peculiar form of motivation to work harder and squelch potential successors to his leadership?

Those close to Vang Pao suggest he should not be held accountable for many of Neo Hom's activities or for various schemes conducted in his name but not necessarily with his blessing. In this way, they suggest, Vang Pao became a widely used and sometimes-abused brand as well as an individual man. Invoking Vang Pao's name became the easiest way for others to make money for themselves. Even people close to him might initiate something and then, once it gains momentum or critical mass, try to drag him along. It was exactly this kind of tactic, some suggest, that got Vang Pao into hot water in 2007. They also insist that the failure of various U.S. agencies to investigate Neo Hom is a sign of the government's neglect, not its collusion—another way in which the United States abandoned the Hmong, even after they got here.

Still, questions remain. If Vang Pao is as respected and powerful as his followers suggest, why would he tolerate such abuse of his name, of his reputation, and of the Hmong people?

FIGHTING BACK

With the establishment of Lao Family Communities in 1977, the Hmong began the process of taking more and more responsibility for their own welfare and development. But mutual assistance efforts were not reserved to "here and now" issues like literacy, job training, and delinquency mitigation. Like so many who had come before them, the Hmong also set about the task of preserving their cultural heritage. "The younger men and women coming to the United States," observes Txong Pao Lee, director of the Hmong Cultural Center, "likely . . . left their family behind. They didn't know how to [perform] traditional [rituals], so they converted to Christianity." Some conversions were less a matter of faith than one of practicality and gratitude. The old traditions were dying; Christianity was the dominant religion in the United States, and many churches sponsored Hmong families looking for a home in America.

According to Tou Geu Leepalao, the eighteen-clan elder council decided in 1982

to create [an] organization to preserve Hmong customs and traditions in this country . . . [W]hen Hmong people went to get married, they didn't know how to do it in the traditional way . . . When somebody died, some did not know how to conduct a traditional funeral ceremony . . . We said that the Hmong people have their own way of doing things . . . [A]t the end of the year, when we want to celebrate the New Year, we can't just go anywhere we want without the proper authorization . . . At that time there was an American named Dr. Kathie. [She] came and told us, "It would be a good thing for you to start this. If you don't, your cultural practices will disappear— your children will lose them."

The elders were concerned that if they started such an organization "the Americans" might not like it. Dr. Kathie told them to move ahead and not to worry; "the Americans" would never think like that.

"Dr. Kathie" was Kathleen Culhane-Pera, a board member and family physician with a background in medical anthropology and a growing affinity for the Hmong people:

[W]e had some really wonderful discussions ... But then there was also the [challenge of the] running of the organization. How do you run a 501(c)(3) ... and get the funding and get a board and be a nonprofit organization? ... We had ... [been at] three different locations when I was on the board ... [T]hen they decided to really extend themselves financially and physically and go into the building on University [Avenue, in St. Paul,] ... with this wonderful vision. And I was skeptical ... We can't afford it, and how can we extend ourselves, and ... would that mean that we could go up in flames? I think some people ... had that same concern, but they were really influenced by this vision of ... a Hmong building and it would have Hmong businesses in there and a place for Hmong Cultural Center to really have a presence and an influence.

Today the Hmong Cultural Center offers lessons in a variety of cultural practices, including wedding and funeral rituals, singing, and traditional instrument playing. Its adjacent resource center holds a wide array of Hmong-related videos and publications, and its former director, Dr. Mark Pfeifer, still edits the peer-reviewed *Hmong Studies Journal*. Organizations designed to help and edify various segments of the Hmong community proliferated.

Lee Pao Xiong, whose father had pushed him onto a plane leaving Long Tieng in May 1975, came to Morgantown, Indiana, with his family, sponsored by a Mennonite church. By the fall of 1976, they moved to St. Paul to be closer to family. When he was in junior high, he bought a short-wave radio: "I was always listening to ... 'Voice of Free China,' which Taiwan broadcast, and then 'Voice of America' ... That's where I got interested in learning Chinese, [and] pursuing international relations." While attending college at the University of Minnesota, Xiong applied for an internship in Washington, DC, and was assigned to Michigan senator Carl Levin: "I came back and changed my major to political science after that." Xiong had missed seeing Hmong people and eating Hmong food while in Washington. After working in a variety of political positions in Minnesota, he joined Hmong Youth Association as a counselor. A year later, the director left, and Xiong was offered the job.

At the time, gang activity was on the rise, particularly "smash and grab" activities, where kids would drive into gun shops and scoop all the guns into the car and drive off . . . They would go into houses and tie people up, then rob them . . . [Y]oung women . . . were getting married while they were in junior high and high school . . . So I created a mentorship program, basically identifying . . . working mentors [who] would have lunch with the mentees once a month so they could have a conversation, explore various career options . . . We would take them to college—this was like 1990, 1991. I think that was part of being in Washington, DC, seeing how important education was [for me] . . . [O]ne agency that will remain nameless came to me and said, "Lee Pao, what are you wasting all this money for working with all these lost kids?" And I said, well, these are our kids. Whenever they commit a crime—front-page news— they didn't say, "This is another person's kid"; they said, "This is a Hmong kid."

Xiong and Hmong Youth Association began working closely with policemen like Bob Fletcher and Joe Mollner as well as with Lao, Vietnamese, and Cambodian organizations to coordinate efforts to help at-risk youth. With Xiong's encouragement, Fletcher and Mollner led an initiative to secure state funding for a Southeast Asian gang prevention program, which was sponsored by state senator Randy Kelly. Next, they coordinated efforts with similar Vietnamese, Lao, and Cambodian agencies to apply for federal money. "[W]e called ourselves the Southeast Asian Community Coalition for Youth and Families. And we . . . got a million dollars, divvied up the money, and coordinated the services—basically, 'You take care of this gang group; I take care of that gang group,' and 'You take care of this age group; we'll take care of the parents over here.'" Agencies also shared case files to ensure that money wasn't wasted and that no one slipped through the cracks.

Unfortunately, as Hmong organizations grew in number and influence, they began to divide along political lines. Members of Lao Family sometimes viewed newer organizations as competitors at best—and as Communist conspirators at worst.

The greatest conflict was between Lao Family, led by General Vang Pao's "faction," and Hmong National Development (HND), led by Dr. Yang Dao. As mentioned in section four, Vang Pao and Yang Dao had been very close in Laos. But with the evacuation of Long Tieng, the two men ended up on opposite sides of the world: Vang Pao in Montana, then California; Yang Dao in France. Yang Dao has been accused by Vang Pao's adherents of telling Hmong to stay in Laos and then leaving himself. Once settled in Ban Vinai refugee camp, Yang Dao received death threats. Vang Pao's supporters say these threats were for causing the deaths of many whom he had encouraged to stay in Laos. Yang Dao insists these threats came because he encouraged the Hmong to migrate to Western countries instead of staying in Thailand and waiting for General Vang Pao's return. Whatever the cause, the rift between the two men must not have been too great, for in 1982 Yang Dao was invited to join Neo Hom. He accepted the position of deputy secretary-general. But by 1985, Yang Dao had grown disenchanted: "When I met with Mr. Hugh Tovar in the U.S. embassy in Bangkok on August 4, 1975, . . . [h]e told me . . . 'my government . . . will never come back like before' . . . I always advised the administration of [Neo Hom] . . . to use political means, diplomatic means, economic means . . . Prince Sisouk na Champassak . . . had the same idea. But the others were military, so their idea was to go back and to fight with armed resistance!" When the prince died in May 1985, Yang Dao had no ally in the organization.

The prince's death also coincided with Neo Hom's ill-fated intrigues in Laos and increasing allegations within the Hmong community about the organization's corruption. Yang Dao noted, "Many people complained to me . . . [O]ne day I went to California. I heard that a man in the organization went from Santa Ana to Sacramento and then came back to Santa Ana with forty-six thousand dollars, and this money disappeared." Wives complained that they had no food in the house because "our husbands just sent the money to Neo Hom." With Yang Dao's departure from Neo Hom in 1985, the war of words between supporters of Vang Pao and Yang Dao and the animosity between their respective organizations increased.

Tensions also developed between Lao Family and Hmong American Partnership (HAP), an organization cofounded by Hmong attorney Christopher Thao and Robert Anderson of the American Refugee Committee. One of HAP's first proposed initiatives was sending medical and educational aid to villages in Laos. This program was interpreted by many Hmong veterans as an attempt to collaborate with the Communist Lao government.

While still working for Hmong Youth Association, Lee Pao Xiong was offered the top post at HAP, which he accepted in January 1993: "One of the members of my board . . . came to my office and slammed the door. He basically said, 'You think that if you go over there, you're going to be able to change Hmong American Partnership. It's a Communist organization . . . The house is possessed with evil spirits, so we're going to destroy it. So if you go there, we're not going to back down, even though we know you and we care about you, you're going to go down with the house.'"

At the end of that week, Xiong received a typed letter with a bullet enclosed:

Hey Mr. Lee Pao

You came to the right place at the right time, and the right target that we need. Made sure you have a life insurance left for your wife. We have a Mac 22, hand gun with Micro good long distance shot . . . We will shot your head below your ears even right or left, depend to the right time. We are follow your white car, license plate No: 873 almost three weeks now. You won't have another options, friend Lee Pao. You will find this enclose gift right on your head for sure . . .

See you soon,
Mr. Shoua Vang
Asia gang McDonough area

Xiong was not the only one receiving threats. J. Kou Vang had left his job in Appleton, Wisconsin, and moved to the Twin Cities to be HAP's director of finance. By that time, says Vang, the Twin Cities had already developed a reputation as "the epicenter of the Hmong community in the United States . . . I thought that anything good will come out of here, and anything *bad* will come out of here, and if you're going to make yourself into somebody, then you need to do it here." Vang remembered the Hmong proverb, "'after you sharpen your knife, you need to go try it out.' Well, I've *sharpened* my knife. I've gone to college, I have three degrees, I graduated in three years—quite honestly I thought . . . I walked on water, and so I needed to come and test out my blade." He continued,

When I first came up here, Hennepin County was in the midst of welfare reform . . . [It] was viewed . . . as the Hmong organizations' way of creating work for themselves—Lao Family and Hmong American Partnership—and that because these two organizations didn't have anything to do, they went and lobbied the county to change welfare laws so they had stuff to do! . . . [A]nd I had bullets sent to me and saying, "Hey, would you please go kill yourself so that we don't have to do it for you?" And we had picketing and stuff of that nature, and on the one hand I was scared shitless but on the other hand it was so exhilarating, I was like, "Man, people are sending me bullets! This is incredible!"

In a way, the struggles between various Hmong organizations were a sign of success. As a community the Hmong were becoming more integrated into American culture, more upwardly mobile economically, and more politically savvy. But many continued to struggle. As the press reported stories of "bride kidnappings," gang and spousal violence, and other problems, observers who knew little or nothing of what the Hmong had endured before coming to America began voicing ignorant and ugly opinions. A particularly notorious incident in Minnesota occurred on June 9, 1998, when the KQRS "morning crew" commented on a tragic story involving a thirteen-year-old Hmong girl accused of killing her child. Tom Barnard, the radio crew's lead personality, commented that these Hmong "should assimilate or hit the goddamn road." Upon hearing that the girl faced a ten-thousand-dollar fine, Barnard retorted, "That's a lot of eggrolls."

At the time, Cy Thao was an emerging visual artist and head of the Center for Hmong Arts and Talent (CHAT). "I think the whole KQRS thing . . . was a defining moment for my generation, within our community, anyway . . . [W]e felt like we needed to voice our opinion about what [Barnard] said . . . We're fighting that minority status thing . . . [but] we felt like, well, we're Americans just as much as anyone, and we're not leaving anytime soon. So we protested and got advertisers from his show to drop." Indeed, by October, Texaco, Mystic Lake Casino and Hotel, the Mall of America, U.S. West, Perkins Family Restaurants, and Norwest Corporation had pulled their advertisements from the show.[19]

But even in the midst of voicing their displeasure and exercising their rights as citizens, this strategy created controversy within the Hmong community. As Thao recalls, elders and younger adults disagreed

on whether it was even appropriate for us to go ask for an apology. For those of us who had just graduated from college, we were like, "We have every right to ask for this." . . . [But] the older generations are like, "No, we shouldn't, because this is not our country. What if they don't like us, and they do more, and we can't live in this state anymore?" . . . And we said, "No, we're not moving. They can't do that to us, and we've got to fight it. We got to stand up for something." The older generation wanted appeasement, and we said, "No, we demand an apology" . . . And we did it and it turned out well.

Though Barnard remained unrepentant, KQRS issued an apology, promised to remove an offensive Asian character named "Tak" from the morning crew repertoire, and put staff through sensitivity training—to no discernable effect.

"I think from that moment," remembers Cy Thao, "those of us who were part of it realized that if we organized well and worked together, we could really shape our community. Our next logical step would be to get more involved in the political process because we knew that was where all the decisions were made. And we didn't want to talk about the decision after it's already been made. We wanted to be in the forefront and make those decisions."

The tide was turning for the Hmong community. They were no longer merely refugees fleeing a war-torn home and an increasingly unfriendly host country. With significant help from their new neighbors, great resolve to adjust once again to a pervasively alien and relentlessly homogenizing environment, and a strong desire to keep their extended families together and provide their children with opportunities most of the elders had never enjoyed, they were becoming a part of the fabric of the countries in which they settled. As with other refugees, that adjustment came at a price: the knowledge that friends and loved ones left behind were often still fighting the battles and suffering the indignities they had escaped; and the pain of seeing their treasured culture vanish from the consciousness of their children and grandchildren.

epilogue

I didn't set out to write a book. My initial goal was to encourage my Hmong students to ask their parents about the history they'd rarely been told. Many took this opportunity, but then they were understandably ready to move on to other things. I, on the other hand, was only beginning to be enthralled by the story I have partly tried to convey in these pages. Even as I was catching up on what I'd missed, the story continued to unfold.

In November 2003, Vang Pao made an announcement to a stunned St. Paul, Minnesota, audience. He had met with Vietnamese officials in Amsterdam and struck a deal: he would support normalized trade relations between Laos and the United States if Vietnam pushed Laos to stop persecuting Hmong still hiding in the forests. Those in attendance were incredulous. After spending twenty-five years planning for a return to Laos, most were unwilling to abandon the cause. Perhaps they continued to call Vang Pao their leader, but they had no intention of following him now.[1]

In late 2003, the Thai government announced it would close a large settlement of Hmong people near the Buddhist temple of Tham Krabok. The influence of the temple's abbot, Phra Chamroon Parnchand, had provided significant protection from Thai authorities. There were no fences, people came and went freely, and most earned their own living. In 1999, the abbot died. "The Thai military moved in . . . put concertina wire all around the village . . . and started controlling access in and out," says Jim Anderson, member of a delegation to Tham Krabok led by St. Paul mayor Randy Kelly. Thai authorities believed this "quarantine" was necessary because Tham Krabok had become the new "beachhead" for the Hmong insurgency. "[T]he Thais announced in April of 2003 that they were going to do this registration for everybody in the camp without any link to resettlement," says Anderson, "so a lot of people were very skeptical . . . [and] either left the camp . . . or refused to come forward . . . [T]hen . . . the announcement was made they were no longer eligible for resettlement. So there were lots of split families."

Some, like Wa Toua Lee, were working outside the camp. Lee's family, having no relatives in America, Australia, or France who sent them money, went to farm in Phetchabun province. By the time they learned of the opportunity to resettle, Tham Krabok was closed and they were forbidden entry.

More than 60 percent of the settlers were under the age of eighteen; about 15,500 applied for resettlement. "There was also a relatively small group of old soldiers who still said, 'I'm not going,'" says Anderson. "But for the first time we were seeing wives and grown children saying, 'OK, that's fine, but *I'm* going.' Some of the old soldiers . . . were very frightened, because there was a lot of bitterness in the camp that the decisions they had made . . . years ago had resulted in the loss of those years . . . [T]hey were feeling really intimidated by some of the younger folks in the camp—very new, novel kind of experience."[2]

Those Hmong who began arriving in the United States in late 2004 faced most of the challenges of those who had come earlier but also a few new ones. They witnessed the progress and relative prosperity enjoyed by other Hmong who came years before. With no federal housing programs, they searched for apartments at regular market rates. Many stayed in homeless shelters or packed in with relatives eager but ill prepared to host them. Most were embraced by the Hmong American community, but some found themselves derided or ignored by kinsmen now Westernized enough to be ashamed or suspicious of them. Some non-Hmong complained about more poor immigrants coming into their community.

These difficulties were not helped by a terrible incident that occurred on November 21, 2004. Minnesota state representative Cy Thao received a call that day from a *St. Paul Pioneer Press* reporter. "He said he wanted to know about Hmong hunting . . . There was this Hmong hunter [Chai Soua Vang] who shot these white hunters in Wisconsin . . . He explained it to me, and right away I knew they were going for the Hmong angle . . . I just want them to report fairly. If it's truly a story about the Hmong community, then [OK], but if it's one guy who's Hmong, you can't . . . drag the whole community into the story."

It was a grim tale indeed. One Hmong hunter in a tree stand where he did not belong was confronted by several white hunters—though only one of them was armed. The nature and intensity of the argument will never be known for certain, but soon five people lay dead and a sixth perished the following day. Hmong organizations felt compelled to make statements on behalf of the whole community and were the recipients of a significant amount of hate mail. But people also responded with understanding and compassion. Theresa Hesebeck's brother Denny Drew was killed by Chai Vang; her husband, Lauren Hesebeck, was wounded. She wrote to the *Eau Claire Leader-Telegram*,

"We would like everyone to know that we do not hold the Hmong community responsible for this act . . . [T]hey did not pull the trigger. I would like to ask anyone who is trying to make this a racial issue . . . please stop this and know that it is a dishonor to all of our loved ones."[3]

On January 6, 2007, Green Bay, Wisconsin, resident Cha Vang, in the United States for fewer than two years, was out hunting, separated from the rest of his friends, when he encountered Peshtigo resident James Nichols. According to Nichols, who was arrested after appearing at a Marinette hospital with a noncritical gunshot wound, the two argued after Nichols accused Vang of interfering with his hunting. Vang shot without provocation, he said, so he returned fire. Rather than reporting the incident to the police, Nichols tried to camouflage Vang's body under leaves and debris. During questioning, Nichols said Hmong people were mean and "kill everything . . . that moves." The attorney general reported that Vang was shot from a much closer distance than Nichols claimed—while walking *away* from his killer. Vang was also stabbed six times, including a wound severing his jugular vein, and was found with a three- to four-inch wooden stick protruding from his clenched teeth. Nichols claimed Vang screamed, "I'm going to kill you! I'm going to kill you!" but Vang knew no English.[4]

It would be as wrong to infer any broad attitudes in the white community because of James Nichols's actions as to pass judgment on the Hmong community because of Chai Soua Vang's misdeeds. Both men went to prison, but the wounds from the incidents linger.

In June 2007, I eagerly awaited the commencement of my sabbatical on July 1. I hoped to work on the book that was taking shape in my head, travel to Laos and Thailand to interview Hmong there, and finally engage in an in-depth interview with General Vang Pao when he visited the Twin Cities for the July 4 soccer tournament.

But the trajectory of my sabbatical, and of the lives of many in the Hmong American community, took a sharp turn on Monday, June 4, when Vang Pao and eight others, including a West Point graduate named Harrison Jack, were arrested and charged with attempting to overthrow the government of Laos. Thousands of Hmong rallied in Vang Pao's defense, though it was often unclear whether they thought he was innocent or they simply felt betrayed once again by the U.S. government.

After years of ignoring serious allegations concerning fund-raising and insurgency activities, the federal government was now looking at Vang Pao through a post–9/11 lens. After all, in late 2005, attorneys in the Department of Homeland Security began reinterpreting an existing provision of the Patriot Act, classifying the Hmong as terrorists. It seemed very much as if investigators had decided the seventy-seven-year-old was leading an anti-Laos terrorist cell. Their alleged master plan, "Operation Popcorn" (likely written for Chao Fa, not Neo Hom), read like "the outline for a bad movie script. ('Mission One: Bring Down the Power of Leaders . . . Mission Two: Take Over the Government.') It's a delusional fantasy, with no logistics to speak of, no plans for getting . . . black-market weapons and mercenaries to Asia."[5]

To say the least, my plans for the year were in disarray. Clearly there would be no extended interview with Vang Pao, and some of my Hmong friends told me it would be highly unlikely that any Hmong in Laos, even ones who fought for the Pathet Lao, would want to speak to an American who came to ask questions about "the old days." After agonizing over what to do for a few months, I decided to make my journey to Laos and Thailand anyway and hope for the best.

On the morning of November 8, 2007, I awoke in Thailand's Nan province. I'd had mixed success in Laos but interviewed many interesting people in Thailand. My guide and I rode toward Huai Nam Khao (White Water), a village populated by Thai Hmong who fought on the Communist side during the Thai civil war and then received amnesty. But our destination was not the village. Just above it was a camp bearing the same name, a physical manifestation of much that is still unresolved from the Secret War. Huai Nam Khao detention center was filled with Hmong, some of whom were part of the anti-Communist force in Laos during or after the Secret War.

We had been given permission by the Hmong governor of the region, Tsao Toua Lee, to visit the camp, but we were still unsure whether we would be admitted. No press were allowed in, nor any humanitarian agencies other than Doctors Without Border (MSF).* There were so

---

* *Médecins Sans Frontieres.* In July 2009, MSF left Huai Nam Khao, saying conditions imposed by the Thai military threatened its impartiality and ability to deliver care. MSF remained in place until the Catholic Office for Emergency Relief and Refugees took over.

many children and so few schools that everyone between the ages of seven and fifteen attended classes only one day a week. One of the three schools had outside funding to provide lunch. The Thai government's attitudes toward the Hmong were evident from signs posted in Thai, Lao, Hmong, and English:

ACTIVITIES NOT TO BE DONE
1. No more immigration
2. No permanent residence in Thailand
3. No transfer to third countries

ACTIVITIES TO BE DONE
1. Provide basic living utilities
2. Strict [obedience] to Thai law
3. Obey Khao Kho Combined Task Force's regulations
4. Return to original residen[ce][6]

Perhaps the only thing more depressing than touring Huai Nam Khao was the suspicion that at least a few individuals, upon seeing a tall, white American walking through the camp, thought he might actually be able to help.

Conditions in Huai Nam Khao were such that every child (ages seven to fifteen) was able to attend school only one day each week.

I watched from the van's rearview mirror as my guide spoke with the guards at the gate. I shot a couple pictures of the scene in case this was the end of our journey. But after radio contact with their superiors, the guards allowed us in.

We met first with the Thai colonel in charge, who initially struck me as a good-humored man doing his best in a difficult situation. That impression changed markedly over the course of our visit. After talking briefly about camp conditions, population (about 7,700 at that time), and routines, the colonel gave us a tour of the crowded schools and the Baptist and Seventh-day Adventist churches located outside the concertina wire of the camp proper. The colonel was particularly fond the churches: "They teach people to be good."

Huai Nam Khao's population was divided into at least four separate groups: those who had lived at Tham Krabok but missed the opportunity to register for migration to the United States; Lao "forest people" who had a legitimate fear of persecution back in Laos; Thai Hmong who tried to "blend in" and see where it would lead; and "economic opportunists" who on their own or through the persuasion of Hmong or Thai human traffickers sold their property, made their way to Thailand, and expected to be accepted for migration to a third country. Throughout our time together, the colonel insisted, "This is not a refugee camp." To him, Nam Khao was simply a place where Hmong were being held until they were sent back to Laos.

The colonel arranged for me to speak with three Hmong ranging in age, they said, from thirty-two to one hundred. Even the youngest had a stern visage shaped by years of hard living. The colonel remained. First he put down a recording device but then decided to have my guide translate the Hmong and English exchanges into Thai as well. When he didn't like my questions, he substituted his own. And his response to almost every answer given by the three men was some variation of, "Things have changed in Laos. You have no reason to fear. Why don't you go back home?" Finally, in frustration, the youngest of the three turned to the colonel and said coldly, "If you are going to send me back to Laos, just kill me now." Was this an expression of genuine fear, a manifestation of ignorance bred by years of isolation and misinformation in the forests of Laos, or grandstanding in the hopes of making a point and impressing an American stranger who might help?

After a little more than an hour of frustration, I thanked the three men for their time, gave each a small amount of cash, and sent them on their way before the colonel could harangue them any further. Before they left, he gave each of them a lollipop. I almost expected him to pat them on the head and say, "good boys." When I asked to be let inside the camp, the colonel allowed it but also escorted me wherever I went. Again, I felt compelled to cut my visit shorter than I would have liked, because the colonel made it clear at every turn that he was "the law" and could do as he pleased. During the course of our visit, we interrupted private meetings, a shaman "riding the bench" (the colonel insisted that we stand next to the shaman "in action" while he took our picture), and medical consultations with MSF staff, who loudly protested. The colonel couldn't have cared less. (When I saw the staff later,

I was relieved to have the opportunity to apologize.) As we left, the colonel repeated another of his mantras: "You write only good things! Only *good* things!"

I was back in America six weeks later when the *New York Times* ran an article on Hmong "jungle fighters" still hiding in Laos. The timing seemed odd. No major American newspaper or magazine had run such a story before. *Time* magazine was poised to publish a story in April 2003, written by Andrew Perrin and accompanied by vivid and disturbing images from Philip Blenkinsop, but it was pulled from the American edition (allegedly to make room for a story on Laci Peterson's murder). I found the *Time* article online and was reading through it when I let out an audible gasp. Looking back at me from one of Blenkinsop's photographs, squatting on the ground with rifles in hand, were two of the men I had met at Huai Nam Khao. Here, it seemed to me, were individuals who had reason to fear returning to Laos.[7]

More than thirty years after the Secret War's end, there are still victims and body counts in its aftermath. There are numerous causes for this ongoing tragedy, few if any heroes, and plenty of blame to go around.

First, the various countries involved in this enduring debacle are playing right into the hands of the groups most interested in its perpetuation. Laos continues to forbid UNHCR monitoring of Hmong who surrender from their hiding places or who return (or are forced) from Thailand.* If someone goes back to Laos and drops out of sight—something easily reported in this age of ubiquitous cell phones—Laos maintains its image as a country that kills or abuses Hmong, even if those Hmong have broken laws or tried to contact members of the resistance. Hmong "humanitarian organizations" raise hell and engage in name-calling that entrenches the animosity of Communist hard-liners in Laos and anti-Hmong elements in Thailand, who ramp up discussions about forcible repatriation, and the cycle continues on and on.[8]

Thailand still doesn't officially admit its participation in the Secret War, preferring to ensure its share of Lao hydroelectric power and the

---

* The Lao PDR *did* ask MSF in 2007 to work with Hmong returnees, but according to MSF Thailand director Gilles Isard the request was never formal and "we had the impression that the Lao authorities would easily fool us." By 2008, realizing UNHCR would never be allowed into Laos, MSF made a proposal to the Lao ministry of health and ministry of foreign affairs, but officials claimed they could take care of the situation themselves. In August 2008 Isard asked for support from the Thai government, which was refused.

contracts to build and finance the dams that produce it. Meanwhile, Lao ethnic populations are moved or their living conditions seriously compromised so forests can be clear-cut for industrial tree plantations, mines, and reservoirs; hydroelectricity is generated to power the mining industry; and most of Laos's gold, copper, timber, rubber, and hydroelectric power are sent to Thailand, Vietnam, and China. Corrupt bidding practices line the pockets of those accepting bids from corporate suitors.[9]

The United States, despite accepting thousands of Hmong from Wat Tham Krabok, is also to blame. In failing to monitor Vang Pao, the CIA allowed him and Neo Hom to chart their own path and make their own rules. At the same time, government officials turned a deaf ear to cries for intervention in Laos and Thailand, in large part because many of those in the State Department had heard it all before. Pleas to help those hiding in Laos or penned up in Thailand were old, tired refrains coming from long-discredited voices still crying wolf.

To many who have watched the long, disappointing decay of their dream to return to Laos, talk of "imminent" revolution, the crises in Tham Krabok, in Huai Nam Khao, and even in the forests of Laos are merely deceptive ploys fabricated by con men. When the cries for a revolution wore thin, Neo Hom changed its theme to "human rights" and "humanitarian crises" reported by a dubiously named "Fact Finding Commission." Its success in escaping scrutiny from law enforcement encouraged imitators. *All* of the various Hmong "resistance" organizations, whether Neo Hom, one of the Chao Fa groups that splintered after the murder of Pa Kao Her in 2002, or the so-called Hmong World Congress and *its* rivals, the World Hmong People's Congress and the Hmong ChaoFa State of Northern Laos, have members whose primary desire is to perpetuate the message of a "humanitarian crisis" that keeps donations coming in.* Since they profit from the suffering of people in Laos, Huai Nam Khao, and elsewhere, they have no real interest in seeing that suffering end. It is hard to imagine, should Huai Nam Khao be closed, that another "hot spot" will not emerge near the Lao/Thai border.

While most Hmong accord General Vang Pao respect for what he

---

* All of these organizations have websites easily accessible to the general public. There are also myriad Hmong chat sites and discussion groups that openly exchange ideas—often in English— about the agendas and reputations of various groups.

accomplished in Laos, far fewer speak admiringly of anything he has done since. Vang Pao's legacy is now tarnished, even after all the charges against him were dismissed on September 18, 2009; Dr. Yang Dao is seen by some as too eager to accept as gospel the information he receives from Thai or Lao sources. When twenty-eight Hmong children and one adult disappeared from Huai Nam Khao in December 2005, Yang Dao insisted the Lao were not involved. In March 2007, when many of those missing turned up in Laos, the girls alleging they were sexually exploited by Lao soldiers, Yang Dao had to eat his words.

It is a testament to the human spirit and the ongoing adaptability of the Hmong people that despite all these troubles and more, they are not merely surviving but thriving in the West.

An entrepreneurial spirit and a sense of mutual dependence have served them well. According to a 2005 Federal Reserve Bank of Minneapolis study, 90 percent of Hmong businesses got started using personal resources; in many cases, extended family members provide the lion's share of labor needed to make the business a success. Even the Hmong of French Guiana, numbering a little more than two thousand, produce between 50 and 60 percent of the nation's fruits and vegetables. This figure is not surprising to anyone who lives in a community with a significant Hmong population and shops at farmers' markets, where Hmong often dominate.[10]

Rising participation in business and in education have also led to rising home ownership rates. While lagging significantly behind other immigrants who came to the United States in the same period, the Hmong have caught up with a vengeance: home ownership rates, which stood at less than 10 percent nationally in 1990, had risen to between 35 and 40 percent by 2000. In the Twin Cities area and larger Wisconsin communities, the rate was 54 percent. The buying power of Hmong in St. Paul in 2000 was estimated at $203 million, money that helped sustain neighborhoods in Frogtown, the Phalen corridor, and elsewhere. "The largest single new home ownership [population] in the suburbs," said former St. Paul mayor George Latimer in 2007, "are the Hmong . . . Part of that, of course, is that our overly individualistic, materialistic tradition is still foreign to them, and the idea of . . . families living together and pooling their resources is not . . . [T]hat's how they're able to put together opportunities for housing and the rest." For some, greater wealth has meant finally owning a piece of land where they and their family can farm or moving to a different state in a more rural setting with a more temperate climate. Hmong communities have grown not only in Minnesota and Wisconsin but also in Georgia, Missouri, Oklahoma, and South Carolina.[11]

Despite ongoing challenges, the Hmong community still treasures education, evidenced by an explosion of Hmong professionals and Hmong with advanced degrees. According to a survey conducted by Christian Hmong Fellowship, there are almost four hundred Hmong with terminal degrees, a far cry from the day, little more than thirty-five years ago, when Yang Dao stood alone. Hmong doctors, lawyers, teachers, real estate agents and developers, auto repairmen, musicians, artists, and storytellers are now common in the community. In the mid-1990s, Tou Ger Xiong, a Hmong comedian, storyteller, and rapper, emerged as one of the first Hmong media personalities, sharing his message of cross-cultural and cross-generational understanding. The first anthology of Hmong literature, *Bamboo Among the Oaks,* edited by pioneer Mai Neng Moua, was published in 2002. Seexeng Lee's iconic art focusing on aspects of Hmong culture has made him one of the most widely renowned artists in the Hmong community and beyond. Kao Kalia Yang's poignant, lyrical memoir, *The Latehomecomer,* published in 2007, won wide acclaim and numerous awards. And in May 2008, Tou Saiko Lee, a Hmong rapper and hip-hop artist who uses his art to reflect on his cultural heritage, was featured in *New York Times Magazine.* In St. Paul alone there are two separate bilingual Hmong newspapers, *Hmong Times* and *Hmong Today,* filled with advertisements from Hmong businesses, clinics, and consultants. Hmong festivals, art fairs and exhibitions, and, of course, soccer tournaments and New Year celebrations draw tens of thousands of people each year. And there is still money to be made sewing the traditional *paj ntaub* and selling all manner of goods from Hmong in Southeast Asia. The Internet, cell phones, CDs, and DVDs have kept the worldwide Hmong community together in ways that would have been impossible twenty-five years ago.[12]

Perhaps most impressive is the speed with which Hmong people have become a political force. In a sign of how significantly Hmong attitudes and opportunities had changed in America, it was a Hmong woman who first won elected office when Choua Lee, her husband appearing with his arm around her on campaign posters, was elected to the St. Paul School Board in 1991. Ya Yang of Wausau, Wisconsin, and

Thai Vue of La Crosse, Wisconsin, were elected to similar posts in 1993. After appointment to the Omaha, Nebraska, human relations board, Lor Mong Lo was elected to the city council in 1994 and eventually became council president. Another milestone was reached in 2000 when President Bill Clinton appointed Lee Pao Xiong to the President's Advisory Commission on Asian Americans and Pacific Islanders. Paul C. Lo, appointed to the Merced City School District Board of Trustees in 1999, was elected to the post in 2001, becoming the first Hmong elected official in California.

The year 2002 was especially important politically in the Hmong American community. In Minnesota, Mee Moua won a special election in January, becoming the first Hmong to serve as a state senator. In November, Cy Thao, who in 2000 had run unsuccessfully for a seat in the Minnesota House of Representatives as an independent candidate, won election as a Democrat. Then, in November 2006, Blong Xiong was elected to the Fresno city council.

While the Hmong have reason to take great pride in their community, they are also thankful for the many ways in which various organizations and individuals helped make their dreams of success a reality. Just two of the many possible examples of this support are George and Nancy Latimer. While George, as mayor of St. Paul from 1976 to 1990, was the more visible figure, it was his late wife Nancy who did most of the heavy lifting: "I was really inattentive and . . . paying attention to being mayor . . . And I can remember Nancy telling me about Jane Kretzmann," who worked in a stateside refugee camp in 1975 and came to Minnesota in February 1976 to work for Lutheran Social Services, helping refugees. "Nancy would get really moved by what she learned from [Jane], and she was with the St. Paul Foundation, and Paul Verret gave her a pretty wide berth of things that she could work on. So everything I ever knew or heard about the Hmong was through Nancy." She began, with Kretzmann's help, to create a newsletter that was distributed "to every possible venue . . . We started getting Hmong translators, and we got our first Hmong police person, and we had all those firsts . . . [E]verywhere I go, I brag about our community, which has elected Hmong to the school board, to the state senate, and to the house of representatives, and people are just amazed that in that short window of time they can take leadership positions, and the first lawyer and the first physicians . . . [I]t's just thrilling."

From Latimer's perspective, this kind of community spirit was inspired by the understanding that "we all stand on the shoulders of those who came before us. And if you spend a little time with a group of people in St. Paul, any church basement or rec center, talking about this, they'll all think back to when they or their parents or grandparents came, and it's a vastly different place they came from, but you know what? There's a tie there that is pure American; that cord is as old as our country."

That cord now binds the Hmong community to this country, and this country to them. Now it is the Hmong people's turn to look over their shoulders and think with empathy and understanding about those who have come here after them. Ger Vue was talking with one of his Hmong friends, who started complaining about Somali drivers. "It's so hard to explain things to them since they don't understand. They disregard the 'Employees Only' sign and park in designated areas where they shouldn't." Vue replied, "Hey, take it easy. They're the new Hmong! Remember, we only have thirty years of experience on them."

"It is hard to hate someone," a friend once said, "if you know their story." Whether discussing the ways in which the Hmong have been manipulated by the French, the United States, Thailand, Laos, Vietnam, and each other, noting the eagerness with which some dismiss or ridicule the struggles of immigrants and refugees, or reviewing the tragedy of the two shooting incidents in Wisconsin, one is reminded of how little time we often take to know and understand each other. We sacrifice the enduring for the expedient, public good for personal glory.

I have tried, to the best of my admittedly limited ability, to tell the history of the Hmong people through the voices of those who lived it themselves. It is my hope that these stories will be used to better understand the Hmong experience but also to ask, "What other stories are out there? What do other people have to say? How many of my other neighbors may I come to better understand and appreciate, and how can I help them better understand and appreciate my community?" Asking questions and seeking to know more, it seems to me, is always better than resting on things we have always assumed to be true. That is a journey I am still undertaking, and in the years to come, I hope I will know more and see things more clearly than I do now. The journey is never done.

THank you / ua Tsaug

My Hmong students, especially Tou Thao, Peter Vang, Kelly Vang, Marly Moua, Lee Vang, Tou Lee, Kia Lee, Jena Vue, Nao Thao, Mai Neng Vang, Youa Vang, Ka Youa Vue, Dao Vue, Dia Lee, and others have been generous with their time, patient with my ignorance, and bold in their willingness to connect me with and translate for members of their family and their community. Cheryl Chatman provided important financial assistance during the early stages of this project. Peter Vang won a Jay and Rose Phillips community service scholarship and used it to conduct critical Hmong-language interviews. He has most generously supported my work well after he had any reason to feel obligated.

Gary Yia Lee is the man through whom manuscripts of any length about the Hmong people ultimately travel. I learned a great deal from Gary during his fifteen months as scholar in residence at Concordia University. He also generously served as my unpaid guide and coordinator through Australia; the kindness and hospitality of his thoughtful wife, Mai Lee Yang Lee, are remembered to this day. Sao Lee and his wonderful wife Choua Yang hosted me during my stay in Innisfail and served as my translators. Pao and Trudy Saykao Thao, Blong Saykao Thao, and Chai Xiong and Mao Saykao Thao provided great help and hospitality while I was in Melbourne. I am deeply indebted to those in Laos who led me by the hand and connected me to valuable resources. Danai Chowwiwat helped with travel arrangements in Thailand. Apisit Seksantisakul and Montree Chowwiwat were my guides and translators in Thailand. Of course, I am grateful to all of those around the world who generously shared their stories.

Lee Pao Xiong, director of the Center for Hmong Studies at Concordia University, has been a constant sounding board, abundant resource, and wise advisor. I thank him for his guidance and support, even when he disagreed with me. Inspiring writer and generous spirit Kao Kalia Yang has offered many thoughtful comments on various drafts of this book. Mary Beth Bloom, Joel Halpern, Eleanor Heginbotham, Greg Norman, Susan Pratt, and Mel Shelby provided me with helpful feedback while reading chapters out of the goodness of their hearts.

Jim Anderson, Ernie Kuhn, Vint Lawrence, Mike Lynch, Lionel Rosenblatt, and Mac Thompson kindly reviewed sections over which they had expertise and provided essential feedback. Timothy Castle, Chia Youyee Vang, Franklin Ng, Robert Entenmann, Keith Dyrud, Grace Dyrud, Mitch Ogden, Seexeng

Lee, and former St. Paul mayor George Latimer reviewed the final manuscript and provided insightful comments. Long Yang helped me wrestle with various thorny issues. Mac Thompson, Mike Lynch, Ernie Kuhn, Vint Lawrence, Roger Warner, Hugh Tovar, Grant Evans, Mark Pfeifer, and General Richard Secord kindly replied to e-mails and phone calls about various and sundry details.

My friend and colleague Thomas Saylor introduced me to Greg Britton at Minnesota Historical Society Press, who accepted my proposal and encouraged me to move ahead. As a result, Shannon Pennefeather, my kind, patient, and highly skilled editor, has been saddled with my work, and deserves both my thanks and my apologies. MHS staff—Pam McClanahan, Mary Poggione, Alison Aten, and Leslie Rask—have all been wonderful. Thanks to the late and much-revered Will Powers for art direction and to Cathy Spengler for her lovely cover and page design.

The Concordia University Faculty Development Committee provided crucial financial support for my travels to Laos and Thailand. My friend and department chair David Woodard supported my efforts to find time to write. Many friends and colleagues at Concordia were especially generous, lending an ear and offering helpful advice.

I am grateful to Paul White, one of the "old Lao hands," and to D. Hulcher for permission to use a few of their fabulous photographs. Diane Schuessler transcribed the vast majority of the English language interviews for me, and as a result could probably have written this book herself. The indefatigable Marlin Heise and the staff of the Hmong Archives were helpful in providing useful, unique resources. Fong Lor was a tremendous help with last-minute translation work.

My thanks to Fred Bartling, Jeff Burkart, Clarke Chambers, Keith Dyrud, George Green, Andrea Hinding, John Howe, Paul Marschke, Byron Marshall, Lary May, David Noble, and the late Rudy Vecoli, my undergraduate and graduate history professors and mentors. I hope this work reflects well on you. My apologies to the people who will be justifiably upset with me when they don't see their names here because I forgot them at a critical moment. *Mea culpa!*

My parents raised me and love me even though I probably didn't turn out the way they'd hoped. I am grateful for all they have done for me over the years and know I can never come close to repaying them. I love you both very much. Finally and most importantly, I thank my lovely, patient, and steadfast wife and partner Janet, without whom few things are possible and nothing is worthwhile.

notes

NOTES TO INTRODUCTION

1. Christopher Robbins, *The Ravens: The Men Who Flew in America's Secret War in Laos* (New York: Crown Publishers, 1987), 65–67. As one American pilot remembered, Lee Lue "would go anywhere against all odds, and most [of the other Lao and Hmong pilots] would follow for fear of losing face."

2. Robert Cooper, ed., *The Hmong: A Guide to Traditional Lifestyles* (Singapore: Times Editions, 1998), 13.

3. Thomas Spencer Jerome, "The Case of the Eyewitnesses," in Robin W. Winks, *The Historian as Detective: Essays on Evidence* (New York: Harper & Row, 1969), 187, 190.

4. Catherine Dupree, "Cushioning Hard Memories," *Harvard Magazine* 106:6 (July/August 2004).

notes to section 1

1. Stephanie Coontz, *The Way We Never Were: American Families and the Nostalgia Trap* (New York: Basic Books, 1992).

2. Oscar Handlin, *The Uprooted: The Epic Story of the Great Migrations that Made the American People* (New York: Grosset & Dunlap, 1951); John Bodnar, *The Transplanted: A History of Immigrants in Urban America* (Bloomington: Indiana University Press, 1985); Werner Sollors, *The Invention of Ethnicity* (New York: Oxford University Press, 1989).

3. Recent DNA studies concluded that "Hmong populations had experienced more contact with the northern East Asians, a finding consistent with historical evidence." B. Wen, H. Li, S. Gao, et al., "Genetic Structure of Hmong-Mien Speaking Populations in East Asia as Revealed by mtDNA Lineages," *Molecular Biology and Evolution* 22:3 (April 2005): 725–34. See Keith Quincy, *Hmong: A History of a People* (Cheney: Eastern Washington University Press, 1995), 1–11; Jane Hamilton-Merritt, *Tragic*

Mountains: The Hmong, the Americans, and the Secret Wars for Laos, 1942–1992 (Bloomington: Indiana University Press, 1993), 5–6; Anne Fadiman, *The Spirit Catches You and You Fall Down: A Hmong Child, Her American Doctors, and the Collision of Two Cultures* (New York: Farrar, Straus and Giroux, 1997), 16. Fadiman, 294, called Quincy's *History* her "indispensable historical reference," yet despite being published by an academic press, his book includes no footnotes to document his sources. Robert Entenmann, "The Myth of Sonom: The Hmong King," *Hmong Studies Journal* 6 (2005): 1–14.

4. Yang Dao, *Hmong at the Turning Point* (Minneapolis, MN: WorldBridge Associates, 1999), xiii.

5. This and other myths have numerous versions, though the gist of the story is essentially the same. I have chosen to share this one because it is different from others that have been published and therefore offers the prolific reader a different perspective.

6. Nicholas Tapp in Cooper, *The Hmong*, 108.

7. Piriya Panasuwan, *Chao Fa: A History That Could Be True* (Chiangmai, Thailand: Benya Publishing House, 2000), 57–58.

8. Hugo Bernatzik, *Akha and Miao: Problems of Applied Ethnography in Farther India* (New Haven, CT: Human Relations Area Files, 1970), 305. Tapp in Cooper, *The Hmong*, 106.

9. It's difficult to know exactly how widespread this story is, but in a conversation with four nonrelated Hmong elders, all four of them were familiar with it. This version was told by an elderly Hmong gentleman named Nhia Yer Yang. Xai Thao later told her daughter a slightly different version of the story (perhaps no less misogynistic) in which all the women killed their husbands because they thought they had no choice but to do as the king commanded. Their crime was more of blind obedience than heartless cunning and ambition.

10. In addition, F. M. Savina, the first of these to arrive in Southeast Asia, is remembered by many Hmong for his role in stopping the widespread French executions of Hmong who had participated in a bloody rebellion against the heavy burden of French taxation (the so-called *Guerre du Fou*, or Madman's War, led by Hmong messianic figure Pa Chay from 1918 to 1921). The Hmong Romanized Popular Alphabet (RPA) was co-established in 1952 by William Smalley, Yves Bertrais, and Linwood Barney. A different writing system, *Pahawh Hmong* or "Chao Fa script," was propagated by another Hmong messianic figure, Shong Lue Yang. Yang's story, and that of his embattled writing system, is told in William Smalley, Chia Koua Vang, and Gnia Yee Yang, *Mother of Writing: The Origin and Development of a Hmong Messianic Script* (Chicago: University of Chicago Press, 1990).

11. Cooper, *The Hmong*, 18, 19.

12. William Geddes, *Migrants of the Mountains: The Cultural Ecology of the Blue Miao of Thailand* (Oxford: Clarendon Press, 1976).

13. Another opportunity to meet a prospective spouse, says Sao Lee, "was at a wedding party—all the girls sitting at a long table on one side, and the boys sitting on the opposite side. They started drinking rice wine and singing [Hmong traditional songs] back and forth . . . The very best singer could usually find a boyfriend or a girlfriend, because if you were a good singer, then girls or boys would just fall in love with you, even if you were not very handsome or beautiful."

14. Cooper, *The Hmong*, 60.

15. Cooper, *The Hmong*, 58.

16. Gretel Schwoerer-Kohl in Cooper, *The Hmong*, 81–82.

17. Cooper, *The Hmong*, 22–25.

18. Sucheng Chan, *Hmong Means Free: Life in Laos and America* (Philadelphia, PA: Temple University Press, 1994), 2–3.

19. Hamilton-Merritt, *Tragic Mountains*, 19. Martin Stuart-Fox, *Laos: Politics, Economics, and Society* (London: Frances Pinter, 1986), 18.

20. Gary Yia Lee, "Ethnic Minorities and National Building in Laos," *Peninsule* 11/12 (1985–86): 215–32; Grant Evans, *A Short History of Laos: The Land in Between* (Crows Nest, NSW: Allen & Unwin, 2002), 55–58. Different sources suggest that Pa Chay was killed by fellow Hmong, by Khmu, or by Kha.

21. Gary Yia Lee, "Ethnic Minorities," 215–32.

22. Touxa Lyfoung, *Touby Lyfoung: An Authentic Account of the Life of a Hmong Man in the Troubled Land of Laos* (St. Paul, MN: The author, 1996), 34.

23. Keith Quincy, *Harvesting Pa Chay's Wheat: The Hmong and America's Secret War in Laos* (Spokane: Eastern Washington University Press, 2000), 46.

24. Quincy, *Pa Chay's Wheat*, 497. Quincy says that in this second version of the story, May became ill after her father's death, and a shaman told him that she would get well only if he retrieved the lock of hair from her father's grave, which he did, angering LoBliayao's sons. The version featured in the main narrative of Quincy's book is attributed to "a member of the Vue clan (1985)" while the footnoted version is ascribed to "a member of the Yang clan (1985)."

25. Chan, *Hmong Means Free*, 7–11; Hamilton-Merritt, *Tragic Mountains*, 20–21; Lyfoung, *Touby Lyfoung*, 46–49; Quincy, *Hmong: A History*, 46–49.

notes to section 2

1. Hamilton-Merritt, *Tragic Mountains*, 21–25; Arthur Dommen, *The Indochinese Experience of the French and the Americans* (Bloomington: Indiana University Press, 2001), 74–75.

2. Gary Yia Lee, "Minority Policies and the Hmong in Laos," in M. Stuart-Fox, ed. *Contemporary Laos: Studies in the Politics and Society of the Lao People's Democratic Republic* (St. Lucia: Queensland University Press, 1982), 199–219.

3. Hamilton-Merritt, *Tragic Mountains*, 29–31, 34.

4. Kenneth Conboy with James Morrison, *Shadow War: The CIA's Secret War in Laos* (Boulder, CO: Paladin Press, 1995), 1.

5. Gary Yia Lee, "Minority Policies."

6. Conboy and Morrison, *Shadow War*, 1–2. According to Pa Cha Kong, "those two who went and married a wife from a different country, the people considered that their royal lineage was fouled, so they did not support them to become the next king . . . And so this is part of the reason for the family to fight against each other for the royal king position."

7. Dommen, *Indochinese Experience*, 92–95; A. J. Langguth, *Our Vietnam: The War 1954–1975* (New York: Simon and Schuster, 2000), 55. Dommen, *Indochinese Experience*, 97, shares another story in which Ho requested six Colt pistols (still in their original wrappings) from Colonel Paul Helliwell, head of OSS in China. Upon receipt, Ho made presents of them to leaders of Vietnamese nationalist factions, "who drew the intended conclusion that Ho had obtained access to stocks of fresh American arms."

8. Dommen, *Indochinese Experience*, 98–108.

9. Zalin Grant, *Facing the Phoenix: The CIA and the Political Defeat of the United States in Vietnam* (New York: W. W. Norton and Sons, 1991), 51. This quote is taken from an interview conducted by Michael Charlton of the BBC.

10. Correspondence with Gary Yia Lee, August 12, 2008. Ernie Kuhn, whose wife was Tiao Saykham's stepdaughter, says both men were awarded the Legion of Honor award by the French. "I have always thought that CAS (Lair) was remiss in not bringing in Chao Saykham, the Phuan governor and "heir" to the ancient Phuan Kingdom. (Whenever Chao Saykham was mentioned with embassy people, the response always was that he was pro-French.) There also should have been some accommodation for Touby." G. C. Gunn, "Road Through the Mountains: The Origins of Nationalism and Communism in Laos, 1930–1954" (PhD Thesis, Monash University, 1985).

11. L. G. Barney, "The Meo of Xieng Khouang Province, Laos," in Peter Kunstadter, ed., *Southeast Asian Tribes, Minorities, and Nations* (Princeton, NJ: Princeton University Press, 1967), 275; Conboy and Morrison, *Shadow War*, 2; Gary Yia Lee, "Minority Policies." Arthur Dommen in Andrea Matles Savada, ed., *Laos: A Country Study* (Washington, DC: GPO for the Library of Congress, 1994), http://countrystudies.us/laos/ (accessed May 5, 2008).

12. Conboy and Morrison, *Shadow War*, 2–4. "Pathet Lao," says Conboy, was really the name given to the military wing of the "cosmetically re-shaped Neo Lao Issara" when the group met in Ho Chi Minh's "mountain redoubt" of Tuyen Quang in August 1950. But "Pathet Lao" was the only name that stuck.

13. Grant Evans, e-mail correspondence with the author, May 28, 2008.

14. Conboy and Morrison. *Shadow War*, 7, states that 95 percent of all GCMA were Hmong.

15. Dommen, *Indochinese Experience*, 208.

16. Conboy and Morrison, *Shadow War*, 4–8.

17. Dommen, *Indochinese Experience*, 208.

18. Fred Walker in Hamilton-Merritt, *Tragic Mountains*, 55, 57–60.

19. "Rapport Concernant la Conduite des Operations en Indochine sous la Direction du General Navarre," in Georgette Elgey, *Histoire de la Ive Republique* 2.1: 641–722.

20. Conboy and Morrison, *Shadow War*, 13–14.

21. Conboy and Morrison, *Shadow War*, 15–16.

22. Dommen, *Indochinese Experience*, 326.

23. Hamilton-Merritt, *Tragic Mountains*, 70.

24. Dommen, *Indochinese Experience*, 329–30.

25. "Sarit Thanarat," *Encyclopedia of World Biography*, http://www.bookrags.com/biography/sarit-thanarat/ (accessed June 4, 2008).

26. Vientiane Embassy to State, telegram 248, August 5, 1958, *FRUS 1958–1960* XVI, Microfiche Supplement, Fiche 5, Document 82, in Dommen, *Indochinese Experience*, 357–58.

27. Dommen, *Indochinese Experience*, 369–78; Vientiane Embassy to State, August 5, 1958.

28. Conboy and Morrison, *Shadow War*, 20–25.

29. Hamilton-Merritt, *Tragic Mountains*, 74; Conboy and Morrison, *Shadow War*, 25.

30. Conboy and Morrison, *Shadow War*, 26; Hamilton-Merritt, *Tragic Mountains*, 76.

31. Jack Mathews in Conboy and Morrison, *Shadow War*, 32.

32. Roger Warner, *Shooting at the Moon: The Story of America's Clandestine War in Laos* (South Royalton, VT: Steerforth Press, 1996), 7. The stories about Kong Le, his motives for his coup—even his ethnicity—are numerous. Kenneth Conboy says he was Lao Theung, Arthur Dommen says Phu Thai, and many others simply call him Lao. Jim Chamberlain says he was half Bru and half Lao. While Kong Le said the coup was a result of his dissatisfaction with foreign influence, Dommen, *Indochinese Experience*, 389–91, collected a variety of alternative explanations. Most compelling is the story that Kong Le led his coup with the guidance of Phoumi Nosavan, who informed him that the cabinet would be absent on August 9. Phoumi and Kong Le were close, and it is possible (though there is no hard evidence) that Kong Le staged the coup at his behest and for his benefit. Phoumi, however, was prevented from returning from Luang Prabang to Vientiane by French authorities. The French, said a former intelligence agent, used Kong Le's coup to double-cross Phoumi and put Souvanna Phouma back in power. (Phoumi was also out of favor with the king, who held him responsible for the escape of Souphonouvong and his confederates.) A day after the coup, journalists in Vientiane wondered about French complicity: Kong Le's public statements were in perfect French. Quincy and Dommen disagree about the level and timing of Kong Le's anti-Americanism. According to Quincy, *Pa Chay's Wheat*, 148, Kong Le was already blaming the United States for Laos's woes in a stadium speech he delivered two days after the coup. Wrote Dommen, "There was no concern for the safety of Americans . . .

It was not until later, when the American decision to support Phoumi became apparent, that the statements of the High Command of the Revolution turned anti-American."

33. Hamilton-Merritt, *Tragic Mountains*, 80.

34. Gary Yia Lee, "Minority Policies."

35. Hamilton-Merritt, *Tragic Mountains*, 27, 51–53, 199.

36. Conversations with several Hmong elders, none of whom wished to be identified. Some versions of the story accuse Vang Pao of murder.

37. Dommen, *Indochinese Experience*, 404–5.

38. Dommen, *Indochinese Experience*, 431.

39. Conboy and Morrison, *Shadow War*, 58; Warner, *Shooting at the Moon*, 16.

40. Grant, *Facing the Phoenix*, 145.

41. Timothy Castle, *At War in the Shadow of Vietnam* (New York: Columbia University Press, 1993), 38.

notes to section 3

1. Arthur M. Schlesinger, *A Thousand Days: John F. Kennedy in the White House* (Boston: Houghton Mifflin, 1965), 163–64; Clark Clifford, *Counsel to the President: A Memoir* (New York: Random House, 1991), 342–44. Fred I. Greenstein, "Taking Account of Individuals in International Political Psychology: Eisenhower, Kennedy and Indochina," *Political Psychology* 15:1 (March 1994): 62–66. It's likely that Eisenhower warned against *unilateral* action by the United States but also indicated that Laos was central to the effort to stop the spread of Communism.

2. Thomas Ahern, *Undercover Armies: CIA and Surrogate Warfare in Laos* (Washington, DC: Center for the Study of Intelligence, 2006), xv. The book was only declassified—still with numerous redactions—in 2009.

3. The last role was more important later in the war, when most of Sam Neua province was Communist controlled. Hamilton-Merritt, *Tragic Mountains*, xvii–xviii.

4. Ernest Kuhn, interview by Arthur Dommen on behalf of the Association for Diplomatic Studies and Training Foreign Affairs Oral History Project, Foreign Assistance Series, Library of Congress, Washington, DC.

5. Yang says the commander of his unit was a former Pathet Lao soldier named Xai Vang.

6. Castle, *War in the Shadow*, 40.

7. "There wasn't anything at all secret about Air America['s existence or] where its offices were," says former helicopter pilot Larry Fraser. "The secret was that it was owned by the CIA . . . We might have suspected it, but it was presented as a legitimate corporation." Les Strouse, a good friend of Aderholt's, knew right away. Director George Doole "gave me a complete briefing on the company . . . [W]e had people working Air America for seven years that didn't know it belonged to the CIA, and that surprised the hell out of me." In September 1965, Bird & Sons was sold to Continental Airlines and renamed CASI (Castle, *War in the Shadow*, 59). Charles Weldon, *Tragedy in Paradise: A Country Doctor at War in Laos* (Bangkok: Asia Books, 1999), 53.

8. Conboy and Morrison, *Shadow War*, 21, 64–66; Castle, *War in the Shadow*, 32.

9. Dommen, *Indochinese Experience*, 439–40.

10. Conboy and Morrison, *Shadow War*, 65–66.

11. Dommen, *Indochinese Experience*, 442–45, 447–48, 450.

12. Warner, *Shooting at the Moon*, 39.

13. Conboy and Morrison, *Shadow War*, 62.

14. Conboy and Morrison, *Shadow War*, 70–72. Jer Xiong Yang remembers being trained in Sam Thong in July 1961. "No one lived [there] yet. It was only jungle and trees . . . At that time there were six American trainers and eight Thai trainers [who worked with us for] three months."

15. Shong Leng Xiong, audio tape, 2005, Center for Hmong Studies, Concordia University, St. Paul, MN.

16. Conboy and Morrison, *Shadow War*, 88–89.

17. Warner, *Shooting at the Moon*, 63–64; Conboy and Morrison, *Shadow War*, 90–91.

18. Weldon, *Tragedy in Paradise*, 24–25.

19. Weldon, *Tragedy in Paradise*, 25.

20. Conboy and Morrison, *Shadow War*, 91.

21. Sutayut Osornprasop, "Thailand and the American Secret War in Indochina, 1960–1974" (PhD diss., Cambridge University, 2006), 119–120, 126.

22. Osornprasop, "Thailand and the American Secret War," 119–120, 126.

23. Chao Huy Ngoc, "North Vietnam–Pathet Lao Alliance During the Vietnam War: (Vietnam's Official Perspectives)" (presentation, Vietnam Center Conference, Lubbock, TX, April 13, 2009). Mr. Ngoc kindly sat with me to review his statistics and to clarify his statements.

24. Weldon, *Tragedy in Paradise*, 18–29.

25. Weldon, *Tragedy in Paradise*, 55–56.

26. Mike Lynch, interview (2006) and follow-up e-mails (2009).

27. Ahern, *Undercover Armies*, 101, 144.

28. Alfred McCoy, *The Politics of Heroin in Southeast Asia* (New York: Harper and Row, 1972).

29. Warner, *Shooting at the Moon*, 112.

30. Ahern, *Undercover Armies*, 146, 150–51.

31. Ahern, *Undercover Armies*, 163–64.

32. Richard Helms, *A Look Over My Shoulder: A Life in the Central Intelligence Agency* (New York: Ballantine Books, 2003), 253; Presidential Appointment Book, John F. Kennedy Presidential Library, Boston, MA. The meeting was between 5:00 and 6:00 PM.

33. Douglas Blaufarb, *The Counterinsurgency Era: U.S. Doctrine and Performance, 1950 to the Present* (New York: Free Press, 1977), 157–59.

34. Lieutenant Colonel Hartley, air force, oral history, from Castle, *War in the Shadow*, 82.

35. Bill Lair, interviewed by Steve Maxner. Vietnam Center. Available at: http://star.vietnam.ttu.edu/scripts/starfinder.exe/0?path=v.olsingle.txt&id=olsingle&pass=&search=CTGYP=Bill+Lair*&format=SINGLE (accessed July 2009).

36. See also Ahern, *Undercover Armies*, 236, where an anonymous pilot says he "had hardly unbuckled his parachute harness

when Hmong guerrillas appeared and guided him to the nearest village, where he was ceremoniously offered boiled eggs and tea."

37. Jim Ragsdale, "Hmong Soldiers Put American Soldiers First," *St. Paul Pioneer Press*, May 15, 2005. See also Curry's book, *Whispering Death: Our Journey with the Hmong in the Secret War for Laos* (iUniverse, Inc., 2004).

38. Weldon, *Tragedy in Paradise*, 96.

39. Weldon, *Tragedy in Paradise*, 51–53.

40. Westermeyer was not assigned to the hospital but worked out of Vientiane as Weldon's deputy.

41. Castle, *War in the Shadow*, 80–81. In his memoir *Obbligato, 1939–1979: Notes on a Foreign Service Career* (New York: Norton, 1984), 216, ambassador William Sullivan recounts how he decided to deceive Vang Pao after doctors told him that his arm would atrophy without the insertion of a metal extender to replace the bone that had been shot away. Traditional Hmong belief teaches that no foreign objects should be in the body. But Sullivan decided what Vang Pao didn't know was good for him: "I . . . elaborated at some length on the way in which the steel would eventually melt as it was warmed by the body, and would ultimately depart from the body just like bad spirits." Between medical exams and airport inspections, Vang Pao must certainly have learned of this deception.

42. Weldon, *Tragedy in Paradise*, 122–23.

43. Ahern, *Undercover Armies*, 175–76.

44. Warner, *Shooting at the Moon*, 177.

45. Warner, *Shooting at the Moon*, 185. Theodore Shackley, *Spymaster: My Life in the CIA* (Dulles, VA: Potomac Books, 2005), 138–39.

46. Castle, *War in the Shadow*, 77; Charles Stevenson, *The End of Nowhere: American Policy Toward Laos since 1954* (Boston: Beacon Press, 1972), 217.

47. Timothy Castle, *One Day Too Long: Top Secret Site 85 and the Bombing of North Vietnam* (New York: Columbia University

Press, 1999), 25, 26. There were four tactical air navigation aids, or TACANs, installed in Laos: Phou Kate, near Lima Site 44 (April 1966), Skyline Ridge, a mountain crest just above Long Tieng (May 1966), Pha Thi (September 1966), and Muang Phalane or Lima Site 61 (March 1967). "Using the TACAN system, 'the aircraft transmitted an interrogator pulse to a ground station, and received back range and bearing information.' While its accuracy was not precise, TACAN was the best ground navigation system then available in Southeast Asia," 26.

48. Castle, *One Day*, 27–33, 61.

49. David Corn, *Blond Ghost: Ted Shackley and the CIA's Crusades* (New York: Simon and Schuster, 1994), 153.

50. Warner, *Shooting at the Moon*, 211, 212; Castle, *One Day*, 82.

51. Castle, *One Day*, 76–79, 81–82; Corn, *Blond Ghost*, 136.

52. Castle, *One Day*, 61–62, 87–89, 96–98, 109. The final comment of this paragraph was made by Dr. Castle during the Q&A portion of a speech he gave at the Vietnam Center Conference in Lubbock, TX, on March 13, 2009. Sullivan cable from http://www.aiipowmia.com/sea/phouphati.html (accessed July 2009); U.S. casualty numbers from CHECO (Contemporary Historical Evaluations of Combat Operations). Report available at: www.aiipowmia.com/reports/lima.html (accessed July 2009). Castle, *War in the Shadow*, 96, says a former Pathet Lao commander he interviewed told him "Some injured Americans were captured at the site and sent to North Vietnam."

53. Warner, *Shooting at the Moon*, 228, 251–52.

54. Warner, *Shooting at the Moon*, 270–71.

55. Conboy and Morrison, *Shadow War*, 201–3.

56. Ahern, *Undercover Armies*, 312.

57. Warner, *Shooting at the Moon*, 272, 274.

58. Conboy and Morrison, *Shadow War*, 210.

59. Near Xieng Khouang, in a cave complex called Tham Kap, Hmong troops found "300 tons of medical supplies, including medicine from such faraway places as Iraq.

In one chamber were three-tier hospital beds sufficient for an estimated 1,000 patients. Other chambers served as operating rooms, with one containing a pair of X-ray machines" (Conboy and Morrison, *Shadow War*, 210, 211, 213). Warner, *Shooting at the Moon*, 274–75.

60. Castle, *War in the Shadow*, 106; Warner, *Shooting at the Moon*, 277.

61. Hamilton-Merritt, *Tragic Mountains*, 226–27.

62. Warner, *Shooting at the Moon*, 301; Osornprasop, "Thailand and the American Secret War," 186.

63. Weldon, *Tragedy in Paradise*, 248–50.

64. Brian Moser, dir., *Disappearing Cultures: The Meo* (Granada Films, 1972).

65. The most provocative data related to Hmong population and mortality during the Secret War were shared by Heng Thung in a November 2007 interview. An optical physicist hired by USAID to conduct aerial surveys of rice and poppy production, Thung also supervised a population survey of the Hmong people served by USAID in 1971. While USAID was dropping enough rice for 250,000 people, Thung's survey concluded there were only 150,000 Hmong being served. USAID, said Thung, always announced in advance when it was going to count heads. Families gathered relatives from nearby villages to be counted, grossly inflating USAID's statistics. After he announced his findings, USAID cut its rice budget. Thung's superior told him, "If you are invited to Long Tieng, the answer is no." Thung said he later helped Yang Dao conduct a survey commissioned by Vang Pao, asking Hmong refugees where they wanted to live. Family members from 1,900 households were also asked their name, gender, and age. When the forms were all gathered and the age distribution was charted, it was, said Thung, "a perfect Christmas tree . . . We didn't have an age gap . . . Where were all the casualties?" Thung's data suggested the stories about a whole generation of Hmong men being wiped out, necessitating the recruitment of twelve- and thirteen-year-old boys, were a myth.

Heng Thung died in January 2009, making his assertions difficult to prove.

66. Warner, *Shooting at the Moon*, 149.

67. Smalley, Vang, Yang, *Mother of Writing*, 29–38. Some of Vang Pao's former soldiers named the men who killed Shong Lue.

68. Smalley, Vang, Yang, *Mother of Writing*, 150.

69. Osornprasop, "Thailand and the American Secret War," 190, 193–94, 203–4, 211.

70. Castle, *War in the Shadow*, 116.

notes to section 4

1. Evans, *Short History of Laos*, 165–75; Quincy, *Pa Chay's Wheat*, 361.

2. Lee, "Minority Policies."

3. Chan, *Hmong Means Free*, 44.

4. From Gayle Morrison, *Sky Is Falling: An Oral History of the CIA's Evacuation of the Hmong from Laos* (Jefferson, NC: McFarland & Co., 1999), 27.

5. Moua Lia in Hamilton-Merritt, *Tragic Mountains*, 342.

6. Yang See in Morrison, *Sky Is Falling*, 77.

7. Jack Knotts in Morrison, *Sky Is Falling*, 187–88.

8. Yang See in Morrison, *Sky Is Falling*, 48.

9. Yang See still has photographs and his diary from 1975, which he also used to type up an account of his activities during these days entitled "Story Never Told."

10. Though not certain, May 13 is the best choice. In Morrison, *Sky Is Falling* (110), Aderholt says he received a phone call on May 13. He told the author the call came on "a Sunday morning," which would have been on May 11. Former CIA station chief Dan Arnold states (Morrison, 111) the process of "sheep-dipping" the C-130 (stripping it of all identifying insignia) might have taken twenty-four hours, which means if Hoff was contacted on the thirteenth, the plane might not have arrived in Long Tieng until the fourteenth, the last day of the airlift. To confuse matters further, Hamilton-Merritt, *Tragic Mountains* (343–44), says the C-130 piloted by Hoff arrived in Long Tieng on

May 11 and never returned. Jack Knotts, the helicopter pilot who evacuated Vang Pao and Jerry Daniels, told Morrison (112), "[Hoff is] getting all this money for each trip. He's *racing* back and forth . . . The rest of us pilots had ongoing contracts and we weren't paid anything extra." Aderholt stated that Hoff and his crew each received five thousand dollars for the entire mission. On a tape recording made between May 12 and 14, 1975, Dave Kouba, who spoke with Hoff at Udorn on May 14, says Hoff made two flights on the thirteenth and two on the fourteenth. Since the C-130 could carry more people than the two C-46s combined, its presence was obviously crucial. Strouse estimates the capacity of the C-130 at about 170, maybe more. In an e-mail to the author (September 26, 2007), Richard Secord wrote, "The EWP [emergency war plan] payload would have been well over 35,000 lbs., depending on density altitude. Some pilots would have no doubt gone with 40,000+." Given the Hmong's small stature, it's likely capacity was limited more by deck area than weight.

11. Ly Teng in Morrison, *Sky Is Falling,* 102; Xiong Moua in Morrison, *Sky Is Falling,* 91–92.

12. Chong Ge Yang in Morrison, *Sky Is Falling,* 137–43.

13. Quotes from Kouba and Knotts are from Kouba's tape recording.

14. Mac Thompson is a self-made expert on many aspects of the Secret War. He has copies of Les Strouse and Al Rich's flight books, knows as well as anyone what the capacity of a C-130 might have been, and has calculated roughly 3,000 to 3,500 people were flown out of Long Tieng to Nam Phong or Udorn. He figures another 8,000 or so made it on their own to Nong Khai and were then trucked down to Nam Phong.

15. Dommen, *Indochinese Experience,* 936–37.

16. Evans, *Short History of Lao,* 185; Hamilton-Merritt, *Tragic Mountains,* 337; Quincy, *Pa Chay's Wheat,* 394. Hamilton-Merritt attributes this quote to Phoumi Vongvichit, a former tax collector who

collaborated with the Japanese during their occupation of Laos, sided with the Viet Minh, and gained a prominent position in the new Pathet Lao government: he was the vice prime minister with whom Yang Dao argued to avert an invasion of Long Tieng. In American political history, the "bloody shirt" refers to the practice of referencing the blood of martyrs, the nefariousness of their killers, or the guilt of a side that started a war or pogrom against others. After the Civil War, for example, Republicans were often accused of "waving the bloody shirt" at Democrats, meaning they undermined Democrats' credibility by continuing to blame them for the Civil War and all the deaths that came in its wake.

notes to section 5

1. Parts of this quote are from the author's conversation with Lair, while others come from a speech he made before the dedication of the Lao, Hmong, and American Veterans' Memorial in Sheboygan, WI, on July 15, 2006.

2. Quincy, *Pa Chay's Wheat,* 460.

3. Warner, *Shooting at the Moon,* 367; Mac Thompson, e-mail correspondence with the author, April 12, 2008; Quincy, *Pa Chay's Wheat,* 443–45.

4. Mr. William McNitt, archivist at the Ford Presidential Library, "checked both the President's Daily Diary (a log of all of his meetings and telephone calls) and the White House Central Files Name File," and found no "evidence of any contacts between the General and the White House nor any documents about the General written by others" (e-mail correspondence with the author, May 13, 2009). Tony Kennedy and Paul McEnroe, "The Covert Wars of Vang Pao," Minneapolis *Star Tribune,* July 3, 2005.

5. INS log book, 1976 (information provided by Mac Thompson).

6. Harold Meinheit, e-mail correspondence with the author, January 13, 2008.

7. Stephen A. Garrett, "Human Rights in Thailand: The Case of the Thammasat 18," *Universal Human Rights* 2:4 (October–December 1980): 43–56.

8. Chia Youyee Vang, *Hmong in Minnesota* (St. Paul: Minnesota Historical Society Press, 2008), 11. U.S. resettlement, says Vang, "is designed . . . as a public-private partnership, with [NGOs] participating in every step of the process . . . The primary agencies involved in resettlement of the Hmong were U.S. Catholic Conference . . . Lutheran Immigration and Refugee Services . . . and Church World Services."

9. Lynellyn D. Long, *Ban Vinai: The Refugee Camp* (New York: Columbia University Press, 1993), 40, 41, 47; Gil Loescher and John Scanlan, *Calculated Kindness: Refugees and America's Half-Open Door, 1945 to the Present* (New York: Free Press, 1986), 180; Kao Kalia Yang, *The Latehomecomer: A Hmong Family Memoir* (Minneapolis, MN: Coffee House Press, 2008), 46, 47.

10. Including Shong Leng Xiong and Paj Ntxheb Vaaj.

11. Jonathan B. Tucker, "The Yellow Rain Controversy: Lessons for Arms Control Compliance," *The Nonproliferation Review* 8:1 (Spring 2001): 29–32; see also U.S. State Department, Bureau of Verification, Compliance, and Implementation, "Case Study: Yellow Rain," October 1, 2005. The bee dung theory was supported by several observations: 1) the pollen grains were too concentrated to have been windborne; 2) no two spots had the same pollen composition, and even spots on adjacent leaves contained different types of pollen grains: this kind of variability would not occur if the material had been artificially spread; 3) the pollen grains were hollow, suggesting bugs had eaten them and excreted the undigested parts; 4) the pollen showed no tendency to disperse, making it highly unlikely it could serve as a "carrier" for a toxin.

12. Rebecca Katz, "Yellow Rain Revisited: Lessons Learned for the Investigation of Chemical and Biological Weapons Allegations" (diss., Princeton University, 2005).

13. Matthew Meselson and Julian Perry Robinson, "The Yellow Rain Affair: Lessons Learned from a Discredited Allegation" (revised version of a paper given in 2006, kindly provided by Dr. Meselson); Katz, "Yellow Rain Revisited," 73: "There were discrepancies in the refugee reports of attacks, but the volume and weight of the accounts would lead a reasonable person to conclude that some type of chemical attack was happening."

14. Merle Pribbenow, "Yellow Rain: Lessons from an Earlier WMD Controversy," *International Journal of Intelligence and Counterintelligence* 19:4 (2006): 741.

15. Katz, "Yellow Rain Revisited," 74, 75.

16. Long, *Ban Vinai*, 47.

notes to section 6

1. From Martin's review of Vernon Briggs, *Mass Immigration and the National Interest* (Armonk, New York: M. E. Sharpe, 1992) in *Industrial Labor Relations Review* 48:1 (October 1994): 176.

2. Yang, *The Latehomecomer*, 102.

3. This makes estimating the number of Hmong in France particularly difficult, though the most common figure seen in print is fifteen thousand. Khou Xiong, "Hmong in France: Assimilation and Adaptation," *University of Wisconsin–La Crosse Journal of Undergraduate Research* VII (2004).

4. Sanford J. Ungar, *Fresh Blood: The New American Immigrants* (Urbana: University of Illinois Press, 1998), 192.

5. Tony McEnroe and Paul Kennedy, "The Covert Wars of General Vang Pao," Minneapolis *Star Tribune*, June 5, 2007.

6. McEnroe and Kennedy, "Covert Wars."

7. Hamilton-Merritt, *Tragic Mountains*, 471–79.

8. Quincy, *Pa Chay's Wheat*, 448–49, 450. "By-Laws of the United Lao National Liberation Front," 1; "The United Lao National Liberation Front: Policies on Internal Affairs and International Relations," 12. Provided to the author by Colonel Carl Bernard.

9. Ruth Hammond, "Rumors of War," *Twin Cities Reader,* October 25–31 and November 8–14, 1989, and "Sad Suspicions of a Refugee Rip-Off," *Washington Post,* April 16, 1989; Quincy, *Pa Chay's Wheat,* 451.

10. Michael Ross, "Probe Links 'Reagan Doctrine' to Covert Aid to Laos Rebels," *Los Angeles Times,* January 23, 1993, 10. The three key figures in this plan were John LeBoutillier, former congressman from New York, Ann Mills Griffiths, executive director of the National League of Families of American Prisoners and Missing in Southeast Asia, and Lieutenant Colonel Richard Childress, director of Asian Affairs for the NSC. Griffiths allegedly accepted tax-deductible donations on LeBoutillier's behalf, with the understanding that the funds would be sent to an account in Thailand that would be used to pay Lao rebels to search for evidence regarding U.S. POWs/MIAs. Childress "put the National Security Council stamp of approval on the operation for hesitant contributors." Almost $200,000 of private funds were collected, but another $400,000 had been wired to the Thai account "from international sources," including banks in South Korea and the Middle East. Many of the details of this scheme and broader attempts to aid anti-Communist forces in Laos are still unclear. There remains an outstanding FOIA request for "documents related to U.S. prisoners of war in Laos, China, Vietnam and the Soviet Union as well as information regarding the involvement of Richard Armitage, Richard T. Childress and Colonel Oliver North in transporting materials to Laos and Vietnam and their involvement in P.O.W. issues": see http://www.gwu.edu/ ~nsarchiv/NSAEBB/NSAEBB182/ tenoldest.htm (accessed July 2009).

11. Wade insists that the U.S. State Department was as eager as the Thai government to see refugees from Laos barred from Thailand.

12. Quincy, *Pa Chay's Wheat,* 455–56; Hamilton-Merritt, *Tragic Mountains,* 488–89. Rick Wade, who reviewed this section and verifies these events, says that it was common for the Lao to round up those they captured and put them in caves, "maybe to hide them from satellites, I don't know." When word of these activities leaked out, alleges Wade, the Lao went back and cleaned bones and other evidence of their atrocities.

13. Sources from Neo Hom insist that General Singlaub had a more substantial relationship with Vang Pao until the split, claiming Singlaub has distanced himself since Vang Pao's arrest in June 2007. "A Fledgling Alliance," *Time* (June 17, 1985); Mark Hemingway, "My Dinner with Jack," *The Weekly Standard* 11:27 (March 3, 2006). According to at least one published report, Her and his rebels were funded in part by a small amount of U.S. money siphoned away from funds allocated for Cambodia.

14. Letter from Wade to Bernard, August 3, 1986, courtesy Carl Bernard. CMA founder Tom Posey is profiled in Holly Sklar's *Washington's War in Nicaragua* (238) as "a former Marine Corporal, John Bircher and Ku Klux Klansman . . . On an approved US Treasury application to become a firearms dealer, Posey wrote, 'I plan to buy weapons and ammo to send to El Salvador.' CMA . . . provided men, training, arms, and other supplies to the contras. 'We like to think of ourselves as missionary-mercenaries,' explained Posey."

15. "Against All Odds: The Laotian Freedom Fighters," at www.heritage.org/research/ asiaandthepacific/hl96.cfm (accessed January 2009). A full-text version of the transcript was provided to the author by Carl Bernard.

16. Relating to the helicopter infiltration, Caristo says,"We hoped that they would make contact with the local Hmong and gather intelligence from [them, hoping] blood would be thicker than politics, and they would . . . set up trail watch . . . [and] road watch teams and report to us." The team came under immediate fire by North Vietnamese local militia, soon became the targets of regular NVA forces, and lasted less than a couple of weeks before returning to Laos.

17. Wade and others insist Vang Pao was not in the area when these events occurred. Claudia Rosett, "A Lonely Lao Fight for Freedom," *Wall Street Journal*, June 13, 1990; Bryan Johnson, "Bombs, Rockets Answer Laotian Challenge," *The Globe and Mail*, February 22, 1990; Keith Richburg, "Insurgency in Laos Seeking to Emerge From Anonymity," *Washington Post*, February 11, 1990; Ruth Hammond, "Rumors of War," October 25, 1989, 6; Quincy, *Pa Chay's Wheat*, 455–57. Rick Wade insists that several of the provisional government's activities occurred on Lao soil: "There were camps along the border that were *inside* Laos." The original proclamation of the new government, he says, was in Cher Pao Moua's base in Xieng Khouang.

18. Anonymous, e-mail correspondence, 2009.

19. Melanie Evans, "'Free Speech' Wins in KQRS Case," *Minnesota Daily*, November 15, 1998.

noTes To ePILogue

1. Stephen Magagnini, "Some Call Gen. Vang Pao 'King of the Hmong,'" *Fresno Bee*, July 18, 2009.

2. "Long Wait Is Over: Hmong from Wat Tham Krabok Begin Arriving in US," *US Refugee Admissions Program News* 2:3 (July 23, 2004), 2.

3. Theresa Hesebeck, letter to the editor, *Eau Claire Leader-Telegram*, December 23, 2004. The other five people killed were Mark Roidt, Al Laski, Jessica Willers, Joey Crotteau, and Robert Crotteau.

4. From now inactive link, http://wfrv.com/local/local_story_016121114.html (accessed June 11, 2008).

5. Roger Warner, "On Exaggeration, Context and the Wages of a Covert War," *St. Paul Pioneer Press*, June 20, 2007.

6. Information from the colonel I interviewed and a young teacher I met during our tour.

7. Thomas Fuller, "Old U.S. Allies, Still Hiding Deep in Laos," *New York Times*, December 17, 2007.

8. E-mail correspondence with author, July 28, 2009.

9. In an address to the Field Correspondents Club of Thailand on December 13, 2008, Shannon Lawrence of International Rivers stated that the Lao government was attracting sufficient foreign investment "to build nearly 30 new dams by 2020. Thailand is the biggest consumer of Lao hydroelectricity . . . Thai companies, such as the Electricity Generating Company of Thailand, or EGCO, Ratchaburi, and GMS Power are some of the main dam builders in Laos. And Thai financial institutions, including Thai XM and private banks, are also important players." International Rivers, "Power Surge: The Impacts of Rapid Dam Development," September 2008. See www.internationalrivers.org/en/southeast-asia/laos (accessed August 25, 2009).

10. Patrick F. Clarkin, "Hmong Resettlement in French Guiana," *Hmong Studies Journal* 6:1 (2005): 27.

11. Michael Grover and Richard M. Todd, "Why Did Hmong Homeownership Lag in the Central Valley?" (report) Federal Reserve Bank of Minneapolis, May 2004; Mark Pfeifer, "U.S. Census Releases 2005 American Community Survey Data for Southeast Asian Americans. See http://www.hmongstudies.org/2005ACSArticle.html (accessed August 25, 2009). Bruce Corrie, "Hmong Community an Asset to St. Paul," *St. Paul Pioneer Press*, May 27, 2004.

12. See http://christianhmongfellowship.org/doctors6.html (accessed August 25, 2009). *Terminal degree* in this context refers to anyone with a PhD, EdD, DMin, ThD, PsyD, MD, DO, PharmD, DDS, DMS, DPM, OD, DMD, DC, or JD.

LIST OF interviewees

These and scores of other interviews were collected between 2002 and 2009 under the auspices of the Hmong Oral History Project (HOHP). Several full-text interviews and other information are available at the project website: http://homepages.csp.edu/hillmer/Hmong_OHP.html.

All Hmong names are arranged by clan name. Some elders from Laos (Vang Pao, Yang Dao) are still best known by the traditional arrangement of clan name first. Hence, Vang Pao, for example, will be found in the Vs rather than the Ps.

General Harry C. "Heine" Aderholt (2006), Jim Anderson (2005, 2007), Anonymous (several) (2006–8), Father Luc Bouchard (2006), Fred Caristo (phone, 2009), Dr. Dia Cha (2005), Dr. Jim Chamberlain (2007), Dr. Kathleen Culhane-Pera (2007), Mhor Dang (2007), Larry Fraser (2007), Dennis Grace (2006), Ruth Hammond (2009), Chai Her (2007), Chris Her (2006), Reverend PaMang Her (2004), Wang Her (2003), Paul Herr (2006), Chay Heu (2009), Captain D. L. "Pappy" Hicks (2008), Xuwicha Hiranprueck (2007), Dr. Rebecca Katz (2008), Pa Cha Kong (2007), Tom Kosel (2007), Jane Kretzmann (2007), Ernie Kuhn (2007), Bill Lair (2006), George Latimer (2007), J. Vinton Lawrence (2006), Fay Chia Lee (2006), Dr. Gary Yia Lee (Lee Yia) (2005, 2006), Mai Lee Yang Lee (2006), Nor Lue Lee (2006), Ong (Adam) Lee (2006), Pao Lee (2006), Sao Lee (2006), Seexeng Lee (2006, 2007), Txong Pao Lee (2007), Wa Toua Lee (2007), Chong Toua Lo (2007), Boua Long (2006), Chia Deng Lor (2008), Fong Lor (2009), Shep Lowman (2008), Mike Lynch (2006), Win McKeithen (2007), Carol Mills (2007), Lieutenant Colonel Gao Moua (2003), Karry Moua (2002), Mee Moua (2005), Lionel Rosenblatt (phone, 2006), Steve Schofield (2006), General Richard Secord (2006), General John Singlaub (phone, 2009), Bill Snyder (2005), Les Strouse (2007), Choua Thao (2007), Cy Thao (2006), Khu Thao (2002), Mai Lee Thao (2005), Pa Seng Thao (2004), Xai Thao (2004), Mac Thompson (2007), Heng Thung (2007), Hugh Tovar (phone, 2007, 2009), John Tucker (phone, 2008), J. Kou Vang (2006), Captain Joua Bee Vang (2007), Keith Vang (2005), Ly Vang (2007), Nhia Lor Vang (2002, 2009), Nao Her Vang (2007), Pa Xe Vang (2007), General Vang Pao (2005), Tong Vang (2007), Dr. Rudolph Vecoli (2007), Kathleen Vellenga (2007), General John W. Vessey, Jr. (2006), Ger Vue (2008), Xao Vang Vue (2004), Rick Wade (phone, 2008, 2009), Dr. Patricia Walker (2007), Tom Ward (2007), Dr. Roy Wehrle (2006), Dr. Joe Westermeyer (2007), Charles Whitney (2007, 2008), Leng Wong (2007), Chia Xiong (2006), Lee Pao Xiong (2005, 2007), Phoumee Xiong (2003), Colonel Shong Leng Xiong (2006), Vang Chou Xiong (2003), Colonel Xai Dang Xiong (2005), Chia Cher Yang (2006), Dr. Yang Dao (2006, 2007, 2009), Edward (Vue) Yang (2007), Jer Xiong Yang (2006), Kao Kalia Yang (2007), Long Yang (2006), Nao Cha Yang (2007), Nhia Yer Yang (2007), Pa Sher Yang (2003), Yang See (2009), Wa Yang (2007), Won Chuck Yang (phone, 2008), Xai Xue Yang (2006), Zong Khang Yang (2006), Tony Zola (2007)

INDEX

PICTURE CREDITS

Maps on pages vi and vii: CartoGraphics, Inc.

page 4: PARU Archives

pages 5, 117, 189, 240–41, 294, 295: Paul Hillmer

page 13: D. L. "Pappy" Hicks

page 23: Chertong Vang

pages 31, 57, 66, 177: Lao National Museum

page 34 top, 208–9, 217, 219, 221, 223, 233, 238: D. Hulcher

pages 34 bottom, 83, 94, 100, 105, 110, 113, 126 left: Paul White

page 35: Lee Pao Xiong

pages 53, 56: Lieutenant Colonel Nenglo Yang, courtesy Noah Vang

page 60: Nor Lue Lee

page 78: Yeng Kong Yang, courtesy Hmong Archives

page 126 right: Choua Thao, courtesy Lee Pao Xiong

page 139: Carol Mills

page 144: Mike Lynch

page 156: Long Yang

page 164: Dave Kouba, courtesy Les Strouse

page 168: Joua Bee Vang

page 185: Sao Lee

pages 214, 267: Seexeng Lee

page 226 left and right: Dr. Gary Yia Lee and Mai Lee Yang Lee

page 240 left: Peter Vang

page 241 right: Eric Menzhuber

page 252: Ly Vang

page 265: Tzianeng Vang

page 280: Fred Caristo

A People's History of the Hmong was designed and set in type at Cathy Spengler Design, Minneapolis. The typefaces are Chaparral and Questal. Printed by Sheridan Books, Ann Arbor.